Sadlier-Oxford

Master the Conventions

GRAMMAR FOR WRITING

Grades 9–12

COMPOSITION
USAGE
GRAMMAR
MECHANICS

COMPOCOMPOCOMP
SAGEUSAGEUUSAG

welcome to
Grammar for Writing

Grammar for Writing is a new program for today's secondary school students. It offers a complete course in grammar, usage, and mechanics—with an emphasis on writing—intended to help build the communication skills needed in a rapidly changing world.

The program takes the "mystery" out of grammar and helps develop better and more confident writers.

Grammar for Writing illustrates how the rules of grammar, usage, and mechanics—the conventions of standard English—can help students develop writing that is not just "correct" but powerful and persuasive, too.

Grammar for Writing has been designed with today's students in mind. Grammar rules are presented and explained in a clear and simple manner so that students can grasp them quickly and apply them to their writing immediately.

"Research studies clearly and consistently show that the most effective way to help students use the conventions of writing is to teach grammar in the context of writing."

Beverly Ann Chin

AUTHORSHIP

A broad-based team of experienced curriculum specialists and professional writers, working under the direction of *Beverly Ann Chin*, professor of English at the University of Montana and past-president of the National Council of Teachers of English (NCTE), developed the new *Grammar for Writing* series to help prepare today's secondary students to be effective writers in school, on writing assessments, on standardized tests, for college admission and placement, and for the workplace.

COMPO
USAGE
GRAM
MAR
MECHAN
OSITION

Sadlier-Oxford introduces *Grammar for Writing*, Grades 9–12:
a course in grammar, usage, and mechanics with an
emphasis on writing at each grade level.

Program Features

- **Informal, student-friendly tone**
- **Practical, two-page lesson format**
  Rules + Examples + Practice Exercises
- **Strong emphasis on writing**

- **Composition** unit (Chapters 1–3) at each grade level provides seven writing workshops teaching the types of writing often required of students.

- **Abundant exercises** include cooperative activities and practice with revising, editing, and proofreading.

- **Flexible lesson format** allows students to write exercises alone, with a partner, in small groups, or with the whole class.

- Emphasis on **persuasive writing** in *Write What You Think* exercises encourages critical thinking.

- Mid-chapter **reviews**, chapter reviews, and cumulative reviews reinforce lesson concepts.

- Four-page **tests** in standardized test format follow the grammar, usage, and mechanics sections in each student book.

- Chapter openers feature striking **photos** as writing prompts and real **student writing models**.

- **Teacher's Edition** includes answers to exercises and valuable teaching tips.

new!

fourth course Gr. 9

fifth course Gr. 10

sixth course Gr. 11

complete course Gr. 12

Begin with Writing

"Grammar for Writing helps students communicate effectively with a variety of audiences and for different purposes."

Beverly Ann Chin

Enriching Your Vocabulary

Just as word knowledge aids students' listening and reading comprehension, an effective speaking and writing vocabulary is critical to developing writing skills.

Authentic Writing

Models of published works set the expectation that students will learn to write clearly, coherently, and expressively.

Student Writing ▶

Authentic student models make writing relevant.

COMPOSITION
Lesson 3.4

Enriching Your Vocabulary

Voracious comes from the Latin verb *vorare*, meaning "to swallow up, eat greedily, or devour." This versatile adjective may be used in both a literal (concrete) and a figurative (an abstract) sense. A person who has a *voracious* appetite is likely to eat huge quantities of food. Someone with a hunger for knowledge may be a *voracious* reader.

Reference to the poem "The Rime of the Ancient Mariner" by Coleridge

Thesis statement

Example

An

Gen

52

Writing About Literature: Analyzing Fiction

When you write about a story or novel, you usually create one of three kinds of essays. The three serve very different purposes.

1. In a **personal response** essay, you write about how you felt and what you thought as you read, about the passages that seemed particularly meaningful, and about the other works that the story reminded you of.

2. In an **evaluation**, you write about how good or bad the work is. Your evaluation is based on objective **criteria**, or standards, that are used to measure the excellence of a literary form. For example, here are two criteria for measuring a short story:
   • The characters are believable.
   • The plot engages the reader's interest.

3. In a **literary analysis**, you discuss one or more of the **elements of fiction**: characters, plot, setting, point of view, and theme.

The following excerpt is from a long literary analysis of Ernest Hemingway's novel *The Old Man and the Sea*. Here, Carlos Baker discusses the feelings that the main character, Santiago, has for birds and fish while he is battling a marlin.

Hemingway's Ancient Mariner
an excerpt from an essay by Carlos Baker

[1]According to the ancient mariner of Coleridge, "[h]e prayeth best who loveth best all things both great and small." [2]Along with humility, pride, and piety, Hemingway's ancient mariner [Santiago] is richly endowed with the quality of compassion. [3]Of course, he is not so foolish as to love all creatures equally. [4]He dislikes, for example, the Portuguese men-of-war, whose beautiful "purple, formalized, iridescent, gelatinous" bubbles serve to buoy up the "long deadly purple filaments" which trail a yard behind them in the water and contain a poison which will paralyze the unwary passersby. . . . [5]He has another set of enemies in the water of the tropic sea.

Internet
Visit us at
www.sadlier-oxford.com

STUDENT WRITING
Expository Essay

**What I Learned About Life
from Selling Shoes**
by Katherine Ivers
high school student, Meriden, Connecticut

I know you're asking, "What could you possibly learn from selling shoes?" But the vast knowledge I have acquired from this minimum-wage job will last a lifetime.

Hired right before Christmas, I was about to receive a crash course in responsibility. Amid the decorations, elevator music, and hordes of customers, I learned my first lesson—patience. This virtue, unbeknownst to the six million crazed customers waving and shoving shoes in my face, is the only reason many of them were not bludgeoned to death by a high heel.

Another very important lesson is stress management. I faced the triple necessity of balancing honors courses at school, holding down a part-time job, and retaining a social life. . . .

I also learned to master quickly the art of budgeting time. I eat dinner, talk to my boss, and study for a trig quiz in fifteen minutes. Going to the bathroom can wait. In the shoe department, I learned something else that surprised me: Men and women are different! I never saw a man try on a pair of shoes and inquire whether they made his ankles look fat. On the other hand, I never saw a woman so anxious to get out of the mall that she purchased any shoe without trying it on. I learned to appreciate and adapt to these differences.

I learned, too, that physical fitness plays an important role. How many people get

---

Writing Workshops

In-depth lessons set the stage for students to see themselves as readers, writers, and communicators.

Writing About Literature:
Analyzing Fiction

Exercise 19 Organize and Draft Your Essay

Before you start writing, review your notes. Choose two or three of your most important points. Then sit down and start writing—anywhere in the essay. Do not worry about perfect sentences. Just get your ideas down in sentences and paragraphs so that you will have something to revise.

- **Introduction, body, conclusion** Make sure you have included everything that belongs in each of the three basic parts.

- **Title** Think of a possible title; try out several. Your title should suggest both the work and your essay's focus.

> **A Literary Analysis**
> INTRODUCTION
> • Author and title of work
> • Brief plot summary
> • Thesis statement
> BODY
> • Major point 1
>   Support, support
> • Major point 2
>   Support, support
> CONCLUSION

Exercise 20 Revise and Edit Your Essay

Let the draft sit awhile. Then use the four revising strategies suggested in Lesson 1.3. Read for accurate content, clear organization, and appropriate style for your purpose and audience. As you and your peer editors revise, ask these questions:

- Is the essay coherent, or well-organized?

- Are the general statements clearly expressed bu...

- Have you elaborated enough to support or "pr...

- Is everything unified, or directly related to, the...

Exercise 21 Edit, Proofread, and Pub...

Double-check each quotation for accuracy and al... satisfied that you have corrected all errors in gra... papers with a partner to check for any you may h...

You might form two reading-and-discussion grou... novels. Take turns reading aloud papers to the ap... have read the work you have written about, see i... they have comments or ideas to add. Your group... novels that members might enjoy.

You might also compile a "lit crit" anthology of e... Then share the anthology with other English clas...

Step-by-Step Exercises

Lessons lead students through the writing process with exercises providing hands-on practice. Students develop and use strategies for assessing their final compositions before presenting their writing to different audiences.

Writing Strategies

Detailed strategies point out critical writing suggestions, enabling students to communicate clearly in many different situations.

COMPOSITION
Lesson 2.3

Coherence

❧ Each of your paragraphs should be **coherent**; that is, its sentences should be sensibly organized so that your reader can follow your thoughts easily.

STRATEGIES FOR WRITING COHERENTLY

1. Be Clear Express your thoughts simply and directly.

2. Guide the Reader Use signposts that show the reader what lies ahead and how thoughts relate to one another. Some signposts are transitional expressions like those on page 27. Others are pronouns and synonyms (words that mean almost the same thing), which refer to terms you have already used. Repeating key words or terms also improves coherence.

3. Put Your Thoughts in Order Arrange information so that "first things come first."

The following list includes four common ways of organizing paragraphs and essays. Unless you have a good reason not to do so, choose one of these orders as a framework.

- **Chronological Order** Organizing your writing chronologically means telling about events in the order in which they occurred. Use chronological order for narrative paragraphs, which may tell a true story or a fictional one; for writing about a historical event; and for describing steps in a process.

- **Spatial Order** Organize your paragraph spatially when you want to describe a person, an animal, a place, or an object. Include details in an orderly way; moving from left to right, top to bottom, near to far, or inside to outside.

- **Order of Importance** Organize your paragraph by degree of importance when trying to persuade your audience. State the least important reasons and other details first, and end with the most important ones—or the reverse.

Strengthen Grammar and Usage Skills

"*Grammar for Writing helps students use writing strategies and the writing process to communicate with different audiences for a variety of purposes.*"

Beverly Ann Chin

Writing Hints · · · · · · · · · · · ·

Students learn practical advice for applying the skills of grammar, usage, and mechanics to their own paragraphs and essays.

Combining Sentences: Inserting Phrases

GRAMMAR
Lesson 6.6

✒ Combine related sentences by inserting a phrase from one sentence into another sentence.

Sometimes, you must alter the words from one sentence to create a phrase for another sentence. Sometimes, you can simply pick up a phrase from one sentence and move it to another sentence.

ORIGINAL Benny was traveling through Europe. He visited several circuses.
COMBINED **Traveling through Europe**, Benny visited several circuses. [participial phrase]

ORIGINAL Lisa plays in a band. The band is in New York. Janet and Rebecca are the other members of her band.
COMBINED Lisa plays **in a band in New York with Janet and Rebecca**. [prepositional phrases]

ORIGINAL We have time. We will buy the tickets at the ticket window. The ticket window is by the third-base line.
COMBINED We have time **to buy the tickets at the ticket window by the third-base line**. [infinitive phrase containing two prepositional phrases]

ORIGINAL My uncle enjoys something. He enjoys walking briskly.
COMBINED **Walking briskly** is something my uncle enjoys. [gerund phrase]

Often there is more than one way to combine sentences. Here are two other versions of the last sentence.

COMBINED To walk briskly is something my uncle enjoys. [infinitive phrase]
COMBINED My uncle enjoys walking briskly. [gerund phrase at end]

In addition to creating a verbal or a prepositional phrase to put in another sentence, you can convert a sentence to an appositive phrase (see Lesson 6.2) and transfer it to another sentence.

ORIGINAL My uncle lives in St. Louis now. He is an immigrant from Russia.
COMBINED My uncle, **a Russian immigrant**, lives in St. Louis now.

Chapter 6 • Phrases **161**

Enriching Your Vocabulary

The adjective *apt* comes from the Latin *aptus*, which means "suited, fitted, or appropriate." The class valedictorian offered *apt* advice to the new graduates. *Aptitude*, as used on page 162, is derived from *aptus* and the suffix *-tudo* (condition or quality). Do you have an *aptitude* for a particular sport?

Writing Hint

Too many prepositional phrases in sentences can make them confusing and singsongy. Avoid this problem by breaking apart and rewording sentences.

The cashmere sweaters are **on the rack next to the ties on display in front of the shirt counter.**

The cashmere sweaters are displayed **on a rack.** They're **next to the ties.** You'll find the ties displayed **in front of the shirt counter.**

Complete Course, page 161

Sentence Combining ▲

Frequent lessons teaching sentence combining give students the practice they need to master this valuable skill.

Skill Building

Thorough and clear presentation of grammar and usage concepts builds skills that students apply to their own writing.

Using Object Pronouns

USAGE
Lesson 10.2

Object Pronouns	
SINGULAR	**PLURAL**
me, you, him, her, it	us, you, them

🖊 Use an **object pronoun** when the pronoun functions as the direct object (DO), indirect object (IO), or object complement (OC) of a sentence or a clause.

      IO   IO   DO
My father gave Dolores and **me** the keys to the car.

         DO
We thanked **him** for the keys.

         DO   DO OC
The family counselor made **you** and **me us.**

🖊 Use an object pronoun when the pronoun functions as the object of a preposition (OP) in a sentence or clause.

         OP   OP
Dad handed the keys to Delores and **me.**

     OP   OP
For both of **us,** driving Dad's car was a big responsibility.

P.S. Don't become confused by the many terms that include the word *object.* Just get a general sense of how an object differs from a subject.

Exercise 4 **Choosing the Correct Pronoun**

Underline the pronoun in parentheses that correctly completes each sentence.

1. Every actor in his heart believes everything bad that's printed about (he, him). —Orson Welles

2. There is nothing which (we, us) receive with so much reluctance as advice. —Joseph Addison

3. Everything intercepts (we, us) from ourselves. —Ralph Waldo Emerson

4. A man in passion rides a horse that runs away with (he, him). —Thomas Fuller

5. We shape our buildings; thereafter, they shape (we, us). —Winston Churchill

See Grammar, Lesson 5.7, for more on direct and indirect objects and Lesson 5.9 for more on object complements.

Editing Tip

Avoid this common error: "between you and I." Always say or write, "between you and me."

Step by Step

To decide whether to use a subject pronoun or an object pronoun:

1. Decide what function the pronoun performs in the sentence.

2. If the pronoun is the subject or a predicate noun, use a subject pronoun.

3. If the pronoun is a direct object, an indirect object, an object complement, or the object of a preposition, use an object pronoun.

Cross References

References help students find related material throughout the book.

P.S. Features

Students begin to recognize that some rules and definitions are more important than others.

Step by Step

Strategies familiarize students with an alternate presentation of the more complex concepts of grammar.

Working Together

Frequent opportunities for students to work cooperatively help them realize that there are many ways to revise, edit, and proofread the same material.

Working Together

Exercise 14 **Writing Paragraphs**

The information in the table is about mean, or average, verbal and math scores of college-bound seniors from 1988 to 1997. Use the information in the table to write one or more paragraphs about trends in the Scholastic Aptitude Test (SAT) scores over that ten-year period. Exchange papers with a partner, and make suggestions for improving each other's paragraphs. Try combining related sentences by inserting phrases.

Refer to Composition, Lessons 3.4 and 3.5, to find strategies for writing an expository paragraph and essay.

SAT Mean Verbal and Math Scores of College-Bound Seniors										
	1988	**1989**	**1990**	**1991**	**1992**	**1993**	**1994**	**1995**	**1996**	**1997**
VERBAL SCORES	505	504	500	499	500	500	499	504	505	505
Males	512	510	505	503	504	504	501	505	507	507
Females	499	498	496	495	496	497	497	502	503	503
MATH SCORES	501	502	501	500	501	503	504	506	508	511
Males	521	523	521	520	521	524	523	525	527	530
Females	483	482	483	482	484	484	487	490	492	494

Source: The College Board

162 *Chapter 6 • Phrases*

Master the Mechanics of Writing

"Grammar for Writing helps students apply knowledge of writing conventions — punctuation, capitalization, and spelling — to their own writing and to the writing of others."

Beverly Ann Chin

Mechanics ▶

The conventions of mechanics include punctuation, capitalization, and spelling.

Thematic Practice Sets

Thematically related exercises encourage students to apply their new skills.

Complete Course, page 315

Semicolons

MECHANICS
Lesson 14.2

A **semicolon** can show that two or more ideas are closely related.

🖊 Use a semicolon to join independent clauses in a compound sentence *without* a coordinating conjunction.

Claude McKay was a great poet and essayist of the Harlem Renaissance; McKay did not write much after 1930. [Semicolon alone joins two independent clauses.]

Claude McKay had few equals as a poet; **however**, his novels were not as well crafted. [Semicolon (before conjunctive adverb) joins two independent clauses.]

Claude McKay had few equals as a poet; **as a result**, his poems still appear in textbooks. [Semicolon (before transitional expression) joins two independent clauses.]

Claude McKay was a great poet and essayist of the Harlem Renaissance, **but** he did not write much after 1930. [With a coordinating conjunction, a comma joins two independent clauses.]

You may use a semicolon between independent clauses joined by coordinating conjunctions if either clause contains a comma. But you don't have to.

She was the last one to read; but when she recited her poems, we were glad we'd stayed.

🖊 Use a semicolon to separate items in a series when one or more of the items contain a comma.

McKay was born in Upper Clarendon Parish, Jamaica; Langston Hughes was born in Joplin, Missouri, but grew up in Lawrence, Kansas; and Countee Cullen, born in Louisville, Kentucky, and adopted by a Methodist minister, grew up in New York City.

Common Conjunctive Adverbs

accordingly	meanwhile
also	moreover
besides	nevertheless
consequently	otherwise
furthermore	still
however	then
indeed	therefore

Common Transitional Expressions

as a result	in fact
for example	in other
for instance	words
from that	on the other
point on	hand
in addition	that is

Editing Tip

Do not use a semicolon between an independent clause and a dependent clause or phrase.

We read poems by Langston Hughes who is probably the best known of the Harlem Renaissance poets.

Exercise 3

Some of the
colons. Re
proper pu

1. Khalil
poets

2. Jean T
his lat

Exercise 4 Combining Sentences into Compound Sentences

On a separate piece of paper, combine each set of independent clauses into a compound sentence. Do *not* use coordinating conjunctions. You may introduce conjunctive adverbs and transitional expressions. Check your combined sentences for proper punctuation.

1. Zora Neale Hurston believed that folklore was priceless. It constitutes the art of the people, who never recognized it as art.

2. Hurston was a self-styled literary anthropologist. She used literary techniques to shape oral narratives.

3. She created a new literary language. The language reflected the poetry in the oral culture of rural blacks in the South.

4. Hurston wrote four novels, a memoir, and more than fifty shorter works. She was more prolific than any black woman writer had been before.

5. Hurston grew up in Eatonville, Florida. Eatonville was the first incorporated black community in the United States.

6. Hurston's mother was a teacher in Eatonville. Hurston's father served three terms as mayor there.

7. Hurston worked while in high school and college. She worked as a maid, waitress, and manicurist.

8. As an English major at Howard University, Hurston began writing short stories and poems. She joined the literary club there.

316 *Chapter 14 • Punctuation: All the Other Marks*

Complete Course, page 316

Skills Instruction

Concrete instruction focusing on relevant mechanical skills
helps improve students' understanding of writing conventions.

Quotation Marks

Lesson 14.3 shows italics (underlining) for certain works of art. This
lesson tells when to use quotation marks for shorter works and for other
purposes as well.

● Use **quotation marks** for titles of short works.

POEMS	"Ode to a Grecian Urn" "The Lake Isle of Innisfree"
SHORT STORIES	"Araby" "The Fall of the House of Usher"
ARTICLES	"Going Out of Our Gourds Over Pumpkins"
SONGS	"The Star-Spangled Banner" "Penny Lane"
SINGLE TV PROGRAMS	"Rescue at Sea" (an episode of *American Experience*)
PARTS OF BOOKS	Part I, "Essays and Memoirs"

● Use quotation marks at the beginning and end of a direct
quotation, but not with an indirect quotation.

Introduce a short, one-sentence quotation with a comma or a
colon; introduce a quotation that is a long sentence or more
than one sentence with a colon.

> Of T. S. Eliot, critics wrote, "Eliot was better equipped than any
> other poet to bring free verse into the twentieth century."

When only a word or two is quoted, use a lowercase letter if the
quoted words do not begin the sentence.

> T. S. Eliot referred to W. B. Yeats as "the greatest poet."
> [no capital letter in quotation]

● Use single quotation marks for titles or quotes within a quotation.

> Brenda asked, "Have you read T. S. Eliot's poem 'Gerontion'?"

● The following rules apply to quotation marks with other marks.

Commas and periods These marks g

> "Dinner is ready," he announced.

Semicolons and colons These marks
quotation mark.

> Here are three reasons I like "Araby":

**Question marks and exclamation
quotation marks if the quotation is a d
go outside if the whole sentence is a q

> "Did everyone read the poem**?**" she a
> Was she surprised when you said, "No

Editing Tips

Features help students
avoid the pitfalls of
writing by alerting them
to possible problem areas
and common errors.

Editing Tip

Don't use two question
marks with a single
quotation mark.

Do you know the line after
"Where have all the flowers
gone"**?**

Don't use quotation
marks for nicknames or
slang.

His nickname is "Spike";
he's a "yuppie."

after death.

10. Eavan Boland dedicated her 1967 book of poems, "New Territory," to
    her mother.

Exercise 8 — Write Your Own Exercise

On a separate piece of paper, write one or more complete sentences for
each item below. Mention actual titles wherever possible, but leave out all
punctuation marks. Then exchange papers with a classmate. See if you agree
on how to punctuate each sentence.

1. Your thoughts about an episode of a TV program you watched recently
   (Make up a name for the episode if you don't remember it.)
2. A song that you've heard recently
3. A direct quotation (actual or made up) at the beginning of a sentence
4. A quotation within a quotation
5. A short story or magazine article you've read and your thoughts about it
6. A poem you've read and your thoughts about it
7. A title of a chapter of a book you are reading and a summary of that chapter

Abundant Practice ▶

Thorough exercises
reinforce lesson
concepts.

Instructional Support

Teacher's Edition

- **Presents ideas and prompts for students' writing**
- **Includes strategies for effective grammar instruction**
- **Provides assessment rubrics for evaluating students' writing**
- **Supplies checklists for revising, editing, and proofreading**
- **Provides answers on the page and in the Answer Key**

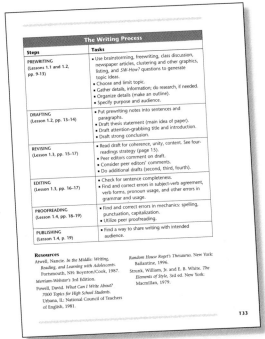

	The Writing Process	
Steps	**Tasks**	
PREWRITING (Lessons 1.1 and 1.2, pp. 9–13)	▪ Use brainstorming, freewriting, class discussion, newspaper articles, clustering and other graphics, listing, and *SW-How?* questions to generate topic ideas. ▪ Choose and limit topic. ▪ Gather details, information; do research, if needed. ▪ Organize details (make an outline). ▪ Specify purpose and audience.	
DRAFTING (Lesson 1.2, pp. 13–14)	▪ Put prewriting notes into sentences and paragraphs. ▪ Draft thesis statement (main idea of paper). ▪ Draft attention-grabbing title and introduction. ▪ Draft strong conclusion.	
REVISING (Lesson 1.3, pp. 15–17)	▪ Read draft for coherence, unity, content. See four-readings strategy (page 15). ▪ Peer editors comment on draft. ▪ Consider peer editors' comments. ▪ Do additional drafts (second, third, fourth).	
EDITING (Lesson 1.3, pp. 16–17)	▪ Check for sentence completeness. ▪ Find and correct errors in subject-verb agreement, verb forms, pronoun usage, and other errors in grammar and usage.	
PROOFREADING (Lesson 1.4, pp. 18–19)	▪ Find and correct errors in mechanics: spelling, punctuation, capitalization. ▪ Utilize peer proofreading.	
PUBLISHING (Lesson 1.4, p. 19)	▪ Find a way to share writing with intended audience.	

Resources

Atwell, Nancie. *In the Middle: Writing, Reading, and Learning with Adolescents.* Portsmouth, NH: Boynton/Cook, 1987.

Merriam-Webster's 3rd Edition.

Powell, David. *What Can I Write About? 7000 Topics for High School Students.* Urbana, IL: National Council of Teachers of English, 1981.

Random House Roget's Thesaurus. New York: Ballantine, 1996.

Strunk, William, Jr. and E. B. White. *The Elements of Style,* 3rd ed. New York: Macmillan, 1979.

T33

Writing Process Guidelines ▲

- List the steps of the writing process
- Provide strategies for teaching each of the steps
- Help customize instruction for varying ability levels

▼ Annotated Teacher's Edition Pages

Provide convenient on-page answers and annotations

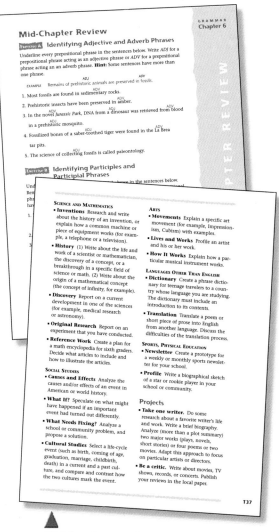

GRAMMAR
Chapter 6

Mid-Chapter Review

Exercise A Identifying Adjective and Adverb Phrases

Underline every prepositional phrase in the sentences below. Write *ADJ* for a prepositional phrase acting as an adjective phrase or *ADV* for a prepositional phrase acting an an adverb phrase. **Hint:** Some sentences have more than one phrase.

EXAMPLE   Remains of prehistoric animals are preserved in fossils.

1. Most fossils are found in sedimentary rocks.
2. Prehistoric insects have been preserved in amber.
3. In the novel *Jurassic Park*, DNA from a dinosaur was retrieved from blood in a prehistoric mosquito.
4. Fossilized bones of a saber-toothed tiger were found in the La Brea tar pits.
5. The science of collecting fossils is called paleontology.

Exercise B Identifying Participles and Participial Phrases

CHAPTER REVIEW

SCIENCE AND MATHEMATICS

- **Inventions** Research and write about the history of an invention, or explain how a common machine or piece of equipment works (for example, a telephone or a television).
- **History** (1) Write about the life and work of a scientist or mathematician, the discovery of a concept, or a breakthrough in a specific field of science or math. (2) Write about the origin of a mathematical concept (the concept of infinity, for example).
- **Discovery** Report on a current development in one of the sciences (for example, medical research or astronomy).
- **Original Research** Report on an experiment that you have conducted.
- **Reference Work** Create a plan for a math encyclopedia for sixth graders. Decide what articles to include and how to illustrate the articles.

SOCIAL STUDIES

- **Causes and Effects** Analyze the causes and/or effects of an event in American or world history.
- **What If?** Speculate on what might have happened if an important event had turned out differently.
- **What Needs Fixing?** Analyze a school or community problem, and propose a solution.
- **Cultural Studies** Select a life-cycle event (such as birth, coming of age, graduation, marriage, childbirth, death) in a current and a past culture, and compare and contrast how the two cultures mark the event.

ARTS

- **Movements** Explain a specific art movement (for example, Impressionism, Cubism) with examples.
- **Lives and Works** Profile an artist and his or her work.
- **How It Works** Explain how a particular musical instrument works.

LANGUAGES OTHER THAN ENGLISH

- **Dictionary** Create a phrase dictionary for teenage travelers to a country whose language you are studying. The dictionary must include an introduction to its contents.
- **Translation** Translate a poem or short piece of prose into English from another language. Discuss the difficulties of the translation process.

SPORTS, PHYSICAL EDUCATION

- **Newsletter** Create a prototype for a weekly or monthly sports newsletter for your school.
- **Profile** Write a biographical sketch of a star or rookie player in your school or community.

Projects

- **Take one writer.** Do some research about a favorite writer's life and work. Write a brief biography. Analyze (more than a plot summary) two major works (plays, novels, short stories) or four poems or two movies. Adapt this approach to focus on particular artists or directors.
- **Be a critic.** Write about movies, TV shows, records, or concerts. Publish your reviews in the local paper.

T37

▲ Writing Across the Curriculum

- **Gives teachers a variety of writing ideas and projects**

Introduction and Conclusion

❏ Does the introduction make you want to read more? What suggestions can you make for improving it?

❏ Does it introduce the topic and the main idea?

❏ Does the conclusion end the essay strongly?

You may want to offer students variations on peer checklists from time to time. One option is to generate mode-specific checklists such as the ones below or even assignment-specific checklists. (See also the discussion of rubrics on pp. 52–55.)

Mode-Specific Checklists

Checklist for Persuasive Writing	❏ Is the writer's opinion clearly stated? ❏ Does the writer give at least two reasons to support that opinion? ❏ Are the reasons themselves supported by convincing evidence (facts, statistics, examples, anecdotes, quotations, and so on)? ❏ Do you understand what the writer wants the reader to do? ❏ Has the writer persuaded you? Why or why not?
Checklist for Narrative Writing	❏ Does the beginning make you want to read more? ❏ Does the writer *show* characters in action and let you hear what they say, or does the writer simply *tell* you about characters? ❏ Does the writing include sensory details? ❏ Are the writer's comparisons relevant and illuminating? ❏ Has the writer used specific nouns and vivid verbs (especially, as alternatives for *said*)? ❏ Is the ending satisfying?
Checklist for Descriptive Writing	❏ Can you picture the setting? ❏ Does the writing include specific sensory details? ❏ Are the comparisons fresh? ❏ Does the organization of details (for example, proceeding from near to far, left to right, or top to bottom) make sense? ❏ Does the description establish an overall mood? What is it?

Editing and Proofreading

As previously mentioned, this series separates the revising task (which focuses on content, style, and organization) from the editing task (which focuses on grammar and usage). Proofreading is the stage of the writing process when students look for mechanical errors in spelling, punctuation, and capitalization. These checklists provide references either for the teacher or the student.

Editing Checklist

❏ Is every sentence grammatically complete (not a fragment or a run-on)? *Lesson 5.1*

❏ Do subjects and verbs agree in number and gender? *Chapter 9*

❏ Are the correct forms of pronouns used? *Chapter 10*

❏ Does each pronoun clearly refer to an antecedent? *Lesson 10.5*

❏ Are verb tenses used consistently, unless there is good reason to vary them? *Chapter 8*

❏ Are the correct forms of irregular verbs used? *Chapter 8*

❏ Are the correct forms of plural nouns and the comparative forms of adjectives and adverbs used? *Chapter 4*

Proofreading Checklist

❏ Is every word spelled correctly? Check a dictionary if you're unsure. *Chapter 16*

❏ Have homonyms been confused (*their* instead of *there*, for example)? *Chapter 16*

❏ Do proper nouns and proper adjectives begin with capital letters? *Chapter 15*

❏ Does every sentence begin with a capital letter and end with an end punctuation mark? *Chapters 13 and 14*

❏ Are commas used correctly in all of their many uses? *Chapter 13*

❏ Is dialogue punctuated correctly? *Lesson 14.6*

Resources

In the classroom, students should have access to several copies of a good college dictionary and a dictionary-style thesaurus.

Grammar for Writing and ELL Problems

Problem Area in English	Comment	Grammar for Writing Treatment, Fourth Course
ADJECTIVE CLAUSES	Forming and positioning adjective clauses cause problems for speakers of Asian languages, of Arabic and Hebrew, and even of Latin-based languages.	Lesson 7.2
ARTICLES	ELL students often leave out the article before a singular count noun.	Lesson 4.4
CAPITALIZATION	Arabic, Chinese, and Hebrew do not use capital letters; Dutch and German capitalize some forms of the second-person pronoun; German caps all nouns.	Chapter 15
EXPLETIVES	Spanish speakers sometimes omit subjects, saying "Is raining."	Chapter 5 covers the "It is raining" sentence structure.
HOMOPHONES	Speakers of Asian languages in particular may be confused by the concept of words sounding alike but having different meanings.	Chapter 12
NEGATION	Multiple negation is common in French and Russian, among other languages.	Lesson 11.3
PLURALS	Some Asian languages have no plural forms for nouns.	Lesson 4.1, Chapter 9, Lesson 16.4
PREFIXES AND SUFFIXES	These word parts are absent in Asian languages.	Lesson 16.3
PREPOSITIONS	English distinguishes between *in* and *on*; Spanish uses *en* for both.	Lessons 4.7 and 6.1
SILENT LETTERS	There are no silent letters in Spanish.	Chapter 16
SUBJECTS, DOUBLE	Some languages add personal pronouns as suffixes or prefixes, leading ELL speakers to say, "Maria she is pretty."	Lessons 5.2, 5.5, 10.1
TENSES	▪ Certain English verbs don't work in the present progressive, but ESL students may say or write, "I am knowing the answer." ▪ In some languages, time is not signaled by word endings but rather by words that native English speakers would call adverbs.	Lessons 4.3 and 8.5
WORD ORDER	▪ In some languages, word order determines the part of speech. For example, the verb is the last word in sentences in Turkish, Korean, and Japanese. ▪ In Russian, subject and object may switch places without affecting meaning.	Lessons 5.1, 5.2, 5.8, 5.9, and 13.1

▲ **Practical Teacher Checklists**

- Checklists for evaluating types of writing
- Checklists for monitoring the writing process

◀ **Support for English Language Learners**

- Shows how specific content in English might pose difficulties in another language and where to find help within *Grammar for Writing*

Assessment

Ongoing Assessment ▶ in the Student Edition

- **Mid-Chapter and Chapter Review Exercises**
- **Cumulative Review of Units**
- **Grammar, Usage, and Mechanics Tests**

...in the ▶ Teacher's Edition

- **Rubrics for Evaluating Students' Writing**

...and in the Student Test Booklet ▶

Also available is a student Test Booklet for each grade level. The Test Booklets extend testing and assessment opportunities and include comprehensive standardized chapter tests that review and reinforce new concepts. A Diagnostic Test and a Mastery Test help teachers identify problem areas and place students within the program.

Technology

www.sadlier-oxford.com

Portfolio Projects

At the beginning of each chapter of *Grammar for Writing*, an Internet prompt directs students to the Sadlier-Oxford website, where they will find a portfolio project suggestion incorporating the concepts from the chapter. Teacher suggestions support each project with assessment suggestions and teaching guidelines.

STUDENT WRITING
Narrative Essay

Working Pride
by Lacey Waldron
high school student, El Cajon, California

As I drove to my job interview on a sunny Saturday afternoon, my palms began to sweat. This was my first job interview, and I wanted to make sure I did everything perfectly. I thought to myself, "What should I say? How should I act?" As I came up to a white duplex that read "DR. McDONALD'S OFFICE," I started to panic. Looking at the clock, I realized I had ten minutes until I had to be in the office. I kept reminding myself that everything would be okay, but that was very hard to believe as my stomach began to turn in circles. After parking my car and fixing myself up, I slowly walked up to the office. Turning the knob of the large, oak door, it was time—time to suck up my fear and put my best foot forward. The first person that I met as I walked through the door was a lady named Mary. Mary seemed like she was a very kind hearted woman. She made me feel at home instantly. Before I knew it, a man who was skinny and had gray hair came walking out; it was Dr. McDonald.

I walked over and met him halfway, and he said, "You must be Lacey." I shook his hand firmly and remembered to make eye contact. I also remembered what my mom had advised me minutes earlier and told myself to relax. After a short interview, Dr. McDonald finished by saying, "I will call you and tell you when I want you to start working." I thanked him, shook his hand again, and walked out to my car.

"I GOT IT!" I said, "I GOT THE JOB!!" I couldn't wait to tell my mom the good news!

Getting my first job has really affected my life; it teaches me responsibility and gives me something to do rather than to get into trouble. My parents also seem to look at me as more responsible, and that's enough of a reward for me. Having money of my own has its ups and downs at times. But having the job that I am proud of is a valuable achievement that can never be forgotten.

Lacey Waldron organizes her personal narrative chronologically—in the order the events happened. She uses transition words and expressions such as *after, first,* and *before*. She also includes dialogue to make the reader feel close to the action. In the last paragraph, Lacey explains the significance of the event—what the incident meant to her.

Reread Lacey's essay and notice that each sentence is a little different from the one before. As you work on sentences in this chapter, think about how you can manipulate them communicate your ideas in an interesting way.

124 Chapter 5 • Parts of a Sentence

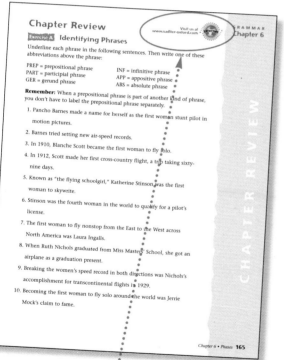

Chapter Review

Exercise A Identifying Phrases

GRAMMAR
Chapter 6

Underline each phrase in the following sentences. Then write one of these abbreviations above the phrase:

PREP = prepositional phrase
PART = participial phrase
GER = gerund phrase
INF = infinitive phrase
APP = appositive phrase
ABS = absolute phrase

Remember: When a prepositional phrase is part of another kind of phrase, you don't have to label the prepositional phrase separately.

1. Pancho Barnes made a name for herself as the first woman stunt pilot in motion pictures.
2. Barnes tried setting new air-speed records.
3. In 1910, Blanche Scott became the first woman to fly solo.
4. In 1912, Scott made her first cross-country flight, a trip taking sixty-nine days.
5. Known as "the flying schoolgirl," Katherine Stinson was the first woman to skywrite.
6. Stinson was the fourth woman in the world to qualify for a pilot's license.
7. The first woman to fly nonstop from the East to the West across North America was Laura Ingalls.
8. When Ruth Nichols graduated from Miss Masters' School, she got an airplane as a graduation present.
9. Breaking the women's speed record in both directions was Nichols's accomplishment for transcontinental flights in 1929.
10. Becoming the first woman to fly solo around the world was Jerrie Mock's claim to fame.

CHAPTER REVIEW

Chapter 6 • Phrases **165**

Publishing Hyperlinks

In each Chapter Review, an Internet prompt directs students to discover hyperlinks to student writing and publishing websites, as well as a list of creative ways for students to publish their writing, both on-line and in print publications.

ALTERNATE ASSESSMENT OPPORTUNITIES

ON THE INTERNET
- Chapter-specific portfolio project assignments
- Opportunities for long-term projects

TEACHER SUPPORT
- Suggestions for providing support for projects

Content Overview

	UNIT I: COMPOSITION									UNIT II: GRAMMAR																
	Writing Workshops									Parts of Speech								Phrases					Clauses				
	The Writing Process	Writing Paragraphs	Writing Essays	Narrative Writing	Persuasive Writing	Expository Writing	Writing About Literature	Research Paper	Special Writing Tasks	Combining Sentences	Parts of a Sentence	Subjects and Predicates	Sentence Fragments	Run-on Sentences	Direct and Indirect Objects	Predicate Nominatives and Adjectives	Object Complements	Prepositional Phrases	Participial Phrases	Gerund Phrases	Infinitive Phrases	Appositive Phrases	Adjective Clauses	Adverb Clauses	Noun Clauses	Sentence Structures	Parallel Structure
Fourth Course Grade 9	■	■	■	■		■	■	■	■	■	■	■		■		■		■	■	■	■	■	■	■	■	■	
Fifth Course Grade 10	■	■	■	■	■	■	■	■	■	■	■	■	■	■	■	■	■	■	■	■	■	■	■	■	■	■	■
Sixth Course Grade 11	■	■	■	■	■■	■	■	■	■	■	■	■	■	■	■	■	■	■	■	■	■	■	■	■	■	■	■
Complete Course Grade 12	■	■	■	■	■■	■	■■	■	■	■	■	■	■	■	■	■	■	■	■	■	■	■	■	■	■	■	■

UNIT III: USAGE

Using Verbs
- Regular and Irregular Verbs
- Verb Tenses
- Active Voice
- Mood

Agreement
- Person and Number, Compound Subjects
- Indefinite Pronouns

Using Pronouns
- Subject and Object Pronouns
- Who or Whom?
- Agreement with Antecedents

Using Modifiers
- Degrees of Comparison
- Double Negatives
- Misplaced and Dangling Modifiers
- Usage Handbook

UNIT IV: MECHANICS

Punctuation
- End Marks and Abbreviations
- Commas in a Series
- Compound Sentences and Phrases
- Colons and Semicolons
- Italics
- Quotation Marks
- Dashes, Parentheses, Brackets, Ellipses
- Titles

Capitalization
- Organizations, Religions, School Subjects
- Historical Events, Documents, Periods
- Calendar Items, Brand Names
- Business Writing

Spelling
- Spelling Rules
- Prefixes and Suffixes
- Noun Plurals
- Commonly Misspelled Words

KEY

■ = Lesson(s) dedicated to listed topic

sixth course

SADLIER-OXFORD
GRAMMAR
FOR WRITING

Teacher's Edition

Sadlier-Oxford
A Division of William H. Sadlier, Inc.
New York, New York 10005-1002

Teacher's Edition: ISBN: 0-8215-0321-9
Student Edition: ISBN: 0-8215-0311-1

123456789/05 04 03 02 01 00 99

CONTENTS

Introduction to Sixth Course

Grammar for Writing Sixth Course is one part of a new grammar and composition program for high school students, grades 9–12. This book provides a full year's work—all the grammar and writing that students need to know plus assignments and exercises to fill the school year. Used together with a literature program and literature-based writing assignments, this book gives you a powerful component to a complete language arts program for students.

This series emphasizes grammar as it applies to writing. It has a user-friendly tone. Its minilessons zoom right to the essentials. Its teaching is prescriptive—with easy-to-follow rules, definitions, instruction, and examples. Students are encouraged to view good grammar not as a list of rules that must be memorized for their own sake but as a valuable tool that can help them improve their writing.

Grammar for Writing prepares students for standardized testing.

The grammar, usage, and mechanics sections address the conventions of standard English that students need to know for state assessment tests and national tests, such as the PSAT and SAT. The three Grammar, Usage, and Mechanics Tests in standardized test format (error recognition and error correction) prepare students for the writing exam in the PSAT test. Two-page Mid-Chapter, Chapter, and Cumulative Reviews reinforce and test students' understanding of writing and grammar concepts. In addition, there is a separate forty-eight page Test Booklet.

Grammar for Writing helps students meet the standards for writing.

In the writing sections and throughout the text, students learn to express and develop their ideas coherently and to write concisely. In Chapter 3, "Writing Workshops," students proceed step-by-step through the writing process as they write for a variety of audiences and for different purposes. They conduct research on issues that interest them, using libraries and electronic databases. The text gives students repeated practice in revising and editing samples of poor writing. Students correct errors in grammar, usage, and mechanics; they use sentence-combining strategies to improve the flow of their writing.

Use *Grammar for Writing* with students of varying ability levels.

Exercises can be done individually by students needing to learn, review, and practice a particular grammar, usage, or mechanics concept. Frequently, exercises are done cooperatively with a partner or small group. You might pair LEP (Limited English Proficiency) students with more proficient students to create an informal tutoring-buddy system. Give mainstreamed ELL (English Language Learner) students many opportunities to *hear* standard English used correctly. You might have them read aloud corrected exercise sentences and paragraphs, for example, and use small-group activities to give ELL students speaking and listening practice. Advanced students might go over lessons and exercises with less advanced students. Challenge these students to do more writing, create new exercises, and turn their Write What You Think exercises into longer papers.

Use *Grammar for Writing* with a variety of schedules.

At the beginning or end of a class period, students can work on minilessons (the teaching text and exercises). You might go over the teaching text in class and assign the exercises to be started in class and finished as homework. Students can also meet in writing groups or with partners to work on both cooperative-learning exercises marked by the Working Together label and ongoing writing projects, such as the exercises in Chapter 3. Students can meet regularly in writing groups and in peer editing sessions.

If the whole class shows repeated weakness in one grammar concept (say subject-verb agreement), set aside a block of time to go over the appropriate lesson(s) carefully. Assign the exercises as group, partner, or individual work; and meet as a class or in small groups to compare exercise answers. Comparing finished writing is especially useful when students do a Revising and Editing Worksheet exercise (see page 98). Since there are no single right answers to these worksheets, students will learn even more by seeing and discussing how other groups or teams have revised the flawed writing samples.

Grammar for Writing improves students' critical thinking skills.

The Write What You Think exercises throughout the book give students practice in developing, supporting, and evaluating arguments on real-life issues. Students develop and strengthen their persuasive skills by giving logical reasons and evidence to support their opinions.

In most of the lessons in Chapter 3, a series of questions, marked by a Critical Thinking label, leads students to analyze professional models of writing. These questions might be used as an assignment or as a prompt for class discussion.

Features and Benefits of Grammar for Writing

Throughout the book, *Grammar for Writing* honors its commitment to teach the fundamentals of grammar through the context of writing. The following charts itemize how both the unit called "Composition" and the units called "Grammar," "Usage," and "Mechanics" incorporate features that help today's students express their thoughts clearly and succinctly.

Unit: Composition	
Feature	**Benefit**
LESSONS	Students spend more time working on writing assignments than reading about writing.
EASY-TO-SCAN LISTS OF ADVICE	Students can locate strategies, directions, and other help faster than is possible with extensive, run-on instruction.
WRITING HINTS	Students learn that writers consider not only important, general principles—such as coherence—but also practical, specific problems—such as "How can I figure out if this topic is too broad?" and "How should I publish this piece?"
"WRITING WORKSHOPS" SETUP	Students realize that regardless of what they write, they can *always* apply the multistage writing process.
COOPERATIVE-LEARNING EXERCISES *Working Together*	Students learn that *every* writer needs an editor; students learn that a writing prompt may stimulate many different responses.
Modes of Writing	**Benefit**
NARRATIVE	Students tell a story—a fictional or true narrative. They use steps, critical events, or chronological order.
PERSUASIVE	Students learn to convince a reader. They use well-reasoned arguments, persuasive language, and emotional appeals in order of importance.
EXPOSITORY	Students explain or inform; they state the main idea. They use facts, examples, quotations, statistics, and definitions presented in a logical order.

Units: Grammar, Usage, Mechanics

Feature	Benefit
SUCCINCT INSTRUCTION	Students quickly move on to exercises.
COOPERATIVE-LEARNING EXERCISES *Working Together*	Students realize that a particular sentence-level problem may yield a variety of solutions.
"WRITE WHAT YOU THINK" EXERCISES	Students doing these persuasive-writing activities get ongoing practice in supporting an opinion with reasons and examples.
WRITING HINTS	Students learn that the end purpose of grammar, usage, and mechanics is applying those skills to paragraphs and essays.
EDITING TIPS	Students, forewarned of common errors, have a head start in working through exercises instead of feeling trapped or tricked by them.
STEP-BY-STEPS	Students exposed to an alternative presentation of the more complex concepts have a greater chance of understanding them.
P.S. NOTES	Students begin to recognize that some rules and definitions are more important than others.
REVISING AND EDITING WORKSHEETS	Students get opportunities to see that all drafts need revising and editing—and that multiple solutions exist.
REVIEWS, REVIEWS, REVIEWS	Students learn, through mid-chapter, chapter, and cumulative reviews, that in reviewing any written material they must be on the lookout for several potential sentence-level problems—that real writing doesn't neatly present only one problem at a time.
TESTS IN STANDARDIZED FORMATS	Students lose some fear of test taking by developing competence in error-recognition and error-correction question formats.
ENRICHING YOUR VOCABULARY	Students develop vocabulary skills by being exposed to words used in context and by immediately reading the meanings of these words in a sidebar.

The Role of Grammar in Improving Students' Writing

by Beverly Ann Chin

Grammar is the sound, structure, and meaning system of language. All languages have grammar, and each language has its own grammar. People who speak the same language are able to communicate because they intuitively know the grammar system of that language—that is, the rules of making meaning. Students who are native speakers of English already know English grammar. They recognize the sounds of English words, the meanings of those words, and the different ways of putting words together to make meaningful sentences.

However, while students may be effective speakers of English, they need guidance to become effective writers. They need to learn how to apply their knowledge of grammatical concepts from oral language to written language.

Effective grammar instruction shows students what they already know about grammar, and it helps them use this knowledge as they write. By connecting their knowledge of oral language to written language, teachers can demystify abstract grammatical terminology so that students can write—and read—with greater competence and confidence.

What Does Research Say About Grammar and the Teaching of Writing?

Strong research evidence suggests that the most beneficial way of helping students improve their command of grammar in writing is to use students' writing as the basis for discussing grammatical concepts. Researchers agree that it is more effective to teach punctuation, sentence variety, and usage in the context of writing than to approach the topic by teaching isolated skills (Calkins, 1980; DiStefano and Killion, 1984; Harris, 1962).

As students revise and edit their writing, teachers can provide grammar instruction that guides students in their attempts to identify and correct problems in sentence structure and usage. For example, if a teacher sees that many students are writing sentences containing misplaced modifiers, the teacher can present a minilesson on this concept using examples from student writing. The teacher can have students edit their own and each other's drafts for this problem.

Integrating grammar instruction into the revising and editing process helps students make immediate applications, thus allowing them to see the relevance of grammar in their own writing.

To What Specific Aspects of Writing Does Grammar Contribute?

Because writing is a complex activity for many students, teachers should focus on the grammatical concepts that are essential for the clear communication of meaning.

Research on the teaching of grammar since the early 1900s shows that grammar instruction that is separate from writing instruction does not improve students' writing competence (Braddock and others, 1963; Hillocks, 1986). In addition, research indicates that the transfer of formal grammar instruction to writing is not applicable to larger elements of composition. Through detailed studies of students' writing, Shaughnessy (1977) concludes that the best grammar instruction is one that gives the greatest return for the least investment of time. Shaughnessy advocates four important grammatical concepts: the sentence, inflection, tense, and agreement. She recommends that teachers encourage students to examine grammatical errors in their own writing. She also cautions teachers not to overemphasize grammatical terminology to the detriment of students' ability to understand and apply the concepts.

Weaver (1998) proposes a similar approach to teaching grammar in the context of writing. She writes, "What all students need . . . is guidance in understanding and applying those aspects of grammar that are most relevant to writing." In a chart as reproduced here, Weaver proposes five grammatical concepts that enable writers to show improvement in sentence revision, style, and editing.

A minimum of grammar for maximum benefits

1. Teaching concepts of subject, verb, sentence, clause, phrase, and related concepts for editing
2. Teaching style through sentence combining and sentence generating
3. Teaching sentence sense through the manipulation of syntactic elements
4. Teaching both the power of dialects and the dialects of power
5. Teaching punctuation and mechanics for convention, clarity, and style

(Weaver, 1998, pp. 21–23)

Rather than striving to teach all grammatical concepts to all students, teachers should prioritize and provide instruction on the grammatical elements that most affect their students' ability to write effectively. Teachers should also be sensitive to individual students' readiness to learn and apply grammatical concepts.

How Does Sentence Combining Improve Writing?

Sentence combining is the strategy of joining short sentences into longer, more complex sentences. As students engage in sentence-combining activities, they learn how to vary sentence structure in order to change meaning and style. Numerous studies (Mellon, 1969; O'Hare, 1973; Cooper, 1975; Shaughnessy, 1977; Hillocks, 1986; Strong, 1986) show that the use of sentence combining is an effective method for improving students' writing. The value of sentence combining is most evident as students recognize the effect of sentence variety (beginnings, lengths, complexities) in their own writing.

Hillocks (1986) stated that "sentence-combining practice provides writers with systematic knowledge of syntactic possibilities, the access to which allows them to sort through alternatives in their heads as well as on paper and to choose those which are most apt" (150). Research also shows that sentence combining is more effective than freewriting in enhancing the quality of student writing (Hillocks, 1986).

Hillocks and Smith (1991) show that systematic practice in sentence combining can increase students' knowledge of syntactic structures as well as improve the quality of students' sentences, particularly when stylistic effects are discussed as well. Sentence-combining exercises can be either written or oral, structured or unstructured. Structured sentence-combining exercises give students more guidance in the ways to create the new sentences; unstructured sentence-combining exercises allow for more variation, but they still require students to create logical, meaningful sentences. Hillocks (1986) reports that, in many studies, sentence-combining exercises produce significant increases in students' sentence-writing maturity.

Given Noguchi's (1991) analysis that grammar choices affect writing style, sentence combining is an effective method that helps students develop fluency and variety in their own writing style. Students can discover sentence variety, length, parallelism, and other syntactic devices by comparing their sentences with sentences from other writers. They also discover the decisions writers make when they revise sentences for their effect on readers.

Teachers can design their own sentence-combining activities by using short sentences from student writing or other appropriate sources. For example, teachers who notice many choppy sentences in students' writing can place these sentences on an overhead for all their students to read. Teachers can then ask different students to combine orally the short sentences in a variety of ways. As students share their different sentence combinations, their teacher can show students how they are naturally applying grammatical concepts such as clauses, phrases, modification, conjunctions, appositives, antecedents, and verb forms.

By participating in oral and written sentence-combining activities, students discover the relationships among meaning, sentence structure, usage, and punctuation. When presented as a revising strategy, sentence-combining activities help students identify short, choppy sentences in their own writing, leading them to combine their ideas in more fluid and sophisticated ways. As students generate more complex sentences from shorter sentences, they discover how the arrangement of phrases and clauses affects meaning and their readers.

What Strategies Can Teachers Use to Teach *Grammar for Writing*?

Grammar instruction is most naturally integrated during the revising, editing, and proofreading phases of the writing process. After students have written their first drafts and feel comfortable with the ideas and organization of their writing, teachers may wish to employ various strategies to help students see grammatical concepts as language choices that can enhance their writing purpose.

For example, teachers can help students revise for effective word choices in a writing conference. As the teacher and student discuss the real audience(s) for the writing, the teacher can ask the student to consider how formal or informal the writing should be. The teacher can remind the student that all people vary their level of language (formal to informal) in oral conversations, depending on their listeners and the speaking context. The teacher can then help the student identify words that change the level of formality of the writing.

Teachers can help students revise boring, monotonous sentences by having a partner read aloud the writing to the student writer. As the partner reads the writing aloud to the writer, both the partner and the writer can recognize when too many sentences begin with "It is" or "There are." Both the partner and the writer can discuss ways to vary the sentence beginnings. After the writer revises the sentences, the partner can read the sentences aloud, and both can discuss the effectiveness of the revision.

Teachers can help students edit from passive voice to active voice by presenting a minilesson. In editing groups, students can exchange papers and look for verbs that often signal the passive voice, such as "was" and "been." When students find these verbs, they can read the sentence aloud to their partners and discuss whether the voice is passive and, if so, if the sentence might be strengthened with an active-voice verb. The student writer can decide which voice is most effective and appropriate for the writing purpose and audience.

Teachers can help students become better proofreaders through peer editing groups. Based on the writing abilities of students, teachers can assign different proofreading tasks to specific individuals in each group. For example, one person in the group can proofread for spelling errors, another person for agreement errors, another person for fragments and run-ons, and another person for punctuation errors. As students develop increasing skill in proofreading, they can become responsible for more proofreading areas. Collaborating with classmates in peer editing groups helps students improve their own grammar skills as well as understand the importance of grammar as a tool for effective communication.

As teachers integrate grammar instruction into writing instruction, they should use the grammar terms that make sense to the students. By incorporating grammar terms naturally into the processes of revising, editing, and proofreading, teachers help students understand and apply grammar purposefully to their own (student) writing. Strategies such as writing conferences, partnership writing, grammar minilessons, and peer response groups are all valuable methods for integrating grammar into writing instruction.

How Does the Teaching of Grammar Relate to the National Content Standards for Students?

The National Council of Teachers of English and the International Reading Association (1996) published *Standards for the English Language Arts*, which defines "what students should know and be able to do with language" (p. 1). While the twelve content standards are presented as a list, they are closely intertwined and emphasize the complex interactions among language skills. Standards 4, 5, and 6 most directly address students' ability to write.

Standard 4: "Students adjust their use of spoken, written, and visual language (e.g., conventions, style, vocabulary) to communicate effectively with a variety of audiences and for different purposes" (p. 3).

Standard 5: "Students employ a wide range of strategies as they write and use different writing process elements appropriately to communicate with different audiences for a variety of purposes" (p. 3).

Standard 6: "Students apply knowledge of language structure, language conventions (e.g., spelling and punctuation), media techniques, figurative language, and genre to create, critique, and discuss print and nonprint texts" (p. 3).

According to the standards:

By closely observing students' writing processes and carefully reading their work, teachers can see which aspects of language structure are giving students trouble and help them learn these concepts through direct instruction and practice. It is also important for students to discover that grammar, spelling, and punctuation are useful not only in the context of fixing problems or mistakes; they can be studied effectively in a workshop context in which students work together to expand their repertoire of syntactic and verbal styles. When students connect the study of grammar and language patterns to the wider purposes of communication and artistic development, they are considerably more likely to incorporate such study into their working knowledge (p. 37).

The national content standards for English language arts are based on professional research and the best classroom practices. While the standards acknowledge the importance of grammar concepts, they clearly recommend that students learn and apply their knowledge of grammar for the purpose of effective communication. By embedding grammar instruction into writing instruction, teachers can positively affect students' actual writing skills.

References

Braddock, R., Lloyd-Jones, R., and Schoer, L. *Research in Written Composition.* Urbana, IL: National Council of Teachers of English, 1963.

Calkins, L. M. "When Children Want to Punctuate: Basic Skills Belong in Context." *Language Arts* 57 (1980): 567–73.

Cooper, C. "Research Roundup: Oral and Written Composition." *English Journal* 64 (1975): 72.

DiStefano, P., and Killion, J. "Assessing Writing Skills Through a Process Approach." *English Education* 16,4 (1984): 203–7.

Harris, R. J. "An Experimental Inquiry into the Functions and Value of Formal Grammar in the Teaching of Written English to Children Aged Twelve to Fourteen." Ph.D. Diss., University of London, 1962.

Hillocks, G., Jr. *Research on Written Composition: New Directions for Teaching.* Urbana, IL: ERIC Clearinghouse on Reading and Communication Skills and the National Conference on Research in English, 1986.

Hillocks, G., Jr., and Smith, M. "Grammar and Usage." *Handbook of Research on Teaching the English Language Arts.* Edited by J. Flood, J. M. Jensen, D. Lapp, and J. R. Squire. New York: Macmillan, 1991, 591–603.

Mellon, J. C. *Transformational Sentence-Combining: A Method for Enhancing the Development of Syntactic Fluency in English Composition.* NCTE Research Report No. 10. Urbana, IL: National Council of Teachers of English, 1969.

National Council of Teachers of English and the International Reading Association. *Standards for the English Language Arts.* Urbana, IL: National Council of Teachers of English, 1996.

Noguchi, R. R. *Grammar and the Teaching of Writing: Limits and Possibilities.* Urbana, IL: National Council of Teachers of English, 1991.

O'Hare, F. *Sentence-Combining: Improving Student Writing Without Formal Grammar Instruction.* Urbana, IL: National Council of Teachers of English, 1973.

Shaughnessy, M. P. *Errors and Expectations: A Guide for the Teacher of Basic Writing.* New York: Oxford University Press, 1977.

Strong, W. *Creative Approaches to Sentence Combining.* Urbana, IL: ERIC and the National Council of Teachers of English, 1986.

Weaver, C. *Lessons to Share on Teaching Grammar in Context.* Portsmouth, NH: Heinemann, 1998.

Why Grammar?

The definitions of grammar vary. In this series, the term *grammar* means not only the description of parts of speech and parts of a sentence but also the topics often labeled usage and mechanics.

The question about whether to teach grammar—and, if so, how—has confronted secondary-school English teachers for years. From the 1960s through the 1980s, university-level scholarship argued against formal grammar instruction. But teachers at middle school and high school levels have had to face several unsettling realities that have surfaced in the wake of this argument.

- Some students—even native English speakers—haven't mastered the conventions of standard written English.

- Some students are not scoring well on standardized tests that require recognizing and correcting sentence-level errors.

- Some parents have demanded that schools teach their children writing skills that will get them into college, land them better entry-level jobs, and advance them in a chosen career.

In this age of raising standards, it is the philosophy of this series that all students need to know and use the conventions of standard English. To accomplish this goal, students need thorough and coherent teaching and practice. The random coverage of grammar in integrated literature anthologies is not sufficient to help students meet the standards.

How to Engage Students in the Study of Grammar

The following suggestions will help improve the study of grammar in secondary-school classrooms.

Tell Students Why They Are Using *Grammar for Writing*

To succeed in high school, on tests, and in college, students must be able to use conventions of standard English. They are learning skills and habits to last a lifetime. In jobs that require them to deal with the public (such as customer service representatives, sales personnel, and professional jobs), employees need to be able to use standard English. Companies require that their white-collar employees write and speak correctly because they represent the company. In business letters, memos, and e-mail, employees must express themselves according to the conventions of standard English.

Acknowledge That Students Already Know Grammar

Native speakers of English start speaking at a very early age. They learn where to place which words. *Grammar for Writing* helps students get around the spots that give most writers trouble. Students will be more open to embarking on a study of grammar if they realize there really is a limited number of concepts to deal with in order to improve their writing.

"P.S." Feature

The little P.S. feature at the end of many lessons reassures students that they don't need to memorize or remember all of the terms in the lesson. It tells them which terms are important—and why.

Grammar Concepts

1. subject-verb agreement
2. verb forms and tenses
3. pronoun-antecedent agreement
4. pronoun reference and case
5. degree of modifiers
6. positioning of modifiers
7. run-on sentences and fragments
8. spelling
9. punctuation
10. commonly confused words

The Writing Process

The writing process movement dates back to the early 1970s, when Donald Murray published his article, "Teaching Writing as a Process Not a Product." Faculty members at the University of New Hampshire (including Donald Murray, Donald Graves, Lucy Calkins, Nancie Atwell, and Thomas Newkirk) gave the writing process movement a home, training teachers and reporting on writing process theory in action. "Children want to write," Donald Graves wrote in 1983 (*Writing: Teachers and Children at Work,* Heinemann). "They want to write the first day they attend school." Today, the writing process movement dominates English classrooms from kindergarten through college.

Writing Workshops

At the core of the writing process are minilessons, peer response groups, and writing workshops (see Chapter 3). In a writing workshop, students complete a sustained writing activity in stages that involve planning, drafting, and revising. Prewriting (the planning stage) and revising (the improving stage) are most heavily emphasized.

You will find a writing workshop in each of the lessons in Chapter 3 of the Sixth Course book. All of these workshops, listed on the following page, deal with the common types of writing that students are asked to do throughout their school career:

How to Use Them These writing workshops are flexible and can be used in different ways to meet your classroom needs. With the whole class, you might read and discuss the professional model and go over the Writing Strategies that appear in each workshop. Notice that in each workshop the exercises take students step-by-step through the writing process. By the time they complete all of the exercises, students will have completed a finished piece of writing of the type specified in the workshop. Students may work in small groups or with partners to talk about the critical thinking questions following the model and to give each other feedback on the exercises. If you prefer, students can work through the exercises individually—in class or as homework.

Writing Groups Try to make the writing groups heterogeneous, with a mixture of students of different ability levels. You might even try to have a mix of different learning styles in each group. A comfortable number for a writing group is four to six students. ELL students who are mainstreamed into regular English classes will benefit from speaking/listening interactions with members of their small writing groups.

Using the Writing Process

Emphasize to students that the writing process isn't the same for everyone. Some students like to outline carefully; others just plunge ahead from rough notes and start writing. Some begin writing with a title and introduction; others find it easier to start with the body and do an introduction and conclusion later.

Explain also that the process is recursive; that is, students can return to an earlier stage to gather more information. Or they may try out a topic and find that it just doesn't work, so they discard that topic and start over again in the topic selection process. Some teachers require students to do several drafts, revising each one. Others focus on just one draft. Many teachers don't separate revising and editing; they consider all the tasks to be revising.

Resources

Atwell, Nancie. *In the Middle: Writing, Reading, and Learning with Adolescents.* Portsmouth, NH: Boynton/Cook, 1987.

Merriam-Webster's 3rd Edition.

Steps in the writing process may have different names, but basically it goes like this:

The Writing Process	
Steps	**Tasks**
PREWRITING (Lessons 1.1 and 1.2, pp. 9–14)	▪ Use brainstorming, freewriting, class discussion, newspaper articles, clustering and other graphics, listing, and *5W-How?* questions to generate topic ideas. ▪ Choose and limit topic. ▪ Gather details, information; do research, if needed. ▪ Organize details (make an outline). ▪ Specify purpose and audience.
DRAFTING (Lesson 1.2, pp. 14–15)	▪ Put prewriting notes into sentences and paragraphs. ▪ Draft thesis statement (main idea of paper). ▪ Draft attention-grabbing title and introduction. ▪ Draft strong conclusion.
REVISING (Lesson 1.3, pp. 15–17)	▪ Read draft for coherence, unity, content. See four-step revising strategy (page 15). ▪ Peer editors comment on draft. ▪ Consider peer editors' comments. ▪ Do additional drafts (second, third, fourth).
EDITING (Lesson 1.3, pp. 15–17)	▪ Check for sentence completeness. ▪ Find and correct errors in subject-verb agreement, verb forms, pronoun usage, and other errors in grammar and usage.
PROOFREADING (Lesson 1.4, pp. 18–20)	▪ Find and correct errors in mechanics: spelling, punctuation, capitalization. ▪ Utilize peer proofreading.
PUBLISHING (Lesson 1.4, pp. 19–20)	▪ Find a way to share writing with intended audience.

Graves, Donald. *Writing: Teachers and Children at Work*. Portsmouth, NH: Heinemann, 1983.

Powell, David. *What Can I Write About? 7000 Topics for High School Students*. Urbana, IL: National Council of Teachers of English, 1981.

Random House Roget's Thesaurus. New York: Ballantine, 1996.

Strunk, William, Jr., and E. B. White. *The Elements of Style,* 3rd ed. New York: Macmillan, 1979.

Purposes of Writing

Help students see that there are many reasons for writing—now and in the future. Basically, these can be broken down into three categories: personal writing (self-expression), real-life writing, and writing for school.

Personal Writing

Writing as self-expression began to be emphasized in the mid-1960s, when progressive teachers introduced journals, freewriting, and other kinds of personal writing into the classrooms. James Moffett (1973) sees self-expressive modes of writing as a way of engaging student writers, even those with limited English proficiency. Everyone has stories to tell, ideas and feelings to communicate.

Journals/Diaries Encourage students to start a special notebook in which they record ideas and experiences. They might also include a list or description of "things I like"; or they can tape into their notebook excerpts from articles, poems, songs, cartoons/comic strips, photos, and ads that they find appealing. Over the course of months, such a journal becomes a rich source of topic ideas and details. Remind students to include in these journals or diaries only those things they're willing to share with their classmates.

- **Writing Logs** Prewriting notes, ideas for writing topics, proofreading logs, reflections on their writing experiences

- **Reading Logs** A record of books they've read and their comments, questions, and responses; responses to particular stories and poems, novels, essays they've read

- **Learning Logs** A record of important ideas and concepts they've learned

Sketchbooks Some students may want to create a sketchbook. They might sketch people, places, objects, and events from memory or direct observation. Encourage them to express what they've sketched in words, too. They might write on the back of a sketch or, if they're using a looseleaf notebook, interleave sketches and written descriptions.

Creative Writing Encourage students to write original poems and stories in conjunction with their study and discussion of literature genres. These may be individual, partner, or group efforts. Share finished works in class—on bulletin boards, in oral readings, or in a class newsletter or literary magazine. Tell students who are interested in creative writing to look for student writing contests and magazines (print and electronic) that publish student writing.

Real-life Writing

Experienced teachers know that students are motivated when they write for a real-life purpose and a specific audience. Here are just a few of the real-life writing situations students may engage in.

Forms, Applications, Résumés Students must follow directions and develop the ability to summarize and express ideas clearly and concisely.

All Kinds of Letters Some letters are social (thank-you notes, friendly letters, and pen-pal letters) and chatty. Others are business letters (order letters, complaint letters, letters to the editor) and formal. Students need to write in the appropriate form and language.

Research As part of their research projects, students may write letters requesting information or interviews. They may need to write letters of acknowledgment and thanks.

E-mail Students may write formal e-mail messages (requesting information, asking questions of an expert) and informal messages to friends and family. They need to learn the "netiquette"—the accepted conventions for writing e-mail messages.

Persuasion Students express and support their opinions when they write a critical review (see "Writing Workshop," p. 48), proposals for solving a school or community problem, and letters to elected representatives. The Write What You Think exercises throughout the Student Edition (see, for example, p. 104) give them repeated practice in writing for persuasive purposes.

Work At work, students may write letters, memos, and reports. Their writing must communicate ideas clearly and concisely.

Writing for School

Students know how important writing skills are in all their classes. Here are just a few of the reasons to write in school.

Reports In history, science, math, and other classes, students are asked to research, organize, and communicate ideas in written and oral reports. (See "Writing Across the Curriculum," pp. T36–T37.)

Paragraphs Paragraph practice helps students gain skill in expressing and developing their ideas. (See Chapter 2, pp. 22–35, for lessons devoted to developing paragraph-writing skills.) In the minicontext of writing a single paragraph, students develop all of the following:

- a natural voice
- flow (sentences that read smoothly in a sequence)
- coherence (ideas that are easy to follow)
- unity (ideas and supporting details that stick to a topic).

Essays By the end of the Sixth Course, students should be applying their paragraph-writing skills to longer papers. (See Chapter 3, "Writing Workshops," pp. 37–76.) Encourage students to write as much as they need to in order to express what they want to say.

Writing for Tests Increasingly, an essay question or two will appear as part of standardized tests. This is part of the performance assessment movement—students are graded on how well they accomplish a writing task in the given time frame. They must formulate, develop, organize, and express their ideas in a limited time. The skills they learn in practicing paragraph development (Chapter 2) and in the writing workshops (Chapter 3) will stand them in good stead on essay tests.

Writing for a Wider Audience Within the context of school, students have many opportunities to use their writing for a real purpose and audience.

- a school paper (articles, letters to the editor, critical reviews)

- a literary magazine or classroom newsletter of students' creative writing

- speeches for school-wide campaigns (elections, assemblies, rallies)

- scripts (school radio broadcasts and theater productions)

- press releases and publicity (school events and productions)

Writing Across the Curriculum in *Grammar for Writing*

Writing-across-the-curriculum programs began in the late 1960s with several researchers at the University of London Institute of Education. These researchers proposed that writing should be an essential part of students' learning in all classes, not just in English, from kindergarten through university level. In some American schools, this policy manifests itself by encouraging teachers in all subject areas to give writing assignments, which they then help their students carry out according to the writing-process paradigm with, at times, advice from English-teacher colleagues. In other American schools, writing across the curriculum remains the purview of the language arts department in hopes that students' interest will be sparked with a variety of writing opportunities.

The following are some cross-curricular writing assignments—in addition to those that can be found throughout *Grammar for Writing*—that students can explore either under your guidance in English classes or under the guidance of subject-area teachers.

Writing Ideas

All of the following suggestions can be done as individual projects, or students can work with partners or small groups. Students should be willing to publish—that is, share—what they've written, making sure it's the best writing they can produce.

SCIENCE AND MATHEMATICS

- **Inventions** Research and write about the history of an invention, or explain how a common machine or piece of equipment works (for example, a telephone or a television).

- **History** (1) Write about the life and work of a scientist or mathematician, the discovery of a concept, or a breakthrough in a specific field of science or math. (2) Write about the origin of a mathematical concept (the concept of infinity, for example).

- **Discovery** Report on a current development in one of the sciences (for example, medical research or astronomy).

- **Original Research** Report on an experiment that you have conducted.

- **Reference Work** Create a plan for a math encyclopedia for sixth graders. Decide what articles to include and how to illustrate the articles.

SOCIAL STUDIES

- **Causes and Effects** Analyze the causes and/or effects of an event in American or world history.

- **What If?** Speculate on what might have happened if an important event had turned out differently.

- **What Needs Fixing?** Analyze a school or community problem, and propose a solution.

- **Cultural Studies** Select a life-cycle event (such as birth, coming of age, graduation, marriage, childbirth, death) in a current and a past culture, and compare and contrast how the two cultures mark the event.

ARTS

- **Movements** Explain a specific art movement (for example, Impressionism, Cubism) with examples.

- **Lives and Works** Profile an artist and his or her work.

- **How It Works** Explain how a particular musical instrument works.

LANGUAGES OTHER THAN ENGLISH

- **Dictionary** Create a phrase dictionary for teenage travelers to a country whose language you are studying. The dictionary must include an introduction to its contents.

- **Translation** Translate a poem or short piece of prose into English from another language. Discuss the difficulties of the translation process.

SPORTS, PHYSICAL EDUCATION

- **Newsletter** Create a prototype for a weekly or monthly sports newsletter for your school.

- **Profile** Write a biographical sketch of a star or rookie player in your school or community.

Projects

- **Take one writer.** Do some research about a favorite writer's life and work. Write a brief biography. Analyze (more than a plot summary) two major works (plays, novels, short stories) or four poems or two movies. Adapt this approach to focus on particular artists or directors.

- **Be a critic.** Write about movies, TV shows, records, or concerts. Publish your reviews in the local paper.

- **Write your memoirs.** Write not just about one personal experience—but several (see pp. 37–41). Give the book of memoirs to family members, or put it in a drawer and take it out in the year 2025.

- **Write about your heritage.** What holidays do you celebrate, and how do you celebrate them? What customs and traditions do you follow? What sayings did you hear as you were growing up? Work with other students to write a multicultural memoir about holidays.

- **Interview relatives or neighbors who are senior citizens.** Ask what they remember about their early days, what life was like where and when they grew up. Summarize your interview into discrete articles and send them to the local paper of the senior citizen's hometown.

- **Do a Foxfire project.** Interview students, teachers, family members, and neighbors. Find out what they know how to do well. Get step-by-step directions to do a particular project; add photographs, diagrams, and drawings. Publish a how-to flyer or booklet.

- **Make life better.** Work to solve an actual school or community problem. Do some research. Consider possible solutions. Write a proposal to someone in charge, and lobby whoever is in power. Write editorials and letters to the editor in support of your issue.

- **Write creatively.** Set some parameters on content and language.

Encourage interested students to write original short stories, poems, or essays. Have an open mike (microphone) night or day in class with students reading what they've written. Invite other classes, parents, and families. Have students research places that publish student writing, and have them send in their work. Counsel them in advance about rejection slips.

- **Make up writing prompts on topics that will interest students.** Have students clip newspaper articles, summarize local news, and so on. Post them in the classroom and discuss them with students. This activity is a great way to interest students in community events, government, and voting. Make up brief prompts you're sure students can respond to in writing without further research. For example:

> You've been asked by the principal to come up with a proposal that will improve the school. Write your proposal and defend it.

Resources

Fulweiler, Toby, and Art Young, eds. *Programs That Work: Models and Methods for Writing Across the Curriculum.* Portsmouth, NH: Boynton/Cook, 1990.

"Ideas for Teachers" column in *English Journal.* Urbana, IL: National Council of Teachers of English, 1996.

Moffett, James. *Student-Centered Language Arts and Reading, K–12: A Handbook for Teachers.* Boston: Houghton Mifflin, 1973.

Step-by-Step Revising, Editing, and Proofreading

Many of your students would probably be happy turning in their first draft as a final paper. Help them to understand that the revising, editing, and proofreading stages in the writing process raise the standards for their own writing. What they learn from repeated practice in revising and peer editing sticks: Over the course of a year, students produce better organized, better written first drafts based on what they've learned through revising and editing.

Note that this series distinguishes between revising and editing—two steps that many teachers lump together as revising. We've separated these steps because it's hard for students to look critically at a piece of writing and see everything at once:

- **Revising** is concerned with content, organization, style, and word choice (see p. 15 in the Student Edition and the four-step strategy for revising).

- **Editing** involves grammar and usage concerns.

- **Proofreading** refers to checking for errors in spelling, capitalization, and punctuation.

Self-Editing

Encourage students to let their first draft sit a while so they can approach it with "fresh eyes." Before they share their drafts with one or more peer editors, encourage them to do a round of self-editing. They can use the Revising and Editing checklists (see pp. T41–T43) that you gave them as handouts at the beginning of the year. They can also refer to the four-step revision strategy on p. 15 of the Student Edition.

Peer Editing

In the days before peer editing, teachers spent a lot of their evenings marking up student papers with red pen or pencil, filling margins with abbreviations such as *Awk* (Awkward), *Frag* (Fragment), and *Sp* (Spelling). Peer editing has not only helped lighten your paper load; it is also one of the most powerful tools of the writing process. Whether students comment on each other's papers in **writing groups** or one-on-one as a single writer and **peer editor**, they develop skills and strategies that transfer to their own writing:

- They learn what to look for in evaluating a draft.
- They learn to ask questions about organization and content.
- They learn from others' approaches to the same assignment.
- They even learn to be tactful in expressing their comments.

It's important to get the peer editing process underway as soon as students have completed their first draft and have had a chance to do some self-evaluation of it—so writers don't lose momentum. If margins are at least an inch on either side, peer editors may write comments directly on their own copy (printed or photocopied) of the draft. In some high-tech classrooms, drafts are posted on a computer. Students might write their comments directly under the draft or even e-mail their comments to the writer.

Forming Writing Groups

Writing process expert Nancie Atwell reports that in her classes she lets students choose the classmate or classmates they think can help them on the part of a paper they are struggling with at the time. "In the writing workshop," she says, "small groups form and disband in the minutes it takes for a writer to call on one or more other writers, move to a conference corner, share a piece or discuss a problem, and go back to work with a new perspective on the writing" (*In the Middle: Writing, Reading, and Learning with Adolescents*, p. 41).

You may want to organize students into groups that stay together for several weeks or throughout the time devoted to one writing workshop. Such stable groups work well with block scheduling and with ongoing projects. Students get to know and trust each other as they try out topic ideas,

discuss specific writing problems, and share their drafts and revisions.

The same group might work together on a writing project—for example, a compare and contrast paper or any of the project ideas mentioned on pages T37–T38. Think of having a writing group do speaking/listening and media projects, too: perhaps a panel discussion with a question-and-answer period on a problem or issue that the group researches, or maybe a multimedia project.

Peer Editing Abbreviated

Depending on your class, you might use a brief peer editing checklist such as the following; or the longer, more detailed checklists that follow:

Brief Peer Editing Checklist

What Are the Strong Points?
- What are the best parts of the paper?
- What has the writer done especially well?

What Are the Weak Points?
- What parts of the paper need more work?
- Do you have any questions about the paper?
- Can you make any specific suggestions for improving the writing?

Revising in Greater Depth

Here is a much more detailed Revising Checklist, one that students may refer to when revising their own work and when commenting on each other's papers. You might want to produce another version of this checklist (and the editing and proofreading ones as well) for students to refer to throughout the year. This checklist applies to expository writing, the kind of writing that students are most often asked to do in school (a comparison and contrast essay, for example, or a critical review). In addition, see the following revising questions, which refer specifically to persuasive, narrative, and descriptive writing.

Revising Checklist

Purpose and Audience
❑ How well does the writing accomplish its intended purpose?

❑ Are the language and details appropriate for the intended audience?

Main Idea
❑ What is the main idea? Is it clearly and directly stated?

Supporting Details
❑ How well does the writer develop the main idea and major points? Are there enough interesting supporting details?

❑ Would the writing be improved by dropping or by adding information? Where? What's missing?

❑ Do you have unanswered questions? What are they?

❑ Would adding details make the writing more interesting? Where? What kind of details would you suggest?

Organization
❑ How well can you follow the writer's ideas?

❑ Would a different organization help?

❑ Do any parts of the draft stray from the main idea?

Sentence Style
❑ Do transitions help the reader follow ideas?

❑ Can unnecessary words, details, and sentences be dropped?

❑ Do sentences read smoothly? Can some be combined?

❑ Do sentence lengths, beginnings, and structures vary?

Voice
❑ Does the writing sound natural? Are word choices and sentence structures awkward and difficult?

❑ Is the writing appropriate for the intended audience?

Word by Word
❑ Are words used precisely? Can you find vague, overused words that should be replaced? Would vivid verbs and specific nouns improve the writing? Where?

❑ Are the sentences overloaded with too many modifiers or too many prepositional phrases?

❑ Can you spot any clichés?

Title
❑ Does the title capture the reader's interest? Does it accurately reflect the paper's content?

Introduction and Conclusion

❏ Does the introduction make you want to read more? What suggestions can you make for improving it?

❏ Does it introduce the topic and the main idea?

❏ Does the conclusion end the essay strongly?

You may want to offer students variations on peer checklists from time to time. One option is to generate mode-specific checklists such as the ones below or even assignment-specific checklists. (See also the discussion of rubrics on pp. T53–T54.)

Mode-Specific Checklists	
Checklist for Persuasive Writing	❏ Is the writer's opinion clearly stated? ❏ Does the writer give at least two reasons to support that opinion? ❏ Are the reasons themselves supported by convincing evidence (facts, statistics, examples, anecdotes, quotations, and so on)? ❏ Do you understand what the writer wants the reader to do? ❏ Has the writer persuaded you? Why or why not?
Checklist for Narrative Writing	❏ Does the beginning make you want to read more? ❏ Does the writer *show* characters in action and let you hear what they say, or does the writer simply *tell* you about characters? ❏ Does the writing include sensory details? ❏ Are the writer's comparisons relevant and illuminating? ❏ Has the writer used specific nouns and vivid verbs (especially, as alternatives for *said*)? ❏ Is the ending satisfying?
Checklist for Descriptive Writing	❏ Can you picture the setting? ❏ Does the writing include specific sensory details? ❏ Are the comparisons fresh? ❏ Does the organization of details (for example, proceeding from near to far, left to right, or top to bottom) make sense? ❏ Does the description establish an overall mood? What is it?

Editing and Proofreading

As previously mentioned, this series separates the revising task (which focuses on content, style, and organization) from the editing task (which focuses on grammar and usage). Proofreading is the stage of the writing process when students look for mechanical errors in spelling, punctuation, and capitalization. These checklists provide references for either the teacher or the student.

Editing Checklist

❑ Is every sentence grammatically complete (not a fragment or a run-on)? *Lessons 5.1, 5.3, and 13.6*

❑ Do subjects and verbs agree in number and gender? *Chapter 9*

❑ Are the correct forms of pronouns used? *Chapter 10*

❑ Does each pronoun clearly refer to an antecedent? *Lesson 10.5*

❑ Are verb tenses used consistently, unless there is good reason to vary them? *Lesson 8.4*

❑ Are the correct forms of irregular verbs used? *Lessons 8.2–8.3*

❑ Are the correct forms of plural nouns and the comparative forms of adjectives and adverbs used? *Lessons 11.1, 11.2, and 16.4*

Proofreading Checklist

❑ Is every word spelled correctly? Check a dictionary if you're unsure. *Lesson 16.1*

❑ Have homophones been confused (*their* instead of *there*, for example)? *Chapter 12*

❑ Do proper nouns and proper adjectives begin with capital letters? *Chapter 15*

❑ Does every sentence begin with a capital letter and end with an end punctuation mark? *Chapter 13*

❑ Are commas used correctly in all of their many uses? *Lessons 13.2–13.6*

❑ Is dialogue punctuated correctly? *Lesson 14.5*

Resources

In the classroom, students should have access to several copies of a good college dictionary and a dictionary-style thesaurus.

Vocabulary

In many lessons, you'll find an extra feature: Enriching Your Vocabulary. One word from an example or exercise sentence is explored in depth. These vocabulary side features give the word's origin, meanings, related forms, and some information about how and when the word is used. Some of them also offer an example sentence that uses the vocabulary word. In the Sixth Course, words highlighted in the vocabulary side features have been drawn from Sadlier's *Vocabulary Workshop* program.

How to Use These Vocabulary Features

Make sure students digest these features by taking a few minutes to go over each one—whenever you can fit these features in—with the whole class. Here are some suggested activities for using these side features and for helping students to acquire new vocabulary words:

- **Create your own exercise.** This type of exercise appears occasionally in the Grammar, Usage, and Mechanics chapters. Ask students to think of other example sentences using the word in the Enriching Your Vocabulary feature. Have them do this as an individual writing assignment or, better yet, ask volunteers to write example sentences on the board. Discuss with the class as a whole or in small groups whether the example sentences use the words precisely.

- **Check a dictionary.** Try to have several good dictionaries in class (an unabridged dictionary and two or three different college dictionaries). Ask students to compare the etymologies and meanings given in several dictionaries: Do they agree with the vocabulary note in the text and with each other? This kind of activity gives students practice in dictionary skills, which will help them work independently to discover the meanings, origins, and usage of unfamiliar words they find in their reading.

- **Create new vocabulary features.** Once you've covered several of the vocabulary features, ask students to imitate the approach. Have each student write an original Enriching Your Vocabulary feature for one unfamiliar word they come across in a literature selection, newspaper, or magazine—even one that they hear on television or radio. Have students share their features with the class or a small group. You might do this on a weekly basis.

- **Keep a vocabulary notebook.** Have students keep a notebook (or part of a notebook) devoted to new words they encounter in their reading. Encourage them to include words from other subjects, too. For each entry, they might list brief definitions and example sentences. On a regular basis, you might have students get together in small groups to teach each other the words they've recorded in their notebooks.

- **Compile a dictionary.** As an ongoing cooperative activity, you might have students work in small groups to create their own minidictionaries for a field that interests them: computer jargon, sports terms, music terminology, and so on. Give students a choice of which group to join, but limit group size to four or five.

- **Introduce word puzzles and games.** Enrich your classroom with word puzzles and games (crossword puzzles from the newspaper, anagrams, and so on) that students can use when they've completed their classwork. Encourage students to work together in teams to make up other puzzles, word games, and puns.

Other Approaches to Vocabulary Study

Here are some other tried-and-true ways to enlarge students' vocabulary:

Reading and More Reading Many studies show that the most effective way for students to enlarge their vocabulary is through the sustained silent reading of books that they choose. Assemble a classroom library that includes a wide range of materials for students with varying abilities. You might work with a school or public librarian (media specialist) to create a minilibrary containing books designed to appeal to your students. Emphasize multicultural content and authors, popular young adult (YA) fiction, and interesting nonfiction. Add the classics that you think will appeal to your students. Students might meet in reading groups to discuss what they're reading and to recommend books to each other. You might have them write critical reviews or present oral reports. They can write in reading logs—noting their informal responses and questions about what they have read.

Context clues Teach or review the skills needed to use **context clues**, the words and sentences surrounding an unfamiliar word that help students guess its meaning. Give students example sentences showing the following kinds of context clues: definitions, appositives, synonyms, comparison/contrast, and other kinds of clues embedded in surrounding sentences.

Internet Explain to students that another tool for improving vocabulary might be using the following recommended Internet sites:

http://www.m-w.com/netdict.htm
The thesaurus link gives related words, contrasted words, and antonyms. Recommended for all high school grade levels.

http://www.thesaurus.com/ This is Roget online. It offers extensive lists. No antonyms are given. It is a fairly sophisticated site and best for the higher grades.

Connecting Technology to Grammar for Writing

Computers make both writing and researching so much easier. Students love working—as well as playing—on computers, but if your students and classrooms do not have access to computers, that fact won't affect the quality of students' writing. Assure them that excellent writing still arrives in longhand on ruled paper (or however you require that it be turned in).

Word Processing: Writing on the Computer

The positive side of word processing is that both revising and editing is a snap and that printed papers are clean and legible. The negative side of word processing is that it's easy for students to copy others' papers and turn in the work as their own. You can avoid plagiarism by requiring students to hand in various stages of their work, such as prewriting notes, outlines, and lists of sources.

Here are the basic skills students must know in order to produce papers on a word processing program:

- how to create and save documents
- how to set margins and line spacing
- how to select fonts (encourage them not to get too fancy)
- how to print documents

Writing Process

Word processing can be used for every stage in the writing process. Here are some specific suggestions:

Prewriting

- To gather ideas for topics, students can use the computer for freewriting, brainstorming, and listing. For freewriting, tell students to turn down the brightness on the monitor so they're not distracted by what they've already written.

- Students can take notes on the computer instead of on note cards. Encourage students to set up separate documents for each source. When they organize their notes, they'll work from printouts of their notes and can highlight the information they find most useful. Just as note cards should have a heading and note the page number of the source, so too students should put in headings and note page numbers whenever they take notes.

- Working with printouts of their notes, students can easily draft and rework an outline on a computer, using tabs for indenting.

Drafting

- Remind students how important it is to save their work regularly and to back up their documents in case of a power failure or computer crash.

- Assure students that there is no "right" way to write on a computer. Some students (those who say they "think better" writing in longhand and those who are new to keyboarding) may prefer writing and revising in longhand. That's acceptable, too. Remind them to leave wide margins and extra space around their handwritten drafts so that there's room to revise. As preparation for revising, double spacing is a good idea so that there is room to revise on computer printouts.

Revising

The best part of word processing is revising. It's easy to replace, insert, move, and delete words, sentences, and paragraphs.

- Encourage students to try out changes and various different versions and to read aloud to themselves what they've written. If they don't want to "lose" a version of their writing, they can keep the original, make a copy, and revise on the copy.

- Some students find it easier to print out a draft, revise in longhand in pencil or pen, and then keyboard their changes. Others prefer revising directly on-screen. Any way that works is fine.

Proofreading

Most word processing programs have built-in grammar and spell checkers. Make sure students realize that these aren't foolproof. Students still must proofread their own papers carefully; exchanging papers with a peer proofreader is an extra safeguard. Students should proofread first drafts, revised drafts, and the final paper.

- Advise students to proofread by reading the whole paper slowly. Reading aloud to themselves might help.

- Warn students that a spell checker won't detect extra words, missing words, and words used incorrectly. As long as a word is spelled correctly, the spell checker approves. For instance, it lets the two errors in this sentence pass unnoticed:

  Mickey order too pizzas with peppers, mushrooms, and olives.

- Grammar checkers will alert students to errors in capitalization; as well as commonly confused words; hyphenation errors; misused words; double negatives; passive construction; punctuation, sentence structure and subject-verb agreement problems; wordiness; and so on. However, no grammar checker is foolproof. A grammar checker may indicate an error when there is no error, and it may make suggestions that are incorrect. Tell students that the responsibility for correct grammar in their writing is theirs alone.

- Encourage proofreading skills in your class by insisting that students who use word processors turn in a clean final paper—without ink corrections or whiteout.

Harnessing Software for Grammar for Writing

Invite students to list and discuss the features of software that make writing easier for them. Raise their consciousness about the connections between technology and their writing assignments. Make sure that at least the following dozen features are at the top of your students' lists:

1. networking and e-mail For helping one another generate ideas during prewriting and for sharing responses to one another's drafts; for distribution—that is, publishing—of finished documents across the aisle or around the world

2. outlining software For help in organizing main ideas and details during prewriting and later

3. cut-and-paste function of a word processor For moving words, sentences, paragraphs, and sections during revising and editing

4. find-and-replace function of a word processor For global replacement of one term or spelling for another at any stage

5. save and save-as functions of a word processor For easily comparing and contrasting drafts

6. thesaurus tool on a word processor For quickly finding alternative vocabulary during any stage

7. spelling tool on a word processor For superficial proofreading (Students must do their own proofreading if they want to catch problems with homophones, typographical errors, and so on.)

8. grammar tool on a word processor For sentence-level analysis (Students must decide whether to accept the tool's suggested revision.)

9. drawing programs, page-design programs, and other features of desktop-publishing software For professional formatting and the inclusion of nontext material (e.g., photographs, drawings) in reports

10. online searches to locate pertinent documents For getting information and facts for research projects

11. discussion groups Whether synchronous or not, to provide access to people seriously interested in and often well informed about topics that students are researching

12. hypertext links For direct access to online sources that a student has used in putting together a research report and that readers may want to review for themselves

Evaluating Internet Information

Emphasize to students that they should not believe everything they read, see, or hear on the Web. Information gleaned from a Web site could be coming from a twelve-year-old, a university library, or a business. Students must learn to evaluate information they find on the Web for bias, accuracy, and current information. They should get in the habit of double-checking what they find on the Web in additional sources.

To evaluate information, students need to know where it is coming from—literally. They must notice and make deductions based on the top-level domain, the three letters at or toward the end of a Web site's address. The following letters have meaning.

- **.gov** A local, state, or national government [Information from such a source is generally reliable.]

- **.edu** An educational institution [The source may be a research department at an eminent university or a fourth-grade class.]

- **.org** An organization [Any organization may have an agenda—that is, a bias—which students must take into consideration.]

- **.com** A commercial—that is, business—source [Students must consider whether the site's information is biased to encourage purchases or other commercial interaction.]

- **.net** A network [Anyone can create a home page and post it here.]

Reliable Sites for Teachers and Students

You and your students may enjoy identifying Web sites helpful to class work by searching with key terms such as *standard English*, *grammar*, and *OWL* (for "online writing lab"). The following are sites that have been checked for reliability and suitability. Remember that Web sites are in constant flux and that sites change overnight. Do your own screening before recommending them to your students.

English as a Second Language

http://www.comenius.com This site includes "Fluency Through Fables" and "The Weekly Idiom." There are interactive features. There are links for many languages.

Grammar, Usage, Mechanics

http://andromeda.rutgers.edu/~jlynch /Writing/ The site is very clear and helpful on relevant grammatical issues.

http://webster.commnet.edu/HP/pages /darling/original.htm This takes the student to a site called "Guide to Grammatical Writing." There are features on sentences, paragraphs, essays, forms of communication (e.g., business letters), and grammar.

Research on the Web

http://www.marlboro.edu/~jsheehy/ writing/ This site is called the Clear Writing Program. It is full of useful information and includes links for *writing* as well as research.

http://ipl.org/teen/aplus/aplus.htm Here, students can access the writing process pages, the Web research pages, and a variety of links. This site is geared to teens.

Writing Process

http://owl.english.purdue.edu This site is geared more toward teachers than toward students, though students will find the writing links useful. These include over 130 handouts on the writing process, grammar, punctuation, job searches, business letters, ESL, and so on. There are extensive lists of Web research links and links to the Purdue libraries.

Using *Grammar for Writing* with English Language Learners

Variously called ESL (English as a Second Language) students, EFL (English as a Foreign Language) students, nonnative speakers, English-language learners (ELL), and multilingual writers, students for whom English is not a first language give you a chance to raise everyone's consciousness about the respect that all languages and dialects deserve. Here are some strategies for giving ELL students a chance to talk about languages and demonstrate what languages other than English sound and look like:

- Conduct an informal survey at the beginning of the term, asking students

  - What other languages do you speak, read, and write besides English?

  - What language(s) do you speak at home?

  - What language(s) besides English have you studied in school? How well do you speak it? Write it? Read it? Understand it when it is spoken to you?

  - How did you learn the rules for forming sentences in your first language? In the other language(s)?

- Give native English speakers a chance to hear the sounds of other languages by asking ELL students to translate into their native language and orally deliver conversational sentences based on the following English ones:

  - Hi. My name is _____.

  - I am _____ years old.

  - My hobbies are _____.

  - The kind of music I like best is _____, and _____ is one of my favorite songs.

  - Good-bye for now.

- Ask ELL students to identify ways in which their first language differs from English. Encourage them to talk about what is giving them the most trouble in learning to speak and write English.

Recognizing Problem Areas for ELL Students

The table on the next page identifies some of the problems ELL students have with English. It lists chapters and lessons from the *Grammar for Writing* series to which you can direct students with those problems.

Grammar for Writing and ELL Problems

Problem Area in English	Comment	Grammar for Writing Treatment, Sixth Course
ADJECTIVE CLAUSES	Forming and positioning adjective clauses cause problems for speakers of Asian languages, of Arabic and Hebrew, and even of Latin-based languages.	Lesson 7.2
ARTICLES	ELL students often leave out the article before a singular count noun.	Lesson 4.4
CAPITALIZATION	Arabic, Chinese, and Hebrew do not use capital letters; Dutch and German capitalize some forms of the second-person pronoun; German caps all nouns.	Chapter 15
HOMOPHONES	Speakers of Asian languages in particular may be confused by the concept of words sounding alike but having different meanings.	Chapter 12
NEGATION	Multiple negation is common in French and Russian, among other languages.	Lesson 11.3
PLURALS	Some Asian languages have no plural forms for nouns.	Chapter 9, Lesson 16.4
PREFIXES AND SUFFIXES	These word parts are absent in Asian languages.	Lesson 16.3
PREPOSITIONS	English distinguishes between *in* and *on*; Spanish uses *en* for both.	Lessons 4.7 and 6.1
SILENT LETTERS	There are no silent letters in Spanish.	Chapter 16
SUBJECTS, DOUBLE	Some languages add personal pronouns as suffixes or prefixes, leading ELL speakers to say, "Maria she is pretty."	Lessons 5.2, 5.5, 10.1
TENSES	■ Certain English verbs don't work in the present progressive, but ESL students may say or write, "I am knowing the answer." ■ In some languages, time is not signaled by word endings but rather by words that native English speakers would call adverbs.	Lessons 4.3 and 8.4
WORD ORDER	■ In some languages, word order determines the part of speech. For example, the verb is the last word in sentences in Turkish, Korean, and Japanese. ■ In Russian, subject and object may switch places without affecting meaning.	Lessons 5.4, 5.8, and 5.9

Assessment in *Grammar for Writing*

The *Grammar for Writing* series has assessment built right in. In this age of assessment and accountability, you'll want some ongoing measures of how well students are doing in the course of the term. The series offers the following different types of assessment in each Student Edition and Test Booklet:

Objective Evaluation

- **Mid-Chapter and Chapter Reviews** In each book, Mid-Chapter Reviews and Chapter Reviews help students review the grammar, usage, and mechanics concepts learned in the preceding lessons. Each review is broken down into exercises that focus on one lesson or one particular grammar, usage, or mechanics problem.

- **Cumulative Reviews** At the end of Chapters 7, 12, and 16, a two-page Cumulative Review covers the preceding chapters in that section. Use these Cumulative Reviews as mastery tests or diagnostic tests depending on your classroom needs.

- **Grammar, Usage, and Mechanics Tests** These objective tests differ from the Cumulative Reviews; the tests incorporate the standardized test format of the PSAT writing exam. Test items include both error recognition and error correction. Again, you may use these materials either as mastery tests or diagnostic tests. Note that the optional assessment component of *Grammar for Writing*, the *Grammar for Writing Test Booklet*, contains test items in standardized-test formats, as well as other kinds of items.

Lightening the Paper Load

Consider letting students help you in scoring objective tests. Have students exchange papers and score them as you go over answers in class; ask for volunteers to give the answers. A whole-class discussion of test items gives students a chance to ask questions. This will reinforce understanding and help students who may still be confused.

Evaluating Responses to Writing Exercises

Grammar for Writing includes many writing exercises that can't be scored objectively, such as the exercises in the Composition Unit (Chapters 1–3), as well as the exercises based on notes, exercises with paragraphs needing revision, and the Revising and Editing Worksheets or Editing and Proofreading Worksheets in the grammar, usage, and mechanics sections (Chapters 4–16). It's up to you to decide whether—and how—to grade these writing exercises or to simply check that students have completed them.

Revising and Editing Worksheets

These one-page themed exercises are examples of poor writing. Students are directed to work individually or with a partner or group to improve the writing. Typically, instructions ask students to correct errors covered in the preceding lessons and to combine sentences and eliminate fragments and run-ons. *There is no single correct answer to any of the revision exercises in the Student Edition.*

What students will learn from these exercises—especially by comparing their revisions and edits with those of their classmates—is that there are many workable solutions to writing problems and many different ways to communicate the same idea. This empowering insight should make students more confident as they revise and edit their own writing. To get the most benefit from the Revising and Editing Worksheets, direct students to compare revisions (sentence-by-sentence or paragraph-by-paragraph) in a whole-class session.

It is impossible to give students' work on the Revising and Editing Worksheets a percentage score; these worksheets contain many errors and invite many ways to revise and edit. Also, remember that students may be working with partners or a group, so the final result is a shared effort. If you feel you must record a number score, try judging the revisions on a 1–4 scale (with four being "excellent"). Give students points for each of the following criteria, and then find the average score.

The revised and edited version:

- communicates ideas and information clearly.

- is made up of complete sentences (no fragments or run-ons) that read smoothly and naturally.

- has no errors related to the chapter's content.

- has no (or very few) errors in grammar and usage.

- uses punctuation correctly.

- spells words correctly.

Rubrics for Evaluating Students' Paragraphs and Essays

You can measure students' original writing using the rubrics on p. T54, which help to identify students' performance levels. Note that the rubrics are generic (they apply to all types of essays) and are based on a six-point scale. (You may find that in your classroom a four-point scale, beginning at Level 4, is more suitable.)

At the beginning of the term, share these (or your own) rubrics with students as a handout that they can keep in their notebooks. Let students know exactly what your standards are, so that they know what to aim for. You might also give students copies of essays from unidentified writers as an example of each level of performance. Reading and discussing these sample essays will clarify for students what you expect of them.

Writing Performance Levels

	The student's writing
LEVEL 6	<ul><li>consistently pursues a strong central purpose across a complex range of ideas, skillfully engages the reader, and shows exceptional insight into the subject.</li><li>includes main ideas that are developed comprehensively and are supported with a variety of logical reasons and detailed examples.</li><li>is skillfully organized.</li><li>shows a distinctive style through the skillful and expressive use of vocabulary, phrasing, and sentence structure.</li><li>demonstrates essentially error-free control of grammar, punctuation, capitalization, and spelling.</li></ul>
LEVEL 5	<ul><li>consistently pursues a central purpose, holds the interest of the reader, and shows insight into the subject.</li><li>includes main ideas that are developed and supported by a variety of reasons and examples.</li><li>is effectively organized.</li><li>shows an emerging style through the effective use of vocabulary, phrasing, and sentence structure.</li><li>consistently demonstrates the accurate use of grammar, punctuation, capitalization, and spelling.</li></ul>
LEVEL 4	<ul><li>shows a consistent purpose, communicates to the reader, and connects to the writer's knowledge of the subject.</li><li>includes main ideas that are organized, developed, and supported by reasons and examples.</li><li>shows a suitable vocabulary, phrasing, and sentence structure</li><li>generally demonstrates the accurate use of grammar, punctuation, capitalization, and spelling</li></ul>
LEVEL 3	<ul><li>shows a purpose but may be inconsistent in communicating to the reader or connecting to the writer's knowledge of the subject.</li><li>includes main ideas that may be organized or partially developed and supported by some reasons and examples.</li><li>may show an imprecise use of vocabulary, phrasing, and sentence structure.</li><li>includes some errors in the use of grammar, punctuation, capitalization, and spelling.</li></ul>
LEVEL 2	<ul><li>attempts to connect the writer's knowledge to the subject and may not show a purpose.</li><li>is typically brief, unorganized, and underdeveloped.</li><li>may include frequent errors in the use of grammar, capitalization, punctuation, and spelling.</li></ul>
LEVEL 1	<ul><li>is too brief or disorganized to communicate to the reader.</li><li>may not connect the writer's knowledge to the subject.</li><li>typically includes many errors in the use of grammar, capitalization, and spelling.</li></ul>

Writing Portfolios

The movement for performance assessment has gained strength over many years. Today, writing portfolios, an essential part of performance assessment, are part of most English classrooms. Writing portfolios give students tangible evidence that their efforts pay off. The portfolios can be made available for review by students' new teachers in subsequent terms.

Many teachers have students create two different kinds of writing portfolios:

- **A works-in-progress portfolio** For every finished piece of writing, students include prewriting notes, outlines, early drafts, revised drafts, and even a brief reflection on their writing experience. Students may also include journals, sketches, logs, and notes about their reading.

- **A best-efforts portfolio** This portfolio shows only the *finished pieces of writing*, examples of what students think are their best writing efforts.

Teacher-Student Conferences

An integral part of performance assessment is teacher-student conferences. One-on-one conferencing helps you assess performance and motivates students to raise their own standards.

Test Booklet

For every course of *Grammar for Writing*, a separate Test Booklet is available for purchase. The Test Booklet contains a separate test for every chapter as well as a Diagnostic Test and a Mastery Test. Items take standardized test formats: error recognition and error correction.

Here is an example of an error recognition question from the Sixth Course Mastery Test.

Directions: Fill in the circle of the letter for each sentence that contains an error.

1. Ⓐ Ⓑ Ⓒ Ⓓ

    A. He and I are on the school paper together.

    B. Of the two of them, she is the best skater.

    C. Just between you and me, our band needs work.

    D. Michel or Suki are representing our grade at the conference.

Note that there are two incorrect sentences; both B and D should be filled in.

Here's why:

B is incorrect. The sentence should use the word *better*, not *best*, because only two people are being compared, so the comparative form is needed.

D is incorrect. The verb should be *is*, not *are*. Two singular subjects connected by *or* take a singular verb.

Diagnostic Test

A four-page Diagnostic Test appears at the beginning of each Test Booklet. You may use this test at the beginning of the school term to determine students' strengths and weaknesses. Each question on the Diagnostic Test is devoted to a single problem area.

Tallying class results will also reveal the grammar, usage, and mechanics skills that the class as a whole needs to learn and review. Use the Diagnostic Test scores and the errors on students' first batch of papers to decide which textbook lessons to use with the whole class and which lessons should be reserved for individuals or small groups.

Mastery Test

Use the four-page Mastery Test to assess the progress students have made during the term. You might plan to hold brief individual conferences with each student to discuss the student's work as a whole and to identify those skills that still need work.

Students whose Mastery Test scores indicate that they are still having trouble (with subject-verb agreement, for example) might work together in small groups to review appropriate lessons and to go over the exercises together.

You might ask these students to create their own exercise items in the style of exercise items in the Student Edition. For example, a pair of students working together might write five sentences that test knowledge of appositives (similar to Exercise 9 on page 222 of the Sixth Course, for example). Exercise writers can then exchange exercises with another team and work together to answer the exercise questions. Finally, both teams (writers and exercise takers) can get together to see if their answers agree.

Chapter Tests

Most Chapter Tests are four pages; a few are two pages long. The Chapter Test focuses entirely on concepts taught in the chapter lessons. In addition to error recognition and error correction items in a standardized test format, many Chapter Tests end with a writing prompt. Four-page tests may also contain a paragraph to be revised.

Writing Prompts

These are a variety of writing exercises that are similar to the Write What You Think exercises in the Student Edition. Students are asked to express an opinion on a topic or issue related to the content of a preceding exercise. They don't need any additional information to express and support an opinion.

Paragraph Revision

Some of the four-page Chapter Tests contain paragraphs that students are to revise. These are similar to the revision exercises found in the Student Edition.

Test Book Answer Key

A separate Answer Key is provided with each package of student Test Booklets.

Answer Key

Chapter 4

Exercise 14 Combining Sentences

1. "The Prologue" is a poem written by Anne Bradstreet, the first woman author in the American colonies.

2. Henry James, a novelist, wrote about relationships among mostly British and American people.

3. Washington Irving wrote "The Legend of Sleepy Hollow," a story in which a headless horseman appears, in the early nineteenth century.

4. I heard a recording of Gwendolyn Brooks, an African American poet, reading poems about love from her Pulitzer Prize-winning collection, *Annie Allen*.

5. Did you ever read *Moby Dick*, a famous novel about a whale that was written by Herman Melville in 1851?

Chapter 5

Exercise 1 Identifying Sentence Fragments

Answers will vary. Sample answers are given.

1. S

2. President Bush proposed a manned space mission to Mars in 1989.

3. This was the twentieth anniversary of the *Apollo 11* moon landing.

4. S

5. However low the costs for new methods of space exploration, it's still very expensive.

6. S

7. Recently, the public seems interested in this trip.

8. A meteorite, showing microscopic signs of ancient life, was discovered on Antarctica.

9. Experts debate whether it's better to send astronauts or a robot into space.

10. Scientists plan to use the International Space Station, due to be completed in 2004, to explore Mars.

MID-CHAPTER REVIEW

Exercise B Combining Sentences

Answers may vary. Sample answers are given.

1. Coffee cups and some of his closest friends may appear in a George Segal sculpture.

2. The artist George Segal lives on an old chicken farm in New Jersey, and he uses the henhouses as his studio.

3. In plaster, he casts the forms of everyday objects, but he doesn't paint them.

4. One sculpture contains plaster molds of real people, as well as a restaurant counter, stools, and a coffee cup.

5. A scene of plaster Holocaust victims from World War II shocks people who see this in San Francisco, and a scene of plaster people on a bread line during the Great Depression saddens those who view it at the FDR Memorial in Washington, D.C.

Exercise 12 Correcting Run-on Sentences

Answers may vary. Sample answers are given.

1. Giovanni da Verrazano and Henry Hudson explored the waterways around New York in 1524 and 1609; Verrazano sailed for the French and Hudson for the Dutch.

2. In 1623, European settlers traveled to New York with the Dutch West India Company. They farmed on the lower end of the island of Manhattan.

3. Many newcomers from England came to New York; they were invited by the Dutch West India Company.

4. New York, called New Amsterdam by the Dutch, came under English control in 1664. Dutch influence on the island of Manhattan remained strong.

5. The colors of the Dutch flag are the colors of today's New York City flag. The Dutch word for *farm—Bowery—*is the name of a section in Manhattan.

6. New York City became the first capital for the nation. George Washington worshiped in Manhattan's St. Paul's Chapel.

7. By the 1870s, William M. ("Boss") Tweed firmly controlled politics in New York; his power came from political corruption.

8. *The New York Times* exposed political scandals in 1871. The corrupt Boss Tweed spent the next seven years in and out of jail, where he died in 1878.

CHAPTER REVIEW

Exercise C Combining Sentences

1. Fairy tales and nursery rhymes are popular literature for children.

2. Are you familiar with the nursery rhymes of Elizabeth, or Mother Goose, a real person from Boston, Massachusetts?

3. She married Isaac Goose and became the stepmother of his ten children.

4. A son-in-law used the name Mother Goose and wrote a collection called *Mother Goose's Melodies for Children* in 1719.

5. Before the appearance of a real Mother Goose in Boston, there lived in France a writer named Charles Perrault, who wrote children's stories.

6. *The Tales of My Mother Goose* was the title of a collection of popular stories by the French writer Charles Perrault, which was published in 1697.

7. Though unknown, it is believed that he borrowed the name *Frau Gosen* from German folklore.

8. Some folklorists believe that Perrault is not the same as the German Mother Goose; others feel sure the authors are one and the same.

Chapter 6

Exercise 2 Combining Sentences with Appositives
Answers will vary. Sample answers are given.

1. Carl Lewis, an extraordinary runner, won many gold medals in Olympic track events.

2. His younger sister Carol also competed as a long jumper.

3. He was born in Birmingham, Alabama, an industrial city, in 1961.

4. At his college, the University of Houston, he came to national attention.

5. He earned three medals, all gold, at the 1983 World Championships in Helsinki.

6. In 1984, Carl Lewis broke the record held by Jesse Owens, the previous greatest runner in U.S. history.

7. Carl Lewis's 1984 Olympic record, four gold medals, has not yet been surpassed.

8. He earned his four gold medals in three solo events and in the relay, a four-man race.

9. In the 1996 Atlanta Olympics, his final competition, he won another gold medal.

10. The gold medalist was thirty-five years old then, an advanced age for an Olympian.

MID-CHAPTER REVIEW

Exercise B Writing with Appositives
Answers will vary. Sample answers are given.

1. *Fin de siècle*, a French term, means "end of the century."

2. Did you know that Juanita became the new restaurant host, the *maître d'hotel*, yesterday?

3. Our debate team captain, Germaine, helps us feel a positive group spirit that the French call *esprit de corps*.

4. Eureka, a town in California, is named after a Greek word that means "I have found it."

5. Eating outside at the Italian restaurant Cafe Alfresco is not unusual since *alfresco* means "outdoors" in Italian.

6. *Canoa*, a Haitian word, became the English word *canoe*.

Exercise 14 Combining Sentences by Inserting Phrases
Answers will vary. Sample answers are given.

1. Rudolfo Anaya is a well-known American author whose hometown, Pastura, is a small New Mexican town.

2. *Bless me, Ultima* is his first novel, in which he begins to show interest in Mexican American folklore.

3. As a boy, Anaya liked Saturdays because on that day of the week he read in the Santa Rosa library, staying there until late in the day.

4. The young Anaya listened to *cuentos*, traditional Spanish stories, and became interested in writing.

5. A tradition of oral storytelling is part of Mexican American culture, and the imagination of a young Mexican American writer, like Rudolfo Anaya, is sparked by this form of storytelling.

6. La Llorona, a crazy spirit who shouts and cries about lost loved ones, is in some of Anaya's stories that are based on *cuentos*.

7. Anaya also writes novels about real-life, modern people who live in New Mexico.

8. In 1992, *Albuquerque*, a novel about a Hispanic boxer, was published.

9. There are many readers of Anaya who learn about Hispanic culture and the Southwest when they read his work.

10. He was interested in writing mysteries, a genre he had not yet tried, so he published one.

CHAPTER REVIEW

Exercise C Combining Sentences
Answers will vary. Sample answers are given.

1. Growing up in Rutherford, New Jersey, William Carlos Williams enjoyed what he calls a typical American boyhood.

2. To earn a living, his father traveled throughout the Caribbean and Latin America as a salesman.

3. While in Cuba, William Carlos Williams's father met Raquel Helene Hoheb, his future bride.

4. Mrs. Williams taught her children about art, a subject she had studied in Paris.

5. The Williamses chose to expose their children to many cultures and to both the Spanish and English languages.

6. In his poetry, Williams included ideas from other cultures.

7. Writing prescriptions in his practice was part of the reason that Williams liked to write short lines of poetry.

8. Influenced by meeting other poets, Dr. Williams wrote poems in addition to practicing medicine.

9. His wife Flossie became the subject of many of his poems throughout his career.

10. By publishing *Al Que Quiero! (To Him Who Wants It),* Williams became well known for his nontraditional poetry.

Chapter 7
Exercise 12 Combining Sentences with Adjective Clauses
Answers will vary. Sample answers are given.

1. The American workforce of the 1980s, which was considered too big and inefficient, stagnated the economy.

2. In the next decade, when the economy grew stronger, the workforce became smaller and more efficient.

3. Many economists who study spending habits advise people not to spend too much or too little when the economy changes.

4. Sudden changes in the economy that occur from time to time often change a person's spending patterns.

5. People, who fuel the economy, should know that economists warn against going into debt in both good and bad economies.

6. Optimism may shrink margins of safety, which people try to maintain, and allow credit card debts to grow out of control.

Exercise 13 Combining Sentences with Adverb Clauses
Answers will vary. Sample answers are given.

1. In Greek mythology, the leaves never fell from trees in autumn until Persephone made this happen.

2. Odysseus finally finds his way home from the Trojan War even though many forces tried to stop him.

3. As long as people respected and revered the Greek gods and goddesses on Mt. Olympus, they often helped humans.

4. At times, if people insulted a god, the gods would punish people.

5. The three-headed guard dog, Cerberus, had to be confronted <u>when a person approached the gates of Hades</u>.

6. The god Zeus threw thunderbolts <u>whenever he wanted to display his strength or anger</u>.

Exercise 16 Identifying Parallel Structure in Sentences

Answers will vary. Sample answers are given.

1. Cross-country travel in 1870 was exhausting, uncomfortable, and expensive.

2. Stagecoaches were the fastest, safest, and most reliable way to travel.

3. No one expected a woman to drive a stagecoach because taking a physical job was not what most women did, because men always drove stagecoaches, and because no woman had ever applied for the job.

4. You may have heard of an unusual woman who lived in the 1870s, used the name "Charley," and drove a stagecoach.

5. Charley kept her identity hidden by cutting her hair short, by wearing scruffy men's clothes, and by acting like the other drivers.

6. Charley was known among stagecoach drivers to be honest with money, to work reliably, and to always be polite to passengers.

7. After her death, the stagecoach company, her co-workers, and her passengers were amazed to find out she was a woman.

8. Like the stagecoach drivers, Pony Express riders worked long hours, ate few meals, and seldom slept.

9. The Pony Express was a mail service that lasted for only eighteen months and that the transcontinental railroad put out of business.

10. For a Pony Express rider, getting a letter from the East to the West required changing horses many times, knowing how to avoid danger, and being able to sleep in the saddle.

Exercise 19 Varying Sentence Beginnings

Answers will vary. Sample answers are given.

1. In January 1876, Jack London was born in San Francisco to parents known by the public as eccentrics.

2. Due to a family financial crisis, he went to work at age thirteen.

3. His first of many world adventures was a voyage to the Bering Sea on a ship trying to catch seals.

4. Jack London's motto was to earn a living as a "vendor of brain" rather than as a laborer.

5. He wrote a 4,000-word essay for a newspaper contest, which brought him his first earnings as a writer, one night in 1895.

6. When he was nineteen, though he was self-taught, he successfully passed exams that allowed him to graduate from high school.

7. Jack London sailed off on the *Klondike* for his first Yukon adventure after a brief college experience.

8. Though they provided a wealth of material for his most famous work, *The Call of the Wild*, the perilous conditions in the Yukon weakened Jack London's health.

9. *The Call of the Wild*, finished in five weeks, became a famous novel.

10. He continued to travel after he got married and had two daughters.

Chapter Review

Exercise C Combining Sentences with Clauses

1. There are few major parts in this play even though the cast of characters is surprisingly long.

2. When you receive a cue from the director, please begin reading your lines.

3. Martin Anderson, who received the lead male role, had never performed on stage before.

4. Critics from the school newspaper attended the opening performance so that they could write reviews.

5. Whenever students wrote and performed a play, the townspeople were willing to come.

Grammar Test: Chapters 4–7

Exercise 3 Combining Sentences
Answers will vary. Sample answers are given.

1. Eudora Welty, whose parents came from the North, was born in Jackson, Mississippi, in 1909.
2. Have you read her famous novel *The Optimist's Daughter*, which won the Pulitzer Prize?
3. She began to write short stories in 1931 when she moved home to Mississippi permanently.
4. Before 1931, Eudora Welty had graduated from the University of Wisconsin and had taken a course in advertising at Columbia University in New York City.
5. Readers gain an understanding of life in the South through Eudora Welty's characterizations and through the vivid twists of humor in her writing.

Chapter 8

Exercise 9 Using the Active Voice

1. Robert Frost read the poem at President John F. Kennedy's 1961 inauguration.
2. Miller Williams recited a poem for the 1997 inauguration of President Bill Clinton.
3. Authors have read their poems at various presidential inaugurations.
4. A team of doctors tested a new surgical procedure.
5. Researchers at UCLA developed a cure for brain cancer.
6. The HMO denied coverage of the experimental procedure.
7. Some health professionals recommend herbal treatments.
8. Antibiotics cure some infectious diseases.
9. Practitioners of holistic medicine can treat major diseases as well as simple aches or pains.

10. Many people drink herbal tea as a remedy for anxiety.
11. Landmark Healthcare, Inc., did a survey to find out how many people used alternative medicine in the year 1998.
12. The survey showed that health care is growing in popularity.
13. Forty-two percent of the adults surveyed in the study used some type of alternative medicine.
14. The people surveyed turned most often to herbal therapy, chiropractic care, and massage therapy.
15. In general, people who are surveyed do not usually employ alternative medicine as a replacement for traditional care.

CHAPTER REVIEW

Exercise B Using the Active Voice

1. A team of researchers conducted experiments.
2. Margo recited the poem after the break.
3. The strong wind propelled the sailboat.
4. Beavers built the dam.
5. Polish poets won the Nobel Price for Literature twice in the last twenty years.
6. The world's fastest runner earned the gold medal.
7. The photo technician repaired the shutter in my camera.
8. An award-winning scenic designer created the play's set.
9. The pharmaceutical company developed a lifesaving drug.
10. The animal shelter produced a calendar featuring illustrations of cats.

Chapter 10

Exercise 15 Editing a Paragraph
Answers will vary. Sample answers are given.
   [1]Some people say the best cars are the old ones. [2]My friend Mike restored a 1969 Mustang. [3]He painted it with a shiny black paint that had sparkles in it. [4]The car shone and glittered when he drove by. [5]The interior was immaculate; [6]its upholstery was

leather that had crinkled with age. ⁷The dashboard was polished and gleaming. ⁸When Mike turned the key, the engine made a low insistent rumble. ⁹It was hard not to look at that beautiful car when he drove past.

Chapter 11

CHAPTER REVIEW

Exercise D Revising A Paragraph
Answers will vary. Sample answers are given.

¹Professor Michael Bleyman was not afraid of roaring and leaping tigers or lions. ²Bleyman founded a special farm in North Carolina to provide a home for abandoned or abused big cats. ³Named as the successor to Bleyman after his death, Nancy Schonwalter abandoned her old job as a video producer. ⁴The Carnivore Preservation Trust is maintained only by Schonwalter and volunteers, without government funds. ⁵Neighboring farmers aren't afraid of the big cats wandering freely around the preservation. ⁶When he began saving big cats, Bleyman once had to catch an escaped tiger roaming around his neighbor's land. ⁷A chain-link fence now surrounds the twenty-year-old animal preserve. ⁸People from the Carnivore Preservation Trust once rescued a tiger that was emaciated and tied to a tree in downtown Houston, Texas. ⁹Nancy Schonwalter might approach a newly rescued tiger without fear in order to gain its acceptance. ¹⁰One of the only major problems for the Trust is finding enough big-cat food for the animals, which costs around $350,000 a year.

Chapter 13

Exercise 5 Revising Sentences
Answers will vary. Sample answers are given.

1. To understand today's table manners, study the dining habits from the past.
2. Using only their fingers, ancient Romans ate their meals.
3. Using every finger but the pinkie and ring finger, aristocrats also ate with their hands.
4. When it was introduced in the eleventh century, the fork shocked aristocrats.
5. In the 1500s, aristocrats still resisted the fork.
6. Before tableware was mass-produced, everybody carried knives.
7. Estimated to be six thousand years old, an ivory spoon was unearthed in Egypt.
8. To celebrate an engagement, the Welsh give a fiancée a carved, wooden spoon.
9. At Chinese and Japanese restaurants, I always ask for chopsticks.
10. Before the eighteenth century, innkeepers did not provide cutlery.

CHAPTER REVIEW

Exercise C Revising Sentences

1. The Chicago Symphony Orchestra, which is the third oldest symphony in the United States, was founded in 1891.
2. Samuel Barber wrote music for the poems of Pablo Neruda, the Chilean poet.
3. The cymbals, not only the drums, are considered percussion instruments.
4. David Del Tredici, who studied music in California and New York, wrote many pieces of music based on *The Adventures of Alice in Wonderland.*
5. Pablo Casals not only became a master cellist but also founded a yearly festival in Puerto Rico.
6. Yo-Yo Ma, the famous cellist, gave his first recital at six years of age.
7. *Rhapsody in Blue,* the first musical composition to combine jazz with classical music, was written by George Gershwin in the 1920s.
8. The classical concert pianist whom many consider to be the greatest of the twentieth century was Vladimir Horowitz.

Exercise D Proofreading a Paragraph
Answers will vary. A sample paragraph is given.

How can you demonstrate that light travels faster than sound? Well, do you experience thunder or lightning first? Most people will say lightning, and they're correct. You may not know it, but thunder and lightning occur at the same time. Yet light travels faster than sound, doesn't it? Consequently, we see the lightning bolt, which strikes first, before we hear the crash of the thunder. To discover how far away lightning is striking, you can use a formula. First, you count the seconds between a lightning strike and the sound of thunder that follows. Next, you divide by three. Your quotient tells you the approximate distance to the lightning in kilometers.

Chapter 14

Exercise 10 Punctuating Dialogue

[1]As Dora and Alex walked along the lake shore, they heard a strange and haunting sound. [2]"What's that?" Dora asked. [3]"Do you hear that, Alex?"

[4]"It's probably just the wind on the water," Alex answered. "Nothing to worry about."

[5]Dora and Alex continued walking along the water's edge and talking about the band they hoped to form in September when they got back to the city. [6]"Okay," [7]Alex muttered to himself. [8]"A bass guitar, a rhythm guitar, a keyboard player, and a drummer will be enough."

[9]"Well," Dora sniped. [10]"Don't forget the lead singer. [11]I mean, that's my part, isn't it?"

[12]Alex walked quietly ahead; then he broke the silence. [13]"The band needs a name and a really good song."

[14]"If we can get a good beat, we can come up with some lyrics," Dora added. [15]"Isn't that a weird sound?" she said, referring to the wind rustling in the background, a sound that seemed to follow them.

[16]"I think it's the wind whipping up the lake water," [17]Alex answered. [18]"Hey!" he exclaimed. "What about that for our name?"

[19]"You're right!" [20]Dora immediately agreed. [21]"We can call our band Cool Breeze," she said, "and we should add a wind instrument to our band."

[22]"How about a flute, a piccolo, or a harmonica?" Alex asked her. [23]"How's this for a song title: 'Wind Over Water'?"

Chapter Review

Exercise C Adding Punctuation to Dialogue

[1]"Watch out for the spiders' webs," Vladimir warned. "This place is full of them."

[2]Lucy slowly turned the doorknob of the old fishing cabin, opened the creaky door, and exclaimed, "Wow! [3]No one's been here for ages."

[4]Vladimir asked, "Have you ever seen such old stuff before?"

[5]"No, never," Lucy answered. [6]She walked over to the bookshelves and looked at the dusty books on the shelves and said, "They're ancient."

[7]Vladimir opened one cracked, leather-bound book to page thirty-three, where he found a handwritten note. [8]He turned to Lucy and blurted out, [9]"This note says: 'The Vlonsky family'—that's my mother's maiden name—'came to this fishing cabin with their neighbors, the Nicholas family, in 1965.'" [10]Vladimir wondered aloud, "Could it be that no one has been here since then?"

[11]"I can't believe it," Lucy gasped.

[12]Then Vladimir said, "My parents and grandparents often told me about this place."

[13]When Lucy picked up another book—*To the Memory of Childhood* by Lydia Chukavskaya—she found another handwritten note. [14]She read aloud, "We, the Vlonsky family, have enjoyed our first American holiday in this cabin: Memorial Day, May 30, 1965."

Chapter 16

Exercise 4 Proofreading a Newsletter

[1]**Weird Sounds**

[2]Neither the city police chief nor the residential neighbors of the Tip Top Bread Factory can locate exactly where a weird, high-pitched sound is coming from. [3]A group of Tip Top employees has decided to intercede in the investigation. [4]These employees will report their findings in the next issue or concede defeat.

[5]**Proceed Without Caution**

[6]Without a doubt, the height of our success as a community is demonstrated in the way we spend our leisure time together.

[7]To achieve this goal, our citizens place no ceiling on what they can do to succeed in creating fun activities for everyone, young and old. [8]So, on Saturday, don't recede into the background and reign as a couch potato king or queen, or make an excuse such as "My niece is visiting." [9]There's no reason to weigh your options carefully, either. [10]Seize the moment, and join one of eight community groups—from the foreign film club to the woodworking club (which made the sleigh for last year's winter parade) to the bongo club.

Exercise 6 Writing New Words
Sample answers are given. Students may think of others.

Prefixes	Suffixes
anti-British	development
antidefamation	entertainment
antisegregation	establishment
antismoking	involvement
preadmission	builder
prearrange	hotter
preempt	reporter
pretheater	upper
postdate	agreeable
postseason	breakable
postsurgical	changeable
postwar	noticeable
unable	diligence
unaffected	emergence
unattractive	occurrence
unhappy	reference
subcategory	dryness
submarine	goodness
subspecialty	readiness
subzero	shyness
react	adventurous
readjust	courageous
redesign	monstrous
reintroduce	poisonous

CHAPTER REVIEW

Exercise A Proofreading a Letter
[1]Dear Editor:

[2]As a citizen, let me seize this opportunity to thank you for your piece on recycling aluminum cans. [3]I have often attempted to intercede in my neighborhood's recycling plans—but without success. [4]For people to succeed with this kind of environmental effort, they must be truly dedicated to their cause. [5]Our local efforts to recycle have been less than enthusiastic, if not downright distressing.

[6]Your article in last Wednesday's paper opened people's eyes to the importance of providing new strategies for saving and reusing natural resources. [7]Let me commend you on some of your recommendations. [8]In particular, I endorse the exciting idea of enlisting ninety-five student volunteers during summer vacation.

[9]I look forward to the next receipt of my newspaper, which I hope unveils more information on this important subject.

[10]Sincerely yours,
E. L. Wichester

CUMULATIVE REVIEW: CHAPTERS 13–16

Exercise B Adding Punctuation to Dialogue
[1]Steve asked Laura, "Have you read *The Red Badge of Courage*, the Civil War novel by Stephen Crane?"

[2]Laura answered, "No, but I have read two of his short stories: 'The Open Boat' and 'The Blue Hotel.'" [3]"Do you know anything about Crane?" Laura asked, "because I'd like to know."

[4]Steven opened their textbook and read aloud: "Stephen Crane was born on November 1, 1871, and died on June 5, 1900. [5]His short life was full of questions and mysteries. [6]At times, he lived the high life; other times, he was penniless. [7]Scholars and readers are continually interested in his life, which few completely understand."

[8]Laura was interested in what Steve read. [9]"You know," Laura said, "I have a CD called *The Open Boat*."

[10]Steve asked, "Is the name taken from the Stephen Crane story?"

[11]Laura exclaimed, "I bet it is!"

[12]Steven stated: "Writer's titles should remain theirs alone, I think, unless they give the title to someone else."

sixth course

SADLIER-OXFORD

GRAMMAR
FOR WRITING

Phyllis Goldenberg   Carol Domblewski

Elaine Epstein   Martin Lee

Senior Series Consultant

Beverly Ann Chin
Professor of English
University of Montana

Series Editor

Phyllis Goldenberg

Sadlier-Oxford
A Division of William H. Sadlier, Inc.
New York, New York 10005-1002

Reviewers

Dr. Muriel Harris
Writing Lab Director
English Dept.
Purdue University
West Lafayette, IN

Keith Yost
Program Director,
Humanities and
Language Arts
Tomball, TX

**Ellen Young
Swain**
English Teacher
Cimarron High
School
Cimarron, NM

Mel Farberman
Asst. Principal
of English
Cardozo High School
Bayside, NY

Galen Rosenberg
English Dept.
Coordinator
Los Altos High School
Los Altos, CA

Patricia Stack
English Teacher
South Park School
District
Library, PA

Donald L. Stephan
Retired English
Dept. Chair
Sidney High School
Sidney, OH

Rose F. Schmitt
English Teacher
Florida Air Academy
Melbourne, FL

Cary Fuller
English Teacher
Rye Country
Day School
Rye, NY

Roxanne Hoblitt
English Teacher
Belgrade High School
Belgrade, MT

Brad Rinn
English Teacher
Roseville High School
Roseville, CA

Barbara A. Mylite
UFT Teacher Center
Specialist
New York City Board
of Education

Patrick O'Reilly
English Teacher
Freeport High School
Freeport, NY

Peter J. Accardi
English Teacher
Chaminade High
School
Mineola, NY

John Manear
English Dept. Chair
Seton-La Salle
High School
Pittsburgh, PA

Carolyn Phipps
English Teacher
Wooddale High
School
Memphis, TN

Wanda Porter
English Dept. Head
Kamehameha
Secondary School
Honolulu, HI

Student Writers

Michael Arcaro
Scarsdale, NY

Michael Berkowitz
New York, NY

Emily Broxterman
Overland Park, KS

Matisa Childs
Coral Gables, FL

Steve Gangemi
The Lawrenceville
School (a prepara-
tory school)
Lawrenceville, NJ

Adele Grundies
La Mesa, CA

Keane Kaneakua
Kaneohe, HI

Rudy Lewis
The Lawrenceville
School (a prepara-
tory school)
Lawrenceville, NJ

**Pia Lindstrom
Luedke**
Pasadena, CA

Sara McCann
Gig Harbor, WA

Suzanne O'Kelley
Eugene, OR

Rusty Ryan
Cambridge, MA

Sara Wechter
Norwalk, CT

Alex Zane
Pottsville, PA

Acknowledgments

Every good faith effort has been made to locate the owners of copyrighted material to arrange permission to reprint selections. In several cases this has proved impossible.

Thanks to the following for permission to reprint copyrighted materials.

Excerpt from "Dust Storm" reprinted with the permission of Simon & Schuster Books for Young Readers, an imprint of Simon & Schuster Children's Publishing Division, from *The Invisible Thread* by Yoshiko Uchida. Copyright © 1991 Yoshiko Uchida.

"Down with Curfews; Up with Children" by Nadine Strossen from IntellectualCapital.com. Copyright © 1996 by Nadine Strossen. Reprinted by permission of the author.

"'Romeo' Takes a Bold Bard Departure" by Todd McCarthy. Reprinted by permission of *Variety* Magazine. Copyright © 1996 *Variety* Magazine.

Excerpt from "Literacy: A Family Affair" by Anita Merina from *NEA Today*. Copyright © 1995 The National Education Association of the United States. Reprinted with permission.

"Antigone" from *Sophocles, the Oedipus Cycle: An English Version* by Dudley Fitts and Robert Fitzgerald, copyright 1939 by Harcourt Brace & Company and renewed 1967 by Dudley Fitts and Robert Fitzgerald, reprinted by permission of the publisher. **Caution:** All rights including professional, amateur, motion picture, recitation, lecturing, performance, public reading, radio broadcasting, and television are strictly reserved. Inquiries on all rights should be addressed to Harcourt Brace & Company, Permissions Department, Orlando, FL 32887-6777.

Excerpt from "Sophocles" by Morton W. Bloomfield and Robert C. Elliott from *Great Plays, Sophocles to Albee*. Copyright © 1975 by Holt, Rhinehart, and Winston. Reprinted by permission of the publisher.

Excerpt from "Reform and the Triangle Shirtwaist Company Fire" by Hadley Davis. Copyright © 1998 The Concord Review. Reprinted by permission of *The Concord Review*. *The Concord Review* is the only quarterly journal in the world for the academic work of high school students of history. Submit essays for consideration to *The Concord Review*, P.O. Box 661, Concord, MA 01742. Will Fitzhugh, 800-331-5007, http://www.tcr.org

Excerpt from Untitled essay, "I think I began to grow up..." from Princeton University. Copyright © 1997, 1998 myEssay.com. Reprinted by permission of myEssay.com.

Photo Credits

Corbis/ Hulton Deutch: Ch. 5; Corbis: Ch. 16
FPG International/ Ron Chapple: Ch. 13
Liaison Agency/ Hulton Getty: Ch. 12
Nonstock/ Annamari Mikkola: Ch. 3; Marcie Jan Bronstein: Ch. 8
Photodisc: Ch 14
Photonica/ The Picture Book: Ch 2
Tony Stone Images/ Robert Stanton: Ch. 1; Hulton Getty: Ch. 4; Chris Shinn: Ch. 6; Jon Riley: Ch. 7; Joe McBride: Ch. 9; David Madison: Ch. 10; Nick Dolding: Ch. 11; J&M Studios: Ch. 15

ISBN: 0-8215-0311-1   123456789/05 04 03 02 01 00 99

Dear Student:

This book is designed to take the mystery out of grammar and to help you become a better, more confident writer. *Grammar for Writing* does just what its title suggests: it shows how the rules of grammar, usage, and mechanics—the conventions of standard English—can make your writing not just correct but more powerful and persuasive, too.

As a student, you are being challenged to write correctly and effectively not only in your English classes but also in social studies, science, and history classes as well. High schools all over America have raised their expectations for graduates. If you have taken a standardized test recently or are preparing to take one soon, you know this only too well. The writing sections of these tests have grown more rigorous and more demanding than ever.

However, there are reasons to speak and write well other than to score well on standardized tests. People judge you by the way you write and speak. Your use of English is evaluated in the writing you do in school, on job and college applications, and in many different kinds of careers. That doesn't mean that you have to say, "To whom am I speaking?" when a friend calls, but you should be able to speak and write correctly when the situation calls for it—in a formal speaking or writing assignment, on a test, and in an interview. The more you practice using standard English, the more comfortable and confident you will become when you write and speak.

As you become a more confident writer, you will find new excitement in recording your thoughts, ideas, opinions, and experiences. You will also see that communicating effectively is the most important way to influence others. As you write about the topics you care about, you will find that people in every part of your life—your teachers, your peers, your bosses, your parents, and your community—gain respect for you and are influenced by the things you write and say.

No textbook can make writing easy. Good writers work hard and revise their work often to find just the right words to move their audience. Consequently, in *Grammar for Writing* you will find a lot of exercises called "Write What You Think." These exercises are designed to help you develop clear, logical arguments to persuade people that your opinion is right. These exercises will sharpen your thinking as well as your writing skills.

Of course, you already know how to write. You've been doing it for years. No one has to prove to you that writing is important—it just *is*. But your writing can always be improved, and the best way to improve it is to learn and practice the skills and strategies in this book. In *Grammar for Writing*, we have tried to present the rules of grammar as simply as possible; whether you are merely refreshing your memory or are learning the concepts for the first time, you'll be able to understand the rules and apply them to your writing.

All of the skills you learn and practice in this book—grammar, writing, thinking—will last you a lifetime.

Good luck, and study well!

CONTENTS

COMPOSITION

GRAMMAR

USAGE

MECHANICS

The Writing Process

Prewriting

 Prewriting refers to all the thinking, planning, and organizing you do before you actually start writing.

To come up with topics and main ideas to write about, as well as details that elaborate on those topics, try out one or more of the following prewriting strategies.

1. **Writer's Notebook** Keep a special notebook or folder in which you jot down experiences and thoughts about anything that interests you.

Your notebook will be like an album of souvenirs from various thought journeys. You can include quotations, cartoons, poems, and magazine or newspaper clippings in your notebook. Try to jot down the reasons why these items captured your interest. Later on, you can look through your writer's notebook and expand them into writing assignments or essays. Use the following writer's notebook entry as a model.

> *Wed. 9/17*
>
> *Gave my campaign speech for class president. Someone in the audience called out, "Are you an innovator, Annette?" Did that person or anyone else understand my 'peer justice' idea? Hope no one noticed my shoes. I almost (but didn't) trip as I stepped off the platform because the laces were untied! I meant to sound as much a poet as a politician. How did it go? Well, next week's election will tell.*

2. **Brainstorming** Focus on a single word or idea, and list everything that comes to mind.

If you're working with a partner or group, have one person act as a recorder. When you've completely run out of ideas, review what you've written, and check or circle those ideas that seem the most promising. Use the brainstorming list on the following page as a model.

Writing Hint

All five prewriting strategies covered in this lesson deal with *narrowing a topic*. Narrowing is a key to successful writing. How can you tell if a topic is too broad, too narrow, or just right?

- If you can break your topic down into more than five subtopics, it may be too broad. Consider writing about one of the narrower subtopics.

- If you cannot break your topic down into more than two subtopics, it may be too narrow already. Think more broadly.

ASSIGNMENT: *Choose an issue that you can campaign for in your run for class president. Write about how you can make a difference.*

BRAINSTORMING NOTES:

lack of selection in the cafeteria   school lunches
the most successful junior prom   enthusiasm for yearbook
potholes in the parking lot and frequent vandalism of student cars
better communication between administration and students
wider variety of language courses offered to juniors

3. Freewriting This strategy is similar to brainstorming but involves nonstop writing.

Focus on one word or topic. Pretend your mind and pencil are on automatic pilot, and begin writing. Don't stop writing for three to five minutes. If you get stuck on the first word, repeat that word until another finds its way onto the page. Don't look back, and don't worry about the structure of your sentences or spelling at this point.

TOPIC: *How to win an election*

Talk with voters; don't walk around school with a sour or bored expression, even on a bad day. What about speeches—are they more effective if they're formal or informal in style, written or spoken spontaneously? Campaign where voters gather—in the front hall before homeroom. Yes, that's not bad, campaigning. I could focus on the best places to campaign, or all the possible places—that's a big topic. I'll keep it to the best places only.

4. Clustering (also called **mapping** or **webbing**) Create a cluster diagram to explore a topic, to break a large topic into smaller parts, or to gather details.

First, write your topic (or any word or phrase) in the middle of a piece of paper, and then circle it. Around the circled topic, write subtopics or related words and phrases. Circle each new word or phrase, and connect it to your original topic. Each new word or phrase may have subtopics, too. Keep going until you run out of thoughts. Refer to the example on the following page.

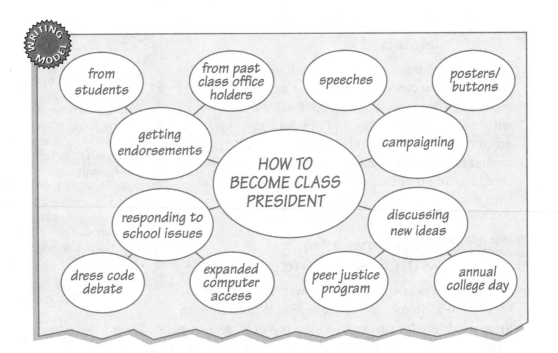

5. *What If?* Questions Write questions about subjects that
interest you in order to explore a range of topics.

For a discussion of
outlining, audience,
and purpose,
see **Composition**,
Lesson 1.2.

You might ask yourself *What If?* questions about a broad topic
that you need to narrow down. For example, if a teacher assigns
you the general topic "Issues at School," you might make a list
similar to the following:

What if students were not required to wear school uniforms?

What if the school cafeteria offered a vegetarian menu?

What if students acted as teachers and administrators for a day?

Try combining a few of the prewriting strategies. For example, a notebook
entry or a *What if?* question might lead you to a topic for writing. You might
brainstorm or freewrite to narrow down the topic or to think about related
details; then you could organize your thoughts by clustering.

Exercise 1 Starting a Writer's Notebook

Start a writer's notebook. Use a small notebook or a folder that you can carry around, or set aside a section of your loose-leaf notebook. Create two entries—one for yesterday and one for today. Jot down notes about your experiences, thoughts, and observations for both days. For this assignment, you should write notes that you'd be willing to share with a writing group.   Encourage students to make a dedicated writer's notebook to keep throughout the school year.

Exercise 2 Exploring a Topic with Freewriting

After you've made entries in your writer's notebook for two days, choose one of the topics. Write a one- to three-word title for the topic on the top of a piece of paper. Then write nonstop for three minutes. **Hint:** If you have trouble getting started, write and repeat the phrase "I think" until you complete the sentence with an idea. Repeat the process whenever you become stuck. Don't be concerned about your spelling, grammar, or sentence structure at this point.   Students' topics will vary.

Exercise 3 Thinking of Topic Ideas

For each of the following items, think of three or four topics to write about. Use at least three different prewriting strategies—the technique suggested in parentheses or one of your own choosing—to help you generate writing topics.
Students' topics will vary.

1. cultural traditions (brainstorming)

2. an event in history (*What if?* questions)

3. the Internet (clustering)

Exercise 4 Narrowing a Topic

Choose two of the broad, general topics below. For each topic, suggest three limited topics that you could cover in a three-page paper.   Students' topics will vary.

TOO BROAD	Natural disasters
LIMITED	Eyewitness account of 1989 earthquake in San Francisco
	Damage that was caused by hurricane-force winds
	The effects of drought on farm families

1. Colleges
2. Sports

3. Driving
4. Endangered Species

5. Movies

Prewriting and Drafting

🖊 Use your prewriting notes to create an **outline**. Your outline may include more details than the one at the right, or you may choose to write your outline in full sentences. Either way, your outline should help guide your writing.

🖊 Consider your **writing style**. Your writing style is determined by your audience as well as by your purpose for writing.

Your **audience** is the person or persons who will read what you write. Ask yourself how much your audience might already know about your writing topic. For example, in an essay about basketball, an audience of players or fans will already know such technical terms as "slam dunk." You won't need to explain such terms. On the other hand, people unfamiliar with the game will not understand the technical terms. Your writing style or word choice will depend a great deal on your audience.

The **purpose** for your writing may be to describe, to inform, to tell a story, to persuade, to entertain, or any combination of these.

Considering your purpose will help you make sound decisions about how much background and supporting details to include in your draft. For example, if your purpose is to persuade your classmates to attend the opening game of the girls' basketball team, you might choose persuasive and energetic language as you write. If your purpose is to explain the procedures for basketball tryouts, your language might be formal and unemotional.

Together, your audience and purpose for writing will determine your style—the manner in which you express your thoughts.

🖊 **Drafting** is the next step in the writing process. You will start by putting your thoughts on paper and into sentences and paragraphs.

Once you have your limited topic, some prewriting notes, a rough outline, and a clear idea of whom you're writing for and why, you're ready to begin your first draft. Now try some of the drafting strategies described on the following page.

Rough Outline
The Alamo

History Prior to Battle

   Mission of San Antonio de Valero (1718)

   Fortress for Texan Revolutionaries (1835)

Battle for the Alamo (1836)

   Mexican Forces

   Texan Forces

History After Battle for the Alamo

   Famous saying: "Remember the Alamo!"

   Alamo bought by Texas

   Area restored

DRAFTING STRATEGIES

1. **Focus.** Find a quiet place, and avoid doing other activities while you draft. If drafting seems impossible, take a break and then try again.

2. **Start Early.** Allow enough time to let your draft sit awhile (overnight is ideal) before you revise, edit, and proofread it. Don't procrastinate—that is, don't put things off. You will need time to think and revise.

3. **Think in Sentences.** Write complete sentences, and vary their structures and lengths. Read some sentences aloud, or say them in your head to develop your sense of sentence awareness. Make sure they sound good together.

4. **Make Appropriate Changes.** Follow the general direction of your outline, but feel free to add details and to use the thoughts that come to you.

Exercise 5 **Drafting Part of a Report**

The outline on page 13 grew out of information on the note card below. Draft two or more paragraphs using some or all of this information. First drafts will vary.

> *Originally a Franciscan mission—San Antonio de Valero, built in 1718*
>
> *Texan revolutionaries occupied the Alamo (1835)—becomes fortress*
>
> *Problem: only 150 Texans*
>
> *Santa Anna—Mexican general leads thousands of Mexican soldiers to reclaim Alamo for Mexico.*
>
> *Thirteen day siege at Alamo—ended on March 6, 1836. Only 32 more Texans arrive at the fort as reinforcements.*
>
> *Fight ended in hand-to-hand combat. Famous American frontiersmen died, including Davy Crockett and Jim Bowie.*
>
> *Building bought by state of Texas (1883). Restored (1936–1939).*

Exercise 6 **Drafting a Paper**

Write a first draft using the prewriting notes you made in Exercise 4 on page 12. Consider your audience and purpose, and make a rough outline. Work with a partner to clearly summarize your topic, main ideas, and supporting details. When you're ready to start writing, follow the strategies suggested in this lesson.

Students' papers will vary. Students will be asked to revise this draft on page 17 in Lesson 1.3, Exercise 9.

Revising and Editing

◗ When you **revise** and **edit**, you shape your draft into its almost final form.

When you revise a draft, you reshape and rewrite your material to make it clearer, more focused, and easier to understand. Revision may involve adding new content, deleting redundant thoughts or phrases, or changing the organization of your information.

Reread your paper four times—once for content, once for style, once for organization, and once for word choice. Use the questions that follow as a checklist to make sure your ideas and presentation are clear.

REVISING QUESTIONS

1. **Content** Does your paper adequately summarize your main ideas? Do you need to add or cut supporting details? Do you need more background information? Is everything relevant, or related, to your main idea(s), or have you wandered off track?

2. **Style** Do your sentences read smoothly? (Try reading them aloud.) Have you varied sentence beginnings, lengths, and structures? Can you combine sentences with related ideas within a paragraph? Are ideas expressed clearly? Would adding transition words or phrases help? Are there unnecessary or repeated words, phrases, or sentences you can cut?

3. **Organization** Do you grab the reader's attention with a lively opener? Is information presented in a logical order—that is, an order that makes sense to the reader? Try to change the order of paragraphs and to present information differently. Will that change improve your paper and help it read more logically?

4. **Word choice** Have you used words that are too general or vague? If so, replace them with more precise words. Have you used a cliché or an overworked word (such as *great*, *nice*, or *bad*)? If so, find fresh words to express your ideas. (Use a thesaurus to find synonyms.) Does your writing sound stilted with too many fancy words? Have you used appropriate vocabulary for your intended audience? Have you explained or defined any technical terms?

The next step, editing, deals with correcting mistakes in grammar and usage, as well as with altering sentence variety and flow to sharpen and streamline your writing. Editing fine-tunes your revision.

Enriching Your Vocabulary

The adjective *redundant* means "using more words than needed; wordy; unnecessary to the meaning." It comes from a Latin word, *redundare*, meaning "to overflow," and it has a connotation of overwhelming readers with unnecessary and irrelevant information.

EDITING STRATEGIES

1. **Sentence completeness** Are any fragments or run-ons posing as sentences? Does every sentence begin with a capital letter and end with an appropriate punctuation mark?

2. **Verbs** Do all present-tense verbs agree with their subjects? Are verb tenses consistent and correct?

3. **Pronouns** Do all the pronouns agree with their antecedents? Are pronoun references clear?

4. **Adjectives and adverbs** Are adjectives modifying nouns and pronouns? Are adverbs modifying verbs, adjectives, and other adverbs? Are comparisons complete? Do comparisons use *-er/more* and *-est/most* forms correctly?

5. **Parallelism of words, phrases, clauses** Does a sentence containing a series of words, phrases, or clauses use the same structure in each item of the series? (See Lesson 7.7 for more on parallel structure.)

◀ **Peer editing** involves giving feedback to your classmates and getting help from them on works in progress. Peer editing can be done with a partner or a small group.

Your peers can either suggest ways to improve a paper or ask questions to help you clarify your ideas. They also can provide positive feedback, pointing to places where your writing succeeds—and why.

> ### Some Questions for Peer Editors
>
> 1. In what specific ways does the writing make me respond positively?
>
> 2. Which sentences or paragraphs fall short of the best writing in this paper? Why?
>
> 3. What is the writer's main idea or ideas? Where, if at all, does the writer lose this focus?
>
> 4. Which details support the main idea well? Which do not add necessary information?
>
> 5. How else could the writer clarify the main idea(s)?
>
> 6. Does the opening grab my attention? Is the ending related to the beginning, and is it interesting as well?
>
> 7. What advice can I give this writer about grammar, usage, or mechanics?

Exercise 7 **Revising an Editorial** *Working Together*

On a separate piece of paper, work with a partner or small group, and use the four revising strategies (content, style, organization, and word choice) to revise the editorial on the following page that a student wrote for a school newspaper. The writer's purpose is to persuade; the audience is made up of students at the writer's high school. Feel free to rewrite, change details, add, or cut in order to maintain focus on the main idea. Consider adding transitions, combining sentences, and making other improvements. Revised editorials will vary.

[1]We who live in smoggy cities such as Los Angeles, California, have too many days with a dirty fog. [2]It's all over our streets. [3]Where does smog come from? [4]A major source is fossil fuels. [5]Fossil fuel is the stuff that sends our cars through the beautiful California landscape. [6]April 22, 1970, was the first Earth Day. [7]Earth Day may seem like ancient history, but the message still matters. [8]I propose that we dedicate ourselves to finding new ways to decrease pollution problems. [9]Problems like smog. [10]We must dedicate ourselves again to a clean environment every April 22. [11]In his last address, in 1963, President Kennedy looked forward to an America "which will build handsome and balanced cities for our future." [12]It's our turn to get cracking. [13]Maybe one of us will become a scientist or an engineer. [14]That person may be figuring out how to burn fuel cleanly. [15]That person may invent an engine that runs on air itself!

Exercise 8 Revising and Editing a Paper

Use the four revising strategies suggested in this lesson, and check a paper's content, style, organization, and word choice. Revise a paper you've written for English or for another class. You can revise a paper you wrote recently or one you wrote a while ago. After you've gone through your paper with the revising questions in mind, look at it again on a sentence-by-sentence level. Ask yourself the editing questions listed in this lesson.

Students' writings will vary. Use the assessment rubrics in the teacher pages to evaluate student writing.

Exercise 9 Peer Editing

1. Revise and edit the paper you drafted in Exercise 6. Use the revising questions and editing strategies to improve your draft.

2. Work with a partner to peer edit your paper. Allow your partner to read your paper without your input. Your partner should respond to your writing using the peer editing questions on page 16 as a guide. Encourage your peer editor to make comments directly on your pages.

3. Review the peer editing comments on your paper, and incorporate those that you feel will improve your writing. Don't be discouraged if you have to rewrite some passages.

Caution peer editors to be positive about the essays they read. Encourage them to suggest possible solutions to problems they find.

Proofreading and Publishing

🖋 When you **proofread**, you search for any mechanical errors and correct them.

The old saying "Don't judge a book by its cover" may be true in some situations. No one likes to be judged on superficial qualities, but readers judge the quality of a person's mind, in part, by the way in which he or she presents ideas in writing. So don't let easily corrected errors in spelling, punctuation, and capitalization keep readers from appreciating your ideas, thoughts, and creativity. Your ability to use conventional standards of English matters.

PROOFREADING QUESTIONS

1. **Spelling** Are words spelled correctly? (Use a college dictionary or a spell checker on a computer.) Have you used a correctly spelled word in an incorrect context (*they're* instead of *their*, for example, or *lie* instead of *lay*—mix-ups that a computer's spell checker won't catch)? Are compound words spelled properly throughout—*earache, Middle Ages, self-consciousness*?

2. **Capitalization** Do proper nouns and proper adjectives begin with capital letters? Are other words appropriately capitalized? Have you capitalized a word that's supposed to start with a lowercase letter?

3. **Punctuation** Are commas, colons, semicolons, quotation marks, and other punctuation marks used correctly? (If you're not sure, review the rules and examples in Chapters 13–14.) Is dialogue punctuated correctly?

4. **Apostrophes** Do contractions and possessive nouns have apostrophes in the right places? Do possessive pronouns have *no* apostrophes?

5. **Hyphens** If words are divided at the end of a line, are the words hyphenated correctly?

6. **Consistency** Is your style consistent? For example, do you write *decision makers* in one paragraph and hyphenate *decision-makers* in another? Do all your technical terms follow accepted usage—*X ray, e-mail, cholesterol*?

Use the proofreading symbols shown on the following page as you proofread your writing.

Proofreading Symbols

CORRECTION	SYMBOL	EXAMPLE
Delete (remove).	ℰ	She set ~~sat~~ down first.
Insert.	∧	I am so thirst∧y.
Transpose (switch).	⌐⌐	I said just, "Sure!"
Capitalize.	≡	Are you going to san francisco?
Make lowercase.	/	We sailed throught the calm Harbor.
Start a new paragraph.	¶	¶She answered, "Certainly!"
Add space.	#	Paolo lives in Rio deJaneiro, Brazil.
Close up space.	‿	Martha has a head ache.

🔹 Keep a **proofreading log**, a record of your spelling, punctuation, and capitalization mistakes.

The act of writing down a mistake usually helps you to remember and avoid making that same mistake again. For insurance, keep your log in a separate notebook or folder, and review it periodically.

🔹 **Publishing** means sharing what you've written.

Writing a paper is something you do alone. But it is through your writing that you can share your ideas with classmates, friends, family, and possibly even wider audiences. Your audience grows every time you let a family member read your writing or every time you read it aloud to a class. Think about publishing your writing in a school anthology or magazine. You can e-mail it to a pen pal, or you can enter it in a contest.

Exercise 10 Proofreading Paragraphs

Find and correct every error in the following paragraphs. Use the proofreading symbols from the chart above.

¹Photography is a fascinating marriage of art and science.

²Louis Jacques Mandé Daguerre, a paris opera set designer, invented the earliest Photograph in 1839. ³That Photograph, named the daguerrotype, began with his work on opera sets.

Publishing Suggestions

WRITTEN WORDS

Magazine of student writing

School or local newspaper

Local or national poetry, story, or essay contest

Class anthology

Writing portfolio

Letters/e-mail

SPOKEN WORDS

Speech

Audiocassette

Oral interpretation

Radio broadcast

Reader's theater

Interview

Debate

MULTIMEDIA

Book with illustrations

Videotape

Performance with music

Bulletin board or library display

Community literature festival

[4]He created illusions ~~threw~~ *through* mechanical tricks and the clever use of ~~lite~~ *light*.
[5]Unfortunately, this ~~brillyant~~ *brilliant* work was destroyed by fire in march 1839, forcing Daguerre out of work.

[6]It was during this ~~idol~~ *idle* time [7]That Daguerre used his mechanical know-how when doing experiments in chemistry and physics. [8]He ~~magiclaly~~ *magically* created photographs from silver-plated copper sheets treated with iodine vapors. the announcement of his discovery in august 1839—just five months after the fire!—astonished paris and the world. [9]Heads of state and royalty rushed to have ~~they're~~ *their* portraits [10]Done by Daguerre.

Exercise 11 · Creating an Editing and Proofreading Exercise

Working Together

Create an editing/proofreading exercise for your classmates. Write one or two paragraphs that have at least ten mistakes (or more if you want) in grammar, usage, spelling, punctuation, or capitalization. Exchange paragraphs with classmates, and see if you can correct all the errors.   Answers will vary.

Exercise 12 · Publishing Your Portfolio

Working Together

Look back at the papers in your writing portfolio, or folder, for this year or last year. For each paper in your portfolio, jot down some ideas on how you might share the portfolio with an audience. Brainstorm additional ideas with your writing group.   Students' ideas will vary.

Writing Effective Paragraphs and Essays

Unity

◖ A paragraph has **unity** (it is unified) when its sentences focus on a single main idea.

Focusing on one main idea as you draft a paragraph will provide a framework that you can later improve upon. Your first draft does not have to include every detail; nor does it require perfect sentence order or final word selection. You will make these changes when you revise and edit. But as you draft, try to keep a clear focus.

◖ A **topic sentence** states the main idea of a paragraph.

A topic sentence in the first or second sentence in a paragraph is like a headline or an announcement of the main idea. Readers will be able to relate supporting details to it. A topic sentence may also fall at the end of a paragraph, where it ties together and summarizes the ideas and details of the preceding sentences.

Not all paragraphs have topic sentences. A paragraph's main idea may be **implied** rather than stated directly, but the main idea must be clear to the reader.

◖ A paragraph that starts with a topic sentence may end with a **clincher sentence** that restates or summarizes the main idea. A clincher sentence is used to strongly restate the main point in the paragraph, to summarize information presented in the paragraph, or to create a transition to a new idea in the next paragraph.

Topic Sentence

WRITING MODEL

Two examples support topic sentence

Transition sentence supports the topic sentence

[1]Not all marathons are like the Boston Marathon; each has its own idiosyncrasies. [2]The mid-winter Atlantic City Marathon is a simple out-and-back course, flat as a billiard table and seemingly almost no challenge—except that it must be negotiated not once but three times. [3]The old New York City Marathon, before the inventive Fred Lebow and his fellow officials devised a course that snakes its way through the city's five boroughs, consisted of tedious repetitions of a villianously hilly roadway through Central Park. [4]Such marathons dull the spirit. [5]Boston is different. [6]Curiously, it is not the world's most presitigious race at that distance (the quadrennial Olympic marathon

Details support
the topic
sentence

Clincher
sentence
strongly restates
the main idea

is), nor its most difficult (the course is more downhill than up), nor even its most scenic (unless you have a liking for freight yards, trolley tracks, and uban sprawl). [7]Nevertheless, it is the single race that captures and summarizes most of what is excellent in marathoning.

—James F. Fixx, *The Complete Book of Running*

SKILLS FOR MAINTAINING UNITY

1. Topic sentence Keep in mind that there's more than one way for a writer to write a topic sentence. For example, Fixx could have written the following topic sentence instead:

> The Boston Marathon may have its quirks, but it remains one of the most important races anywhere.

On the other hand, the following sentences are too weak to act as good topic sentences for the paragraph on the merits of the Boston Marathon.

> Running is inspiring. [**too broad**]
> The course of the Boston Marathon is mostly downhill. [**too narrow**]

2. Effective development of ideas The model paragraph sticks to the main idea. Every sentence adds a piece of important information that builds on what came before. Fixx doesn't clutter his paragraph with unnecessary sentences such as the following:

> Marathoners come from all over to participate in the Boston Marathon.

3. Clincher sentence Fixx's clincher sentence provides closure to the paragraph and adds impact. It also serves as a good transition to his next paragraph, which might focus on those things that are excellent in marathoning.

Exercise 1 Choosing a Topic Sentence

1. If you were going to write a paragraph on the changes in the New York City Marathon, which of the following two topic sentences would you use? Give reasons for your choice on a separate piece of paper.

a. The course change inspired by Fred Lebow revitalized the New York City Marathon, making it one of the most important marathons in the United States today. Sentence *a* helps ask this question: "How did the changes improve the Marathon?" Sentence *b* focuses on Lebow rather than on the changes.

b. Runners can thank Fred Lebow for changing the course of the New York City Marathon.

Elaborating with Supporting Details

◀ **Elaboration**, or **development**, means adding details to support a main idea.

When you present an idea, you keep the reader or listener interested by building supporting details for your main idea and by varying the types of details you give. Within a paragraph, you might include details such as **facts**, **statistics**, **quotations**, **definitions**, **anecdotes** or **incidents**, **examples**, **reasons**, and **comparisons**.

The writer of the following paragraph realized that the first draft did not contain enough specific details to support the topic sentence. Notice the details she added when she revised it.

[1]The December 21, 1913, issue of *The New York World* published something new: the crossword puzzle. [2]It was based on an English
called magic word squares *named Arthur Wynne*
children's game. [3]A journalist ‸created this puzzle, which included
a list of across and down *as they began to appear in every U.S. newspaper.*
‸clues. [4]People enjoyed crossword puzzles‸that appeared. [5]Publishers
which immediately became national best-sellers.
began to print full-length books with crossword puzzles, ‸and they

became popular.

When you start to revise your first draft, think about how to add details that will make your writing colorful. However, try to present new information in each sentence. Don't just say the same thing in different words.

Exercise 2 Improving Unity and Adding Details

■ Review Grammar, Lessons 6.6 and 7.5, for tips on combining sentences by inserting phrases and clauses.

Work with a partner or small group to revise the following paragraph. Cross out any words or sentences that destroy the paragraph's unity. Then, from the list on the next page, select the details that you think would improve the paragraph. Write the letter of the detail where you think it belongs in the paragraph. Then write your revised paragraph on a separate piece of paper. **Hint:** The details can be inserted as phrases and clauses.
Revisions will vary. Sample revisions given.
  [1]Every springtime, Formosa termites enjoy the evening air of New

Orleans, Louisiana. [2]These insects came from Taiwan to the United States

just fifty years ago. ³Like all termites, they are wingless except during mating
      Detail A
season. ⁴When they have wings, they fly in swarms that make it difficult for
            Details B and C
people to see or even breathe. ⁵When just one termite mates, reproduces, and
                  Detail D
settles into a dead-wood habitat, trouble begins. ⁶Park benches, stadium

bleachers, stores, homes, and anything else made out of wood can literally

crumble from the damage done by the destructive Formosa termites.

Details

A. Termites with wings, called alates, seek mates and settle down.
B. New Orleans residents keep their lights off when swarms are spotted, because
   light attracts alates. Alates come indoors through the tiniest building cracks.
C. Fewer than one percent of these termites reproduce.
D. These termites are not harmful to humans, but they can damage anything
   made out of wood.

Exercise 3 **Writing a Paragraph from Notes**

Write a unified, well-developed paragraph about the Amazon River based
on the information on the note card below. You do not need to use all of
the information. Begin your paragraph with a topic sentence.

Students' paragraphs will vary.

Flows from Peru through Brazil in South America for about 2,300 miles

Located near the equator—hot all year long

More than 100 inches (254 cm) of rainfall per year

Surrounded by the rain forest—a warm, wet area with dense plant life

Few human inhabitants in the rain forest because of climate—hot, humid

People who live in the rain forest usually live in ports on the Amazon

*Rubber, wood, gold—natural resources of the Amazon basin, transported
on the Amazon River*

Carries more water than the Nile, the Rhine, and Mississippi combined

*River length nearly equals the distance between the East Coast and the
West Coast of the United States*

Coherence

❧ Each of your paragraphs should be **coherent**—that is, each one should be logically organized so that your reader can follow your thoughts easily. Your writing should flow naturally. Use the following three strategies for writing coherent paragraphs.

STRATEGIES FOR WRITING COHERENTLY

1. Be clear. Express your thoughts simply and directly. Eliminate wordiness, and avoid overly long and complicated sentences.

2. Guide the reader. Use signposts to show the reader what lies ahead and how ideas are related. Signposts can be transition words (see those on page 28). Others are pronouns and synonyms (words that mean almost the same thing) that refer to terms you've already used in your paragraph. Repeating key words or terms also improves coherence.

3. Put your thoughts in order. Arrange information so that "first things come first."

The following list includes five common and effective ways to organize paragraphs and essays. Unless you have a good reason not to do so, choose one of these organizing principles to guide your writing.

- **Chronological Order** Organize your essay in order of time, or chronologically, when you want to describe events in the order in which they occurred. Chronological organization works well for the following types of writing: narrative paragraphs about true or fictional events, expository paragraphs about historical events, and paragraphs that describe steps in a process.

- **Spatial Order** Organize your paragraph spatially when you want to describe a person, an animal, a place, or an object. Describe details in an orderly way: Move from left to right, top to bottom, near to far, or inside to outside.

- **Order of Importance** Organize your paragraph by level of importance when you are trying to persuade your audience. State the least important reasons and details first, and end with the most important ones. In news stories, writers usually reverse this sequence—the most important detail is in the lead sentence.

Writing Hint

Think of a paragraph as a unit of meaning. Start a new paragraph whenever the meaning changes.

- **Logical Order** Organize your paragraph logically to give information in the order a reader needs to know it to understand your key points. Usually, logic determines which details you group together or where you provide background information or definitions of terms. For example, if you were writing about a cross-country trip, you might logically tell about your first stop, then your second, third, and so on.

- **Specific to General/General to Specific Order** Present details in a paragraph so that they either build toward and support a general idea or pare down a general idea to focus on a more specific, exact thought. Thus, if you were writing to persuade readers to protect wildlife, you might start with a specific example of an animal that had been hurt or killed due to careless humans: for example, a manatee that was badly injured by a speeding boat's propellors. You might use that specific detail to lead into a discussion of more general ways to protect wildlife.

The revisions in the following model show how one writer improved coherence in response to the peer editor's notes in the margin.

Use transition for emphasis.

Give examples.

Eliminate wordiness.

Combine sentences.

Give specific details.
Add transition word.

WRITING MODEL

In fact,
¹Owning a business is not just for adults. ²Some teenagers run their own businesses successfully. ³Teenagers might start a business *such as pet care, house cleaning, lawn care, or other fields* in a field in which they have skill or interest.

⁴Any beginning business owner will address certain questions. *For example, he or she* ⁵~~Any beginning business owner~~ must ask, "What are my interests?" *and* ⁶~~They must ask,~~ "What is the potential for making a profit in this business?" ⁷There are other things to think about, too. ⁸Owners must check out government rules about business in the library or *advertising and bookkeeping* *Finally,* on the Internet. ⁹They must think about ~~business details~~. ¹⁰They need to think about whether they need any employees or equipment to run their businesses.

Some Common Transitional Words and Expressions

To show **time**		To show **examples**		To show **order of importance**		To **compare**	
after	first	for example	namely	above all	second	also	likewise
afterward	immediately	for instance	that is	finally	then	and	similarly
at last	later	in addition		first	last	as	too
before	soon	in other words		most important		like	
during	then						
finally	when	To **summarize**		To show **cause**		To **contrast**	
		all in all	finally	**and effect**		although	but
To show **place**		as a result	therefore	as a result	since	however	still
above	inside	in conclusion		because	so	in contrast	yet
across	into	in summary		consequently	so that	nevertheless	
among	off			if . . . then	therefore	on the other hand	
behind	outside	To **emphasize**		for that reason			
below	there	for this reason	again				
between	through	moreover	in fact				
in front of	under	most important					

Exercise 4 **Revising Paragraphs for Coherence**

Work with a partner or small group to improve the coherence of the following paragraphs. Try adding transitional words and expressions, reordering information, and combining sentences. Write your revised paragraphs on a separate piece of paper.   Students' revised paragraphs will vary.

¹The words you speak may be your legacy on earth. ²This seemingly strange statement was supported by the findings of Johanna Nichols at a convention of the American Association for the Advancement of Science in 1998. ³Johanna Nichols is an expert on Native American languages. ⁴For a long time, it was believed that humans walked across the Bering Strait on a land bridge from Asia to Alaska about 11,500 years ago. ⁵Humans slowly made their way southward. ⁶It was also believed that one long migration occurred. ⁷These settlers traveled south to warm regions, then back north when the earth warmed up again.

⁸Nichols's research on the development of Native American languages indicates that there were three migrations before the last Ice Age and one migration (the Eskimo-Aleuts) afterward. ⁹Nichols's research shows that the last migration took place around 5,000 years ago. ¹⁰Nichols dates the first migrations as far back as 40,000 years ago. ¹¹The language you speak might tell where your ancestors lived. ¹²The results of Johanna Nichols's research are based on calculations related to the amount of time it takes a language to develop.

Exercise 5 Writing a Coherent, Unified Paragraph

Choose one of the following assignments, and write a coherent, unified paragraph.
Students' paragraphs will vary.

1. Explain the basic rules of a game or sport for someone unfamiliar with it.

2. Think about a room or building you know well, such as a room in your home, the classroom, a movie theater, or a favorite store. Then write a detailed description of it.

3. Your school is considering placing on the local board of education a student representative who can cast a vote on behalf of the student body. Do you think this would be a good idea? Why or why not? Write a paragraph stating your opinion, and provide reasons to support that opinion.

Exercise 6 Writing a Paragraph from Notes

Write a coherent, unified paragraph based on the following note card. Include a topic sentence.

Willa Cather (1873–1947)—American novelist

Writer who emphasized strong, female characters well before the women's movement or feminism

Writing focused on immigrant characters involved in settling the American West

Raised in Red Cloud, Nebraska

One of few women to graduate from University of Nebraska (1895)

Worked as a journalist and a high school English teacher

Moved to New York City (1906), worked as a magazine editor

Publication of novel O Pioneers! (1913) brought acclaim

Two more well-received novels written in 5 years—The Song of the Lark (1915) and My Ántonia (1918)

Students' paragraphs will vary but should include a clear topic sentence. Students should stick to that topic and support it with related details or ideas from the card, and they should have a logical organization for these ideas. See teacher pages for assessment rubrics.

Purpose

You write paragraphs and essays for a number of purposes. In this lesson, you'll study four of the main **purposes** for writing.

DESCRIPTIVE

When your purpose is to describe a person, a place, an object, or an animal, use the following suggestions.

- **Use sensory details** that appeal to the reader's sense of sight, hearing, smell, touch, and taste. Sensory details help create a **main impression** or **mood** in your writing.

- **Use spatial order** to present the sensory details from left to right, top to bottom, near to far, one direction to another—or in reverse.

Context: writer's location
Smell detail

Sight detail

Sound detail

Touch detail
Change of mood

> ¹As I stood in one corner of the garden, I could smell the lilac's perfume travel to me like the sweetness of the spring. ²I moved to the garden's center and began to weed a patch of wild daisies. ³Behind me, the hibiscus shrubs had just blossomed, each bloom looking like a show-off. ⁴Best of all, a meadow lark sat on the garden fence singing a song of new growth and joy. ⁵When I turned to survey this newcomer in full view, I stepped on a branch of flowering weeds whose thorny stems stung my legs. ⁶Needless to say, the pleasure of my morning in the garden suddenly evaporated.

NARRATIVE

When your purpose is to tell a story, either a fictional story or a true narrative, use the following suggestions.

- Use **specific details** to help make the reader feel like an eyewitness to the events.

- Use **chronological order** (time order) to relate the events in the order in which they occurred.

Quotation gives authenticity to setting

> ¹Monday night "the storm crosses offshore and the first-stage wind surge" passes over the *Satori*. ²The weather radio reports that ocean conditions will ease off briefly and then deteriorate again as the

Chronological organization

storm swings back toward the coast. ³By then, though, the *Satori* might be far enough south to escape the storm's full wrath. ⁴The boat wallows on through Monday night, the barometer rising

Specific details and description

slightly and the wind easing off to the northeast; but then late that night, like a bad fever, the storm comes on again. ⁵The wind climbs to fifty knots, and the seas rise up in huge dark mountains behind

Events create suspense

the boat. ⁶The crew take turns at the helm, clipped into a safety line, and occasionally take a breaking sea over the cockpit. ⁷The barometer crawls downward all night, and by dawn the conditions are worse than anything Stimson has ever seen in her life.

EXPOSITORY

There are several ways to explain and to inform: You can compare and contrast; you can discuss cause and effect; or you can define, classify, or analyze. The following suggestions will help you with expository writing.

- State your **main idea** as early and as clearly as possible.

- Use **facts**, **examples**, **quotations**, **statistics**, and **definitions** as supporting details to develop the main idea.

- Present details in a **logical order** so that they make sense to the reader. Transition words help your reader follow your train of thought (see page 28).

Types of Exposition

Comparison/Contrast The writer explores similarities and differences between two or more subjects.

Cause and Effect The writer examines reasons behind an occurrence (causes) and/or the results of an occurrence (effects).

Classification The writer gathers similar elements and details into a category to distinguish one category from another.

Definition The writer defines a term or concept and elaborates with supporting details (descriptions, comparisons, examples, or statistics).

WRITING MODEL

Main idea stated, showing time of occurrence

¹Last month, a group of entrepreneurs from Tampa, Florida, were searching the Mediterranean Sea for lost treasure. ²Using a

Statistic: distance, fact

robot equipped with a video camera, the searchers were able to view the sea's floor over a half-mile deep. ³The team's director, Greg Stemm, reported the discovery of clay storage jars, called amphoras,

Fact and definition of finding

from an extremely old shipwreck. ⁴Stemm sent his video recording of the discovery to specialized archeologists who tentatively identified the earthen jars as typical of the Carthaginian jars from

Explanation of discovery

around 400 B.C. ⁵Worth a fortune, these jars have been submerged for more than two thousand years.

PERSUASIVE

When your purpose is to convince readers to share your opinion or to encourage them to take action, use the following suggestions:

• Begin with a sentence that **grabs the reader's attention**.

• Include an **opinion statement** that clearly expresses your point of view.

• Present **reasons** and other **evidence** to support your opinion.

• Arrange the supporting details in **order of importance**—from most to least important, or the reverse.

• Include a **call to action**.

Attention grabber

[1]When was the last time you read a handwritten note from a friend that was perfectly legible and in good cursive letters? [2]Chances are this is a distant memory. [3]One of the most basic skills of grammar school—penmanship—is almost entirely overlooked, and elementary school students are getting to high school with virtually illegible handwriting. [4]This neglect by grammar schools

Opinion statement

Reason supports opinion

must stop. [5]For starters, students should not be given a computer keyboard in place of pencil and paper. [6]"Handwriting is a motor skill,"

Quotation supports reason

said a teacher in Glenford, Ohio. [7]"Practice is the only way to perfect any motor skill." [8]However, if this basic skill is not practiced regularly in grammar schools, this shift toward illegible handwriting will

Call to action

continue. [9]In short, grammar schools have a responsibility to instill the habits of good penmanship that will last a lifetime.

Exercise 7 Writing with Different Purposes

Write at least two different kinds of paragraphs. You may use the suggested topics below or choose a topic of your own. Students' two paragraphs will vary. Check that each contains a topic sentence, sticks to and supports its main idea, and is logically organized. See teacher pages for assessment rubrics.

1. A **persuasive paragraph** about high school students leaving school before they graduate to take a job (argue for or against)

2. A **descriptive paragraph** about a special outdoor place

3. A **narrative paragraph** about a discovery, an adventure, or a journey

4. An **expository paragraph** giving information about your school, your community, a specific career, or a celebrity

Writing Essays

A well-written essay begins with an **introductory** paragraph, continues with several more paragraphs constituting the **body** of the essay, and ends with one or more **concluding** paragraphs. In other words, good essays have a definite beginning, middle, and end.

INTRODUCTION

An introductory paragraph has two key missions: to interest readers in reading further and to present them with the overall subject or idea of the essay.

> The **thesis statement** of an essay is the overall idea. It is also called a **claim** or a **controlling idea**.

The thesis statement in the introduction of an essay functions like the topic sentence in a paragraph. Sometimes, the thesis statement appears in an essay's very first sentence. On the other hand, as shown below, the writer may choose to first present readers with an interesting detail and then lead them to the more general thesis statement.

> Baggy pants, baseball caps worn backwards, T-shirts two sizes too big— have you seen a third grader dressing like this recently? Because of wild swings in fashion trends, local school districts are now adopting strict dress codes or uniforms.

Here's what *not* to write:

> This paper that I'm about to write explains why . . .
> In this essay, I'll talk about . . .

> ### Some Ways to Begin an Essay
>
> • anecdote • vivid image
> • example • quotation
> • question
> • bit of dialogue
> • startling statement of fact

BODY

Support and develop your thesis statement by following your introduction with several more paragraphs that contain supporting details, anecdotes, and examples. Use these guidelines to help you draft the body of an essay.

1. **Topic sentences** Think of the body of your essay as a series of main ideas, each one expressed in the topic sentence of a separate paragraph. Each paragraph should contain specific details that support the topic sentence.

2. Organization Decide how you're going to arrange your main ideas. You may choose one of the organizational methods described in Lesson 2.3. Try to begin with first things first—background information—and then move through your main ideas in the order your reader needs to know them. Creating an outline of an essay before you write (see Lesson 1.2) may help you organize the ideas for the body.

3. Focus Avoid repetition, and eliminate wordiness. Ask yourself, "What am I trying to say?"; then say it as clearly as you can.

> **Some Ways to End an Essay**
>
> - summary of main ideas
> - comment on importance of topic
> - thought-provoking question
> - quotation
> - prediction about the future
> - call to action

CONCLUSION

The conclusion of your essay is your chance to wrap up your thoughts, information, or ideas. Try to sum up your main ideas and explain how they support your thesis statement. Your essay will usually conclude with one or two sentences or possibly a full paragraph or more. In the margin, you'll find suggestions for concluding essays.

Here's what *not* to write:

> Well, that's everything I know about this subject. I wish I could tell you more, but that's all I have time for now.

> **Writing Hint**
>
> Your conclusion may echo a thought or phrase from the introduction. This technique encourages readers to view your essay as a whole.

Exercise 8 **Drafting an Introduction**

You are writing an autobiographical, narrative essay about the time you gave a speech to introduce a friend who was running for class president. Here's what happened: You uttered one sentence of the introduction and forgot everything else you had planned to say. You reached into a pocket for your note cards but realized that you had left them at home. Draft an introduction to this autobiographical essay that will make your classmates want to read the whole story. Make up any details that you need.   Students' introductions will vary.

Exercise 9 Writing Body Paragraphs Based on Notes

Review the notes on the card below. Write one or more paragraphs for the body of a research paper about World War II. Give each paragraph a topic sentence, and support each topic sentence with facts. Your audience should be your high school social studies class.

Details of D-Day (background information)

Took place June 6, 1944

Allies crossed English Channel from Great Britain to attack Germans in Normandy (region of France)

Operations involved 11,000 planes, 600 warships, 1,500 tanks, and 175,000 soldiers

Entire operation was secret—surprise attack on Germans

Germans attacked Allies as soldiers stormed out of warships

Huge casualties—6,600 U.S. soldiers killed, wounded, or lost on beaches of Normandy

Due to the huge number of soldiers, enough troops survived the beach, and operation succeeded

Students' paragraphs will vary but should include a clear topic sentence, supporting details, and pertinent background information. See teacher pages for assessment rubrics.

Exercise 10 Drafting a Conclusion

Draft a concluding paragraph for a persuasive essay about a proposed state law that would raise the eligibility age to drive to twenty. Make up any specific details that you need. In your conclusion, state your view of this proposed law and the key reasons behind that opinion.   Students' conclusions will vary.

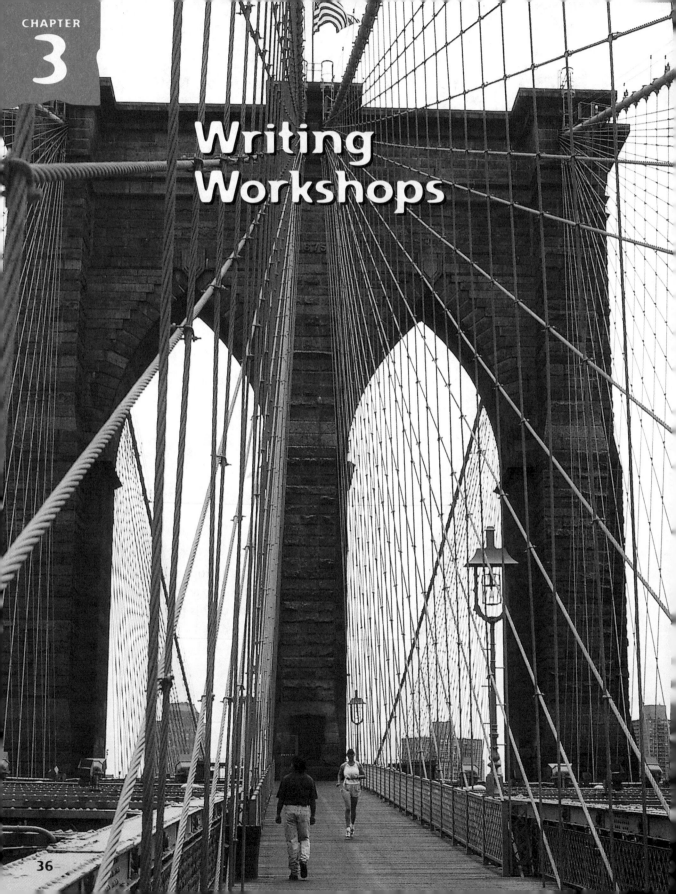

Writing Workshops

Narrative Writing: Personal Narrative

When you write a **personal narrative**, you tell a true autobiographical story that happened in a limited time. You strive to make it interesting, and you reflect on how you felt about the incident then and now.

"Dust Storm" is an excerpt from *The Invisible Thread*, a full-length memoir by Yoshiko Uchida about her experiences in Topaz, a World War II internment camp for Japanese Americans. After the bombing of Pearl Harbor, Hawaii, on December 7, 1941, by Japanese bombers, President Franklin D. Roosevelt issued Executive Order 9066, which required all persons of Japanese descent living in America to forfeit their property and report to such internment camps. Many of the internment-camp barracks were unheated former animal pens. Nonetheless, the internees coped with the difficult circumstances by establishing schools, planting gardens, and organizing group activities.

Dust Storm

from *The Invisible Thread* by Yoshiko Uchida

[1]What people didn't realize was that no matter where they moved in Topaz, they would find the same frustrating conditions. [2]Barren unfinished rooms. [3]Dust everywhere. [4]Sudden water stoppages . . . .

Prepares reader for incident

[5]About a week after we arrived, I encountered my first dust storm. [6]As the afternoon temperatures began to rise, I felt a hot, dry wind and saw murky gray clouds gathering in the sky.

Presents setting

[7]I was walking home with a friend when the wind suddenly became a fierce, ominous living thing, twisting and shrieking and howling at us as though we had incurred its wrath. [8]It flung swirling masses of sand into the air, engulfing us in such thick clouds of dust, we couldn't even see barracks ten feet away.

[9]We ran into the nearest laundry barrack and found the air inside already thick with dust. [10]The flimsy barrack shuddered with each blast of wind, and we heard garbage cans and wooden crates slamming against the building as the wind flung them through the air.

Describes details in chronological (time) order

[11]We crouched near the washtubs for over an hour, waiting for the wind to subside even a little. [12]When it did, we decided to make a run for our homes.

[13]"Be careful, Yo," my friend called.

[14]"I will. [15]You, too."

Quotes dialogue

Includes sensory details — [16]We separated then, and I staggered alone through the billowing dust, weaving as though I were drunk, blown this way and that by the howling wind. [17]Sand blew into my eyes, so I could barely see. [18]It blew into my nose and mouth, so I could hardly breathe. [19]The dust was making me choke, but fear of being swept off my feet and flung into the desert kept me going.

[20]When I finally stumbled into our room, I was covered with dust. [21]It was in my hair and on my eyelashes and in my nose. [22]My mouth tasted like chalk. [23]I found Mama sitting alone, worrying about the rest of us.

[24]"Oh, Yo Chan, I'm so glad you're safe," she said, hugging me.

Reveals feelings — [25]We were worried about Kay and Papa, but there was nothing we could do. [26]We simply covered everything with newspapers and lay on our cots, our faces covered with towels, waiting for the storm to end.

[27]Kay and Papa came home about supper time, covered with dust from head to toe. [28]They had both been caught too far away to run home as I had, but they were safe.

Explains aftermath and impact of events — [29]By sunset the storm had spent itself. [30]When I went outside to look up at the wide encircling desert sky, it had turned glorious shades of pink and gold and lavender. [31]It was hard to believe it was the same sky that only a few hours earlier had spewed out such suffocating terror. [32]It was almost as though the dust storm had never happened, but I knew from our dust-filled room that it had indeed been quite real.

Critical Thinking

After you read the personal narrative, answer the questions below.
Use the following questions to lead a class discussion.

1. What is the main problem that the dust storm creates for people at Topaz? Using time order, summarize what happens to Yoshiko Uchida in this narrative.

2. How do sensory details enhance the author's writing? How would the narrative be different without sensory details?

3. How do the direct quotes affect your response to this event in Yoshiko Uchida's life?

4. Find at least three active verbs in the personal narrative that help you envision this dust storm through the eyes of the writer. Explain how these verbs influence your feelings about the author's experience in Topaz.

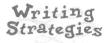 The purpose of a personal narrative is to explain or relate a series of events. Because a personal narrative not only recounts an incident but also reflects on the incident's meaning, use writing strategies that serve these dual purposes.

1. **Select an incident.** An incident is a ministory. It has a **plot** (the series of events), **characters**, and a **setting** (when and where the incident occurred). Since you are the narrator—the person telling the story—you should narrate the incident from the **first-person point of view** using first-person pronouns (*I, me, mine, we, us, ours*).

2. **Watch time order.** A complete event comprises smaller happenings that occur over a period of time. If you write in **chronological order**, you'll start at the beginning and relate the events in the order they occurred until you've recounted the entire incident. You may also use reverse chronological order to recount an incident from its conclusion back to its beginning.

3. **Explain the point of it all.** You write personal narratives to shed light on the personal meaning of life events. To accomplish this goal, you must include details that tell the story clearly as well as details that communicate how and why the event is significant to you. You may write about an incident that influenced you, another individual, or an entire community. Whatever your topic, tell your reader why it is important.

> **Writing Hint**
>
> Envision the incident in your mind as if it were a movie filmed through a camera lens. As the camera pans the incident, select the few sensory details that stand out for you.

4. **Sprinkle the narrative with sensory details.** Describe the incident as you experienced it. Note what you saw, heard, smelled, tasted, or touched. Too many sensory details, however, may numb the reader, so choose only the most relevant ones.

5. **Add dialogue.** Words are powerful, especially exact words that are spoken, so include some direct quotes. If you don't remember the exact words from the event you are narrating, take a guess at who said what. Yoshiko Uchida heightens readers' sensations of the dust storm by first including dialogue between herself and a friend and by later quoting her mother's words.

6. **Include your thoughts and feelings.** Think back on how you felt when the incident was unfolding. How do you feel about it in retrospect? Insert those thoughts and feelings as you write.

Exercise 1 Get Started

Use one or two of the prewriting techniques (writer's notebook, freewriting, brainstorming, clustering, and so on) from Lesson 1.1 to generate some incidents you can write about. Like Yoshiko Uchida, you might focus on something extraordinary that happened to you. You could also concentrate on an incident that changed you or a decision you once made that had far-reaching consequences. The incident or decision can be serious or funny. Think of the incident as if it were a story with a plot, characters, a setting, and a point of view.
Answers will vary. Refer to "Purposes of Writing" in the teacher pages for prewriting suggestions.

Exercise 2 Plan Your Personal Narrative

Create a story map similar to the one below to sort out the relationships among elements in your personal narrative and your feelings or insights about them. Include as many details in your story map as you can.
Answers will vary. Encourage students to err on the side of too many details at this stage of writing.

Story Map

a. What is the **setting?**	
b. Identify the **characters** and describe them.	
c. Identify the **conflict** or event in your narrative.	
d. Why was the event important to you?	

Exercise 3 Draft Your Personal Narrative

As you draft, remember that your audience is your classmates. Your purpose may be to tell an entertaining story or an important one. Note that in addition to the story itself, Yoshiko Uchida shares her feelings about the incident throughout her narrative.   Answers will vary.

- **Make your point clearly**. A personal narrative goes beyond simply describing an incident; you have to explain the meaning the incident had for you. If you spent a day volunteering at a soup kitchen, for example, you might write about how you felt looking at the people in line. What did you learn about them and about yourself through your experience?

- **Zero in on essential events and details**. Sometimes, one piece of dialogue or one telltale action reveals the whole point of your narrative. Look for these kinds of telling quotes or moments and use them to illustrate the point of your narrative. Let them unfold naturally so readers sense their meaning as an integral part of the incident.

Exercise 4 Revise Your Personal Narrative

Try reading your paper aloud to yourself and then to a partner. First, check to make sure the events are organized logically (use either chronological order or order of importance). Listen for active verbs, sensory details, and dialogue. Make any changes to improve the narrative flow. Then go over the essay once more to see if it reads smoothly and if it makes a point the reader can understand. Eliminate unnecessary wordiness and replace general nouns or verbs with precise ones. When you're satisfied with your draft, share it with a small writers' group. Ask the members of the group for their comments, questions, and suggestions, and then decide if you want to revise further.   Answers will vary. Students should refer to Lesson 1.3 for more revising strategies.

Exercise 5 Proofread and Publish

Check your revised paper for errors in grammar, usage, punctuation, capitalization, and spelling. Exchange papers with a partner to see if you've missed any mistakes.   Answers will vary. Students should refer to Mechanics, Chapters 13–16, for additional proofreading skills.

Share your personal narrative with friends and family, especially anyone who might have had a similar experience or who was directly involved in yours. If you enjoyed this assignment, continue to write about incidents that mean something to you as chapters in an ongoing memoir. You might also consider presenting this personal narrative as a gift to a friend or relative.

Persuasive Writing

How do you hold readers' interest, win them over to your viewpoint, and convince them to act on an issue—all at the same time? You write a **persuasive essay** with clear **arguments** that are well supported by evidence. As you read the following essay about curfews, pay attention to the author's argument and her evidence to support it.

Down with Curfews;
Up with Children
by Nadine Strossen

Attention grabber

[1]In San Diego, the American Civil Liberties Union (ACLU) is now representing a group of clients who face criminal prosecution because they engage in the following activities: working in a Rescue Mission soup kitchen; volunteering for "Safe Rides," a program providing teenagers with rides home from weekend parties; acting in plays; and participating in study groups. [2]The dregs of society, eh?

Loaded words make position statement clear.

[3]Why do our clients face arrest for these perfectly lawful—indeed, laudable—activities? [4]Because they are teenagers who live in San Diego, which has been aggressively enforcing a curfew law that bars anyone under eighteen from all public places after 10 P.M. [5]Moreover, many other cities, all across the country, have recently adopted similar policies, putting all teens under virtual house arrest.

States position of curfew supporters

[6]Politicians across the spectrum have applauded these martial law-type measures. [7]In his 1996 "State of the State" address, California Governor Pete Wilson denounced the ACLU's lawsuit against the San Diego curfew, saying, "If anyone ought to be sued, it's the ACLU—for defying common sense."

Logical appeal with evidence: businesses and police oppose curfew.

[8]Our teenage clients and their parents might not agree with the governor—and they would not be alone. [9]The many businesses harmed by the loss of young patrons, and the police officers who would rather pursue real criminals—of all ages—than turn innocent young people into criminals, undoubtedly would join the ACLU in "defying" common sense.

Direct quote by police captain endorses ACLU position.

[10]Significantly, the decision to aggressively enforce San Diego's strict curfew was made by the city council, not police officials. [11]As one police captain reported to the department's assistant chief, "Field officials tend to see this program as a politically inspired boondoggle that has no real relevance to crime problems on their beats."

Statistical evidence on teenage crime

[12]San Diego's arrest statistics bear out the police officers' view that enforcing the teen curfew is a waste of their time. [13]Since the strict enforcement began, the number of juvenile arrests for violent crimes decreased almost four times as much during noncurfew hours as it did during curfew hours. [14]Likewise,

the number of juveniles who were victims of violent crime decreased almost twice as much during noncurfew hours as during curfew hours.

Emotional appeal supported by evidence — [15]Most crimes committed by and against minors occur between 3 and 6 P.M. [16]And, tragically, most violence against young people takes place in their own homes. [17]Under the "logic" of the curfew advocates, should we therefore banish our nation's youth from their own homes? [18]Or hold them hostage there during the midafternoon? . . .

Use of loaded term—"Big Daddy"— supported by concept of constitutional rights — [19]When Big Brother acts like Big Daddy, by imposing a curfew on all children, he violates the constitutional rights of parents and children alike. [20]A federal judge in Washington, D.C., so ruled at the end of October. [21]He struck down the District's 1995 curfew law, which the ACLU challenged on behalf of a group of young people, their parents and grandparents, and a movie theater. [22]Unfortunately, though, the unconstitutionality of the recent rash of curfew laws is far from settled. [23]The D.C. government promptly appealed the ACLU's victory; other lower courts have split on the issue—for example, a federal judge in San Diego upheld its draconian curfew last summer; and the U.S. Supreme Court has never resolved the issue.

Call to action against teenage curfews — [24]We have to hope that when the Supreme Court does face this important issue, it will follow the sound approach of the Washington, D.C., ruling. [25]Along with so many of the faddish policies that are touted as "anticrime," "pro-children," and "pro-family," curfew laws are, in fact, just the opposite. [26]If we really want to do something for young people and their families—as well as for public safety—maybe we should impose strict curfews on all politicians, to stop them from enacting ineffective and dangerous measures.

Critical Thinking

After you read the persuasive essay, answer the questions below.
Use the following questions to lead a class discussion.

1. Which details in the first and second paragraphs make the writer's position clear?

2. To what audience do you think this writer is addressing her essay? Cite details in the essay that make you think this.

3. List two reasons—with specific examples of evidence—that support the writer's opinion.

4. How does the writer either counter or demolish the argument of those in favor of teenage curfews in San Diego? Cite examples from the essay.

5. The next to last paragraph begins with this statement: "When Big Brother acts like Big Daddy. . . ." How do the terms "Big Brother" and "Big Daddy" influence how you feel about Nadine Strossen's argument against teenage curfews?

6. Read the last paragraph aloud. In what way does this paragraph affect your opinion on the subject of curfews for teenagers? What kind of action would you consider taking after reading this essay?

Build Your Vocabulary. Which of these words from the essay can you define: *laudable* (sentence 3), *boondoggle* (sentence 11), *draconian* (sentence 23), *touted* (sentence 25)? Look up the words you don't know in the dictionary, and use the phonetic symbols to pronounce the words correctly. Add these words to your vocabulary notebook.

Writing Strategies

The purpose of writing a persuasive essay is to convince your reader to support your opinion. As you write, include a variety of the following strategies to strengthen your argument.

1. **Present a clear opinion.** Your opinion is the heart of your argument—a concise summary of your entire essay. Make sure it appears at the beginning of your essay in a clear, complete **position statement** or **thesis statement**.

2. **State reasons for your opinion.** Readers usually respond best to arguments that present two or more reasons in support of an opinion. In your essay, write about the reasons that are the most convincing.

3. **Support reasons with evidence.** Evidence comes in a variety of forms. Use the forms of evidence that best suit your argument, but vary the use of those forms within an essay.

   • State **facts** or **statistics** from reliable reference sources.

   • Include **expert opinions** in the form of quotations. (Make sure to identify the expert and use an exact quote.)

   • Drop in **examples** and **anecdotes** (including some drawn from personal experience or observation).

4. **Support reasons with emotional appeals.** Emotional appeals strengthen your argument *only* when accompanied by evidence-supported reasons, which are **logical appeals**. However, emotional appeals alone may offend readers, make them lose

Writing Hint

The words you choose go a long way toward persuading or alienating readers.

1. Identify the members of your audience (their age, their knowledge about a given subject), and use language and evidence that will both persuade this group of readers and hold its interest.

2. Choose words and phrases that make you appear confident and reliable, as well as committed to your viewpoint.

3. Don't waffle by using qualifiers such as *probably*, *maybe*, or *perhaps*.

interest in your ideas, or raise suspicions about the validity of your reasoning. Use emotional appeals carefully.

Loaded words may carry either positive or negative connotations. For example, the word *dregs* often has a negative connotation, which communicates a negative emotion. When Nadine Strossen writes about teenagers as "the *dregs* of society, eh?" (sentence 2), she is heightening readers' awareness of negative feelings toward teenagers with this loaded word. Indeed, she hopes her readers will reject the negativity inherent in the word *dregs* and come around to her viewpoint, which she feels is more positive toward teenagers.

5. **Avoid fallacies of thinking.** These are unproved assumptions communicated when writers **stereotype** (present a fixed idea about all members of a group) and **overgeneralize** (present a conclusion applied to everyone). The words *everyone* or *most* often introduce these kinds of fallacies. So beware!

OVERGENERALIZATION   *Everyone* knows that rock and roll music is painfully uncomplicated. [overgeneralization about the qualities of rock and roll music]

STEREOTYPING   *Most* writers are mere dreamers, not doers. [stereotyping the personalities of all people who write]

6. **Present and demolish counterarguments.** As you write persuasively, acknowledge opposing views and give reasons—along with evidence—to disprove these views.

7. **Conclude with a call to action.** Persuasive writers often conclude by urging readers to take constructive action, such as writing letters, donating money, voting in an election, volunteering, or buying a particular product. A **call to action** effectively reinforces your opinion.

Exercise 6   Choose a Topic

Work with a small group to brainstorm topics for a persuasive essay. Use these hints.   Answers will vary. Suggest that students use the prewriting suggestions in Lesson 1.1.

• The topic must be debatable, not just a matter of personal taste. It should be an issue or question that people disagree about.

• You must have a strong opinion about the topic you choose. But be careful! Some topics are inappropriate for school assignments. Check with your teacher if you suspect that your topic may be inappropriate.

Exercise 7 State Your Opinion

The chart below shows how one writer developed a clear, complete thesis statement for a persuasive essay. With your writing group, complete the chart with other possible thesis statements that are clear and complete on the topics listed. Answers will vary.

Developing a Thesis Statement

Subject of Thesis	Clear, Complete Thesis Statement
Physical Fitness	High school physical education departments should help students develop and maintain individual fitness programs.
Student Government	
Teenaged Volunteers	
Your Topic	

Now, add the topic for your persuasive essay to the chart and develop a clear, complete thesis statement.

Exercise 8 Support Your Opinion

Before you write, think about your audience and choose the reasons, evidence, and emotional appeals that will persuade the members of this audience to embrace your point of view. Write down as many arguments as you can think of to support your opinion.   Answers will vary.

• Choose the two or three strongest arguments.

• Jot down the reasons, evidence, and emotional appeals that support each argument. These notes can serve as a rough outline as you start Exercise 9.

Exercise 9 Draft Your Essay

As you write your draft, support your opinion with the reasons and relevant evidence you outlined in Exercise 8. Keep the following in mind.
Answers will vary. Students should refer to Lesson 1.2 for drafting strategies.

• Provide background information that you think your intended audience will need to understand your subject and to follow your argument.

• Mention your sources and be specific in the evidence you present. Your audience will be impressed that your research is thorough.

• Don't waste words or wander off the subject. Make your argument strong by keeping it tight.

Exercise 10 Edit, Proofread, and Publish

Edit your writing carefully to eliminate unnecessary words and sentences. Tighten your argument by dropping anything that doesn't *directly support* your main point. To influence readers' emotions, selectively include loaded words and emotional appeals in your essay. Share your paper with a writing group, or use the following publishing suggestions.

• Send your persuasive essay to the editor of a school or local newspaper as an editorial or a letter to the editor.

• If you've written on issues that affect government, send your essay to a government representative from your community or state.

• Send your persuasive essay to a local television or radio program with a letter asking the producer to consider addressing the issue on the air.

• Use the position statement in your paper as the starting point for a team debate among classmates.

Answers will vary. Students should refer to Lesson 1.4 for proofreading strategies and publishing suggestions.

Persuasive Writing: Critical Review

When you watch a movie, read a book, or look at a painting or sculpture, you have a reaction to it—either positive or negative. If you write about your reaction and analyze why that work of art makes you feel that way, your essay—or **critical review**—becomes a form of **persuasive writing**. Sometimes, a critical review may summarize the plot and give an opinion about the overall work. But a critical review goes beyond a plot summary and a stated opinion: You must give **reasons** why you feel a particular way about a work of art and support your reasons with **evidence**. The evidence you cite may encompass **comparisons** with other works of the same genre or **emotional appeals** based on your personal reaction.

The review below is one person's opinion about a movie. Think critically about the author's opinion as you read.

'Romeo' Takes Bold Bard Departure
by Todd McCarthy

Attention grabber and thesis statement — [1]No doubt the most aggressively modern, assertively trendy adaptation of Shakespeare ever filmed, this overwhelmingly of-the-moment version of one of literature's most enduring tragic love stories can serve as a litmus test for any viewer's willingness to accept extreme stylistic attitudinizing as a substitute for the virtues of traditional storytelling. . . . [2]Anything but dull, and ultimately saved by the manifestly indestructible qualities of the four-hundred-year-old play, this is decidedly as much Baz Luhrmann's *Romeo and Juliet* as it is William Shakespeare's. . . .

Critiques setting — [3]Luhrmann transports the Montagues and Capulets to Verona Beach and a violent contemporary world dominated by designer guns, customized cars, and incessant music. [4][The] result is simultaneously striking and silly, boldly elaborated and unconvincing, imaginative and misguided. [5]Although arresting in spots, it falls far short of bringing out the full values of the play, and [it] doesn't approach the emotional resonance of Franco Zeffirelli's immensely popular 1968 screen version. . . .

Comparison to earlier film

[6]Luhrmann's biggest set piece is the Capulets' conciliatory masquerade ball, at which Romeo's best buddy Mercutio (Harold Perrineau, grown considerably since *Smoke*) shows up in a white wig and silver-spangled miniskirt to sing a musical number on the stairway. [7]But this doesn't bring the picture alive nearly as much as does Claire Danes, whose Juliet, from the moment she appears, is the picture of youthful purity, spontaneity, and romantic readiness. [8]Her scenes, both with and apart from Romeo, also stand as a welcome relief from the unrelenting cacophony of the rest of the picture, and it is a measure of the director's intent to upend conventional readings

of Shakespeare that he stages most of the famous balcony scene in a swimming pool.

⁹In a literally edge-of-the-world beach sequence, Juliet's enraged cousin Tybalt comes looking for Romeo but kills Mercutio instead, whereupon Romeo turns his world upside down by taking revenge upon Tybalt. ¹⁰Perhaps the greatest anachronism in modern terms is Romeo's subsequent "banishment" from Verona Beach, instead of [his indictment for] murder. . . .

States biggest problem with script

¹¹This is the very rare Shakespeare film not dominated by British-trained theater actors—only Pete Postlethwaite, as Father Lawrence, and Miriam Margolyes, as the Nurse, qualify on this count—so the mostly young Stateside actors are not put in the position of being shown up by them. ¹²However, their relative awkwardness with the language is spotlighted by Danes, who has somehow found a way to both enunciate the Shakespearean lingo and make its meanings lucid and accessible.

Offers opinions of actors with supporting evidence

¹³Playing Romeo as a James Deanish brooder, Leonardo DiCaprio brings youthful energy to the role but neither seems like his parents' son nor much like one of the gang he runs with. ¹⁴He gets his speeches out without undue embarrassment but, [in contrast to] Danes, they don't seem second-nature to him . . . .

Supports opinion by citing specific flaws

¹⁵But it is the transposition of the story to an exotic contemporary setting that is the film's most striking and unmanageable component. ¹⁶Even when the wild stylings, obvious notions, and shrill performances don't work, which is often, the sheer confidence of Luhrmann's audacious conceptions makes an undeniable impression. ¹⁷As irritating and glib as some of it may be, there is indisputably a strong vision here that has been worked out in considerable detail.

Summarizes opinion of strengths and weaknesses

Critical Thinking

After you read the critical review, answer the questions below.
Use the following questions to lead a class discussion.

1. Based on the first two sentences of the review, what do you think the author thinks the movie's strengths are? What does he think the movie's weaknesses are?

2. What evidence does the author give to justify his praise of the actress Claire Danes, who played Juliet?

3. Reread sentences three through five. Identify the emotionally charged language that the author uses to support his negative opinion of the setting for the movie.

4. In his conclusion, the author states both the strengths and weaknesses of the movie. Do you think that this technique improves or detracts from the critical review? Explain your answer.

Build Your Vocabulary. Which of these words from the essay can you define: *litmus test* (sentence 1), *incessant* (sentence 3), *conciliatory* (sentence 6), *cacophony* (sentence 8), *anachronism* (sentence 10), *indictment* (sentence 6), *lucid* (sentence 12), *audacious* (sentence 16)? Look up the words you don't know in a dictionary, and use the phonetic symbols to pronounce the words correctly. Add these words to your vocabulary notebook.

Writing Strategies The purpose of a critical review is to present your opinion of a movie, live performance, book, or other work of art and to persuade your readers that your opinion is correct. Here are some strategies that you can use to persuade readers.

1. **Choose a subject.** Choose a film, book, or artwork you know well and about which you have strong feelings—positive or negative. You may discover a good subject by looking through your writer's notebook.

2. **State your opinion.** Make your opinion of the work clear by using concise language. This opinion statement usually belongs in the first paragraph of your critical review.

3. **Support your opinion.** As in any persuasive writing, support your opinion with reasons and evidence. For example, if you claim that the major weakness of a film or play is the acting, cite examples of it and explain how it affects the overall work.

4. **Know your readers.** How much do you need to explain to your readers about the work you are reviewing? Are they well versed in the subject or essentially unfamiliar with it? Knowing the members of your intended audience will enhance your ability to persuade them. For example, if your readers have never seen the movie or read the book you are reviewing, you may wish to give a brief plot summary. (Be careful not to let the plot summary take over your essay!) If you are writing about a very famous movie, play, or book, such as *Romeo and Juliet*, you can be certain that most of your readers are familiar with the story. A plot summary is usually unnecessary in this case.

Criteria for Movie Reviews

• What kind of movie are you reviewing—adventure, drama, science fiction, romance, comedy, children's feature?

• What element of the film—writing, acting, cinematography, special effects—captivates you the most?

• How do the technical aspects of the film—cinematography, color, special effects, music, lighting—contribute to the overall point of the movie?

• Do the actors succeed in their roles?

• Is the script well written?

• Does the story progress coherently from scene to scene?

---

5. **Organize your essay.** In writing a critical review, you have two
   organizational options: You can present your opinion at the beginning and
   support it with reasons and evidence, or you can build your case throughout
   the review and offer your opinion as the overall summary. In either case, use
   transition words and sentences to help guide your reader through your essay.

Exercise 11 Choose a Subject *Working Together*

In a small group, list books you've read, movies you've watched, or plays
that you have seen in the theater in the last month. Choose one for the
subject of your review, and consider other works in the same category to
use as comparisons. Answers will vary.

• Group the works by genre—that is, adventure, drama, comedy,
  science fiction, and so on.

• Name the characters or the actors and director involved in each book,
  movie, or play.

• Discuss the plot of the work and any other outstanding features,
  such as special effects, a remarkable setting, or effective dialect.

Exercise 12 Explore the Subject and *Working Together*
Develop Your Opinion

Go over the information you listed in your group in Exercise 11. If you are
reviewing a movie, think about your subject in terms of the Criteria for Movie
Reviews on page 50 in this lesson. The aspects for judging books, movies, and
plays listed in the chart below may help you evaluate various elements of the
work that you can mention in your review. Answers will vary.

Movie	Book	Play
location of film	setting	sets
theme	theme	theme
dialogue	writing style	script
casting/acting	characters	casting/acting
directing	movement of plot	stage direction
technical aspects (special effects/music score/etc.)	attention to detail	atmosphere of theater

Exercise 13 State Your Opinion and Organize Ideas

For the work you've chosen to review, summarize your opinion in one or two sentences. You may want to test your opinion out on your writing group. Then list the reasons for your opinion. Organize those reasons—and the evidence supporting each one—in a way that strengthens your argument and makes it persuasive. Draw details from your notes from Exercise 12 to bolster your opinion. Answers will vary. Tell students to make sure their opinions are supported by reasons.

Exercise 14 Draft Your Critical Review

Think of your review in three parts: the introduction, the body, the conclusion. Remember that a critical review is much more than an opinion and a summary of a plot. Answers will vary. Drafts should reflect a coherent structure.

• **Introduction** Grab your reader's attention with an appeal to his or her emotions, a strong thesis statement, or a striking comparison.

• **Body** In the midsection of your review, specify the reasons for your opinion. Cite evidence from the work itself, and detail your own emotional reaction to it.

• **Conclusion** Restate your opinion in an interesting way. Summarize your argument from both the introduction and the body of the review.

Exercise 15 Revise, Edit, and Proofread Your Review

Allow at least a few hours between drafting and revising. Make sure your opinion is clear and specific. Check the order in which you present reasons and evidence. Would a different order be more persuasive? Did you provide enough evidence to successfully persuade your readers? Have a partner read your review and point out paragraphs that succeed and others that could use more work. Finally, check your critical review for mistakes in grammar, usage, punctuation, capitalization, and spelling. Answers will vary.

Exercise 16 Publish Your Review

Share your paper with your writing group. Then discuss where movie or book reviews by teenagers are published. Consider sending your review to a school or community newspaper—or even to a local radio station. Check the Internet web sites where teenagers exchange critical reviews. Publish your review at a site where you can get feedback from students in other schools around the nation. Refer to the teacher pages on "Technology" for Internet resources.

Expository Writing: Problem-Solution Essay

Sometimes in an essay, you identify a **problem** and offer one or more possible **solutions**. Here's an excerpt from an article about how individuals and organizations have addressed the problem of illiteracy and its effects on adults and children.

Literacy: A Family Affair
by Anita Merina

[1]You think America's millions of functionally illiterate adults aren't your problem? [2]Think again: They have kids.

Problem identified

[3]Across the country, there are ninety million adults who can't read at a fifth grade level. [4]Forty million of them can barely read or write at all. [5]These are tragic numbers for America—devastating when you consider that children of functionally illiterate adults are twice as likely as other kids to be functionally illiterate themselves.

[6]"We're facing an intergenerational crisis of illiteracy," says Sharon Darling, president of the National Center for Family Literacy. [7]"Far too many at-risk children are at-risk because their parents are undereducated, even afraid of school and teachers," Darling continues. [8]"That translates into one generation after another of parents not having the confidence to go into schools and take part in their child's education."

Problem explained in more detail through quotation

[9]Statistics show that a child whose parent dropped out of high school is six times more likely than average to drop out, too.

Statistic supports seriousness of problem.

[10]"If you could get parents to come back and finish their educations," Darling says, "you could make them comfortable with school. [11]Then they, in turn, could teach their children by example to enjoy school and learn."

Quotation illustrates problem.

[12]In a nutshell, that's what family literacy programs are all about.

States solution

[13]In the last ten years, the number of family literacy programs across the country has jumped from 500 to more than 5,000. [14]Whether you call the program Even Start, Families for Learning, or Project Literacy, the goal of family literacy programs is the same—stopping the cycle of failure.

Statistic supports solution.

[15]Recent studies show they work. [16]Even though 25 percent of at-risk kids are likely to repeat at least one year prior to fourth grade, not one of the 2,500 three- and four-year-old participants in a family literacy program evaluated in a 1993 study repeated a grade in elementary school. [17]Moreover, once these children entered elementary school, they were reported to be highly motivated to learn and performed well.

Ideas connected with transition word *moreover*

[18]Many educators deal with adult illiteracy every day—some more directly than others.

Anecdote supports literacy programs. [19]Chloe Gentry, an instructional assistant at Jacob Elementary School in Louisville, Kentucky, dropped out of high school to get married. [20]Five years ago, she and her four-year-old son Bradley enrolled in a family literacy program at Schaffer Elementary School.

[21]"When we entered the program, Bradley wouldn't speak. [22]He wouldn't let go of me," Gentry says. [23]"Now he's a happy nine-year-old doing well in all of his classes. [24]Without this program, he might have ended up in a remedial class."

Expert opinion endorses literacy programs. [25]National Education Association member Karen Kitagawa runs a family literacy program in Honolulu, Hawaii. [26]Parents come in four days a week for literacy instruction, math and science, English, parenting classes, and classes with their children. [27]"So many of these adults start with few skills, very low self-esteem, and memories of bad experiences," Kitagawa explains. [28]"By fulfilling these parents' desire to help their children and help themselves, we fill a void in their lives and in our school community."

[29]Robert Mendez is an educator, too. [30]In addition to his job as plant manager at Orchard Elementary School in Los Angeles, he's vice-chair of the California Literacy Foundation, sits on the board of Laubach Literacy, and travels the country speaking to newly literate adults. [31]Mendez has published articles and poetry in magazines, even spoken at a United Nations conference on literacy. [32]But all of these accomplishments pale compared to the satisfaction Mendez gets from helping his son succeed.

[33]"Every day, I sit with my son Matthew and help him with his homework. [34]I read with him, help with his reports, and take him to the library. [35]Doing this brings me closer to him.

Concludes with anecdote and connection to problem [36]"This is what I tell adults who are sometimes frustrated with their progress and think about giving up. [37]I tell them to hang in there, that it isn't important that you read quickly to your child—it's that you care enough to do it. [38]That's your success. [39]Literacy is more than learning to read. [40]It's getting rid of the luggage of guilt and shame. [41]It's realizing you're opening doors to worlds you thought were closed to you. [42]It's realizing that schools aren't places you dread walking into anymore. [43]They're places where you've rediscovered the joy of learning. [44]That's the legacy I want to pass on to my son."

Critical Thinking

After you read the problem-solution essay, answer the questions below.
Use the following questions to lead a class discussion.

1. With a partner, look at the essay and identify which paragraphs (a) introduce and explain the problem, (b) focus on solutions, and (c) present a conclusion. How and where does the writer use statistics, examples, anecdotes, quotations, and expert opinions to clarify and strengthen ideas?

2. There are a number of people whose individual experiences and ideas related to illiteracy are presented in this essay. How do the quotations and anecdotes contribute to the writer's main point, or thesis, about literacy programs?

Build Your Vocabulary. Look at the following words and terms in context, and then take a guess at what each word or term means: *functionally illiterate* (sentence 5), *intergenerational* (sentence 6), and *instructional assistant* (sentence 19). Add the words you don't know to your vocabulary notebook.

 The purpose of a problem-solution essay is to identify a problem and to explain a possible solution to the problem. To make your case strong in a problem-solution essay, you must gather information, present details in a logical order, and express your ideas clearly. The following strategies can help:

1. **Identify a problem.** Leaf through your writer's notebook, and see if you have written about a problem that you feel should be solved. Try brainstorming (page 10) problems that arise in science, medicine, or politics. Consider freewriting (page 10) about a local, national, or international issue that you and your readers feel strongly about. Your problem can be one that already has a working solution or one for which you can propose a solution.

2. **Gather information.** Research the solutions to the problem you've chosen to write about. How have others suggested handling the problem?

3. **Build your case.** Come up with reasons why the solution is effective. Explain the solution using evidence: facts, statistics, quotations, expert opinions, anecdotes, or examples.

4. **Make an outline.** After you've gathered evidence to support your solution, organize this material into an outline to help you figure out the strongest and most logical way to explain that evidence. If appropriate, you may wish to include a step-by-step proposal to implement your solution.

5. **Address any anticipated resistance.** Many social problems— homelessness, drug abuse, high dropout rates, for example—are difficult to solve because there are at least two sides to the issue. In your problem-solution essay, be sure to acknowledge the arguments of those opposed to your solution, and point out why your solution is workable.

6. **Connect ideas.** In writing your essay, make sure that one idea flows seamlessly into the next by connecting ideas with the proper transition words. Highlight similar ideas with words such as *similarly, likewise, also,* and *too.* As you shift from one thought to a contrasting one, guide readers with transitions such as *however, yet, but,* and *on the other hand.* To show that one point results from another, insert transitions such as *if . . . then, when, as a result of,* and *because.*

7. **Maintain a consistent tone.** Some problem-solution essays cry out for a sobering tone; others are more effective when presented with a light touch. Whichever tone you adopt, stick to that tone throughout the essay.

Exercise 17 Choose a Topic

Use one or all of the following suggestions to come up with a topic for your problem-solution essay. Your audience will be your classmates and teachers.
Answers will vary. Students should refer to Lesson 1.1 for prewriting strategies.

• **It's personal.** Interview friends and classmates, or leaf through the advice column in a school or local newspaper to identify a personal problem that teenagers typically experience.

• **It's academic.** Do a survey of your peers to come up with specific school problems that need to be solved. From the responses, choose a problem that interests you.

• **It's political.** Read newspapers and magazines, listen to radio shows, or watch television programs dealing with current events. To find out about community problems, attend a meeting of a local political or volunteer organization, or call the offices of these groups. Choose a political issue that you care about.

Exercise 18 Gather and Organize Information

Brainstorm several possible solutions to the problem you've chosen to write about. Then gather evidence, such as facts, statistics, quotations, expert opinions, examples, and anecdotes. Some of your evidence may derive from printed sources, such as newspapers; other evidence (including anecdotes or quotations) may come from interviews or discussions. Take notes or summarize the evidence supporting each solution. This will help you decide which solution would work best and which evidence supports the reasons for that solution.
Answers will vary. Research may reveal weaknesses in students' topics. Encourage students to adjust their topics based on new information.

Exercise 19 Organize and Draft Your Essay

Use the following instructions to organize and draft your problem-solution essay. Concentrate on getting your ideas down in your draft. Answers will vary.

1. **Define the problem.** In a few sentences, define the problem. Consider introducing the topic with an interesting quotation, statistic, or observation.

2. **Elaborate.** Consider the people in your audience (classmates and teachers) and what they know or might not know about your topic. Present several well chosen details. Be careful not to pile on too many minor or unnecessary details.

3. **Present your proposed solution.** State your solution clearly. Use evidence to explain why the solution solves the problem. Provide facts, statistics, quotations, expert opinions, anecdotes, and examples. Tell why it's better— more workable, less costly, or more comprehensive—than the alternatives.

4. **Conclude your case.** Briefly restate your solution, adding a powerful quotation or question, if appropriate, that provokes your readers to seriously think through the ideas in your essay.

Exercise 20 Revise and Edit Your Essay

Ask yourself the following revision questions to help you improve your essay.

Have I stated the problem clearly and analyzed it clearly? Have I presented a solution that readers can understand? Did I include enough compelling evidence? Have I restated my solution with enough emphasis in the conclusion? Have I eliminated wordiness and inserted transitions to connect one idea to the next? Answers will vary. Students should refer to Lesson 1.3 for more revising strategies.

Exercise 21 Proofread and Publish Your Essay *Working Together*

Reread your paper to check for mistakes in grammar, usage, punctuation, capitalization, mechanics, and spelling. Then ask a partner to check it for mistakes. Answers will vary. Students should refer to Lesson 1.4 for proofreading strategies and publishing suggestions.

• Read your essay aloud to classmates. When you're finished, ask them to summarize the problem you targeted and your solution. Allow time for listeners to ask questions about your solution.

• If another student tackles the same or a similar topic, think about creating student teams to debate the problem. Related essays may be used to develop arguments for either side of the debate.

Writing About Literature: Analyzing Drama

When you write about a play, you take into account a number of factors, such as your overall response to the work, the power of the writing, the strength of the plot, and how each theatrical element interacts with the others. Here are three ways to structure an essay about a work of drama:

1. In a **personal response** essay, you communicate your feelings about what the play means to you.

2. In an **evaluation**, you focus on the strengths and weaknesses of the play. You answer this question: How good is the play?

3. In a **literary analysis**, you take the play apart and look at each element separately—writing, character development, plot, staging, theme. Then you explain how each element contributes to the play and how the elements interact to create an overall effect.

The following excerpt is from a longer literary analysis of Sophocles' *Antigone*. The writer, Eliot Bloomfield, discusses which of the main characters (Antigone or Creon) is the true tragic hero—and why.

Sophocles' *Antigone*
by Eliot Bloomfield

Title and playwright

Main conflict

. . . [1]*Antigone* by Sophocles is based on an incident taken from the history of the royal family of Thebes. [2]The tragedy arises from the conflict of two loyalties—loyalty to God (or the gods) and loyalty to the state. [3]Antigone represents the first and Creon the second. [4]Caught between these two forces is Haemon, Creon's son and Antigone's fiancé. [5]He is torn between filial piety and love for his bride-to-be. [6]The tragedy could have been written around him, but that was not the way Sophocles chose. [7]Rather, [Sophocles] turned his back on Haemon's problem to take up the larger intellectual tragic problems.

Statement about characters and theme

Analysis of title

Notion of tragic hero stems from pride.

[8]Actually, there is a real question in *Antigone* as to who is the tragic hero. [9]That it must be either Antigone or Creon is clear from the play itself, and the title should lend credence to those who favor Antigone. [10]But it is most likely that the title was used by Sophocles merely to indicate the general subject matter. [11]A stronger case can be made for the theory that *Antigone* is Creon's tragedy. [12]It is [Creon's] tragic fault of pride (*hubris*) or obstinacy which brings upon him his doom in the deaths of his son and wife. [13]The chorus points this out clearly throughout the play and especially at the end . . . .

[14]Creon pitted himself against the gods, who demand that honor be paid to the dead, and in his presumption, he was brought low. [15]The Greeks looked

Ideas about
loyalty in Greek
society

⎡ with particular horror at those who refused to allow the dead to be
⎣ buried properly. [16]Such a deed would still arouse indignation today, but
to the Greeks it would be the violation of a religious duty and a true

Explains central
conflict

⎡ sacrilege. [17]It meant that the shade (or soul) of the unburied would not
⎣ be allowed to enter Hades, the abode of the dead.

Writer advances
controversial
interpretation of
the play.

⎡ [18]Although Antigone, in our opinion, is not the tragic hero of this
play, she does more than serve as a mere foil and as opposition to Creon.
[19]She is a majestic and moving figure in her own right. [20]Inflexible and
perhaps somewhat arrogant, she nevertheless moves us in her dignity
and in her defense of a higher morality than the expedient and the
immediate. [21]She is not in love with death, as her grief over her
unmarried state shows, but she is willing to die for what she knows is
⎣ right. [22]She serves as an eternal symbol and warning for all men.

Supports thesis
with idea from
Aristotle's
Poetics

⎡ [23]Aristotle in his *Poetics* held that the playgoer, witnessing a great
tragedy, undergoes a purgation of soul (catharsis) as he pities the
⎣ characters and feels terror for their (and his) human lot. [24]Much ink has
been spilled trying to explain exactly what catharsis is, and the subject
cannot be dealt with here. [25]But the experience should become clear to
those who enter into the spirit of this great drama, whose relevance to
moral and political issues of our own time is strikingly clear.

Critical Thinking

After you read the literary analysis, answer the questions below.
Use the following questions to lead a class discussion.

1. What specific information does the writer convey about the plot, characters,
setting, and theme of *Antigone*?

2. Find two statements in the essay that identify the essay's main idea.

3. How would you describe the style (e.g., formal, informal, academic, friendly)
and tone of this essay?

4. Do you think Eliot Bloomfield makes a strong case for his thesis? Explain
your response.

Build Your Vocabulary. How does context help you understand these terms:
filial piety (sentence 5), *tragic hero* (sentence 8), *sacrilege* (sentence 16), *foil*
(sentence 18), *purgation of soul* (sentence 23)? Underline any other words that
are unfamiliar to you. Look each word up in a dictionary, and add those words
to your vocabulary notebook.

Writing Strategies

In an **analysis** of a play, you evaluate each element separately. You
consider how individual aspects contribute to the play and how the
aspects work together to create an overall effect. Use the following
strategies to develop and write an analysis of a play.

1. **Identify title and playwright.** In the first paragraph, identify the work and the author that you're writing about.

2. **Explain briefly what the play is about.** Write a very short plot summary. You should include the central theme or conflict that drives the action of the play.

3. **Present a thesis statement.** Your thesis expresses your main idea about the play. It may focus on one or more of these elements: **characters**, **plot**, **theme**, and **setting**. Narrow your thesis statement to just one aspect of the play for a three-page essay.

4. **Support what you say.** Find lines in the play that support your thesis statement and explain why you feel they are relevant. Try to find three quotations or events that support your thesis.

5. **Watch your tone.** The tone of your essay should be formal and serious. Avoid contractions, sentence fragments, and slang words.

6. **Use the present tense.** When you refer to characters or events in the plot, use present-tense verbs. For example, Bloomfield uses the present tense in sentence 13 ("The chorus *points* this out clearly . . .").

> **Questions for Analysis**
>
> • **Characters** Are they complex or simple? What motivates them?
>
> • **Conflict, Resolution, and Suspense** What effect does the structure—the division of scenes and acts—have on the action of the play?
>
> • **Theme** What is the overall meaning of the play?
>
> • **Setting and Stage Directions** How do they influence the interpretation of the plot?

Exercise 22 **Prewriting: Choose a Play** *Working Together*

With a writing group, list plays you have read for school or have seen on stage. Go through the list, and share your initial reactions to these plays. If one play resonates strongly with your own experience, talk about why that play touches you. Answers will vary.

Exercise 23 **Prewriting: Develop a Thesis**

If possible, reread your play to reconsider the effect of stage directions, to understand the structure, or to identify the theme. Then choose the literary or dramatic element that stands out most for you, and develop your thesis with that element in mind. Be careful to limit your topic. Consider narrowing your topic to one character, one scene, or one brief dialogue.
Answers will vary. Students should refer to Lesson 1.1 for prewriting strategies.

Exercise 24 Organize and Draft Your Essay

Start writing anywhere in the essay, focusing on two or three of your most important points. Don't concentrate on writing perfect sentences. Just get your ideas down in sentence and paragraph form so you'll have something to revise. Feel free to add new ideas as you write. You can sort out ideas, reorganize, and add or delete words, phrases, and sentences later.
Answers will vary. Students should refer to Lesson 1.2 for drafting strategies.

Exercise 25 Revise and Title Your Essay

Let the draft sit for awhile. After you reread your essay, develop a title that leads the reader to your thesis or simply states the name of the play. Then use the four-step revising strategy suggested in Lesson 1.3. Read for accurate content, clear organization, and appropriate style for your purpose and audience. As you and your peer editors revise your draft, ask questions such as those that follow.

Is the essay coherent, well organized, and easy to follow? Are the general statements clearly expressed and not wordy? Do you cite specific lines from the play to back up each point you make in the essay? Does every point you make in the essay bolster your thesis statement? Is everything unified (directly related to the thesis)? Answers will vary.

Exercise 26 Edit, Proofread, and Publish Your Essay

Double-check each quotation for accuracy, including punctuation. When you are satisfied that you have corrected all errors in grammar, usage, punctuation, capitalization, and spelling, exchange papers with a partner to check for any errors you may have missed.

- If you and several of your classmates write about the same play—or plays in the same genre or historical period—form groups to read your classmates' essays, and then comment on them. After one of you reads an analysis to the group out loud, elicit questions and disagreements from your audience.

- You may wish to bind the essays into a book of drama analysis and make it available in the school library for other students and English teachers to read.
Answers will vary. Students should refer to Lesson 1.4 for proofreading strategies and publishing suggestions.

Expository Writing: Research Paper

A **research paper** is based on a thorough investigation of a limited topic. You may be asked to write a research paper in any of your classes, not just in English class. Consider the following types of research papers:

1. The most common type of research paper **summarizes** or **explains** information you have gathered from several different sources. Your writing **synthesizes** (puts together to form a new whole) what other writers have reported.

2. Another type of research paper adds your own **evaluation**, or opinion, about your topic. For example, in a problem-solution paper based on research, you might focus on a community problem and evaluate the effectiveness of several proposed solutions.

3. A third type of research paper distills and summarizes your own **original research**. In social studies, you might draw conclusions and present findings based on surveys, questionnaires, or interviews you conduct. A science research paper might report your observations and experiments. For this kind of paper, you explain the idea or theory that you begin with and the carefully controlled experiments you conduct to test that theory. As part of an original research paper, you also include a **survey of the literature**, citing published articles related to your investigation.

Note: Many research papers combine an evaluation with a summary or an explanation of the research. In this case, you usually evaluate the research of others and then report your own original research or your own interpretation of the evidence.

In the following excerpt from an original student research paper, the student summarizes and explains a historical incident. Then she evaluates related events, ideas, and legislation that followed it. The paper includes **parenthetical references** to its sources and ends with a **Works Cited** list, both of which are covered later in this lesson.

4-line heading:
Name/Teacher/
Class/Due Date

Hadley Davis
Dr. Alan Proctor
Social Studies
May 1, 1998

Title, centered

Reform and the Triangle Shirtwaist Company Fire

Brief description
and evaluation
of historical
incident

[1]On March 25, 1911, a terrible tragedy struck New York City, a horrifying fire, claiming scores of lives at the Triangle Shirtwaist Company. [2]But the 146 people who perished in the fire did not die in vain. [3]Their deaths sparked a new flame in New York City. [4]The pleas of the working class for better factory conditions, long ignored, were finally heard after the Triangle deaths. [5]For those deaths stimulated a guilty concern over the state of factory safety, a concern which called for action, for change.

Thesis
statement:
Commission
created to
protect workers

[6]And so out of the ashes of the Triangle victims, a Factory Investigating Commission was built, a commission which over a period of four years examined thousands of industrial establishments, listened to hundreds of witnesses, held public hearings, and finally pushed through the legislation needed to reorganize the New York City labor and fire departments, and to insure safer factories for the working class (Stein 209).

Research
sources cited in
parentheses

[7]When Frances Perkins, a member of the Factory Investigating Commission, dubbed the workshops and factories of the clothing industry virtual "fire and death traps," she was not exaggerating (Foner 367). [8]And the fire which began in Washington Square at 4:40 on Saturday afternoon, March 25, 1911, inside the Asch Building—where the Triangle Shirtwaist Company and its 500 employees occupied the eighth, ninth, and tenth floors—was her testimony.

Primary source
further explains
incident and
supports thesis.

[9]The cause of the fire was unknown, but suddenly people on the eighth floor of the Triangle Company began to cry "fire," and, according to one survivor, flames seemed simply "to push up from under" tables (Stein 34–35). [10]The eighth floor of the factory (like all the floors in Triangle) was overcrowded, and the sewing-machine tables were crammed so closely together that there was little aisle space in which to move ("Waist" 5). [11]Furthermore, scraps of the flimsy fabric and paper patterns used to make the shirtwaists lay scattered everywhere and caught fire quickly, only aiding the spread of the flames (Schoener 172). [12]Those on the eighth floor who were able to make an escape rushed to the stairway or pushed their way into one of the two narrow passenger elevators. [13]But within minutes, the entire floor became a "mass of fire" (Stein 36–42). [14]The girls were met at the stairs by the blaze. [15]The elevator ceased to function.

[16]The elevator never even reached the ninth floor, the biggest "fire and death trap" (Foner 367). [17]The ninth floor was the last to learn of the fire. [18]On the tenth, where the offices were located, a phone call of warning

Running head: 1/2 inch from top of paper

was received, and employees climbed onto the roof and managed to escape (Stein 43, 46). [19]However, on the ninth, the most crowded floor, fire simply instantaneously appeared. [20]Many jumped on machine tables (Llewellyn 24). [21]Others, their dresses on fire, ran to the windows, preferring to jump rather than be burned to death ("Waist" 4). [22]Some were caught so unaware that, later, firemen found "skeletons bending over sewing machines" and fifty-eight girls frozen dead in the dressing room (Schoener 171; Foner 359). [23]The people on nine who had the time to escape were, nevertheless, just as trapped: The door to the ninth floor was locked (to keep the girls from stealing cloth during the day); The passenger elevators never came; and the one fire escape that the building possessed quickly collapsed ("Waist" 2; Foner 359). [24]Desperate and with nowhere to turn, more Triangle workers [dove] off window ledges. . . .

Reliable source: *New York Times* verifies information

[25]According to the *New York Times*, "The firemen had trouble bringing their apparatus into position because of the bodies which strewed the pavement and sidewalks" ("Waist" 1). [26]The bodies, said fireman Frank Rubino, "were hitting us all around" (Stein 17). [27]But there was little help the firemen could offer the falling girls. [28]Their ladders were not tall enough to reach the three top floors of the building, and the life nets they had were of no use (Stein 17). [29]This was because, Battalion Chief Edward J. Worth explained, the girls came down with such force that they "went right through life nets, pavement, and all" (Stein 17). [30]The firemen could only drag the dead bodies away and later use pulleys to remove one blackened body after another from the building's remains ("Waist" 2). [31]*The New York Times* reported the morning after the fire that "two girls, charred beyond all hope of identification, were found in the smoking ruins with their arms clasped around each other's necks" ("Waist" 3).

Explains impact of fire

[32]It was this, the drama of the tragedy, which was powerful and poignant enough to reach the public of New York and make it stop to consider the city's factories—that they were unsafe, that they were fire traps. . . .

Summary and evaluation of pre-fire strike

[33]On November 24, 1909, 1,800 waistmakers, including the workers of the Triangle Shirtwaist Company, went on strike as members of the Garment Workers' Union. [34]However, the shirtmakers' demands—unlocked doors and sufficient fire escapes among them—were never met (Wertheimer 309). [35]Rather, Triangle management responded by locking out its 500 strikers and by advertising for replacements (Foner 324). [36]"If the union had won," explained 1909 Triangle Shirtwaist Company striker Rose Safran,

Indented quotation

we would have been safe. [37]Two of our demands were for adequate fire escapes and for open doors from the factories to the street. [38]But the bosses defeated us and we didn't get the open doors or the better fire escapes. [39]So our friends are dead (Stein 168).

Davis 3

Details of public response to fire

[40]At the public funeral for the Triangle victims, the garment workers marched under one banner: "We Demand Fire Protection" (Stein 154). [41]This time, they would be heard: Numerous citizens, ranging from businessmen to suffragists, from priests to East Side workers, met and spoke in the weeks and months following the conflagration (Stein 135). [42]Through these people, the conscience of the city emerged. [43]They aired a sense of public guilt and genuine concern over conditions in factories, conditions which they realized no one had previously taken enough responsibility for (Stein 135). . . .

Topic sentence with supporting details about effect of fire on the workers and lawmakers

[44]The commission took its job seriously. [45]Within the first year of its work alone, it inspected 1,836 industrial establishments in New York and heard a total of 222 witnesses (Stein 209). [46]Throughout this process, it held hearings before the New York legislature and proposed new laws or amendments (*Laws 1911* 1269). [47]The legislature in turn enacted remedial legislation. [48]The four-year term of the commission is, in fact, commonly acknowledged as "the golden era in remedial factory legislation" (Stein 210). [49]The labor laws passed between 1911 and 1919 correspond to the commission's findings—when the commission discovered a problem, change ensued. . . .

[50]In 1912, legislation was enacted requiring the installation of an automatic sprinkler system in factory buildings over seven stories high with more than 200 people employed above the seventh floor (*Laws 1912* 661). [51]Fire Chief John Kenlon had previously reported to the Commission that although an automatic sprinkler system would have cost the Asch Building $5,000, it was his belief that no life would have been lost in the Triangle Shirtwaist Company fire had one been installed (Stein 209). [52]Similarly, it was agreed that the fact that there had been no fire drills at Triangle caused panic when fire broke out ("Waist" 2). [53]And undoubtedly, at Triangle, where fire swept through the building without warning, a fire alarm would have insured an earlier detection of fire—and an earlier escape. [54]Consequently, an addition to the labor law called for both a fire drill at least every three months as well as the installation of a fire-alarm signal system in any factory building over two stories high that employed twenty-five persons above the ground floor (*Laws 1913* 363). [55]Also, during the Triangle fire, scraps of fabric and paper cuttings, which lay in heaps and covered the floor and tables, fed the spread of the blaze (Schoener 72). [56]Hence, a new law ordered that all waste in factories (e.g., cuttings) must be deposited into fireproof receptacles and that no such waste be allowed to accumulate on the floor (*Laws 1912* 658). [57]Thirty bodies were discovered in the shirtwaist company's open elevator shafts after the conflagration,

Davis 4

and so the New York legislature in July 1911 dictated that all elevator shafts in all city buildings must be enclosed ("Waist" 1; *Laws 1911* 1820). . . .

[58]During their strike in 1909, the workers at the Triangle Shirtwaist Company probably sang this popular and optimistic Garment Workers' Union song:

Popular union song lyrics illustrate workers' spirit and resolve.

[59]Hail! [60]The waistmakers of nineteen nine . . .
Breaking the power of those who reign,
Pointing the way, smashing the chain.

[61]We showed the world that women could fight.
[62]And we rose and won with women's might (Foner 345).

Conclusion summarizes impact of fire.

[63]Their strike in 1909 was not successful, but the Triangle waistmakers still "won." [64]By 1914, the law, not factory owners, reigned in the garment industry and in the manufacturing buildings of New York. [65]Although they had died for their cause, the victims of the Triangle Shirtwaist Company fire had pointed the way toward a safer future for the working class.

Davis 5

Works Cited

Book by one author

Foner, Phillip S. *Women and the American Labor Movement*. New York: The Free Press, 1979.

Printed laws of the State of New York

Laws of the State of New York. Albany: New York State, Chapter 561 of 1911 (page 1269); Chapter 693 of 1911 (page 1820); Chapter 332 of 1912 (page 661); Chapter 329 of 1912 (page 658); Chapter 203 of 1913 (page 363).

Llewellyn, Chris. *Fragment From the Fire*. New York: Penguin Books, 1977.

Scholarly work compiled by editor

Schoener, Allon, ed. *Portal to America: The Lower East Side, 1870–1925*. New York: Holt, Rinehart and Winston, 1967.

Stein, Leon. *The Triangle Fire*. Philadelphia: J.B. Lippincott Company, 1962.

Newspaper article

"Waist Factory Fire." *New York Times* 26 Mar. 1911: 1–5.

Wertheimer, Barbara Mayer. *We Were There: The Story of Working Women in America*. New York: Pantheon Books, 1977.

The purpose of a research paper is to provide in-depth information on a limited topic. The following specific strategies apply to all three types of research papers.

1. **Choose and limit a topic.** First of all, choose a topic you would like to know more about. Look through your writer's notebook for ideas or ask "I wonder" questions. Also make sure you choose a topic for which you can find sufficient sources—about five listings in a library index. On the other hand, narrow your topic when there are so many sources that you hardly know where to focus. One way to do this is to name a large topic and list as many smaller topics related to it as you can in order to come up with a limited topic for your paper. Use the following cluster map as an example.

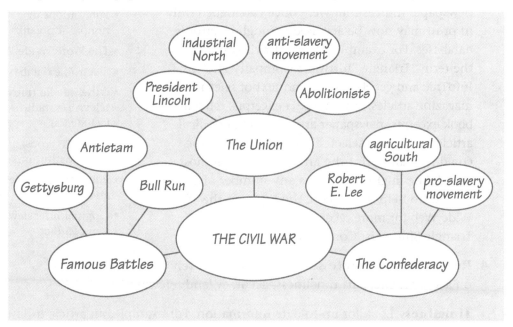

2. **Make a schedule.** Budget your time to keep your focus, and pace yourself through each of the following steps in writing a research paper: (1) choosing and limiting a topic; (2) finding and evaluating sources as well as making bibliography cards; (3) taking notes; (4) drafting a thesis statement and title; (5) developing an outline; (6) writing a first draft; (7) documenting sources; (8) revising; (9) proofreading; and (10) preparing the final manuscript.

For a six- to eight-week assignment, most steps take one to three days; allow about a week and a half for taking notes, writing a first draft, and revising.

3. Look for several sources. Make sure you include both **primary** and **secondary sources**.

A **primary source** is an original text or document, such as a literary work, a diary, a letter, a speech, an interview, or a historical document.

A **secondary source** presents the writer's comments on a primary source. Reference books, biographies, literary criticism, and history and science textbooks are secondary sources.

The Readers' Guide to Periodical Literature and many newspaper indices that were once catalogued only in print may now be accessed through electronic databases. For example, Hadley Davis could enter the term "Triangle Shirtwaist Company Fire" in InfoTrac and get the listing and text of relevant magazine articles, encyclopedia excerpts, reference book excerpts, newspaper articles, and periodical articles. If Hadley selected one of the titles, she could read and print the articles that seem most useful. She might also access any number of search engines to help her explore the topic on the World Wide Web for more recent information on the Triangle Shirtwaist Company fire.

> ### Some Sources to Explore
>
> - Periodicals (newspapers, magazines, journals)
> - Books
> - Reference books (encyclopedias, specialized books such as an atlas)
> - Government publications
> - Publications by nonprofit organizations
> - The World Wide Web
> - Electronic databases
> - Other media (movies, television, radio, CD-ROMs)
> - Museums, zoos, and other institutions
> - Published interviews and surveys
> - Original interviews you conduct

4. Review and evaluate sources. Before you rely on a source, check its timeliness, accuracy, and relevance.

Timeliness Look for up-to-date information. For example, an article in last month's *Atlantic* magazine is a better source for information about juvenile crime than a ten-year-old book.

Accuracy Evaluate your sources for accuracy, and don't believe everything you read. For example, an Internet source from a government or university database is more reliable and unbiased than an individual's home page. You can trust major newspapers (*The San Francisco Chronicle* or *The New York Times*) more than a tabloid.

Relevance Look for information directly related to your limited topic. Detours may be fascinating, but beware. If information isn't relevant to your paper, you will lose precious time researching it and possibly lose your focus.

5. Track sources and cross-reference notes. Record essential publishing information for each source on a **source card** or **bibliography source card**. Your source card should include all the bibiographical information you'll need for your Works Cited list. This includes author, title, publisher, date, and place of publication as well as any other pertinent information. Assign each source card a numeral, and write it in the upper right-hand corner of the card. Then, when you take notes, just indicate the source card number on your notes, and you won't need to rewrite all the source data.

SAMPLE SOURCE CARD

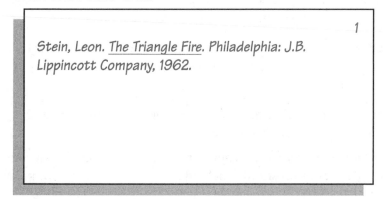

1

Stein, Leon. *The Triangle Fire*. Philadelphia: J.B. Lippincott Company, 1962.

6. Take notes. You may quote a source directly (use quotation marks!) or use your own words. Be sure to write the page number of each note you take on your note card.

When you **summarize**, you state only the most important ideas in your own words.

When you **paraphrase**, you spell out every idea in the same order as in the original, using your own words.

SAMPLE NOTE CARD

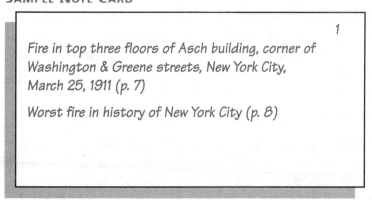

1

Fire in top three floors of Asch building, corner of Washington & Greene streets, New York City, March 25, 1911 (p. 7)

Worst fire in history of New York City (p. 8)

7. **Map ideas in outline form.** Sort your note cards into piles according to main ideas. Based on the information in each pile, make an outline that shows at least three main ideas, in order, with at least two supporting points for each one. Each pile of note cards should be one of your main ideas.

8. **Draft a thesis statement.** Your **thesis statement**, or statement of your controlling idea, comes at the end of the introduction. It tells your readers the main point you're going to make in the rest of the paper.

DRAFT   After the Triangle Shirtwaist Company fire, a commission was appointed.

REVISED   After the Triangle Shirtwaist Company fire, a commission investigated factory conditions and proposed laws to ensure worker safety.

9. **Acknowledge sources.** Always credit sources whenever you directly quote a phrase, sentence, or passage; or whenever you summarize or paraphrase someone else's original idea.

The research paper model on pages 63–66 follows The Modern Language Association (MLA) style for citing sources.

• Use **parenthetical citations** wherever you make reference to a source in your paper. Each citation should include the author and page number of your source.

• Give complete information about each source at the end of the paper in a **Works Cited** list.

For specific rules about citations and bibliographical references, consult the *MLA Handbook for Writers of Research Papers*, 4th edition, by Joseph Gibaldi. Some instructors prefer students to use footnotes or endnotes rather than parenthetical citations. Follow your instructor's guidelines or those in the *MLA Handbook*.

10. **Do not plagiarize.** Using someone else's words or ideas without giving credit constitutes **plagiarism**, which is a serious offense. Plagiarism has prompted lawsuits, job firings, and expulsions from colleges and universities. Borrowing or buying a research paper written by someone else is also plagiarism. Beware: Teachers can tell when the writing in a paper isn't your own.

Exercise 27   **Prewriting: Choose a Limited Topic**

Your teacher may specify a general subject (for example, how the life of a famous American writer or artist influenced his or her work), or you may be free to choose your own topic. Keep in mind the number of pages you have to write when you choose, and limit your topic. If you can choose your own topic, start by listing subjects that interest you, such as politics, space, or endangered animals. Look through your writer's journal to come up with ideas. Then write down questions you have about each listed item. Freewriting about a specific topic may also help you limit your topic.

Answers will vary. Students should refer to Lesson 1.1 for prewriting strategies.

Exercise 28 Prewriting: Gather Information

Write a **direction statement** about what you are planning to research. For example, "I am going to write about the effect of war on the novels of Ernest Hemingway." Use strategies 3–6 on pages 68–69 to begin your research. As you find sources and examine them, keep the following ideas in mind: Answers will vary.

Purpose Your purpose is to give information. You need to provide background information and define technical terms, but also look for new and interesting facts. Try to present information that sheds new light on a topic. Don't just repeat facts that readers already know.

Audience Even though your initial audience will most likely be your teacher and classmates, keep in mind that you may publish your paper more widely.

Exercise 29 Prewriting: Develop an Outline

After you've prepared notes from a number of sources, organize your note cards by main ideas. Do you have enough ideas and strong enough evidence to back up your ideas? Answers will vary.

Too few main ideas Make sure you have at least three or four main ideas. Try dividing a broad main idea into two. If you have fewer than three ideas, consider doing more research.

Too little supporting evidence If you need more evidence to support your ideas, continue researching.

Too much irrelevant information Look through each pile of note cards, and organize them from most to least important. You may choose not to use some of the weakest cards, but don't discard anything. Keep all your notes until your paper is written.

**Plan for
Research Paper**

Title page or heading

Introduction
Attention grabber

Thesis statement

Body
Main idea 1
 Support
Main idea 2
 Support
Main idea 3
 Support

Conclusion
Summary of Thesis

Works Cited Page

Exercise 30 Write a First Draft with Documentation

Start drafting long before your paper is due so that you will have plenty of time
to revise. Apply skills 8-10 from page 70. Don't be afraid to research further to
fill in any holes you find as you draft. Keep the following advice in mind, too.

Answers will vary. Students should refer to Lesson 1.2 for drafting strategies.

Title As you draft, think about a title for your research paper.

Quotations Quotations show that you have done your
research, but only insert quotations that add something
special—a particular tone, a poignant observation, a clever
turn of phrase. Your paper should mostly be written in your
own words.

> ■ **Refer to
> Mechanics,
> Lessons 14.5 and
> 14.6, for the rules
> for punctuating
> quotations.**

Documentation Include your parenthetical citations and complete citations
as you draft. You won't want to try to remember which card held each detail.

Introduction and conclusion Many writers write these parts last, after
they see what they've written in the body of the paper.

Exercise 31 Revise and Edit Your Draft

If you follow a schedule, you should allow yourself more than a week to revise.
Read through your draft many times, focusing on one aspect of your paper for
each reading. Consider one reading for content, one for organization, one for
style, and one for word choice. Check to see that you have arranged your ideas
in the most logical order. Look for places to add transitions within a paragraph
as well as at the beginning of a paragraph. Do the best revising job you can, and
then ask for input from peer editors.

Answers will vary. Students should refer to Lesson 1.3 for additional revising strategies.

Exercise 32 Proofread Your Paper

At this point, check carefully for the accuracy and punctuation of all the
quotations that you have included. Check the style of parenthetical citations
and of your Works Cited list. Make sure that you have provided publishing
information in the right order and punctuated exactly as required.

Answers will vary. Students should refer to Lesson 1.4 for proofreading strategies.

Exercise 33 Prepare the Final Copy and Publish

Do your best to make your paper error free so that your ideas shine through
clearly. Double space your entire paper, including the Works Cited page. Read
the final paper again before you turn it in. If you find any last-minute mistakes
in grammar, usage, punctuation, capitalization, or spelling, correct them neatly
in ink. Finally, for your effort and accomplishment: Congratulations!

Answers will vary.

Special Writing Tasks: Essay Responses

Essay questions measure what you know about a subject and how you think through a subject posed in an essay question. Increasingly, you'll be called on to answer essay questions in a variety of settings, such as on standardized tests, on classroom exams, and in college applications. The following essay was submitted as part of a successful college application.

Essay Question

Moving from high school to college and succeeding in this transition depends on a student's maturity as well as his or her academic skills. What childhood or teenage experience (other than academic) has helped create the person you now are—the person who you feel is ready to succeed in college?

Essay Response

¹I think I began to grow up that winter night when my parents and I were returning from my aunt's house, and my mother said that we might soon be leaving Leningrad to go to America. ²We were in the Metro then. ³I was crying, and some people in the car were turning around to look at me. ⁴I remember that I could not bear the thought of never hearing again the radio program for schoolchildren to which I listened every morning before going to school.

⁵I do not remember myself crying for this reason again. ⁶In fact, I think I cried very little when I was saying goodbye to my friends, relatives, and even to my father. ⁷When we were leaving, I thought about all the places I was going to see—the strange and magical countries I had known only from adventure books and pictures in the world atlas; I even learned the names of the fifty states because their sound was so beautifully foreign and mysterious. ⁸The country I was leaving never to come back to was hardly in my head then.

⁹The four years that followed taught me the importance of optimism, but the notion did not come at once. ¹⁰For the first two years in New York, I was really lost—coming from a school in Leningrad to a Brooklyn yeshiva, and then to Chapin, I did not quite know what I was or what I should be. ¹¹Mother remarried, and things became even more complicated for me. ¹²Some time passed before my stepfather and I got used to each other. ¹³I was often upset and saw no end to the "hard times."

¹⁴My responsibilities in the family increased dramatically since I knew English better than everyone else at home. ¹⁵I wrote letters, filled out forms, translated at interviews with Immigration and Social Security officers, took my grandparents to the doctor and translated there, and even discussed

Attention-grabbing detail

Introduce details of immigration experience

Personal response to upcoming life change

Thesis statement connects immigration with lesson in maturity

Analyzes personal effects of immigration

telephone and utilities bills with company representatives. [16]I spent a lot of time at my grandparents' house and eventually moved in with them.

Explains life lesson

[17]As a result of my experiences, I have learned one very important rule: Ninety-nine percent of all common troubles eventually go away! [18]Something good is bound to happen in the end when you do not give up—and just wait a little!! [19]Of course, troubles need help in getting out of our lives, but I do not mind putting in a little work. [20]For some reason, I believe that my life will turn out all right, even though it will not be very easy.

Interpretation of experience

[21]America gave us freedom and independence. [22]It also made us assume responsibility for ourselves. [23]Nobody can ruin my life unless I let it be ruined. [24]We create our own happiness. [25]It is up to us to use our freedom with responsibility.

Critical Thinking

After reading the essay, discuss your responses to each numbered item below with a writing group.

Use the following questions to lead a class discussion.

1. Summarize how the experience of immigration helped the writer to mature. Outline the essay.

2. Pick out five details in the essay that illustrate the writer's maturity.

3. How does the concluding paragraph tie together the anecdotes that precede it?

4. What kind of person do you imagine the writer to be based on this essay? Describe the character and personality of the writer.

Writing Strategies

You'll face essay questions on classroom tests, on standardized tests, and on college applications. Use the following strategies to improve your responses to them.

1. **Read the question carefully.** Essay questions often have more than one part. Also check for instructions about the required length of your response, the preferred writing style, and other essay elements. Read the question at least twice in order to understand exactly what you're supposed to do.

2. **Find the key words.** Look for the following kinds of **key words** in an essay question, and do what they ask you to do:

   Sample essay questions illustrate key words.

   Analyze Write an **analysis** of a specific topic by taking an idea apart and explaining its separate parts.   **Analyze** the role of the chorus in Sophocles' *Oedipus Rex*.

   Interpret Write an **interpretation** of a topic by stating your ideas about what something means. Support your ideas with examples from the text.
   Interpret Robert Frost's metaphor of the divided road in the poem "The Road Not Taken."

Compare/Contrast Bring out similarities and/or differences between
two elements.   In *To Kill a Mockingbird*, **compare** Atticus Finch's views on shooting the
rabid dog with his children's pride in his marksmanship.

Explain Provide information and reasons to **explain** a particular topic.
Explain how photosynthesis works.

Discuss Expand on a topic in any way you choose.
Discuss how the Holocaust gave birth to the state of Israel.

3. **Make a plan.** Take a few minutes to create a simple outline with words or
phrases that will jog your memory when you write your first draft. Ask
yourself these questions: What is at the core of your outline? What are the
major points you need to make?

4. **Include an introduction and conclusion.** Both the introduction and
conclusion should be brief. They also should grab the attention of the reader.
Consider using a striking detail or anecdote such as the one in the
introduction of the sample essay in this workshop. Think of your essay as
three motions: Introduce something (include a thesis statement), discuss it
(body), tell what you discussed in a different way (conclusion).

5. **Watch your language and use transitions.** Readers are most often
impressed by writing that sounds true to a real person's personality. Avoid
using difficult vocabulary, convoluted sentences, or odd word arrangements
that you think might impress a reader. Transitions will help you move
seamlessly from one thought to another. Look at how the writer of the
sample essay moves from one idea to another with the following transitions:
but, then, as a result, of course. Remember, also, that since the model response
is not an in-class essay, the writer has time to go back and add transitions as
well as polish the writing.

6. **Remember all the stages of the writing process.** Your response will be
fuller and more detailed when you take the time to develop and refine your
ideas by using prewriting, drafting, and revising strategies.

Exercise 34 Select an Essay Question

Choose one of the following questions to respond to in a 500- to 600-word essay
(approximately two double-spaced printed pages).   Answers will vary.

• You are writing a brief autobiography that covers your life from its
very beginning up until right now. Write the next-to-last chapter.

• What life experience has helped to make you the kind of student you now
consider yourself to be?

- Analyze the impact of setting in any literary work.

- Identify an immensely successful American (contemporary or historical), and explain the reasons for his or her success.

Exercise 35 Plan Your Response and Write a Draft

Plan your response and write a first draft, keeping in mind these concepts:
Answers will vary.

Be yourself. Don't write what you think your audience wants to read. Write from your personal feelings and thoughts.

Make a plan. Consider and organize at least two major points with supporting details that answer the question you've chosen.

Write a thesis statement. Let your thesis statement tie together the major points in your outline.

Draft in three parts. For an introduction, lead into your thesis statement with an interesting, attention-grabbing detail, question, or fact. Write about the main ideas from your outline in the body of the response. Add one more interesting detail, and/or restate your thesis in the conclusion.

Exercise 36 Revise, Edit, and Proofread Your Response

Review your response, focusing on each of the following issues:
Answers will vary. Students should refer to Lesson 1.3 for revising strategies.

- **Be concise, and write with confidence.** Use concrete details rather than abstract ideas. Moreover, say it all with confidence. Don't weaken your statements by using words such as *probably*, *maybe*, or *perhaps*.

- **Clarify and simplify.** Delete words or sentences that don't relate directly to your thesis. Add transition words to make your points clear and concrete.

- **Consult your proofreading log.** If your essay is one that you can write over a period of days, go over it carefully to correct errors in usage or any problems in punctuation, capitalization, and spelling.

Parts of Speech

Direct students to
chapter-specific
portfolio projects
on Sadlier-Oxford's
website.

STUDENT WRITING
Research Paper

In War and in Peace
by Michael Berkowitz
high school student, New York, New York

The sun rose slowly over Mount Vernon on December 12, 1799 revealing a cold and wintry day. Aside from periods of rain, sleet, and snow, it seemed like a normal day. Indeed, no one could have foreseen that this day would lead to the death of a great American hero.

Undaunted by the bad weather, Lieutenant General George Washington, who had been retired from the presidency for nearly two years, set out on his daily horseback ride around his five-hundred-acre Virginia estate, Mount Vernon. The harsh weather beat down on Washington, but he continued to ride. After five hours in the cold, he returned to his house and sat down to dinner without even changing his damp clothes. His close friend and secretary Tobias Lear later commented that chunks of snow rested in Washington's hair while he ate (Thane 407).

It continued to snow through the next day. Washington began to develop a cold and a sore throat from being out the day before, so he did not go on his usual rounds. At night, Washington and Lear sat down in the parlor to read. When Washington left the room to go to bed, Lear advised him to take some medicine to get rid of his cold. Washington turned to Lear and replied, "You know I never take anything for a cold. Let it go as it came" (Irving 394).

Between two and three o'clock on the morning of the fourteenth, Washington woke his wife to tell her that he was very ill. He was breathing with great difficulty as he instructed her not to notify anyone until dawn.

Thus, it was not until Mount Vernon was fully awake that its inhabitants learned of Washington's condition. Three doctors were sent for. The first, Dr. James Craik, had been Washington's friend and doctor since Washington was a young man. The other two doctors, Dr. Brown and Dr. Dick, were called at Craik's request (Thane 409). Washington was diagnosed with a throat infection known as "inflammatory quinsy." After a number of futile attempts at bleeding him, the doctors realized they could do nothing to help Washington. Craik took a seat by the fireplace in Washington's room, and there he sat in despair for the rest of the day.

Finally, Washington, barely able to speak, told the three doctors, "I feel myself going; you had better not take any more trouble about me" (Thane 410). Hours later, the first President of the United States died at the age of sixty-seven. . . .

Works Cited
Thane, Elswyth. *Potomac Squire* (New York: Duell, Sloan and Pearce) 1963.
Irving, Washington. *The Life of George Washington*, vol. 4 (New York: Cooperative Publication Society, Inc.) 1859. Reprinted by permission of *The Concord Review*.

Allow time for
students to dis-
cuss the student
writing. Suggest
that they identify
its strengths and
propose possible
improvements.
Use the model
to introduce the
concepts in the
chapter.

The first paragraphs of Michael Berkowitz's research paper are an account of George Washington's final days. This episode is an effective beginning for a thorough research paper on Washington's life as soldier and peacemaker.

In this chapter, you'll take a close look at the different kinds of work that words do—that is, you will learn about the parts of speech. As you do the writing exercises in this chapter, you'll apply what you learn to your own writing.

Nouns

Whatever you name that you experience through your senses, thoughts, and feelings is a noun.

● **Nouns** are words that name persons, places, things, or ideas.

PERSONS	stepfather, Michael Jordan, acquaintance, Grant Hill, scientist
PLACES	avenue, peninsula, Houston, New Mexico, White House
THINGS	jeans, backpack, software, couch, television, music
IDEAS	calmness, freedom, friendship, self-confidence, pleasure

● Nouns that name ideas are called **abstract nouns**. You use abstract nouns when writing or speaking about feelings, characteristics, or qualities. By contrast, **concrete nouns** name things that you can see, hear, smell, taste, or touch.

ABSTRACT	love, innocence, knowledge, endurance
CONCRETE	rain, finger, soil, computer, garage, parakeet

● **Proper nouns** name *particular* persons, places, things, ideas, or events. Always capitalize proper nouns. Some proper nouns contain two or more words. **Common nouns** refer to general, not particular, persons, places, things, ideas, or events. Therefore, they are not capitalized.

COMMON	river, holiday, street, official, battle, ceiling
PROPER	Mississippi River, Earth Day, Richard the Lion-Hearted

Writing Hint

Use nouns that are as specific as possible.
   mansion   *sandy bluff*
The ~~house~~ on the ~~hill~~
      Gulf of Mexico
overlooked the ~~water~~.

● **Collective nouns** name a group of people, animals, or things. Can you think of one or more collective nouns thst name groups to which you belong?

COLLECTIVE	swarm, accumulation, couple, flock, student council

● **Compound nouns** consist of two or more words. Use a dictionary to find out if a compound word is hyphenated, written as one word, or written as two or more words.

COMPOUND	stepson, CD-player, Declaration of Independence, air conditioner

● A **noun phrase** is a group of words that acts like a noun in a sentence. Like other phrases, a noun phrase does not form a complete sentence. You'll learn about the different types of noun phrases in Lesson 6.4.

Exercise 1 Identifying Nouns

Underline all the nouns in the following passage from a travel journal. Look for common nouns, proper nouns, abstract nouns, concrete nouns, compound nouns, and collective nouns. **Hint:** Pronouns such as *I, you*, and *we* do not count as nouns.

¹Our drive from Albuquerque, New Mexico, through the Jémez Reservation stunned me. ²From the bus I photographed dramatic landscapes in the high desert. ³Passing a village, I took pictures of dried red peppers, called *ristras*, which hung in strings outside each adobe home.

⁴We continued into the mountains outside Santa Fe. ⁵My spirits soared when I spotted an elk. ⁶Of course, I took a few snapshots. ⁷Most amazing of all, though, was our visit to Bandelier National Monument. ⁸There we viewed the ruins of prehistoric cliff dwellings and ceremonial sites that belonged to the Pueblo Indians. ⁹The homes are carved into the rock of Frijoles Canyon, overlooking beautifully forested land crisscrossed by freshwater streams. ¹⁰My favorite photograph shows my friend Jesse climbing the last of many steep ladders up to the *kiva*, a sacred cave reserved for ceremonies.

¹¹Our guide explained that this area holds important keys to the past. ¹²The Pueblo Indians did not have a written language, but they did leave behind petroglyphs—drawings etched into rock—and artifacts that reveal much about the beliefs and traditions of these ancient people of the Southwest.

Exercise 2 Adding Nouns to Sentences

Fill in the blanks in each sentence with the kinds of nouns indicated in parentheses. Choose specific nouns to create vivid, clear sentences.
Sample answers shown.

1. The place I would like most to visit is (proper noun) Acadia National Park, located near (proper noun) Ellsworth, Maine.

2. At my favorite spot, the (concrete noun) ocean and the (concrete noun) landscape are unforgettable.

3. When I listen to my favorite (common noun) music, I am overcome with feelings of (abstract noun) happiness.

4. The reporter wrote an in-depth (common noun) piece about a candidate for (proper noun) the U.S. Senate.

5. The sailor bravely steered his (concrete noun) ship through a raging (common noun) storm.

Pronouns

It may seem necessary to repeat nouns in order to communicate ideas. But pronouns break the monotony of repeated nouns and act like a breath of fresh air.

◗ **Pronouns** are words that take the place of a noun or another pronoun.

Most pronouns clearly refer to a noun or a noun phrase in the same sentence or in a preceding sentence. The word or phrase the pronoun replaces is known as its **antecedent**. The arrows in the following sentences point to the antecedents of the **personal pronouns** and their **possessive forms**—the most common pronouns you use.

Aretha played a jazz medley on the trumpet for **her** classmates. **It** captured **their** interest. **She** knew **it** would because **she** believed that the appreciation of jazz could be communicated through **her** performance.

◗ **Indefinite pronouns** express an amount or refer to an unspecified person or thing.
Some lingered outside the theater.
Nobody heard a word the actor said.

◗ **Demonstrative pronouns** point to specific people or things.
This is exactly what the audience wants.
That was a moving performance.

◗ **Interrogative pronouns** begin a question.
When will the play begin? **Who** has the lead? **Where** is it set?

◗ **Relative pronouns** introduce adjective clauses. (See Lesson 7.2 for more on adjective clauses.)
The author **whose** books have won awards visited our school.
The topic **that** the author covered fascinated us.

◗ **Reflexive pronouns** end in *-self* or *-selves* and refer to an earlier noun or pronoun in the sentence. These are called **intensive pronouns** when they are used to add emphasis.
Manuel helped **himself** to a concert program. [reflexive]
I **myself** could never perform on stage. [intensive]

Personal Pronouns

I	you	her
me	he	it
we	him	they
us	she	them

Possessive Pronouns

my	your	his
mine	yours	its
our	her	their
ours	hers	theirs

Some Indefinite Pronouns

all	another
any	anybody
anyone	anything
both	each
either	everybody
everyone	everything
few	many
most	neither
nobody	none
no one	one
several	some
somebody	someone

Demonstrative Pronouns

this	these
that	those

Some Interrogative Pronouns

Who?	Which?
What?	Whom?
When?	Whose?
Where?	

Relative Pronouns

that	whom
which	whose
who	where

Reflexive and Intensive Pronouns

myself	yourself
himself	herself
itself	ourselves
yourselves	themselves

Exercise 3 Identifying Pronouns

Underline all the pronouns in this paragraph, including possessive pronouns that come before nouns.

¹Paul Simon became a rock and roll musician in the 1960s, along with <u>his</u> friend Art Garfunkel. ²Together <u>they</u> performed as Simon and Garfunkel. ³Since then, Paul Simon's musical journey has continued. ⁴<u>He</u> wrote the songs for the movie *The Graduate*. ⁵<u>Few</u> can forget songs like "The Sound of Silence." ⁶To challenge <u>himself</u> further, Paul Simon began to perform on <u>his</u> own in the 1970s. ⁷By the mid-1980s <u>he</u> again became an innovator, creating the album *Graceland* with Ladysmith Black Mambazo, a popular South African group. ⁸Brazilian drummers worked with Simon on <u>his</u> next album, *The Rhythms of the Saints*. ⁹<u>Who</u> could guess <u>that</u> in the 1990s Paul Simon would team up with the Caribbean-born, Nobel Prize-winning poet, Derek Walcott? ¹⁰<u>They</u> co-wrote the musical *Capeman* for the Broadway stage. ¹¹<u>It</u> starred Marc Anthony, a famous Puerto Rican singer. ¹²<u>This</u> last endeavor shows <u>that</u> people continue to challenge <u>themselves</u>, even <u>those</u> as famous as Paul Simon.

Exercise 4 Writing with Pronouns

Work with a partner to create an interview with a performer or musician. Write at least five questions. Then develop answers the performer might give as responses. Try to use each kind of pronoun from page 81 at least once. Underline all the pronouns in your sentences. Students' interview questions will vary. You might ask students to imagine they are on TV conducting their interviews.

Exercise 5 Write What You Think

■ **For more on writing persuasively, see Composition, Lesson 3.2.**

Politicians and other activists have often called for censorship of the lyrics of certain popular music to protect young listeners from negative influences. Do you think a law should be passed that permits the censorship of music of any kind? Write a letter to a member of Congress protesting or supporting the censorship of lyrics in popular music. State your opinion clearly and support it with reasons, facts, and examples. Answers will vary. Give students full credit if they have stated an opinion and attempted to support their opinions. They should also have written grammatically complete sentences that begin with a capital letter and end with an appropriate end punctuation mark.

Verbs

● **Verbs** are words that express an action or a state of being. Every complete sentence has at least one verb.

● **Action verbs** come in two varieties. You can observe some action verbs: *rebound, echo, squirm*. Others express emotions: *envy, despise, cherish*.

> Luis **hit** a double, while Johnny **dashed** for home plate. The fans **hoped** their team **scored**.

Verbs change form to indicate time. (For more about verb tenses, see Lesson 8.4.)

> The audience **applauded**. The audience **applauds**. The audience **has been applauding**.

Some action verbs (V) take direct objects (DO) (For more about direct objects, see Lesson 5.7.)

>   V   DO
> The pitcher **threw** the **ball**.

● **Linking verbs** join—or link—the subject of a sentence with a word that identifies or describes it. (See Lesson 5.2 for more about subjects and predicates.)

> From an airplane, a highway **seems** narrow.

Some verbs can be both linking and action verbs—but not at the same time. They are used as linking verbs only when they precede a word that identifies or describes the subject.

> LINKING VERB   I **feel** much better.   She **remains** a good friend.
> ACTION VERB   I **feel** the bumps.   She **remains** in her seat.

● A **verb phrase** contains a main verb plus one or more **helping** (or **auxiliary**) **verbs** (HV). *Not* (*n't* in a contraction) is never part of the verb phrase.

>   HV   V
> **Could**n't David **meet** us at the movies?
>   HV   V
> She **must have been shopping** for hours.

Linking Verbs: Some Forms of *To Be*

am	is
are	should be
being	was
can be	were
have been	will be
would have been	

Some Other Linking Verbs

appear	become
feel	grow
look	remain
seem	smell
sound	stay
taste	turn

Some Helping Verbs

be (is, am, are, was, were, been, being)
have (has, had)
do (does, did)

can	shall
could	should
may	will
might	would
must	

Writing Hint

To communicate ideas with precision and appeal, use strong verbs rather than a form of the verb *to be*.

His preference **is** comedies. [to be]

He **prefers** comedies. [strong verb]

Exercise 6 **Identifying Verbs**

Underline every verb and verb phrase in the sentences on the following page. **Hint:** Three sentences have two verbs or verb phrases and one sentence has three verbs or verb phrases.

1. In 1857, Samuel Clemens <u>became</u> a Mississippi River pilot in New Orleans and <u>changed</u> his name to Mark Twain.

2. The name *Mark Twain* literally <u>means</u> "a river depth of two fathoms."

3. Mark Twain first <u>worked</u> as a journalist in Nevada and California; he later <u>turned</u> to other forms of writing.

4. Readers <u>enjoyed</u> his humorous essays and tall tales.

5. Twain <u>chose</u> respectability over adventure when he <u>settled</u> in Hartford, Connecticut, and <u>married</u> in 1870.

6. Twain <u>drew</u> on his Western experiences for the anecdotes he <u>used</u> in his popular book *Roughing It.*

7. Using his own childhood memories, Twain <u>began</u> to write the adventures of Tom Sawyer and Huckleberry Finn.

8. The novels *The Adventures of Tom Sawyer* and *The Adventures of Huckleberry Finn* <u>were published</u> in 1876 and 1884, respectively.

9. Everyday speech and realistic American settings <u>remain</u> a hallmark of Twain's greatest novels.

10. Investments in failed business ventures <u>caused</u> Twain's depression later in his life.

Exercise 7 Revising a Paragraph

Strengthen the following paragraph by adding vivid verbs and precise nouns. You can make up details and add, drop, or combine sentences.
Students' revisions will vary.

¹A student got an assignment to write a short story. ²She was confused. ³She needed help. ⁴A friend helped her. ⁵The friend talked about real-life stories. ⁶The girl's preference was a news story that might appear in the newspaper. ⁷The girl and her friend exchanged ideas about a news story. ⁸They decided it would be about a woman who was volunteering her time to help out at a soup kitchen. ⁹While the woman was helping at the soup kitchen, she had an accident. ¹⁰The woman could no longer volunteer at the soup kitchen or work at her job. ¹¹Soon, many of the people she had helped at the soup kitchen started visiting her at home. ¹²Some of them even brought her food. ¹³She realized how much she meant to these people.

Mid-Chapter Review

Exercise A   Identifying Nouns and Pronouns

Underline the nouns and pronouns in the paragraph.

¹Henri Matisse and Pablo Picasso are two world-famous twentieth-century artists who worked in Paris. ²After Matisse died, Picasso remarked, "I have to paint for us both now." ³The two men were well aware of their importance to modern art. ⁴Their extraordinary creativity joined them in people's minds. ⁵In truth, though, they were as different as night and day. ⁶For Matisse, his home was a refuge where he would quietly retreat. ⁷Picasso socialized with many friends, and he could always be found in Parisian cafés and clubs. ⁸Picasso expressed their differences by referring to himself as the North Pole and Matisse as the South Pole. ⁹Few deny the greatness of their contributions to art. ¹⁰Modern art owes much to the great vision of both Picasso and Matisse.

Exercise B   Reviewing Verbs

Underline all the verbs in the paragraph below. Be sure to include verb phrases, too.   Do not penalize students for identifying infinitive phrases as verbs. Infinitives are covered in Lesson 6.5.

¹Exercise and a good diet combine to create healthy minds and bodies. ²Most people know that. ³But not everyone realizes that exercise is as important for teenagers as it is for adults. ⁴Doctors and nutritionists recognize that to ensure a long life of wellness, health routines must begin at an early age. ⁵Teenagers may appear healthy on the surface, but how do they really feel? ⁶Ask teenagers who jog, play sports, or walk vigorously every day how they feel after physical exertion. ⁷Not only do their muscles feel stronger, but their attitudes become more positive and upbeat. ⁸A recent survey of 5,000 sixteen-year-olds in Great Britain showed that those who participated in team sports and other physical activities had low rates of physical illness and emotional distress.

Exercise C   Revising a Report

Revise the following report. Use vivid verbs and specific nouns. Consider inserting pronouns to avoid repeating nouns. Make other changes to improve the report. **Hint:** There is no single correct way to revise the report, and not every sentence needs to be fixed.   Answers will vary. A sample revision is given.

¹When the Civil War ~~happened~~ exploded on April 12, 1860, Mathew Brady ‸was a , an early American photographer,

busy person. ²~~Mathew Brady was an early photographer working in the~~

~~United States.~~ ³~~Mathew Brady himself~~ He had already ~~took~~ taken photographs of presidents as well as other famous people of the United States. ⁴The work

of ~~Mathew~~ Brady, whom people called Broadway Brady, was ~~seen~~ _{exhibited} in his

New York ~~Gallery⁵The photographs of Mathew Brady were known as the~~

"Gallery of Illustrious Americans."

From the
⁶~~The~~ first Civil War battle at Bull Run ~~saw Mathew Brady taking~~

~~pictures, and he continued to take pictures~~ , Mathew Brady took pictures. up to the siege at Petersburg.

was kept in
⁷~~Mathew Brady kept~~ his equipment ~~on a wagon that was called~~ the "what-

With this
is-it-wagon." ⁸~~The~~ equipment ~~of the "what-is-it-wagon" helped Mathew~~

he photographed
~~Brady take photographs of~~ the battle at Antietam, Maryland, in 1862. ⁹~~In~~ These famous

made   the pain and bloodshed in
photographs ~~of the battle at Antietam, Maryland, it is~~ clear ~~that~~ the War

between the States ~~was full of pain and bloodshed.~~ ¹⁰~~The photographs of~~

that   took
~~the battle are famous.~~ ¹¹The photographs ~~Mathew~~ Brady ~~did~~ of ~~President~~

, including one with Lincoln's young son Tad,
Abraham Lincoln are also famous. ¹²~~One of the famous photographs of~~

~~President Lincoln also has his young son Tad in it.~~

the impact of
¹³The work of Mathew Brady is an early example of ~~what~~ photojournalism.

were able to see how war really was by the photos in
is. ¹⁴~~When~~ people at home ~~looked at~~ their newspapers, ~~they saw how war~~

~~really was.~~ ¹⁵Today, we also know more about what the Civil War was like.

those same
¹⁶~~We know what the Civil War was like~~ by viewing ~~the~~ photographs

had such a great impact on the   of his own time.
~~by Mathew Brady~~ that people ~~who lived between 1860 and 1864 viewed.~~

¹⁷Unfortunately, the Civil War cost Mathew Brady a great deal of

money. ¹⁸~~He lost a total of~~ $100,000 in all. ¹⁹After the Civil War, ~~Mathew~~

experienced
Brady ~~had~~ financial trouble. ²⁰~~The financial trouble he experienced after~~

that put an end to   forced him to
~~the war made him stop~~ his photography career altogether and search for

something else to do. ²¹With the help of supporters and the United States

received   as well as
Congress, though, ~~Mathew~~ Brady ~~got~~ an award of money. ²²~~These same~~

~~supporters also got Mathew Brady~~ a medal for his work ~~that honored him~~

an 1876
at ~~a~~ centennial celebration. ²³~~The centennial celebration was~~ in

Philadelphia, ~~Pennsylvania, in 1876.~~

Adjectives

Adjectives help readers picture things accurately and precisely.

● **Adjectives** are modifiers. They give information about the nouns and pronouns they modify.

WHAT KIND?	**slippery** ice, **sophisticated** remark, **brilliant** color, **silent** room
HOW MANY?	**two** months, **several** poems
HOW MUCH?	**more** cake, **less** milk
WHICH ONE?	**worst** movie, **last** train, **that** concert, **third** apartment

A noun may be modified by two or more adjectives.

The **tall**, **majestic** skyscraper loomed before us.

The weather was not only **dry**, but **hot**.

● The adjectives *a* and *an* are called **indefinite articles** because they refer to any one member of a group. The adjective *the* is known as the **definite article** because it points out a particular noun.

INDEFINITE   You can write **a** humorous poem.

DEFINITE   **The** humorous poem you wrote made me howl with laughter.

● **Proper adjectives**, which are derived from proper nouns, always begin with a capital letter.

Southern accent   **Korean** paintings

Mexican pyramids   **Franklin** stove

● Adjectives usually come right before the nouns they modify, but **predicate adjectives** follow a linking verb to modify the subject of a sentence.

The bus trip was **difficult**.

The sky appears **blue** and **clear**.

● When a noun or a possessive pronoun modifies another noun, it functions as an adjective.

Shakespeare sonnet   **baseball** bat

office building   **kitchen** sink

his mitt   **their** wedding

Writing Hint

For more vivid writing, try combining two adjectives, or two words that function as adjectives, to create one specific modifier—a compound adjective. Many compound adjectives are hyphenated.

The mayor retained **decision-making** authority.

A **self-appointed** leader helped the committee solve its problem.

Exercise 8 Identifying Adjectives

Underline the adjectives in the following paragraphs, including proper adjectives, articles, and possessive pronouns.

¹With over <u>four thousand</u> soldiers under <u>his</u> command, <u>the Spanish</u> explorer Francisco Vásquez de Coronado headed north in 1540 from what is now Mexico. ²He was hoping to find <u>the immense</u> wealth of <u>the legendary Seven</u> Cities of Cibola, also known as <u>the Seven</u> Cities of Gold. ³He never found <u>the imaginary</u> cities, but he did explore areas of <u>the southwestern</u> United States. ⁴To escape <u>the dry</u> climate of Arizona, Coronado and <u>his</u> troops marched northeast into New Mexico. ⁵Here he saw <u>the magnificent</u> Rocky Mountains in <u>the</u> distance from <u>his winter</u> campsite. ⁶When <u>his</u> troops later crossed into <u>present-day</u> Texas, they experienced <u>a dramatic</u> change in scenery. ⁷The landscape became <u>barren</u> and <u>flat</u>. ⁸<u>Grass-covered</u> plains stretched to <u>the</u> horizon. ⁹Coronodo and <u>his</u> troops never found <u>the mythical</u> cities of gold they were searching for. ¹⁰When they reached what is now <u>south-central</u> Kansas, they turned back. ¹¹<u>Their long</u> adventure took <u>two difficult</u> years. ¹²Coronado retired to <u>a quiet</u>, <u>uneventful</u> life in Mexico City, <u>richer</u> in knowledge of <u>the North American</u> continent than in gold.

Exercise 9 Revising Sentences to Add Information

Revise the sentences below to give the reader more information and to create more interesting sentences. Underline all the adjectives in your revised sentences.   Revised sentences will vary.

EXAMPLE   The dessert was on the table.
<u>The</u> <u>tasty</u> <u>chocolate</u> cake tempted us from <u>the</u> <u>dining</u> <u>room</u> table.

1. We fished in the pond.

2. The boys ran around the track.

3. Dad slept on the couch.

4. The family drove to the city.

5. Juan swam in the ocean.

6. I read the book on the train.

7. She met friends for dinner.

8. They walked on the beach.

Exercise 10 Writing with Adjectives

Ask a classmate to describe an activity that interests him or her. Listen carefully, take notes, and ask questions. Then write a brief paragraph about what you learned. Include clear descriptions of the activity as well as the reasons your classmate gives for enjoying that activity. Use adjectives to make sentences colorful and sharp.   Students' paragraphs will vary.

Adverbs

To describe an action completely and clearly, you sometimes use a modifier called an adverb.

◖ Adverbs modify, or tell more about, verbs, adjectives, and other adverbs.

MODIFIES VERB	The athlete ran **quickly**.
MODIFIES ADJECTIVE	They swam in a **pleasantly** cool lake.
MODIFIES ADVERB	Who can sit **most** quietly?

Many adverbs may come either before or after the verbs they modify.
Briskly, the horse rounded the bend. The horse rounded the bend **briskly**. The horse **briskly** rounded the bend.

Many adverbs end with the suffix *-ly* (*slowly, modestly, thoughtfully*, for example). However, many common adverbs do not end in *-ly* (*today, much, already*).

◖ Intensifiers are adverbs that answer the question *to what extent?*
The game was the **least** interesting of all.
We ate **too** much food.

Some Common Adverbs That Do Not End in -ly

almost	not (n't)
already	seldom
also	still
always	then
fast	there
here	today
just	tomorrow
late	too
more	well
much	yesterday
never	yet

Some Common Intensifiers

less	rather
least	really
more	so
most	somewhat
nearly	too
only	truly
quite	very
exceptionally	
extraordinarily	

Exercise 11 Identifying Adverbs

Underline the adverbs in each sentence. Draw an arrow to the word the adverb modifies. **Hint:** Four sentences contain more than one adverb.

1. Arizona State University effectively runs an academic "boot camp."

2. It substantially increases the number of minority, college-bound math majors.

3. Sixteen-year-olds develop their math skills quite successfully here.

4. They work cooperatively to solve one hundred math problems nightly.

5. The students study intensely, but they work happily together.

6. Initially, this program helped only thirty-two minority students.

7. The academic "boot camp" has progressed significantly, becoming part of the university's Institute for Strengthening Underrepresented Minority Students in Mathematics and Science.

Step by Step

Adjective or Adverb?

1. Decide which word you need to modify.

   He speaks (*soft, softly*).

2. If you need to modify a noun or pronoun, use an adjective.

3. If you need to modify a verb, adjective, or another adverb, use an adverb.

   He speaks **softly**.

8. Dr. Joaquin Bustoz, a founder of the institute, who is from a minority background himself, generously gives of his time.

9. He hopes some of his students will eventually become teachers, too.

10. Imagine spending a summer day doing ten hours of math that absorbs your attention completely.

Exercise 12 Choosing the Correct Modifier

When you talk with friends, you may mix up adjectives and adverbs. In more formal settings—in school and in business—you need to choose modifiers that correctly fit your sentences. Underline the modifier in the parentheses that correctly completes each sentence.

1. It takes an (extreme, extremely) (creative, creatively) person to develop a new invention.

2. Alexander Graham Bell worked (extraordinary, extraordinarily) hard to perfect his (high, highly) successful invention, the telephone.

3. Marie Curie won a second Nobel Prize in 1911 for her (exceptional, exceptionally) work with (dangerous, dangerously) (radioactive, radioactively) elements.

4. Pi Sheng created one of the first (entire, entirely) (mechanical, mechanically) printing presses in China in 1040.

5. Samuel Morse's first (complete, completely) (accurate, accurately) telegraph message was sent from Baltimore to Washington, D.C., in 1844.

6. Nineteenth-century French physician Rene Laennec invented the stethoscope, a (strange, strangely), foot-long device, to listen to his patients' chest sounds and to diagnose (previous, previously) undetermined heart ailments.

7. Thomas Edison, an (ingenious, ingeniously) inventor, registered more than one thousand patents for such (brilliant, brilliantly) imaginative products as the light bulb, the phonograph, and the movie projector.

8. Basketball fans owe a (deep, deeply) debt of gratitude to James Naismith, who invented the game in 1891 by (clever, cleverly) using two peach baskets and a soccer ball.

Exercise 13 Writing with Adverbs

Picture the way something moves. Imagine a bird in flight, a skater gliding on ice, a basketball player dunking the ball, or a friend walking. Write a paragraph in which you describe in detail the motion you envision. Use adverbs and adjectives to create a vivid, accurate description. Students' paragraphs will vary. Make sure students have included an adequate number of adverbs and adjectives to paint a picture for the reader.

Combining Sentences: Inserting Single-Word Modifiers

◖ You can express your ideas concisely and effectively by combining a series of short, choppy sentences into one flowing sentence. Combine sentences by inserting key words from one sentence into another sentence.

ORIGINAL   The bears lumbered near our campsite. The bears were grizzlies. The bears lumbered sluggishly.

COMBINED   The **grizzly** bears lumbered **sluggishly** near our campsite.

The combined sentence sounds a lot smoother because it avoids unnecessary repetition. Notice that the single words inserted into the sentence work as modifiers—adjectives and adverbs.

ORIGINAL   The eagle dived into the water. The eagle dived instantly. The water was icy.

COMBINED   **Instantly**, the eagle dived into the **icy** water.

Note: Sometimes the key words change form when you combine sentences (in the first example above, *grizzlies* becomes *grizzly*).

ORIGINAL   Members of Congress listened to debates and reports. The debates centered on ecology. The reports were made by congressional aides.

COMBINED   Members of Congress listened to **ecology** debates **and congressional aides'** reports.

ORIGINAL   People testified before Congress. Experts on ecology spoke about groundwater contamination. Congressional aides reported on voter concerns about their water.

COMBINED   **In testimony** before Congress, **ecology experts reported on** groundwater contamination, **while** congressional aides **cited** voter concerns about this **issue**.

Step by Step

Combining Sentences

To combine a series of short sentences:

1. Find the sentence that gives readers the most information.

2. In the other sentences, look for single words that can be incorporated into the sentence identified in Step 1.

3. Insert the single words where they make sense. You may need to change the form of the words you're moving.

4. Test the combined sentence to see if it sounds natural and conveys the proper meaning.

Exercise 14 **Combining Sentences**

Combine the groups of sentences on the following page into single sentences. **Hint:** Drop some words and change the form of others to combine sentences successfully.

EXAMPLE   *Moby Dick* is a novel by Herman Melville. *Moby Dick* is a famous novel. Herman Melville was American.
Moby Dick **is a famous novel by the American Herman Melville.**

See Answer Key.

1. "The Prologue" is a poem. "The Prologue" was written by Anne Bradstreet. Anne Bradstreet was the first woman author in the American colonies.

2. Henry James wrote about relationships among people. Henry James was a novelist. The people he wrote about were mostly British and American.

3. Washington Irving wrote about a headless horseman. The headless horseman appeared in a story called "The Legend of Sleepy Hollow." Washington Irving wrote "The Legend of Sleepy Hollow" in the early nineteenth century.

4. I heard a recording of Gwendolyn Brooks reading poems about love. Gwendolyn Brooks is an African American poet. Gwendolyn Brooks read poems from her Pulitzer Prize-winning collection, *Annie Allen*.

5. Did you ever read *Moby Dick*? *Moby Dick* is a famous novel about a whale. The book was written by Herman Melville. The book was written in 1851.

Exercise 15 **Revising a Paragraph**

Work with a partner to improve the following first paragraph of a story for the school literary magazine. Look for opportunities to combine sentences.

¹The Watson twins live on a street called Shadow Lane. ²Shadow Lane is usually a quiet street. ³It is a winding street. ⁴Tonight, the wind howls fiercely. ⁵The wind howls as fiercely as a pack of hungry wolves. ⁶The people on Shadow Lane usually turn out their lights by nine o'clock. ⁷But the people on Shadow Lane keep their lights burning brightly late into this night. ⁸The people on Shadow Lane have never before heard such a strange sound. ⁹The Watson twins and their parents keep their lights shining brightly in their house, too. ¹⁰The Watson twins are sixteen years old. ¹¹The Watsons live in the first house on the street. ¹²Tonight, the people of Shadow Lane will never forget the Watson twins.

¹³Tonight the people of Shadow Lane will never forget the bizarre night sounds.

¹⁴The names of the Watson twins are Andrea and Clyde.

Extend this exercise by having students continue the story.

Prepositions

Prepositional phrases add color and depth to writing, amplifying the thoughts in a sentence.

◆ **Prepositions** connect a noun or pronoun to another word in the sentence to form a **prepositional phrase**. [For more about prepositional phrases, see Lesson 6.1.]

    beneath the carpet
    toward a greater understanding

Some prepositions are **compound** (made up of more than one word).

    in spite of them
    according to the Constitution

◆ Words that are prepositions in one sentence may be adverbs in another sentence. Look to see if a word starts a prepositional phrase. If it does not, it is an *adverb*.

  ADVERBS   Get **inside** quickly.
              Set the food **down** on the table.
  PREPOSITIONS The treasure is **inside** the cave.
              The mouse ran **down** the clock.

Exercise 16 **Identifying Prepositions**

The following passage is the famous first sentence from *A Tale of Two Cities* written by Charles Dickens. Underline every preposition.

    It was the best of times, it was the worst of times, it was the age of wisdom, it was the age of foolishness, it was the epoch of belief, it was the epoch of incredulity, it was the season of Light, it was the season of Darkness, it was the spring of hope, it was the winter of despair, we had everything before us, we had nothing before us, we were all going direct to Heaven, we were all going direct the other way—in short, the period was so far like the present period, that some of its noisiest authorities insisted on its being received, for good or for evil, in the superlative degree of comparison only.

Some Commonly Used Prepositions

about	during	out
after	except	outside
along	for	over
around	from	since
at	in	through
before	inside	to
below	into	toward
beneath	like	under
beside	near	until
between	of	up
beyond	off	upon
by	on	
down	onto	
but (meaning "except")		
with/without		

Some Common Compound Prepositions

according to	along with
apart from	aside from
as to	due to
because of	in front of
in place of	in spite of
instead of	out of
in addition to	

Writing Hint

In the past, students were taught never to end a sentence with a preposition. British Prime Minister Winston Churchill is said to have challenged this rule by saying: "This is the sort of [English] up with which I will not put." Today, ending a sentence with a preposition is usually acceptable.

What are you looking **for**? Here's the pen I spoke **about**.

Exercise 17 Selecting Prepositions

Complete each sentence with one or more prepositions. Your selection will determine the meaning of the sentence. Choose carefully so that the sentences make sense.

1. A telescope can detect stars ___in___ the Milky Way.

2. The astronauts conducted experiments ___during___ their later orbits.

3. The campers chose dried beef and rice ___in addition to___ a sandwich.
   intead of *or*

4. The experience ___of___ weightlessness was new ___to___ them.

5. ___After___ touchdown, an official walked ___through___ the spacecraft.

6. The cat leapt ___onto___ the counter, where frozen fish was defrosting.

7. The fighter pilots reported some problems ___during___ the test run.

8. The mascot entertained ___between___ innings.

9. Luisa's poodle came in first ___at___ the dog show.

10. The Invisible Man could disappear ___into___ thin air.

Exercise 18 Revising Sentences

Expand the sentences below by adding prepositional phrases. Make up all the details you need to make interesting sentences. Underline all the prepositions in your sentences.

EXAMPLE   Howard drove his car.

In spite of the snow, Howard drove his car over the mountain to school.

1. The parking lot was full.   5. The bus stopped.

2. The lot had potholes.   6. My car needs repair.

3. All parking spots are full.   7. I take the bus.

4. All parking spots are empty.   8. The bus arrives late.

Exercise 19 Writing with Prepositions

Write a brief paragraph in which you explain how you do something. You might write about getting dressed in the morning, making muffins, or scoring a goal in soccer. Try to use some prepositional phrases in your paragraph. When you've finished writing, read your paragraph aloud to yourself. If some sentences sound too monotonous and singsongy, try removing one or more of the prepositional phrases. Students' paragraphs will very. Suggest that students add some humor to this paragraph.

Conjunctions and Interjections

● **Conjunctions** join words or groups of words.

Coordinating conjunctions join words or groups of words that are equal in importance.

> Thunder, lightning, **and** hail hit the area. The thunder **and** lightning finally stopped, **but** the hail kept falling.

Correlative conjunctions are always used in pairs.

> **Either** it's raining **or** snowing. **Both** you **and** I are going dancing.
> **Neither** Lakisha **nor** Abdul took first prize.
> **Just as** thunder rumbles, **so** (too) lightning eventually strikes.

Place correlative conjunctions correctly when you write. The words or phrases joined by a correlative conjunction should play the same role in the sentence. For example, the conjunction might join two subjects or two clauses.

> INCORRECT **Either** people love frog legs **or** hate them.
> CORRECT People **either** love frog legs **or** hate them.
> CORRECT **Either** people love frog legs **or** they hate them.

> INCORRECT **Either** the girls went to the mall **or** to the grocery.
> CORRECT **Either** the girls went to the mall **or** they slept late.
> CORRECT The girls went **either** to the mall **or** to the grocery.

Subordinating conjunctions connect adverb clauses to main clauses. (For more about adverb clauses, see Lesson 7.3.)

> The author smiled **because** a reader asked for her autograph.
> We studied together **so that** we could all pass the test.
> The team needs more practice **since** the game is tomorrow.

● **Interjections** express mild or strong emotion.

Interjections have no grammatical connection to the rest of the sentence. They are set off by a comma or an exclamation point.

> **Darn!** I forgot my book again.
> **No way!** I certainly will not resign.
> She exclaimed, "**Wow!** What a parade!"

Coordinating Conjunctions

and but or
nor yet

Some Correlative Conjunctions

both . . . and
either . . . or
neither . . . nor
not only . . . but also
whether . . . or
just as . . . so (too)

Some Common Subordinating Conjunctions

after	in order that
although	provided that
as far as	since
as long as	so that
as soon as	unless
as though	until
because	when
before	where
if	whereas
while	

Some Common Interjections

aha	ouch
cool	ugh
hey	well
hooray	wow
oh	yo

Writing Hint

Especially when writing dialogue, experiment with placing interjections in the middle as well as the beginning of sentences.

Claire insisted, "I said **No!** at least a hundred times."

Exercise 20 Identifying Conjunctions and Interjections

Underline all the conjunctions and interjections in the sentences below.
Hint: Only two sentences contain an interjection.

1. <u>Both</u> artist Georgia O'Keeffe <u>and</u> the photographer Alfred Stieglitz contributed significantly to American culture.

2. Stieglitz made his reputation <u>not only</u> as a gallery owner <u>but also</u> as a photographer.

3. After art school O'Keeffe's work was ignored, <u>but</u> she later became an important painter.

4. <u>When</u> he first saw her work, Stieglitz exclaimed, "<u>At last!</u> A woman on paper!"

5. <u>Just</u> as many artists loved big cities, <u>so</u> O'Keeffe loved deserts.

6. O'Keeffe painted flowers, <u>yet</u> her work wasn't sentimental.

7. <u>Whether</u> you see them at a museum <u>or</u> find them in a gallery, the paintings and photographs are remarkable.

8. Many people say "<u>Wow!</u>" <u>when</u> they see an O'Keeffe painting.

9. <u>Not only</u> did O'Keeffe paint, <u>but</u> she <u>also</u> posed for Stieglitz.

10. <u>Neither</u> Stieglitz <u>nor</u> O'Keeffe could've predicted their success.

Exercise 21 Writing with Interjections

Work with a partner to write a conversation of at least ten lines of dialogue between two friends. Have the characters discuss movies they love or hate. Include an interjection in each line. Then read the dialogue aloud with your partner. Add, remove, or rewrite interjections to end up with a dialogue that sounds natural.   Students' dialogues will vary.

Exercise 22 Write What You Think

Write a paragraph that expresses your thoughts on the following statement. Support your opinion with facts and examples.

Private foundations and public donations should be the sole supports of fine art and public television and radio in this country. The federal government should end all financial support of those institutions.

Revise and edit your paragraph and be certain that you have used prepositions and interjections correctly.   Suggest that students research information to support their opinions. Answers will vary. Give students full credit if they have stated an opinion and attempted to support that opinion. They should also have written grammatically complete sentences that begin with a capital letter and end with an appropriate end punctuation mark.

Determining a Word's Part of Speech

🔖 A word's part of speech is determined by how the word is used in the sentence. For example, the word *down* can be used as a noun, a verb, an adjective, or an adverb.

NOUN   The football coach explained a first **down**.

VERB   The runner **downed** a quart of water after the race.

ADJECTIVE   The **down** side is that we don't get a raise.

ADVERB   When the tree fell **down**, it damaged my car.

Exercise 23 Identifying Parts of Speech

Identify the part of speech of each underlined word as it is used in the sentence. Use these abbreviations.

N = noun   ADJ = adjective   CONJ = conjunction
P = pronoun   ADV = adverb   INT = interjection
V = verb   PREP = preposition

___ADJ___ 1. W. E. B. Du Bois was an <u>American</u> civil rights leader and author.

___V___ 2. Born and raised in Massachusetts, he <u>graduated</u> from Harvard.

___CONJ___ 3. Du Bois championed <u>both</u> economic <u>and</u> political equality for African Americans.

___PREP___ 4. He co-founded the National Association for the Advancement <u>of</u> Colored People (NAACP) in 1909.

___PREP___ 5. He edited the NAACP magazine, *Crisis,* <u>until</u> 1934.

___ADV___ 6. Du Bois <u>tirelessly</u> worked to help all oppressed people.

___ADJ___ 7. Du Bois encouraged the development of <u>African American</u> literature and art.

___ADV___ 8. He <u>strongly</u> advocated the power of African American-owned businesses.

___N___ 9. Du Bois's international <u>concerns</u> prompted the first Pan African Congress.

___P___ 10. <u>Several</u> of the delegates became leaders of African nations.

Revising and Editing Worksheet

Revise the following draft of a biographical sketch. You may combine sentences, add or delete details, and replace words. Some sentences may not need revising. **Hint:** Watch out for spelling mistakes, too. Students' revisions will vary.

[1]Sitting Bull, a famous native american, deeply understood the Sioux spirit world. [2]Sitting Bull communicated his thoughts and experiences clearly. [3]His father, the warrior and mystic Returns Again, first called his son "Slow," because of the babys quiet, contemplative nature. [4]Years later, Returns Again renamed his son Sitting Bull. [5]Sitting Bull was fourteen years old when his father renamed him. [6]The name was "Tatanka Yotanka" or "Sitting Bull."

[7]As a teenager, young Sitting Bull himself had dreamlike states. [8]In one dreamlike state Sitting Bull heard an animal. [9]Sitting Bull heard an animal calling from a high perch on a rocky butte. [10]Sitting Bull went to the spot. [11]Sitting Bull found an eagle. [12]From that moment, Sitting Bull believed he was going to lead his people.

[13]By 1868, Sitting Bull was considered a leader among the Hunkpapas, a band of Lakota Sioux. [14]Other Sioux leaders signed the treaty of Fort Laramie that required them to live on a reservation in southern south dakota. [15]Sitting Bull could have signed the treaty. [16]Sitting Bull refused to give up any ancestral lands.

[17]Sitting Bull's people suffered. [18]Their suffering was long. [19]After many years of fleeing from the U.S. Army, Sitting Bull and his people finally surrendered. [20]His surrender saved his people from starvation in Canada. [21]Sitting Bull traveled with Buffalo Bill Cody and Annie Oakley in the Wild West Show run by Buffalo Bill Cody and Annie Oakley. [22]Sitting Bull also continued to speak up for his people. [23]Sitting Bull lived until 1890.

Visit us at
www.sadlier-oxford.com ▸ Internet

Exercise A **Identifying Parts of Speech**

In the space provided, identify the part of speech of the underlined word in each of the following sentences about some of the first ten presidents of the United States. Use these abbreviations.

N = noun	ADJ = adjective	CONJ = conjunction
P = pronoun	ADV = adverb	INT = interjection
V = verb	PREP = preposition	

ADJ 1. George Washington was trained as a <u>land</u> surveyor.

_N_ 2. George Washington was the <u>commander in chief</u> of the Continental Army troops.

ADV 3. Washington, of course, <u>eventually</u> was elected president.

CONJ 4. Thomas Jefferson <u>not only</u> became president <u>but also</u> helped plan the capital city, Washington, D.C.

_N_ 5. The War of 1812 occurred during the <u>presidency</u> of James Madison.

PREP 6. James Monroe learned about politics and law <u>from</u> Thomas Jefferson.

ADJ 7. Andrew Jackson was the first <u>presidential</u> nominee from Tennessee.

ADV 8. Martin Van Buren was one of the <u>most</u> unpopular presidents.

_P_ 9. <u>Who</u> can forget the name "Tippecanoe," a battle between the Native American leader Tecumseh and the future ninth U.S. president, William Henry Harrison?

_V_ 10. John Tyler <u>is remembered</u> as the vice-president who became president after Harrison's death.

Exercise B **Revising a Business Letter**

On a separate piece of paper, revise the following draft of a business letter. Make sure to clarify any confusing or awkward phrasing. Feel free to replace words, add new details, combine sentences, and delete words or entire sentences.   Students' revisions will vary.

Dear Ms. Jabbar:

[1]When the New York Yankees won the World Series, it was a big deal

in my neighborhood. [2]Because of that, I wanted to see if you had any special souvenirs from the postseason that I might be able to get. [3]I was interested in such things as pennants, coffee mugs, caps, and other things like that that I could put on display in my room.

[4]I wanted to get things to remind me of all the big moments. [5]Souvenirs of this kind bring back happy memories to me.

[6]When you send me information about the memorabilia you are offering from the postseason, please include information about how I can order this memorabilia. [7]I want to see this information as soon as possible. [8]Rush it to me in the mail. [9]You can also send it on the fax. [10]My fax number is (718) 555-9280.

[11]I would like to thank you very much in advance for sending me this information so I can place my order right away.

Sincerely,

Marisa Fielder

Exercise C Revising a Personal Narrative

On a separate piece of paper, revise the following draft of a personal narrative. Feel free to make any changes that will make these paragraphs stronger and more interesting. Replace words, add specific details, add direct quotes, combine sentences, and cut words or sentences.
Students' revisions will vary.

[1]There was snow everywhere. [2]I had never seen so much snow. [3]The snow was white. [4]The snow sparkled like diamonds under the blue sky.

[5]This was my first time on a ski slope. [6]I had never gone skiing before. [7]I was excited. [8]I was nervous. [9]My friends had gone skiing before. [10]I was the only beginning skier in our Teen Tours group.

[11]Sam used ski poles to begin moving across the slope. [12]He began by putting ski poles in the snow. [13]Sam pushed off using the poles he was using. [14]Sam motioned to me to copy what he was doing. [15]Sam liked to say "way to go." [16]That's what Sam said to me. [17]I copied Sam. [18]I began to move quickly across the mountain slope. [19]I was moving too quickly.

[20]I couldn't turn. [21]I was heading for a tree. [22]Sam yelled for me to fall backwards into the snow. [23]Cherise yelled the same words. [24]I followed the advice of Sam and Cherise. [25]I avoided the tree. [26]With the help of Sam and Cherise, I got up. [27]I brushed off the snow. [28]I tried again. [29]Each time I tried, I got a little bit better. [30]By the end of the day, I could ski down the beginner slope without falling once.

Parts of a Sentence

STUDENT WRITING
Narrative Essay

The Earthquake
by Keane Kaneakua
high school student, Kaneohe, Hawaii

All was well in the city of Kaneohe. It was a cool Saturday morning and the first day of 1984's Christmas vacation. There was an uncommon stillness in the air. All of a sudden, a rumbling under the earth broke the stillness. The rumbling grew immense in a very short amount of time. No one knew what was going on for a few seconds, and then there were screams of fright: "Earthquake!"

The shaking lasted for about five minutes, yet the shaking during those five minutes was enough to level houses and buildings. Then the real chaos of trying to find family and friends and of trying to put lives back together began.

The estimated cost of the damages was about $5,000,000,000. It would take years to put Oahu back together. People scrounged around looking for lost pieces of their lives as if they were putting together a puzzle. Lost family members, pets, and friends were just a few of the major losses resulting from the earthquake.

For ten years, Oahu has shown the physical scars of the earthquake that mentally and physically shook the island. For generations to come, no one will forget the wrath of 1984.

Keane Kaneakua's narrative writing relates the events of a natural disaster in the order in which they occurred. His transition words throughout the essay help guide his readers, and the varied sentence lengths help keep his style lively and interesting.

Reread Keane's essay, and notice that his sentences vary in structure. As you work on sentences in this chapter, think about how you can manipulate them to communicate your ideas in an interesting way.

Allow time for students to discuss the student writing. Suggest that they identify its strengths and propose possible improvements. Use the model to introduce the concepts in the chapter.

Using Complete Sentences

🔹 A **sentence** is a grammatically complete group of words that expresses a thought.

Don't judge whether a sentence is grammatically correct by its length. A short sentence may be as complete as a long one.

> Did the Trinity River flood?
> This afternoon, after two hours of nonstop rain, the Trinity River rose above its banks and flooded Trinity Road.

What makes both of these sentences grammatically correct? First, they begin with a capital letter and end with a punctuation mark—a period, a question mark, or an exclamation point. In addition, all complete sentences do the following two things: (1) name the person, animal, thing, or state of being that the sentence is about and (2) tell what that person, animal, thing, or state of being does or is.

Writing Hint

Occasionally, fragments can be used in informal writing for effect. When you write what people say, in dialogue, or when you write an advertisement, you might use fragments to imitate everyday speech or to create memorable phrases.

Not now.

Okay by me.

Best by far.

🔹 A sentence has one of four purposes.

PURPOSE OF SENTENCE	END PUNCTUATION	EXAMPLES
Declarative sentences make a statement.	period	It rained the day the President visited.
Imperative sentences issue a command or request.	period or exclamation point	Line up in front of the entrance. No talking!
Interrogative sentences ask a question.	question mark	Did you notice the First Lady's red, white, and blue suit?
Exclamatory sentences express a strong feeling.	exclamation point	Wow! His speech really impressed me!

A group of words may begin with a capital letter and conclude with end punctuation, but those words may not express a complete thought.

🔹 A **sentence fragment** is a group of words that is not grammatically complete. Avoid sentence fragments when you write.

FRAGMENT Because the President talked about education. [This doesn't tell *what* happened.]

SENTENCE Students listened because the President talked about education.

FRAGMENT Spoke out on issues concerning education. [This doesn't identify *who* the speaker is.]

SENTENCE The President, who spoke out on issues concerning education, received a standing ovation.

Exercise 1 Identifying Sentence Fragments

Write *S* on the line before each numbered item if the group of words is a
complete sentence. Write *F* if the group of words is a fragment. Correct the
fragments on a separate piece of paper.
See Answer Key for sample corrections to fragments.

___S___ 1. What makes space voyages to Mars fascinating to scientists is the
planet's glow.

___F___ 2. President Bush proposing a manned space mission to Mars in 1989.

___F___ 3. Which was on the twentieth anniversary of the Apollo 11
moon landing.

___S___ 4. The $500 million cost delayed the proposal.

___F___ 5. However low the costs for new methods of space exploration.

___S___ 6. A trip now might only cost $55 million.

___F___ 7. This trip, which the public seems interested in recently.

___F___ 8. Showing microscopic signs of ancient life there, a meteorite
discovered on Antarctica.

___F___ 9. Better to send astronauts or a robot into space experts debate?

___F___ 10. To use the International Space Station by its completion date in 2004
to explore Mars.

Exercise 2 Writing Complete Sentences

With a partner or a small group, come up with five questions you might ask a
NASA official or an astronaut about U.S. space exploration. Then write the
answers the NASA official or astronaut might give. Try to use each of the four
kinds of sentences in your interview. Remember to use capital letters and end
punctuation correctly.

Exercise 3 Write What You Think

Write a paragraph in response to the statement below. Support your opinion
with facts, reasons, and examples. Check your writing to make sure you
eliminate all sentence fragments.

Billions of tax dollars have been spent on space exploration since NASA was
launched four decades ago. That money would have been better spent to
remedy social ills here on Earth, such as poverty, inadequate health care,
crime, and unequal access to a good education.

Answers will vary. Give students full credit if they have stated an opinion and attempted to
support their opinions. They should also have written grammatically complete sentences that
begin with a capital letter and end with an appropriate end punctuation mark.

Subject and Predicate

Every sentence has two essential parts: a **subject** and a **predicate**. The subject names the person, place, thing, or idea the sentence is about. The predicate tells what the subject does or is.

SUBJECT	PREDICATE
The restaurant called Café Aroma	attracts many students.
My classmates Jerry and Elaine	drink coffee all afternoon.

● The **simple subject** is the key word or words in the subject. A simple subject may contain a proper noun, which may be made up of more than one word. The complete subject is made up of the simple subject and all of its modifiers (such as adjectives and prepositional phrases).

● The **simple predicate** is always the verb or verb phrase that tells something about the subject. The complete predicate contains the verb and all of its modifiers (such as adverbs and prepositional phrases), objects, and complements.

You'll review objects and complements in Lessons 5.7 and 5.9.

In the sentences below, all simple subjects and simple predicates are highlighted. Notice that a sentence can begin with either the subject or the predicate.

Don't get confused by contractions. A contraction may contain both the simple subject and part of the verb in a sentence.

You've eaten the whole cake!

The subject is **you**, and the verb is *have eaten*.

COMPLETE SUBJECT	COMPLETE PREDICATE
The **River Restaurant**	**will open** this Monday.
I	**can set** a table blindfolded.
A **cloud** of steam	**rose** off the baked lasagna.
These plastic **plates** and **cups**	**may be placed** in a microwave.

COMPLETE PREDICATE	COMPLETE SUBJECT
Here **steam**	fresh **broccoli** and **carrots**.
In the kitchen **hums**	the **sound** of busy cooks and waiters.

Exercise 4 **Identifying Subjects and Verbs**

Underline the subject (the simple subject) once and the verb (the simple predicate) twice in each sentence of this press release. **Hint:** There is more than one subject or verb in several sentences.

¹The Carson City International Food Festival will take place on the last weekend in September. ²Full meals and delicious snacks will tempt passersby from dawn to dusk. ³All day long will the scents of delicious

foods <u>fill</u> the air. ⁴Visitors and food <u>critics</u> <u>will</u> <u>sample</u> and <u>savor</u> shrimp-filled spring rolls from Vietnam. ⁵<u>Luigi Salerno</u> and his <u>son</u> <u>will serve</u> pizza and pasta. ⁶<u>Café Abyssinia</u> <u>will</u> also <u>show</u> customers how to eat with sheets of traditional Ethiopian bread.

⁷The <u>Barbecue Bistro</u> and the <u>China Coast</u> <u>will</u> each <u>provide</u> hungry festival guests with highly unusual dishes. ⁸If spice and variety are the keys to great cooking, the <u>Barbecue Bistro</u> <u>will win</u> the "spice" category hands down. ⁹<u>Variety</u>, that other essential ingredient of great cooking, <u>will be</u> on grand display at the China Coast. ¹⁰In fact, <u>visitors</u> <u>will smack</u> their lips with every bite from booths at this tantalizing festival coming soon to our city.

Exercise 5 **Writing Complete Sentences**

On a separate piece of paper, write the directions for following the recipe for the Barbecue Bistro's Barn Chile in complete sentences. You may write the recipe as a numbered list or in paragraph form. Use capital letters and end punctuation correctly in your sentences. Students' recipes will vary.

Barbecue Bistro's Barn Chile

large pot with lid

1 pound pinto beans—soak overnight in water, cook in pot until tender on top of stove

onions (2), bell pepper (1), tomatoes (4)—chop
1 pound ground beef (lean)—brown in large skillet

add Barbecue Bistro's Special Spice Mix to beef

vegetables—add to beef, 15 minutes

skillet contents into bean pot

simmer—30 minutes

salt and pepper to taste

(optional) top servings with sour cream, shredded cheese

Correcting Sentence Fragments

You may form complete sentences from sentence fragments by using these three strategies:

1. Attach it. Join the fragment to a complete sentence before or after it.

FRAGMENT Did you ever visit Mt. Rushmore. While on vacation?

REVISED Did you ever visit Mt. Rushmore while on vacation?

2. Add some words. Add the missing subject, verb, or whatever other words are necessary to make the group of words grammatically complete.

FRAGMENT Western legends were chosen. The original figures on Mt. Rushmore.

REVISED Western legends were chosen as the original figures on Mt. Rushmore.

3. Drop some words. Drop the subordinating conjunction that creates a sentence fragment.

FRAGMENT As though nature also sculpted Mt. Rushmore.

REVISED Nature also sculpted Mt. Rushmore.

> **Step by Step**
>
> **The Sentence Test**
>
> To determine whether a group of words forms a complete sentence, ask these three questions:
>
> 1. Does it have a subject?
> 2. Does it have a verb?
> 3. Does it express a complete thought?
>
> If you can't answer *yes* to all three questions, you have a fragment. Correct it.

Exercise 6 Correcting Sentence Fragments

On a separate piece of paper, revise each numbered item to eliminate all sentence fragments. Use the three strategies above to form complete sentences. Revised sentences will vary. Sample answers given.

1. Back in 1885. A lawyer named Charles E. Rushmore named the peak of a rock dome in South Dakota.

2. He believed That the peaks of that dome would some day be carved as human heads.

3. The idea was developed by Doanne Robinson, a South Dakotan.

4. ~~When~~ the state hired an Idaho sculptor named Borglum, known for working on a large scale.

5. At first Borglum was hired by others. To sculpt Robert E. Lee on Stone Mountain, Georgia.

6. Carving Mt. Rushmore. was A more interesting project for Borglum.

7. Borglum's letter of 1925 suggested. Portraying American presidents rather than Western legends.

8. ~~Because~~ materials had to be hauled up the mountain by horse or on foot for over fourteen years.

9. Fortunately, ~~since~~ lack of access protects the carvings from vandals.

10. From 1941 until the present, people ~~marveling~~ *have marveled* at the $990,000 New World wonder.

Editing for Fragments

Improve the paragraph below. If the numbered line is not a sentence, add, omit, or change words and punctuation. Be sure to add capital letters and end punctuation marks where necessary. Make sure every sentence expresses a complete thought. Revised paragraphs will vary. Sample answers given.

[1]One of the most controversial but popular monuments erected in the United States, *is* [2]The 1980 Vietnam Veterans Memorial in Washington, D.C. [3]Maya Lin, an architecture student from Yale, submitted design plans in a contest, *and her* [4]~~That a student's~~ design was chosen over others by a panel of experts! [5]At the monument, people *can* ~~reading~~ the names of those who died or disappeared in the Vietnam War. [6]All the names *have been carved into* ~~on~~ two black granite walls, each 200 feet long. [7]There, beside the two walls, [8]~~S~~tands a realistic sculpture of soldiers from this tragic conflict. [9]In Montgomery, Alabama, another Maya Lin sculpture. [10]~~To~~ *honors* ~~honor~~ the memory of both Dr. Martin Luther King, Jr., and those who died in the Civil Rights movement. [11]The monument that Lin designed. [12]~~It~~ is a circular black granite table. [13]Forty names *that are* engraved on the table. [14]~~Which~~ are the names of those killed during the Civil Rights movement. [15]Water flows. [16]From the center of the table. [17]~~Water~~ *It* also ~~on~~ *cascades down* a wall behind the table. [18]Engraved on the wall, *are* the words that Dr. King quoted from the Bible: ". . . until justice rolls like water and righteousness like a mighty stream." [19]~~Which~~ *The monument* creates a very powerful impact.

Finding the Subject

Every sentence has a subject and a verb which together make a complete thought. You'll need to identify the subject so that you'll know the correct verb form to match it. Chapter 9 focuses on subject-verb agreement.

As you look for subjects, keep the following tips in mind:

● In an **inverted sentence**, the verb (v) comes before the subject (s).

                                v   s

Beneath the lake's surface **swam** a **school** of tropical fish.

                  v   s   s

In the gallery **hung paintings** and **photographs** of marine life.

● The words *here* and *there* are never the subject of a sentence. In a sentence beginning with *here* or *there*, look for the subject after the verb.

            v   s

Here **sprouts** a single **blade** of grass.

          v   s   s

There **will be wildflowers** and cultivated **roses** in the community garden.

In the first example, the word *here* acts as an adverb that modifies the verb *sprouts* by indicating "where." In the next sentence, the word *there* is used as an expletive, which is a word that has no role in the grammar of the sentence except, in this case, to start it.

● The subject of a sentence is never part of a prepositional phrase.

      s

The **lack** of rain created a drought in the state. [The prepositional phrase *of rain* modifies the subject *lack*.]

● To find the subject of a question, turn the question into a statement.

      s

Are **you** the person with the windowbox? [*You* are the person with the windowbox.]

● In a command or request (an imperative sentence), the subject is understood to be *you* (the person being spoken to).

    s

[You] Turn off the garden hose.

          s

Casey, **[you]** tell Joey how to arrange the flowers.

In the second imperative sentence above, the name *Casey* is a direct address but is not the subject.

Writing Hint

Avoid overusing *there* to start sentences. It's easy to avoid this construction.

There are many flowers in Dawson's garden. There are tulips, lilacs, daffodils, and roses in bloom.

There are many kinds of flowers in Dawson's garden. Tulips, lilacs, daffodils, and roses are in bloom.

Underline the subject(s) in each of the sentences below. If the subject is understood to be *you*, write *You* at the end of the sentence.

1. In 1955, <u>Dr. Martin Luther King, Jr.</u>, gained national attention when he staged a bus boycott in Montgomery, Alabama.

2. The <u>buses</u> in Montgomery allowed African Americans to sit only at the back.

3. <u>Most</u> of the people who rode buses in Montgomery were African American.

4. <u>Dr. King</u> and his <u>neighbors</u> decided not to ride the bus.

5. When the African Americans walked to work, bus <u>companies</u> and other <u>businesses</u> suffered.

6. How many days did the <u>boycott</u> last?

7. There were <u>groups</u> of African Americans who formed carpools or stayed home.

8. The nonviolent <u>tactics</u> of the protesters were successful.

9. In December 1956, the <u>U.S. Supreme Court</u> ruled that segregation on buses was unconstitutional.

10. Read an account of the boycott in your history textbook.   You

Exercise 9 **Identifying Subjects**

Underline the subject(s) in each sentence of this school flyer. If the subject is understood to be *you*, write *You* at the beginning of the sentence.

[1]Do <u>you</u> think science is no more than memorizing facts from a textbook or doing a few mildly interesting classroom experiments? [2]You Join the troop of students already signed up to create fascinating projects for the science fair. [3]One <u>group</u> of students is planning to build its own greenhouse to grow healthy, organic foods. [4]Does the <u>idea</u> of inventing your own classroom robot sound more appealing? [5]You Discover the amazing projects you can design using nothing more than your imagination. [6]There are only a few <u>rules</u> to follow in order to submit a project for the fair. [7]In the front hall of the main building <u>you</u> will find the forms and cards to be filled out. [8]Along with our science faculty, two <u>professors</u> from the city university will judge the entries. [9]The winning <u>projects</u> will represent our school in a citywide science fair. [10]Judging from our students' inventive minds, <u>we</u> expect the science fair to generate tremendous interest.

Combining Sentences: Using Conjunctions

● A sentence with a **compound subject** has two or more subjects sharing the same verb. The subjects are joined with a conjunction.

Both Anthony **and** Hannah wrote one-act plays.

● A sentence with a **compound verb** has two or more verbs sharing the same subject. Verbs can be combined with a conjunction.

The student **wrote** the poems **and published** them.

● A **compound sentence** combines two or more simple sentences into a single sentence.

ORIGINAL   Some enjoy writing poetry. Others prefer writing stories.

COMBINED   Some enjoy writing poetry, **while** others prefer writing stories.

ORIGINAL   Teachers and students named the anthology together. Only the students published and distributed the book.

COMBINED   Teachers and students titled the anthology together, **but** only the students published and distributed the book.

● Use these three strategies to combine sentences into a compound sentence.

1. Use a comma and a conjunction to combine the sentences.

ORIGINAL   Kita's story presents a slice of history. It also provides a mystery to keep readers entertained.

COMBINED   Kita's story **not only** presents a slice of history, **but** it **also** provides a mystery to keep readers entertained.

2. Use a semicolon alone to combine the sentences.

ORIGINAL   The main character lives in South Africa. During this time, Nelson Mandela becomes the first native South African president of the country.

COMBINED   The main character lives in South Africa; during this time, Nelson Mandela becomes the first native South African president of the country.

3. Use a semicolon followed by a conjunctive adverb to combine two sentences. A comma always follows the conjunctive adverb.

ORIGINAL   The heroine experiences segregation and prejudice. She survives and lives a long, prosperous life.

COMBINED   The heroine suffers segregation and prejudice; **nevertheless,** she survives and lives a long, prosperous life.

Coordinating Conjunctions

and	or
but	so
nor	yet

Some Correlative Conjunctions

either . . . or
neither . . . nor
not only . . . but also
both . . . and
just as . . . so (too)

Some Commonly Used Conjunctive Adverbs

accordingly	meanwhile
also	moreover
besides	nevertheless
consequently	otherwise
finally	similarly
furthermore	still
however	therefore
indeed	thus
instead	whereas

Some Transitional Expressions

as a result	on the other
at last	hand
for example	otherwise
for instance	such that
in fact	then
likewise	

Exercise 10 Identifying Conjunctions

In the paragraph below, circle each conjunction. Underline each simple subject once and each verb twice.

¹Henry James (1843–1916) was born in the United States, (but) he spent most of his adult life in England. ²Brash, unsophisticated Americans (and) cultured Europeans are the main characters in his novels. ³Isabella Archer, one of his American characters, inherits a fortune (and) moves from New York to England in *Portrait of a Lady* (1881). ⁴She falls for (and) marries the unscrupulous Gilbert Osmond; (consequently) she loses her fortune to him. ⁵This (and) other novels by James are not typical love stories. ⁶Henry James' readers (not only) probe into (but also) understand characters' motives, actions, and beliefs. ⁷Because of this, James is respected as a founder of the modern psychological novel. ⁸James' *Portrait of a Lady* (and) *Wings of a Dove* were recently made into movies; (therefore,) this proves their contemporary appeal. ⁹Curiously, Henry James' brother William was also a famous writer; (however,) William wrote books on philosophy and psychology. ¹⁰William James joked that Henry was the better psychologist; (whereas,) Henry considered William the greater writer.

Exercise 11 Revising a Report

Work with a partner or small group to revise the following passage on a separate piece of paper. Look for ways to combine subjects, verbs, or simple sentences into compound subjects, compound verbs, or compound sentences.
Revised passages will vary but should avoid repetition and use conjunctions correctly.

¹The first part of the word *psychology* has a Greek origin. ²The second part of the word *psychology* also has a Greek origin. ³*Psycho* means "breath or principles of life, spirit, and mind." ⁴*Logy* means "speech or discourse." ⁵These word parts mean that human behavior is based on reasons related to the mind. ⁶These word parts point to the mind's power over people's thoughts, feelings, and actions.

⁷The ancient Greek philosopher Aristotle had a theory about human behavior. ⁸The ancient Greek philosopher Aristotle wrote a book called *De Anima* about his theory. ⁹The ancient Greek philosopher Aristotle wrote his book in the fourth century B.C. ¹⁰*De Anima* states that human behavior is ruled by the heart. ¹¹Modern texts and ideas about human behavior have been influenced by this classic work.

Mid-Chapter Review

Exercise A Identifying Subjects and Verbs

In each numbered item, underline the subject once and the verb twice. If the subject is understood to be *you*, write the word *You* after the sentence. In compound sentences, underline both verbs and both subjects.

1. Can you cope with everyday stress?

2. Here lies the key to emotional challenges.

3. Deal with daily frustrations; don't let them act like roadblocks. You; you

4. Minor failures and disappointments happen to everyone at some time.

5. A well-adjusted person explores problems and solves them one at a time.

6. What if one day everything goes wrong and seems to be backfiring?

7. You or a friend might lash out in response to frustrations.

8. Find a positive strategy to help you cope, or talk yourself out of feelings of intense stress. You; you

9. Many people revise unattainable goals or increase their efforts to reach them.

10. Fight frustration and negativity with positive coping tools. You

Exercise B Combining Sentences

On a separate sheet of paper, combine the sentences in each numbered item. You may need to change or omit words and punctuation. In your revised sentences, underline the subjects once and the verbs twice. Circle the conjunctions and the additional punctuation that you used to combine the sentences. See Answer Key for sample answers.

1. Coffee cups may appear in a George Segal sculpture. Some of his closest friends may appear in a George Segal sculpture.

2. The artist, George Segal, lives on an old chicken farm in New Jersey. He uses the henhouses as his studio.

3. In plaster, he casts the forms of everyday objects. He doesn't paint them.

4. One sculpture contains plaster molds of real people. The sculpture also includes a restaurant counter, stools, and a coffee cup.

5. A scene of plaster Holocaust victims from World War II shocks people who see this in San Francisco. A scene of plaster people on a bread line during the Great Depression saddens those who view it at the FDR Memorial in Washington, D.C.

Exercise C Writing Complete Sentences

On a separate piece of paper, rewrite the paragraphs from the magazine article below to eliminate any sentence fragments and to combine numbered items where appropriate.   Revised articles will vary.

[1]Today, Randy feels frustrated. [2]Today, Randy experiences a stressful situation. [3]Randy must deal with a situation. [4]Involving peer pressure. [5]Many students face peer pressure. [6]Peer pressure may make people feel like they need to belong. [7]Peer pressure may test a person's character. [8]Convictions, too.

[9]What would you do about peer pressure? [10]Because strategies can help you. [11]First of all. [12]Make decisions based on what you care about. [13]Spend time with those you care about. [14]You can ask questions of a group of your peers who want you to join them in an activity that seems as if it might be something you wouldn't do on your own. [15]You can express strongly. [16]Your feelings to the peer group that wants you to join it in an activity you're unsure of or you think is wrong. [17]Another person in the group might object, too. [18]That person may feel the same as you. [19]If you are uncomfortable with a group of peers. [20]Leave. [21]True friends will support your decision. [22]Not ridicule you.

Exercise D Write What You Think

Write a paragraph in response to the statement below. Support your opinion with facts, examples, and reasons. Check to make sure your paragraph contains only complete sentences, not sentence fragments.

Studies prove that smoking is bad for your health and the health of those around you. Cigarettes cause nicotine addiction and should be banned.   Answers will vary. Give students full credit if they have stated an opinion and attempted to support their opinions. They should also have written grammatically complete sentences that begin with a capital letter and end with an appropriate end punctuation mark.

Correcting Run-on Sentences

🔷 A **run-on sentence** is made up of two or more sentences that are incorrectly run together as a single sentence.

One of these five strategies may help you correct a run-on sentence.

1. Separate them. Add end punctuation and a capital letter to separate the sentences.

RUN-ON   New York City celebrated its 100th anniversary in 1998 before January 1, 1898, New York consisted only of the island of Manhattan.

CORRECTED   New York City celebrated its 100th anniversary in 1998. Before January 1, 1898, New York consisted only of the island of Manhattan.

2. Use a conjunction. Use a coordinating or correlative conjunction preceded by a comma.

RUN-ON   Brooklyn did not necessarily want to become part of New York City Manhattan wanted its neighbor within its boundaries.

CORRECTED   Brooklyn did not necessarily want to become part of New York City, **but** Manhattan wanted its neighbor within its boundaries.

3. Try a semicolon. Use a semicolon to separate two sentences.

RUN-ON   The students have to park on the street the parking lot is full.

CORRECTED   The students have to park on the street**;** the parking lot is full.

4. Add a conjunctive adverb. Use a semicolon together with a conjunctive adverb or transitional expression. (See the lists on page 111.) Be sure to put a comma after the conjunctive adverb.

RUN-ON   In the 1940s, fans in Brooklyn cheered for the Dodgers people in Manhattan supported the Yankees.

CORRECTED   In the 1940s, fans in Brooklyn cheered for the Dodgers**; on the other hand,** people in Manhattan supported the Yankees.

5. Create a clause. Turn one of the sentences into a subordinate clause.

RUN-ON   Comic strips made Fiorello LaGuardia a popular mayor in the 1930s he read comics over the radio to the children of New York.

CORRECTED   **By reading comic strips over the radio to the children of New York,** Fiorello LaGuardia became a popular mayor in the 1930s.

Editing Tip

A **fused sentence** is a run-on sentence with no punctuation. A **comma splice** is a run-on sentence with only a comma separating the sentences.

New York City had a total of forty-three newspapers in 1898, *but* only twenty-three were written in English.

Writing Hint

Vary sentence lengths. Short sentences, one after the other, sound as bad as run-on sentences.

CHOPPY
The subway car stopped. The subway car jolted. A tunnel was dark. The train raced through it.

SMOOTH
The subway car stopped, then it jolted forward as the train raced through a dark tunnel.

■ **See Grammar, Lessons 7.1–7.5, for more information on subordinate clauses.**

Exercise 12 Correcting Run-on Sentences

On a separate piece of paper, rewrite each run-on sentence as one or more well-written sentences. Use a variety of strategies. See Answer Key for sample answers.

1. Giovanni da Verrazano and Henry Hudson explored the waterways around New York in 1524 and 1609, Verrazano sailed for the French and Hudson for the Dutch.

2. In 1623, European settlers traveled to New York with the Dutch West India Company they farmed on the lower end of the island of Manhattan.

3. Many newcomers from England came to New York they were invited by the Dutch West India Company.

4. New York, called New Amsterdam by the Dutch, came under English control in 1664, Dutch influence on the island of Manhattan remained strong.

5. The colors of the Dutch flag are the colors of today's New York City flag, the Dutch word for *farm—Bowery—*is the name of a section in Manhattan.

6. New York City became the first capital for the nation George Washington worshiped in Manhattan's St. Paul's Chapel.

7. By the 1870s, William M. ("Boss") Tweed firmly controlled politics in New York his power came from political corruption.

8. *The New York Times* exposed political scandals in 1871, corrupt Boss Tweed spent the next seven years in and out of jail, where he died in 1878.

Exercise 13 Editing a Report

With a partner or in a small group, correct all of the run-on sentences and fragments in this report. Use a variety of strategies, and write your revisions on a separate piece of paper.

[1]Walt Whitman is a famous nineteenth-century American poet, he is also a beloved citizen of New York City. [2]That he was born on Long Island. he [3]Eventually Whitman became the editor of the *Daily Eagle*, a Brooklyn newspaper, poetry also interested him. [4]Because he advocated an antislavery and then position. [5]Whitman lost his job with the newspaper he began to work on a however, group of unusual poems. [6]Whitman published *Leaves of Grass* himself in 1847, the book it did not receive an enthusiastic reception from the reading public. [7]He wrote and a preface anointing himself as the voice of the common people. [8]Today, no one would disagree; most people would consider him a major voice of the American not only experience in the years surrounding the Civil War and beyond. [9]He wrote about but individual pleasures in life he also wrote about President Lincoln after his Although assassination and about different regions of the United States. [10]He may have begun his life as a common man, Walt Whitman became an uncommonly keen observer of our country through his work.

Direct and Indirect Objects

In this lesson, you'll review two kinds of objects: direct objects and indirect objects. Both of these appear in the predicate of a sentence.

🦪 A **direct object** (DO) is a noun or pronoun that receives the action of an action verb. A direct object answers the question *whom* or *what* following the verb.

> DO
> A complete revolution of the Earth around the sun takes a **year**.
> [*Year* answers the question *takes what*.]

> DO
> Mr. Arnold asked **us** how we celebrate the New Year. [*Us* answers the question *asked whom*.]

Not all verbs take objects. When you consider action verbs and linking verbs (see Lesson 4.3), only action verbs take objects. An action verb that takes an object is a **transitive verb**. A verb that doesn't take an object is an **intransitive verb**.

🦪 An **indirect object** (IO) is a noun or pronoun that answers the question *to whom* or *for whom* or *to what* or *for what* following an action verb.

Sentences may have direct objects without indirect objects, but they never have an indirect object without a direct object. Also, the indirect object always appears before the direct object.

> IO   DO
> Babette will hand the **teacher** the **report** on Wednesday.
> [Will hand—*to whom?*—the teacher. *Teacher* is the indirect object; *report* is the direct object.]

> IO   IO   DO
> The reporter gave **John** and **me** a **tour** of the newspaper.
> [Gave—*to whom?*—John and me. Gave—*what?*—a tour. *John* and *me* are the indirect objects; *tour* is the direct object.]

Two sentences may express the same meaning, but one may contain an indirect object while the other contains a prepositional phrase. Neither direct nor indirect objects ever appear in prepositional phrases.

> IO   IO   DO   DO
> Give **Eli** and **me** a **notebook** and a **pen**.

> DO   DO
> Give a **notebook** and a **pen** to Eli and me.
> [*To Eli and me* is a prepositional phrase.]

Enriching Your Vocabulary

The adjective *scrupulous* comes from the Latin word *scrupulosus* and means "conscientiously honest." A bandit might be considered *unscrupulous*. (See Exercise 16.)

Step by Step

Finding Direct and Indirect Objects

To find a direct object:

1. Find the action verb.

2. Ask the question *whom* or *what* after the action verb.

To find an indirect object:

1. Find the action verb.

2. Find the direct object.

3. Ask the question *to* or *for whom* or *to* or *for what* after the action verb.

Exercise 14 Identifying Direct and Indirect Objects

For each sentence from the following product advertisements, write *IO* over an indirect object and *DO* over a direct object. **Hint:** Some direct objects or indirect objects in these sentences may be compound.

1. Wipe & Swipe washes away every speck of dirt.
 DO over "speck"

2. Give yourself the gift of gab with Talk Back software.
 IO over "yourself", **DO** over "gift"

3. Students love the ease of ABC Computers.
 DO over "ease"

4. A swarm of bees can't make honey as sweet as we make Taste O'Honey.
 DO over "honey", **DO** over "Taste O'Honey"

5. You can take us for a ride on your new Olympic exercycle.
 DO over "us"

6. We'll show you the money if you show us a dead Eterno battery.
 IO over "you", **DO** over "money", **IO** over "us", **DO** over "battery"

7. It takes only three minutes for Red Alert Security Systems to respond to our home alarm.
 DO over "minutes"

8. Face Off gel makes your complexion sparkle.
 DO over "complexion"

9. Visit us just one time, and you'll discover a paradise on Earth.
 DO over "us", **DO** over "paradise"

10. Gather one and all for after-school fun and food at Ben's Border Cafe.
 DO over "one", **DO** over "all"

Exercise 15 Writing with Direct and Indirect Objects

With a partner or in a small group, write a paragraph-length advertisement that might be read on the radio. The product or service may be real or made up. Write *DO* over each direct object and *IO* over each indirect object in your paragraph. **Remember:** Don't confuse objects of prepositions in prepositional phrases with indirect objects. Write your advertisement on a separate piece of paper and compare your work with that of other groups of classmates.
Students' advertisements will vary. Direct and indirect objects should be marked correctly.

Exercise 16 Write What You Think

Write a paragraph in response to the statement below. Support your opinion with facts and examples.

The Federal Trade Commission should fine advertisers who make false claims about their products. The fine should equal three times the annual sales of the product to discourage this kind of unscrupulous business practice.

Answers will vary. Give students full credit if they have stated an opinion and attempted to support their opinions. They should also have written grammatically complete sentences that begin with a capital letter and end with an appropriate end punctuation mark.

Predicate Nominatives and Predicate Adjectives

Sometimes, a sentence is incomplete even though it includes a subject (s) and a verb (v).

S   V   S   S   V   S   V

That music sounds. You and I will be. The singer in the band is.

- A **linking verb** needs a **subject complement**—a noun (N) or an adjective (ADJ)—in order to express a complete thought. The verbs *sounds*, *be*, and *is* are some linking verbs.

                ADJ   N

That music sounds **loud**.   You and I will be **friends**.

Subject complements fall into one of two categories—**predicate nominatives** or **predicate adjectives**.

- A **predicate nominative** (PN) is a noun or pronoun that follows a linking verb (LV) and renames or identifies it.

       S   LV   PN

The lead singer in the band is **José Luis**. [*José Luis* is a proper noun that renames the subject *singer*.]

       S   LV PN

The salesperson who can help you is **she**. [*She* is a pronoun that identifies the subject *salesperson*.]

- A **predicate adjective** (PA) is an adjective that follows a linking verb and modifies or describes the subject.

       S   S   LV   PA

The fiddler and the accordion player seem **upbeat**. [The adjective *upbeat* modifies the subjects *fiddler* and *accordion player*.]

        S   LV   PA   PA

Will the CD become **warped** or **scratched**? [The adjectives *warped* and *scratched* modify the subject *CD*.]

■ For more about linking verbs, see **Grammar**, Lesson 4.3.

Editing Tip

In formal speech and writing, a pronoun used as a subject complement takes the subjective case. However, in informal usage, most people consider the object case acceptable. For example, the correct answer to the question, "Who's there?" is: "It is *I*." [*I* is a subjective case pronoun.] But in friendly conversations, people commonly answer, "It's *me*." [*Me* is an objective case pronoun.] See Chapter 10 for more on pronouns.

Exercise 17   Identifying Subject Complements

Underline every predicate nominative and predicate adjective in the sentences below. In the space provided, write *PN* for predicate nominative or *PA* for predicate adjective.

__PN__   1. One of the most respected people in the music world is Quincy Jones.

__PA__   2. To this day, he seems excited about the subject of rock 'n' roll.

<u> PN </u> 3. Early in his career, Quincy Jones was a <u>musician</u>.

<u> PA </u> 4. As an African American on band tours, he often looked <u>angry</u> when confronted with prejudice and segregation.

<u> PN </u> 5. In the 1950s, the most celebrated people in pop music were <u>African Americans</u> and <u>Elvis</u>.

<u> PN </u> 6. Jones became the first African American record <u>producer</u>.

<u> PA </u> 7. His work as a producer seemed <u>strange</u> but <u>exciting</u> to him.

<u> PA </u> 8. In the early 1960s, it seemed <u>improbable</u> that any foreign band would top Americans on the charts.

<u> PN </u> 9. Quincy Jones was a <u>fan</u> of the Beatles and the Rolling Stones before their first American tours.

<u> PN </u> 10. For Quincy Jones, rock 'n' roll remains the quintessential <u>expression</u> of human feelings.

Working Together

Exercise 18 **Writing With Predicate Nominatives and Predicate Adjectives**

With a partner or in a small group, use the sentences below to help you write with subject complements. If a complement you write is a predicate nominative, write *PN* above it. If the complement you write is a predicate adjective, write *PA* above it.   Answers will vary. Sample answers given.

[1]Music you listen to too often may grow ____PA____ <u>monotonous</u>. [2]Do you want to solve this problem? [3]Here is our ____PN____ <u>suggestion</u>. [4]Exchange CDs among your group of friends. [5]Different CDs and cassettes may sound ____PA____ <u>refreshing</u>. [6]Used CDs and tapes are often ____PA____ <u>undamaged</u>. [7]Now your music tastes will look ____PA____ <u>expansive</u>. [8]Your music collection will become ____PA____ <u>dynamic</u> and ____PA____ <u>broad</u>. [9]This may all seem ____PA____ <u>idealistic</u>. [10]Do not grow ____PA____ <u>overwhelmed</u>, please. [11]As your music experience expands, your thoughts will grow ____PA____ <u>broad</u>. [12]Sharing music will now be ____PA____ <u>routine</u> and ____PA____ <u>customary</u>.

Answers will vary. Give students full credit if they have stated an opinion and attempted to support their opinions. They should also have written grammatically complete sentences that begin with a capital letter and end with an appropriate end punctuation mark.

Exercise 19 **Write What You Think**

Write a paragraph in response to the statement below. Support your opinion with facts, reasons, and examples.

Some contemporary music lyrics call on listeners to commit crimes, brutalize women, and use obscenities. CDs that advocate such antisocial behavior and violent acts should be censored or banned.

Object Complements

Certain kinds of action verbs require more than just a direct object to make a sentence complete.

▶ An **object complement** (OC) is a noun, pronoun, or adjective that completes the meaning of a direct object.

**Some Synonyms for
Make and Consider**

appoint	judge
call	name
choose	paint
cut	sweep
elect	think
find	

        S   V   DO   OC
The mole made the burrow **deep**. [*Deep* is an object complement that describes *burrow*, the direct object.]

Only sentences with the verbs *make* and *consider* (along with their synonyms) take object complements.

    S   V   DO   OC
We appointed Mirna **editor** of the school paper. [*Editor* is an object complement that completes the meaning of the direct object, *Mirna*.]

Exercise 20 · Identifying Object Complements

Underline each object complement in the paragraph below. Draw an arrow from the object complement to the direct object it identifies or describes. **Hint:** Two sentences do not contain object complements. **Remember:** Object complements only appear in sentences that use the verbs *make*, *consider*, or their synonyms. Don't consider phrases or clauses to be object complements.

¹Seen from a distance, some bird watchers consider the white ibis a <u>snow goose</u>. ²Flocks of white ibises find fish <u>abundant</u> in shallow water. ³The many marshes of Texas make an appealing habitat for these birds. ⁴Recently, some glossy ibises from the Atlantic Ocean or Eastern Gulf Coast made Texas their <u>home</u>, also. ⁵Did you know that ancient Egyptians thought ibises <u>sacred</u>? ⁶The word *Ibis* names a divine being in the Egyptian language. ⁷Why do others consider these birds <u>special</u>? ⁸For many, these creatures have been made images both <u>exotic</u> and <u>beautiful</u>. ⁹Spot a flock of ibises anywhere, and you'll make the dazzling memory <u>yours</u> forever.

Revising and Editing Worksheet

Revise the following paragraphs to eliminate sentence fragments, run-on sentences, and wordiness. Make any other changes you think will improve the paragraph. **Hint:** Watch out for other errors, including using the wrong case pronouns and incorrect spelling.

[1]If members of the International World Calendar Association (IWCA) had their ~~weigh~~ [way]. [2]Every date in the year would fall on the same day of the month[,] ~~each year.~~ [Each year,] [3]The New Year would be celebrated every Sunday, January 1.

[4]To this day, the Chinese Calendar[,] ~~does not consider January 1 New Year's Day.~~ [5]The Jewish Calendar[,] ~~does not consider January 1 New Year's Day,~~ [and] the Indian Calendar doe~~s~~ not consider January 1 [to be] New Year's Day. [6]There are other reasons to consider[,] ~~to~~ [too]. [7]The American colonies celebrated New Year's Day in March until 1752. [8]To the colonists[, who were farmers,] ~~March seemed the best time of year for celebration. [9]The colonists were farmers.~~ [10]Planting time seemed to be the best time of the year for a celebration of the New Year.

[11]There are 365 days, 5 hours, 48 minutes, and 46 seconds in a year. [12]How do you divide[?] [13]This amount of time evenly[?] [14]What determines the length of a week or month[?] [15]Julius caesar[, the emperor of Rome,] developed a new calendar[.] [and] [16]~~Julius caesar was dictator of Rome; Julius caesar~~ corrected earlier Roman calendars. [17]The Julian calendar has twelve months[; consequently,] [18]Our calendar has twelve months[, too] [Although] [19]Both calendars mark the New Year on January 1[.] [20]~~But~~ the Julian Calendar doesn't add up[, because] it gives every fourth year an extra day[. In addition,] ~~and~~ this original calendar needs 445 days in a year to correct earlier errors in counting the time it takes the earth to revolve around the sun.

[21]The calendar [that] we use[.] [22]~~It~~ is named after Pope Gregory XIII[.] [23]The ~~calender is a~~ Gregorian calendar, ~~it was~~ invented by astronomers[,] ~~and it~~ dropped ten days [between] ~~from~~ October 5 [and] ~~to~~ October 15 in 1582[. in order] [24]To fix an error from earlier calendars. [25]After 1582, the Gregorian Calendar was adopted in Europe[. and] [26]Today, it is used all over the world.

Chapter Review

Visit us at
www.sadlier-oxford.com
Internet

Exercise A Identifying Subjects and Verbs

In each sentence, underline the subject (simple subject) once and the verb twice. If the subject is understood to be *you*, write *You* following the sentence.

1. As a junior, you or a friend may become interested in driving a car.

2. On streets and roads, heed the sign that says, "Student Driver."   You

3. Teenagers in suburbs long to get out on their own in a car.

4. City dwellers, though, enjoy the benefits of public transportation.

5. Nevertheless, students should be trained in the rules of the road.

Exercise B Identifying Complements

Underline the direct and indirect objects, the subject complements, and the object complements in the sentences below. Above each, write *DO* (direct object), *IO* (indirect object), *OC* (object complement), *PA* (predicate adjective), or *PN* (predicate nominative).

1. The work of William Shakespeare remains a mystery for many readers.

2. An English teacher once showed them a movie version of *Romeo and Juliet*.

3. The film of this play seemed understandable and dramatic.

4. The drama coach gave the class instructions on how to read the poetry of Shakespeare, one sentence at a time.

5. Without movie versions, our class considered these plays boring at first.

6. "Movies gave Vicky and me a new insight into Shakespeare," Winston confessed.

Exercise C Combining Sentences

On a separate piece of paper, combine the sentences or sentence fragments in each numbered item into one complete sentence. You may change, add, or omit words and punctuation.   See Answer Key.

1. Fairy tales are popular literature for children. Nursery rhymes are popular literature for children.

2. Are you familiar with the nursery rhymes of Elizabeth, or Mother Goose? Mother Goose is a real person from Boston, Massachusetts.

3. She married Isaac Goose. She became the stepmother of his ten children.

4. Because a son-in-law used the name Mother Goose. The son-in-law wrote a collection called *Mother Goose's Melodies for Children* in 1719.

5. Before the appearance of a real Mother Goose in Boston. There lived in France a writer named Charles Perrault. Charles Perrault wrote children's stories.

6. *The Tales of My Mother Goose* in 1697. The title of a collection of popular stories by the French writer, Charles Perrault.

7. That he borrowed the name *Frau Gosen* from German folklore. It is unknown. It is believed.

8. Some folklorists believe that Perrault is not the same as the German Mother Goose. Others feel sure the authors are one and the same.

Exercise D **Revising Paragraphs**

Revise the following paragraph to eliminate sentence fragments, run-on sentences, and wordiness. Make any other changes you think will improve the writing. Revised paragraphs will vary.

¹I believe that books are superior entertainment to movies, Wilson completely disagrees with me. ²Since he likes movies. ³I read a book about the slave revolt on the ship *Amistad*. ⁴I saw a movie by Steven Spielberg about the slave revolt on the ship *Amistad*. ⁵Although I liked the book slightly more than the movie because of its greater wealth of details. ⁶Wilson read a book version of *Star Wars*. ⁷The movie, he argued, was far superior to any written version of this science fiction tale. ⁸The special effects of *Star Wars* can't be translated easily with words alone, they dazzle the viewer. ⁹That is Wilson's argument. ¹⁰With which I agree, at least about *Star Wars*. ¹¹Someday I will write a detailed novel, someday Wilson will direct the movie. ¹²We will let professional critics decide which version is better.

Exercise E **Write What You Think**

Write one or two paragraphs in response to the statement below. Support your opinion with facts, reasons, and examples.

Only books with lots of action make good movies. Filmmakers should make action-packed movies rather than intellectual or true-life stories.

Answers will vary. Give students full credit if they have stated an opinion and attempted to support their opinions. They should also have written grammatically complete sentences that begin with a capital letter and end with an appropriate end punctuation mark.

Phrases

STUDENT WRITING
Narrative Essay

Sunday Soccer Clinic
By Rudy Lewis and Steve Gangemi
high school students, Lawrenceville, New Jersey

Soccer is the most popular sport on earth, and Sunday is the most uneventful day in Lawrenceville. Combine these two and you get Sunday Soccer, arguably the most inspirational and valuable community-service project on campus. When we first laced on our cleats and headed to the field on a warm autumn day, we were unaware of the impact we were about to have on the lives of forty Trenton children. The first day was full of surprises. The ragtag team of children arrived clothed in anything from dresses and sandals to jeans and boots. Many of the children were unfamiliar with the game of soccer. Few could kick the ball well, and no one knew the rules. Each player was determined to win, and everyone wanted to be a star, but no one realized that the only way to win was through teamwork. As the weeks passed, the skills of the children rapidly improved, and they began to function as a team. By the end of the session, they had a real grasp of the game. But their learning experience went beyond the field. They learned skills which they were able to apply to their lives at home.

Cooperation and communication are key to any group effort. Although it was a valuable experience for the children, it was equally rewarding for us coaches. Sunday Soccer was more than just fulfilling the volunteer requirement; it was also an experience that allowed us to partake in the players' growth, not only as soccer players, but also as individuals. Because we knew that the athletic facilities the children were offered at Lawrenceville would have been otherwise unavailable to them, it was a great pleasure for us to allow them this experience. We also learned just how lucky we are to have the amenities and opportunities that we as students here have. Overall, it was a truly rewarding experience for both the volunteers and the children.

The autobiographical incident above is effective because the authors tell the reader not only what happened but also why those events were significant to them. The reader understands what impact the Sunday Soccer Clinic had on both the children and the coaches.

The essay above is also effective because the authors use phrases to describe and to explain, as well as to combine sentences. As you work on the exercises in this chapter, you will learn to use phrases to improve your own writing.

Allow time for students to discuss the student writing. Suggest that they identify its strengths and propose possible improvements. Use the model to introduce the concepts in the chapter.

Adjective and Adverb Phrases

🐚 A **prepositional phrase** always begins with a preposition and ends with an object (a noun or pronoun).

The modifiers between the preposition and its object(s) are part of the prepositional phrase. The prepositional phrase may have a compound object, two or more objects joined by a conjunction such as *and* or *or*.

PREP   OBJ   ADJ   OBJ   PREP OBJ   OBJ
beside the umbrella and red blanket   for him and me

In the sentence below, each of the three prepositional phrases adds information to the sentence by modifying another word in the sentence.

The students **in the last row** moved **to the first row of the auditorium**.

🐚 An **adjective phrase** is a prepositional phrase that modifies a noun or pronoun in a sentence and answers the questions *Which one?* or *What kind?*

The whale **with the huge blow hole** is a female.

🐚 An **adverb phrase** is a prepositional phrase that modifies a verb, an adjective, or another adverb, and it answers the questions *When? How? Where?* or *To what extent?*

The seagull flew **against the wind**.

Please grill the salmon **for ten minutes**.

Some words function as both prepositions and adverbs, depending on how they are used in a sentence. In the first sentence below, the word *under* is used as a preposition. In the second sentence, the word *under* stands alone and acts as an adverb. **Remember:** Prepositions never stand alone.

PREP
Did the surfboard go **under** the wave?

ADV
Did the diver go **under**?

Writing Hint

Do you "stand *in* line" or "stand *on* line"? It depends on the region of the United States where you live.

For most prepositions, however, certain choices are more appropriate than others.

write *in* pencil/write *with* pencil

dance *with* the music/dance *to* the music

reach *to* the stars/reach *for* the stars

Editing Tip

It's never wrong to use a comma after one introductory prepositional phrase, and you *should* use a comma after two or more. However, don't use a comma when an introductory prepositional phrase immediately precedes a verb.

INCORRECT
In the front closet, is the old TV set.

Underline each prepositional phrase in the sentences below, and draw an arrow to the word each phrase modifies. Label the phrase *ADJ* for adjective phrase and *ADV* for adverb phrase.

■ See
Grammar,
Lesson 4.7, for
a list of
prepositions.

1. The waters of the Gulf Stream begin in Florida. ADJ; ADV

2. The Gulf Stream is unusually warm for ocean water. ADJ

3. The width of the Gulf Stream is about fifty miles. ADJ; ADV

4. Within the Atlantic Ocean, it flows like a river toward Europe and Africa. ADV; ADV; ADV

5. The current flows north from Florida toward Maine. ADV; ADV

6. The Gulf Stream sweeps through the wide Sargasso Sea, located around the Bermuda Islands. ADV; ADV

7. The Sargasso Sea is strewn with seaweed floating on its surface. ADV; ADV

8. The seaweed in the Saragasso Sea is called sargassum. ADJ

9. Sargassum is found in warm seas and has special branches with berry-like air sacs. ADV; ADJ

10. When Christopher Columbus crossed the Sargasso Sea, he believed he was near land. ADV

11. However, sargassum in the Gulf Stream does not usually float near land. ADJ; ADV

12. Early navigators feared becoming entangled in the seaweed. ADV

13. Jean Rhys wrote *Wide Sargasso Sea* after moving to England from the West Indies. ADV; ADV

14. This novel is based on the English classic *Jane Eyre*. ADV

15. Both novels have been made into movies. ADV

Appositives and Appositive Phrases

Imagine that a friend tells you about someone who participated in a national track competition. The friend might communicate one piece of information about that person, then add another detail.

> Lara competed in a national track competition. Lara is the new student in our math class.

Here's a way to combine these ideas into one sentence.

> Lara, the new student in our math class, competed in a national track competition.

◖ An **appositive** is a noun or pronoun that identifies or explains the noun or pronoun that precedes or follows it. An **appositive phrase** is made up of an appositive and all of its modifiers.

In the combined sentence above, the phrase *the new student in our math class* is an appositive phrase. The noun *student* is an appositive that identifies *Lara*.

Essential appositives provide information essential to understanding the sentence.

Do not use commas to set off essential appositives.

> My cousin **Jason** broke the school record in the long jump.
> The California track clubs **the Jaguars and the Coasters** shared first place.

Nonessential appositives provide extra information that is not essential to understanding the sentence.

Use commas to set off nonessential appositives.

> Olga, **the youngest competitor,** took third place in the 100-meter dash.
> Denver, **a city at a high altitude,** hosted a national junior track event.

Exercise 2 Combining Sentences with Appositives

On a separate piece of paper, combine these sentences using appositives or appositive phrases. **Remember:** Use commas to set off nonessential appositives.   See Answer Key.

> EXAMPLE   Carl Lewis was a multitalented track star. Carl Lewis competed in various events.
>
> *Carl Lewis, a multitalented track star, competed in various events.*

1. Carl Lewis won many gold medals in Olympic track events. Carl Lewis was an extraordinary runner.

2. His younger sister also competed as a long jumper. His sister is Carol.

3. He was born in Birmingham, Alabama, in 1961. Birmingham is an industrial city.

4. At his college, he came to national attention. Carl Lewis attended the University of Houston.

5. He earned three medals at the 1983 World Championships in Helsinki. All his medals were gold.

6. In 1984, Carl Lewis broke the record held by Jesse Owens. Jesse Owens was the previous greatest runner in U.S. history.

7. Carl Lewis's 1984 Olympic record has not yet been surpassed. He holds the Olympic record of four gold medals.

8. He earned his four gold medals in three solo events and in the relay. The relay is a four-man race.

9. In his last competition, he won another gold medal. His final competition was the 1996 Atlanta Olympics.

10. The gold medalist was thirty-five years old then. Thirty-five is an advanced age for an Olympian.

Exercise 3 Writing Sentences with Appositives

On a separate piece of paper, write five sentences about a hobby or interest you have, such as playing a sport, painting, gardening, caring for a pet, or playing a musical instrument. Write from your own experience as either a participant or an observer. Try to provide details, either essential or nonessential, as appositives or appositive phrases. After you finish writing, underline any appositives or appositive phrases you included. Students' sentences will vary.

Exercise 4 Write What You Think

On a separate piece of paper, write a few paragraphs in response to the following statement:

The Olympic Games should be abolished because the competition places a premium on winning at all costs.

Support your opinion with facts and examples.
Answers will vary. Give students full credit if they have stated an opinion and attempted to support their opinions. Look for grammatically complete sentences that begin with a capital letter and end with an appropriate end punctuation mark.

Participles and Participial Phrases

A **verbal** is a verb form that functions as another part of speech. There are three kinds of verbals: participles, infinitives, and gerunds.

● A **participle** is a verb form that acts as an adjective by modifying a noun or a pronoun.

You can use a **present participle**, which ends in *-ing*, or a **past participle**, which usually ends in either *-d* or *-ed*. Irregular verbs have irregular participles. [See the list of common irregular verbs in Lessons 8.2 and 8.3.]

Don't confuse a participle with a verb phrase. A verb phrase is formed by placing a helping verb before a participle. It functions as a verb in a sentence. A participle standing alone acts as an adjective in a sentence.

VERB PHRASE	The fire **is burning** slowly.
PARTICIPLE	The **burning** building is collapsing.
VERB PHRASE	The class **has collected** donations for uniforms.
PARTICIPLE	José has the **collected** works of Shakespeare.

● A **participial phrase** is made up of a participle and all of its modifiers. The whole phrase acts as an adjective.
Cheering loudly, we greeted the singer. [modifies *we*]
One teenager held a photograph **signed by the singer herself**. [modifies *photograph*]

P.S. Participles and participial phrases sound more complicated than they are in reality. You use participles and participial phrases naturally when you're talking.

■ See Usage, Lessons 11.4 and 11.5, for more about misplaced or dangling modifiers in a sentence.

Writing Hint

Place a participial phrase close to the word it modifies. Otherwise, you may say something you don't mean.

ORIGINAL
I found a picture of Michael Jackson **surfing the Internet**.

REVISED
Surfing the Internet, I found a picture of Michael Jackson.

Exercise 5 Identifying Participles and Participial Phrases

Underline the participles and participial phrases in each sentence. Draw an arrow to the noun or pronoun it modifies. **Hint:** A sentence may contain more than one participle or participial phrase. Be sure to underline prepositional phrases that are part of the participial phrase.

EXAMPLE Tom saw two murals by Marc Chagall hanging in the Metropolitan Opera House.

1. Marc Chagall painted scenes based on Jewish culture.

2. The talented Chagall first took painting lessons in Vitebsk, Russia.

3. He moved to St. Petersburg, a city filled with artists.

4. He moved to Paris, known as the art center of Europe.

5. In Paris, he missed his intriguing girlfriend, Bella.

6. During a visit home in 1914, the renowned Chagall was prevented from returning to Paris with his bride, Bella, by the outbreak of World War I.

7. Heading the new department of fine arts, Chagall stayed in Vitebsk after the Russian Revolution of 1917.

8. A frustrated Chagall and his wife, Bella, left Russia for good in 1922.

9. An admiring world audience hailed Chagall's paintings depicting dreamlike scenes of life in Vitebsk.

10. Floating animals and people often appear upside down in his paintings.

Exercise 6 Writing with Participial Phrases

On a separate piece of paper, create complete sentences that contain each of the participial phrases below. Place the participial phrase as close as possible to the word it modifies. Share your sentences with your writing group to check that you have not used the phrases as verbs. Students' sentences will vary.

1. shocked by the news

2. satisfying everyone

3. diving for the ground ball

4. fascinated by the movie

5. established long ago

6. cleaning his room

7. stopped in traffic

8. changing trains

Exercise 7 Writing with Participles

Rewrite the art review below by combining sentences and using participles to streamline the narrative. Students' paragraphs will vary.

¹The paintings of artist Elena Gonzales were exhibited this week. ²They were exhibited at the Windswept Gallery. ³They were stunning. ⁴Many of the canvases feature the ocean and the shore. ⁵People are playing in the water. ⁶They are playing on the sand. ⁷Details are striking in the paintings. ⁸She shows every wave, rock, or object on the Maine beach where she lives. ⁹The artist paints driftwood. ¹⁰The artist pays careful attention to every detail. ¹¹*Drifting Driftwood* is her favorite painting. ¹²That painting earned first place in an art show last year. ¹³This reviewer appreciated them. ¹⁴Anyone who loves the sea will treasure these paintings. ¹⁵Directions to the gallery are simple. ¹⁶The gallery has a bright red awning. ¹⁷It is located between Second and Third Streets off Main.

Mid-Chapter Review

Exercise A Identifying Adjective and Adverb Phrases

On a separate piece of paper, underline every prepositional phrase in the sentences below. Write *ADJ* for a prepositional phrase acting as an adjective or *ADV* for a prepositional phrase acting as an adverb. Draw an arrow to the word each phrase modifies. **Hint:** Some prepositional phrases run together.

1. Whitney wanted a job with Frontrunners, a sporting-goods store.   ADJ

2. The store placed help wanted flyers in its display window.   ADV

3. Whitney was looking for business experience and some income.   ADV

4. In spite of the cost of getting a business degree, Whitney was planning on a career in business.   ADV; ADJ; ADV; ADJ

5. Her parents stood behind her decision.   ADV

6. Whitney did not work beyond 7 P.M., so she could still help around the house.   ADV; ADV

Exercise B Writing with Appositives

On a separate piece of paper, combine the two sentences in each numbered item using an appositive phrase. **Remember:** Nonessential appositives that provide extra information are set off by commas.   See Answer Key.

1. Fin de Siècle means "end of the century." It is a French term.

2. Did you know that Juanita became the restaurant host yesterday? She was the new maître d'hotel.

3. Our debate team captain helps us feel a positive group spirit that the French call *esprit de corps*. Germaine is our captain.

4. Eureka is named after a Greek word that means "I have found it." A town in California is named Eureka.

5. Eating outside at the Italian restaurant is not unusual since *alfresco* means "outdoors" in Italian. We ate outside at Cafe Alfresco.

6. *Canoa* became the English word *canoe*. *Canoa* is a Haitian word.

Exercise C Identifying Participles and Participial Phrases

Underline the participles and participial phrases you find in the sentences on the following page. Draw an arrow to the word each participle or participial phrase modifies. **Hint:** Don't confuse a verb phrase with a participle acting as a modifier.

1. Have you seen the Declaration of Independence exhibited at the Smithsonian Institution?

2. This fascinating document proclaimed the separation of the American colonies from Great Britain.

3. On June 11, 1776, members of the Second Continental Congress drafted a working declaration.

4. Thomas Jefferson authored the draft, and Benjamin Franklin made some needed revisions.

5. The completed Declaration was adopted on July 4, the date celebrated as Independence Day.

6. An earlier version predating the famous Declaration was passed on July 2, 1776.

7. The ratified version of the Declaration of Independence called for nationhood and contained the ideas of an ideal government.

8. Borrowing from the philosophers John Locke and Jean Jacques Rousseau, the Declaration embodies the idea of the people's natural rights.

Exercise D **Revising a Paragraph**

Revise the following paragraph. Try to combine sentences and add your own specific details. Correct mistakes you find, such as fragments. Try to use at least one prepositional phrase, one appositive phrase, and one participial phrase in your revision.   Students' revisions may vary.

   [1]Mario stood on line to see a movie. [2]Rochelle was Mario's girlfriend. [3]Rochelle stood on line with Mario. [4]It was raining. [5]All of a sudden, a man in front of Mario started coughing uncontrollably. [6]Rochelle was wondering what she could do to help. [7]The man suddenly fell down. [8]The ground was cold and wet. [9]The man's girlfriend said something was caught in his throat. [10]Rochelle knew the Heimlich maneuver. [11]This maneuver is used to dislodge things stuck in a person's throat. [12]She performed the maneuver. [13]The man stopped coughing. [14]The man felt better.

Exercise E **Write What You Think**

On a separate piece of paper, write a few paragraphs in response to the statement below. Support your opinion with facts and examples.

   Courses in first aid and life-saving procedures such as CPR (cardiopulmonary resuscitation) should be required in every high school in the United States.
   Answers will vary. Give students full credit if they have stated an opinion and attempted to support their opinions. Look for grammatically complete sentences that begin with a capital letter and end with an appropriate end punctuation mark.

Gerunds and Gerund Phrases

Gerunds, like participles, are verb forms. But participles act as adjectives, and gerunds act as nouns in a sentence.

🖎 A **gerund**, ending in *-ing*, is a verb form that acts as a noun.

Whatever a noun can do, a gerund can do, too.
>**Mining** is an occupation. [subject]
>Bob's occupation was **mining**. [predicate nominative]
>Who has attempted **mining** for gold? [direct object]
>Have you given **mining** a try as a possible career? [indirect object]
>Nancy likes to read about **mining**. [object of a preposition]

🖎 A **gerund phrase** is made up of a gerund and all of its modifiers and complements. The entire phrase functions as a noun. **Remember:** Complements, such as direct and indirect objects, are words that complete the meaning of a verb.
>**Being a forty-niner** was an important role in California history. [subject]
>**Panning for gold** seldom brought the forty-niners real wealth. [subject]
>Photographers enjoyed **taking pictures of forty-niners**. [direct object]
>Forty-niners ended a day by **weighing their gold nuggets**. [object of a preposition]

Editing Tip

Nouns and pronouns that modify a gerund are possessive.

INCORRECT
The **chalks** screeching disturbed the class.

REVISED
The **chalk's** screeching disturbed the class.

INCORRECT
We applauded **him** singing.

REVISED
We applauded **his** singing.

Enriching Your Vocabulary

The word *intriguing*, as used in Exercise 9, has the same Latin root as *intricate*. The root, *intricare*, means "to entangle, or embarrass." Thus, an *intriguing* personality is one that incites curiosity and fascination.

Exercise 8 Identifying Gerunds and Gerund Phrases

Underline every gerund and gerund phrase in the sentences below. A gerund phrase may contain one or more prepositional phrases. Count these as part of the gerund phrase. **Remember:** Not every *-ing* word is a gerund; it must function as a noun in the sentence to be considered a gerund.

1. Sonya enjoyed <u>studying photographs</u> at the Oakland Museum one day.

2. <u>Looking at the exhibition of gold miners</u> was both fascinating and surprising.

3. <u>Taking photographs of forty-niners</u> became part of the gold rush experience.

4. One forty-niner, James Woolsey, is pictured <u>holding a huge gold nugget</u>.

5. By <u>paying three or four dollars</u>, Woolsey had his picture taken.

6. The Oakland Museum encouraged <u>reading about the photographs</u> by <u>placing tags beside them</u>.

7. By posing for these photographs, the forty-niners gave themselves dignity.

8. Documenting the presence of Asian miners in California is an 1851 photograph by Isaac Wallace Baker.

9. William Shew promoted photographing miners with their gold in front of the steamers that waited to take them home.

10. By observing photographs of Spanish-Californian miners, Sonya understood her ancestors' past.

 Exercise 9 **Writing Sentences with Gerunds and Gerund Phrases**

On a separate piece of paper, write questions and answers for an interview about future career plans. First, have one partner or a small group write questions about the future careers and activities students might pursue after graduation. Then, have the other partner or small group answer these questions in complete sentences. Include a gerund or gerund phrase in the sentence that represents each question and/or its accompanying answer (see sample below).

Q: Would working in advertising interest you?

A: As a person with artistic ability, I'd consider working in advertising a very intriguing career. Answers will vary.

Exercise 10 **Write What You Think**

On a separate piece of paper, write a few paragraphs in response to the statement below. Support your opinion with facts, reasons, and examples.

> Scientists believe that the rise in asthma in young people today is caused by the rise in air pollution from automobiles. The automobile industry should take responsibility for this pollution and should pay to clean up the air.

Answers will vary. Give students full credit if they have stated an opinion and attempted to support their opinions. Look for grammatically complete sentences that begin with a capital letter and end with an appropriate end punctuation mark.

Infinitives and Infinitive Phrases

An **infinitive** is a verb form that is almost always preceded by the word *to*. An infinitive can play several parts in a sentence. It can be a noun, an adjective, or an adverb.

My uncle likes **to dig** for fossils. [infinitive as noun]

He was the first person **to see** the ancient footprint. [infinitive as adjective]

What was it like **to roam** the ancient earth? [infinitive as adverb]

The word *to* is the *sign*, or *marker*, that begins an infinitive. But don't confuse the infinitive marker *to* with the preposition *to*. **Remember:** An infinitive *to* is always followed by a verb.

INFINITIVE   They began **to dig**.

PREPOSITION   Please give this **to her**.

An **infinitive phrase** is made up of an infinitive and all of its modifiers and complements.

Like participial phrases and gerund phrases, infinitive phrases may contain one or more prepositional phrases.

She began **to sketch the ancient footprint in the rock**.

To become an archeologist takes long study and training.

They asked him **to write an article about his discovery**.

Infinitives sometimes appear without the word *to*. In these cases, the word *to* is understood.

The student helped **[to] organize** the notes.

PS. To use infinitives and infinitive phrases properly, you don't have to worry about whether they are functioning as nouns, adjectives, or adverbs. You use them in everyday speech.

Exercise 11 Identifying Infinitives and Infinitive Phrases

Underline the infinitives and infinitive phrases in these sentences. Remember that an infinitive phrase includes the infinitive and all of its modifiers (including prepositional phrases) and complements. **Hint:** Not every phrase beginning with *to* is an infinitive.

1. Tourists flock to a national park in South Africa <u>to step in the oldest known human footprints on earth</u>.

2. These prints are believed <u>to have been made over 100,000 years ago</u>.

3. How were they able to survive so long?

4. Soon after the prints were made, sand blew in to cover them.

5. Afterwards, the prints turned to stone, which allowed them to endure.

6. These fossils are beginning to shrink because too many people have stepped in them.

7. To preserve these fossils, the South African government has taken action.

8. The original footprint stone was taken to a museum, and a mold was made to replace the original.

9. Archeologists were able to determine that the ancient footprint belonged to a five-foot-three inch tall female.

10. Soon archeologists hope to uncover more ancient prints that show who else walked with her.

Exercise 12 Writing Sentences with Infinitives and Infinitive Phrases

On a separate piece of paper, write five sentences from a speech that the ancient person in Exercise 11 might address to a modern-day audience. What would she say about her experience of being trapped in time? What would she say about the modern world she witnesses? What would she say about any hopes or dreams she has for her descendants? In each sentence, try to include at least one infinitive or infinitive phrase. Underline the infinitives and the full infinitive phrases you write. Here's one way to start:

I can't begin to express my amazement at the speed of modern life.
Students' sentences will vary.

Exercise 13 Write What You Think

On a separate piece of paper, write a message you would like to leave in a time capsule for people of the future. Write your message in paragraph form. Use the instructions below to help you formulate your ideas.

1. Describe some of the thoughts and feelings that motivated people during your lifetime.

2. Describe some important events or discoveries during your lifetime.

3. Explain your own hopes and dreams for humanity.

Students' paragraphs will vary. Look for grammatically complete sentences that begin with a capital letter and end with an appropriate end punctuation mark.

Combining Sentences: Inserting Phrases

Combine short or choppy sentences by using phrases for smooth and seamless transitions. This will help you to express your ideas clearly.

🍃 Combine related sentences by inserting a phrase from one sentence into another sentence.

When you combine sentences, you sometimes pick up a phrase from one sentence and simply drop it into another. Other combinations require slight changes in word forms.

ORIGINAL   The grandfather was telling a story. He told a story about a coyote. The story was told to his grandchildren.

COMBINED   The grandfather was telling **his grandchildren** a story **about a coyote**. [indirect object; prepositional phrase]

ORIGINAL   The grandfather liked telling stories. He was Maria's favorite relative.

COMBINED   The grandfather, **Maria's favorite relative**, liked telling stories. [appositive phrase]

ORIGINAL   Maria was listening to the story. She realized that coyotes had always interested her.

COMBINED   **Listening to the story**, Maria realized that coyotes had always interested her. [participial phrase]

ORIGINAL   People recount their dreams. Dreams may be frightening or fascinating. Telling stories about dreams may help explain them.

COMBINED   **Recounting a frightening or fascinating dream** may help **explain the dream's meaning**. [gerund phrase; infinitive phrase]

ORIGINAL   Maria listened to the details in the story. The details helped her follow what was happening to the coyote.

COMBINED   Maria listened to the details in the story **to help her follow what was happening to the coyote**. [infinitive phrase]

Often there are different ways to combine the same sentences. Here's one more way the last group of sentences could be combined:

COMBINED   **Listening to the details in the story** helped Maria follow what was happening to the coyote. [gerund phrase with two prepositional phrases]

Exercise 14 Combining Sentences by Inserting Phrases

Use phrases to combine the sentences in each numbered item. You may work with a partner or small group. Don't forget to add commas around nonessential appositive phrases. **Hint:** There is more than one way to combine most of these sentences. See Answer Key.

1. Rudolfo Anaya is a well-known American author. Pastura is his hometown. Pastura is a small New Mexican town.

2. *Bless me, Ultima* is his first novel. He begins to show an interest in Mexican American folklore.

3. As a boy, Anaya liked Saturdays. On that day of the week he read in the Santa Rosa library. He stayed there until late in the day.

4. The young Anaya listened to *cuentos*. *Cuentos* are traditional Spanish stories. He became interested in writing.

5. A tradition of oral storytelling is part of Mexican American culture. The imagination of a young Mexican American writer, like Rudolfo Anaya, is sparked by this form of storytelling.

6. La Llorona is a crazy spirit. She is in some of Anaya's stories that are based on *cuentos*. She shouts and cries about lost loved ones.

7. Anaya also writes novels. These are about real-life, modern people. They live in New Mexico.

8. In 1992, *Albuquerque* was published. It is a novel. The novel is about a Hispanic boxer.

9. There are many readers of Anaya. They learn about Hispanic culture and the Southwest when they read his work.

10. He was interested in writing mysteries. He published one. Mysteries are a genre Anaya had not yet tried.

Exercise 15 Writing a Paragraph

Students should combine sentences where possible by using phrases. You may have students exchange paragraphs with a partner and make suggestions for improving each other's paragraphs. Answers will vary.

Conduct a survey on your classmates' reading habits and preferences using the questions below. Feel free to create your own questions. As you survey three classmates, write a one-sentence response, based on each answer. Then, on another piece of paper, write the results of the survey in a paragraph.

1. How many books, on average, do you read in a month?

2. What kind of writing or literary genre (mystery, biography, novel, etc.) do you most enjoy reading?

3. What do you consider the ideal length for a book?

4. What are two qualities you look for in any book you read?

Revising and Editing Worksheet 1

Revise the following biographical sketch on a separate piece of paper. Correct sentence fragments and combine short or choppy sentences by inserting phrases. Make any other changes you think will improve the paragraphs. **Hint:** Watch out for spelling mistakes, punctuation mistakes, and usage mistakes. Answers will vary.

[1]A Navajo artist from New Mexico and Arizona. [2]Carl Gorman was also a World War II hero. [3]He helped create a code. [4]Using the Navajo language. [5]The Navajo language is little-known. [6]This code was so successful that Gorman did not speak about it publicly. [7]Until 1969. [8]He honored the governments request for his silence. [9]After 1969, though, he lectured about successfully inventing the code in the Pacific front. [10]He lectured throughout the country.

[11]The Japanese hoped to break the code. [12]But breaking this code. [13]Demanded more than mere knowledge of Navajo. [14]Apart from 50,000 Navajos, fewer than thirty people understood Navajo when World War II broke out. [15]Navajo is a language without an alphabet. [16]Through cooperation with other Navajo soldiers. [17]Navajo words took on new English meanings. [18]These words were in this code. [19]For example, the Navajo word, *jay-sho*. [20]*Jay-sho* means buzzard. [21]*Jay-sho* translated as "bomber" in this code. [22]It was in this code. [23]Without question, the Japanese was at a disadvantage. [24]Because they couldn't figure out what their enemy was planning to do. [25]They did not understand this amazing way information was safely exchanged. [26]The information was exchanged among Americans.

[27]Carl Gorman was born on the Navajo reservation in Chinle, Arizona. [28]Using Navajo was not permitted in a mission school. [29]He attended a mission school. [30]It became a difficult experience for Gorman. [31]Gorman insisted during his school experience. [32]On speaking his native language despite rules prohibiting it. [33]This was a beloved language to him.

Revising and Editing Worksheet 2

Work with a partner or small group to revise these paragraphs. Write your revised biographical sketch on a separate piece of paper, and compare your response with those made by other pairs or groups of classmates. Correct sentence fragments and combine sentences by inserting phrases to create complete sentences that read clearly and smoothly. Make other changes you think will improve the paragraphs. **Hint:** Watch out for spelling mistakes, punctuation mistakes, and capitalization mistakes. Answers will vary.

¹Between 1840 and 1870, more than a quarter of a million people. ²Traveled in wagon trains on overland trails. ³They traveled across the continental United States. ⁴A new life out West was what they looked for. ⁵Establishing a new life proved to be a difficult task. ⁶They hoped to eventually claim free land in Oregon or California. ⁷Travelers braved bad weather. ⁸They braved treacherous crossings. ⁹The weather was harsh. ¹⁰The crossings were over Rivers and Mountains. ¹¹Iowa is a Midwestern state. ¹²The 2,400 mile trip from Iowa to the West Coast is long. ¹³It marks one of the greatest migrations of modern times.

¹⁴Travelers wrote diaries and journal entries. ¹⁵This allowed them to record the details of this trip, and the trip was amazing. ¹⁶Woman took part in recording the events they experienced that happened along the way. ¹⁷They were from every state in the union. ¹⁸Women would travel the overland trails. ¹⁹It wasn't easy. ²⁰It wasn't easy for anyone. ²¹It was especially difficult for women with small children.

²²Lydia Rudd was one of the many migrants. ²³Lydia Rudd wrote a diary. ²⁴It was written during her trip to Oregon. ²⁵In 1852. ²⁶Her husbands' name was Harry. ²⁷She and her husband hoped to acquire free land threw the Donation Act. ²⁸The Donation act allowed for land. ²⁹Men and women signed up for land through the Donation Act. ³⁰Lydia looked forward. ³¹To land carrying her name alone.

Chapter Review

Exercise A **Matching Definitions**

Match the term in Column 1 with its definition in Column 2. Write the
letter of the definition in the space provided.

___e___ 1. gerund

a. the *-ing* verb form that functions as an adjective

___b___ 2. preposition

b. a verb form that is almost always preceded by
the word *to*

___c___ 3. infinitive

c. a word used to show the relationship between
two words in a sentence, such as *in*, *with*, or *over*.

___a___ 4. participle

d. a noun or pronoun that identifies or explains
the noun or pronoun preceding or following it

___d___ 5. appositive

e. the *-ing* verb form that functions as a noun

Exercise B **Identifying Phrases**

Identify each underlined phrase by writing one of these abbreviations at the
end of the line. **Remember:** A prepositional phrase may be a part of
another kind of phrase. Label the main phrases, not the prepositional
phrases within other phrases.

PREP = prepositional phrase INF = infinitive phrase
PART = participial phrase   APP = appositive phrase
GER = gerund phrase

1. She hoped <u>to learn about the poet and doctor William Carlos Williams</u>. INF

2. <u>Coming from an English and Cuban background</u> influenced this
   American poet. GER

3. Some people questioned the poetry <u>written by a doctor after
   office hours</u>. PART

4. His personal writing style gave rise to a new way of thinking <u>about
   American poetry</u>. PREP

5. One famous poem, "This Is Just to Say," is written as a late-night note
   from Dr. Williams <u>to his wife</u>. PREP

6. This note describes nothing more than some plums <u>enjoyed as a late-
   night snack</u>. PART

7. <u>In its short 28 words</u>, "This Is Just to Say" touches on his marriage. PREP

8. The shattered glass, <u>glittering in an alleyway</u>, is the subject of
   "Between Walls." PART

9. This observation, <u>made by Dr. Williams</u> at work, demonstrates the poetry of everyday life. PART

10. Dr. Williams finds poetry in daily observations or in his relationship with Flossie, <u>his wife of many years</u>. APP

Exercise C **Combining Sentences**

On a separate piece of paper, write one complete sentence from the two sentences in each numbered item. Use the type of phrases indicated to combine the sentences. Add commas where they belong. See Answer Key.

1. William Carlos Williams grew up in Rutherford, New Jersey. He enjoyed what he calls a typical American boyhood. [participial phrase]

2. His father earned a living as a salesman. He traveled throughout the Caribbean and Latin America. [infinitive phrase]

3. While in Cuba, William Carlos Williams's father met Raquel Helene Hoheb. Raquel Helene Hoheb was his future bride. [appositive phrase]

4. Mrs. Williams taught her children about art. This was a subject she had studied in Paris. [appositive phrase]

5. The Williamses made a choice. They chose to expose their children to many cultures and to both the Spanish and English languages. [infinitive phrase]

6. Williams had ideas from other cultures. Ideas can be found throughout his poetry. [prepositional phrase]

7. Williams liked to write short lines of poetry. In part this comes from writing prescriptions in his practice. [gerund phrase]

8. He was influenced by meeting other poets. Dr. Williams wrote poems in addition to practicing medicine. [participial phrase]

9. His wife became the subject of many of his poems throughout his career. Her name was Flossie. [appositive phrase]

10. Williams became well known for his nontraditional poetry. His fame grew when he published *Al Que Quiero! (To Him Who Wants It)*. [prepositional phrase]

Exercise D **Write What You Think**

In some countries ruled by dictators, poetry and other forms of creative expression are censored or banned. In the United States, freedom of expression is a basic right and must be safeguarded.

Write a few paragraphs in response to this statement. Support your position with facts, reasons, and examples.

Clauses

STUDENT WRITING
Persuasive Essay

New Sports Policy a Boon for Athletes
by Rusty Ryan
high school student, Cambridge, Massachusetts

The sports department's new policy of organizing nonvarsity sports according to a player's ability, instead of by age, represents a significant improvement over the former system. As of this season, freshmen are permitted to play on JV [Junior Varsity] teams in soccer and field hockey, and juniors and sophomores can also play on third teams, which were formerly reserved for freshmen. By strengthening the JV program, the new policy has the potential to improve the performances of both JV and varsity teams.

In past years, many students have complained about the "dead end" nature of JV teams. Players who wished to improve their skills and make varsity teams in future years often found themselves at odds with students who merely wanted to fulfill their sports requirement with a minimum of effort. The wide disparity of talent on JV teams prevented ambitious players from improving and frustrated less talented players who often received little playing time.

Under the new system, competitive players, both freshmen and upperclassmen alike, will be able to develop their skills without being held back by less serious athletes. JV teams will be more successful, and varsity teams will benefit because players moving up from JV will have had the experience of playing in a competitive environment.

The system will also provide a more enjoyable environment for less serious players. Although some upperclassmen were disappointed to be cut from JV and have quit the program entirely, those who chose to play on third teams will likely enjoy both the greater playing time and the more relaxed pace. Once the system has been in place for a few years, it will be less of a shock for upperclassmen to be cut from JV, and more will elect to continue playing. Another benefit of the new system is its potential to ease the isolation many freshmen feel from the rest of the school.

The opinion statement of Rusty Ryan's persuasive essay appears in the last sentence of the first paragraph. He supports his statement with background information, with reasons that support his opinion, and even with a response to opposing viewpoints.

One of the reasons that Rusty's essay is effective is that he uses clauses to connect sentences and to give variety to his writing. In this chapter, you'll practice using clauses to express ideas clearly and to vary your own sentences.

Allow time for students to discuss the student writing. Suggest that they identify its strengths and propose possible improvements. Use the model to introduce the concepts in the chapter.

Independent Clauses and Subordinate Clauses

◗ An **independent** (or **main**) **clause** has a subject (S) and a verb (V) and expresses a complete thought.

Like a complete sentence, an independent clause within a sentence can stand alone. That's why it's *independent*!

S   V
Long ago, immigrants came to America from Europe.

V   S   S   S
In the steerage section traveled parents, children, and others.

A **compound sentence** contains two or more independent clauses joined by a conjunction and no subordinate clauses.

INDEPENDENT CLAUSE   INDEPENDENT CLAUSE
One family traveled from Russia, **and** another came from Italy.

◗ A **subordinate** (or **dependent**) **clause** has a subject and a verb but doesn't express a complete thought.

S   V   S   V
because they hoped for a better life   who barely had a penny

Subordinate clauses may appear at the beginning, middle, or end of a sentence.

A subordinate clause is a sentence fragment. It can't stand alone. It must be inserted into or attached to an independent clause.

People **who had money** traveled first class. [The subordinate clause is inserted into the independent clause.]

Immigrants endured difficult journeys **because they hoped for a better life**. [The subordinate clause is attached to the independent clause.]

Exercise 1 Identifying Clauses

On the blank before for each numbered item, write *I* for an independent clause or *S* for a subordinate clause. On a separate piece of paper, revise every subordinate clause to make it a complete sentence.
Students' revisions to subordinate clauses will vary. Sample revisions are given.

___I___ 1. Ellis Island greeted immigrants between 1892 and 1954.

___S___ 2. Whoever entered the United States by the Atlantic Ocean. braved rough seas and uncertain weather.

___I___ 3. New York City's population exploded from 60,000 to over 3 million.
City schools were filled with children

___S___ 4. Who came from Italy, Russia, Ireland, and Greece, among other countries.

  <u> S </u>5. Since many immigrants settled in the Northeast, especially in cities.

 , schools had to adjust to students who couldn't speak English.

  <u> S </u>6. Crowded urban neighborhoods with many immigrants.

 overwhelmed city services.

  <u> S </u>7. ~~Although they~~ Many came because of religious or political persecution.

  <u> S </u>8. Even though the immigrant life was tough, hundreds of thousands made the difficult journey.

Exercise 2   Proofreading Paragraphs

Proofread the following paragraphs, correcting all fragments. **Remember:** You may place a subordinate clause at the beginning, middle, or end of a sentence. You may also change a subordinate clause into an independent clause.

Revised paragraphs will vary.

 [1]The trip many poorer immigrants made in steerage was difficult. [2]Even though the journey may have proved worthwhile over time. [3]Who kept journals about their trip. [4]People included details about the hardships. [5]The ship voyage from a port in Europe to Ellis Island usually took up to two weeks. [6]Although some ships could make it in six days. [7]Because the ship's food was often inedible or against the religious practices of some travelers. [8]Many immigrants ate the little food they could bring on board. [9]Which got stale during the journey.

 [10]Many feared shipwrecks or accidents. [11]When bad weather made the water rough. [12]Morris Raphael Cohen wrote about his fear of an accident. [13]He wrote about the crowded conditions in steerage. [14]Who left Europe because of prejudice. [15]Against Jewish people. [16]Whatever happened mattered less when the Statue of Liberty was spotted. [17]This symbolized freedom. [18]The written memories of immigrants from the turn of the twentieth century reveal. [19]Who among us has a great wealth of spirit. [20]How the human spirit can triumph.

Exercise 3   Writing a Family Narrative

■ Refer to **Composition, Lesson 3.1,** to find strategies for writing a family narrative.

On a separate piece of paper, write a few paragraphs about when and from where your family first came to America. You may need to interview your relatives to gather information. If you don't know these facts, use your imagination to picture your ancestors and what might have motivated them to leave their homeland and travel to a foreign land. If you're a Native American, write a few paragraphs about the early history of your people in the United States.

Students' narratives will vary. Give students full credit if they have stated an opinion and attempted to support their opinions. They should also have written grammatically correct sentences that begin with a capital letter and end with an appropriate end punctuation mark.

Adjective Clauses

In this chapter, you'll review three kinds of subordinate clauses: adjective clauses, adverb clauses, and noun clauses.

⬤ An **adjective clause** is a subordinate clause that functions as an adjective. It modifies a noun or pronoun.

The trumpet player, **who wears a tuxedo**, stands in front.

The trumpet **that she bought** sounds magnificent.

Adjective clauses usually follow the word they modify. They usually begin with an introductory word called a **relative pronoun** or a **relative adverb**. Refer to the list in the side column.

Sometimes, these introductory words are omitted. The sentences below make sense with or without the bracketed words.

Where is the music [**that**] **I bought**?

Rafael is the guitarist [**whom**] **you will accompany on the trumpet**.

Like appositives [see Lesson 6.2], adjective clauses provide information that is either essential to the meaning of a sentence or not essential. An **essential clause** delivers the main message of a sentence. A **nonessential clause** adds extra information but does not contain the main message of the sentence.

When the clause is essential, it must not be set off with commas.

ESSENTIAL   This is the hall **where the orchestra performs**.

NONESSENTIAL   This hall, **where the orchestra performs**, will be remodeled next year.

P.S. You learned about essential and nonessential clauses when you studied appositives in Lesson 6.2. The same rules about commas apply to adjective clauses. In other textbooks, you may see the term *nonrestrictive* used for *nonessential* and *restrictive* used for *essential*. These terms are synonyms.

Some Words That Introduce Adjective Clauses

Relative Pronouns

that	who
what	whoever
where	whom
which	whose

Relative Adverbs

where	why
when	

Editing Tip

Place the adjective clause right next to the word it modifies.

INCORRECT
The book is a best-seller that I'm reading now.

CORRECT
The book that I'm reading now is a best-seller.

Exercise 4 **Identifying Adjective Clauses**

Underline the adjective clauses in the sentences below.

1. Yo-Yo Ma, who is a world-famous cellist, was born in Paris.

2. The two cellos that he plays were made in Italy and Austria.

3. Julliard, where Yo-Yo Ma studied, is a world-class music school.

4. He performs for young audiences <u>who respond enthusiastically</u>.

5. The pianist Emanuel Ax is a musician <u>whom Yo-Yo Ma admires</u>.

6. A program, <u>which Yo-Yo Ma and Emanuel Ax developed</u>, presents family concerts at Carnegie Hall.

7. The city of Hong Kong, <u>which was about to rejoin China</u>, was the site of Yo-Yo Ma's solo performance in 1997.

8. Some music <u>that Yo-Yo Ma has studied</u> comes from China and Africa.

9. Nashville, <u>where country music is king</u>, has invited Yo-Yo Ma to play.

10. Music is the universal language <u>that allows everyone to communicate</u>.

Exercise 5 Identifying Sentences with Adjective Clauses

Read the following paragraph one student wrote about his favorite instrument. Underline the adjective clauses.

[1]At the age of ten, people <u>whom I admired</u> wanted me to play the piano. [2]My parents could not find a piano <u>that would fit in our apartment</u>. [3]In fact, the piano, <u>which had been my instrument of choice</u>, didn't turn out to be my favorite. [4]My favorite instrument, <u>which is in my pocket right now</u>, is the harmonica. [5]The place <u>where I first heard the harmonica</u> was in my own living room. [6]CDs of the blues, <u>which my parents like to play</u>, captured my interest. [7]John Mayall, <u>who is a well-known musician from the 1960s and 1970s</u>, became my favorite harmonica player. [8]Then I listened to folk music <u>that featured the harmonica</u>. [9]Bob Dylan, <u>who became popular in the 1960s</u>, played a terrific harmonica along with a guitar. [10]Now I look for harmonica solos and harmonica players <u>that sound as good as Dylan</u>.

Exercise 6 Writing from Experience

On a separate piece of paper, write five sentences about instruments, musicians, and kinds of music that interest you. When you have finished writing, underline any adjective clauses you have included in your paragraph. Then, exchange papers with a classmate to see if you've underlined all the adjective clauses. **Remember**: Use commas to set off nonessential adjective clauses from the rest of a sentence.   Students' sentences will vary.

Adverb Clauses

◖ An **adverb clause** is a subordinate clause that functions as an adverb. It modifies a verb, adjective, or another adverb.

    Unless it rains, young plants cannot grow. [modifies the verb *can grow*]
    The animals seemed nervous **whenever rolling thunder began.**
    [modifies the adjective *nervous*]
    The rain fell sooner **than we had expected.** [modifies the adverb
    sooner]

An introductory adverb clause is always followed by a comma. You'll find a list of introductory words and phrases for adverb clauses in the side column. When these words or phrases begin an adverb clause, they're referred to as **subordinating conjunctions**.

When words are omitted from an adverb clause, the clause is called an **elliptical adverb clause**. You can see the missing words in brackets below.

    Yesterday's rain fell harder **than today's** [**did**].
    The farmers are more concerned about rainfall **than the**
    merchants are [**concerned about rainfall**].
    We won't worry **as long as you don't** [**worry**].
    Have you ever known anyone **as lucky as Felice** [**is**]?

Exercise 7 **Identifying Adverb Clauses**

Underline the adverb clauses in the following sentences.

1. <u>Where farms now thrive</u>, a desert once covered the

    Great Plains.

2. Sand covered this region <u>before it was inhabited</u>.

3. <u>Until the Dust Bowl of the 1930s</u>, the Great Plains attracted thousands

    of settlers.

4. <u>Though conditions were poor</u>, farmers continued to grow crops.

5. A series of droughts struck the Plains region <u>as the Great Depression</u>

    <u>tightened its grip on the nation</u>.

Subordinating Conjunctions

after	so that
although	than
as . . . as	though
as long as	unless
as soon as	until
as though	when
because	whenever
before	where
even though	whereas
if	wherever
in order that	whether
provided that	while
since	

Writing Hint

Don't interrupt a subject and verb with an adverb clause.

INCORRECT
The goats **because they were hungry** ate all the grass.

CORRECT
The goats ate all the grass **because they were hungry**.

6. <u>Since the grasslands had been cleared for crops</u>, loose, dry soil was swept away with the fierce winds.

7. <u>While the Great Depression made life difficult</u>, the Dust Bowl destroyed lives.

8. A curtain of dust blew all the way to the east coast, <u>although the worst of the damage was in the Plains</u>.

9. Easterners ignored the Dust Bowl <u>until black dust clouds struck them, too</u>.

10. <u>After rain put an end to the Dust Bowl in 1935</u>, floods became the problem.

Exercise 8 **Writing a Paragraph with Adverb Clauses**

On a separate piece of paper, work with a partner to write a paragraph from the following notes about the Dust Bowl days of the 1930s. When you've finished writing, exchange paragraphs with other student pairs and underline the adverb clauses you find.   Students' paragraphs will vary.

Observations at the Watson Farm on the Great Plains in Oklahoma

The farm used to produce a surplus of crops.

Sand dunes now surround the Watson farm.

Cattle cannot find grass easily.

Bean crops don't grow an inch all summer.

Big black cloud of dust races across the plains in Oklahoma.

Neighbors warn one another about the approaching storm.

Sand found covering the crops and grazing lands after the storm.

Family experiences coughing fits from the sandstorm.

Frustration is overwhelming when clouds appear, but no rain falls.

U.S. Congress decides to help those struggling on the plains.

Noun Clauses

🪶 A **noun clause** is a subordinate clause that functions as a noun.

A noun clause can do anything a noun can do. It can act as a subject, a direct object, a predicate nominative, an indirect object, or the object of a preposition. A noun clause may appear at the beginning, middle, or end of a sentence. As in adjective and adverb clauses, certain words usually introduce a noun clause. You'll find some of those introductory words listed in the side column. As in other clauses, you may find modifiers and complements within a noun clause.

Some Words That Introduce Noun Clauses

how	which
if	whichever
that	who
what	whoever
whatever	whom
when	whose
where	why
whether	

Whoever was stealing the precious stones had many accomplices. [subject]

Detectives believed they would never know **what happened to the diamonds**. [direct object]

The anonymous midnight phone call was **what tipped off the police**. [predicate nominative]

The lawyer instructed Betty to testify truthfully about **whether she knew the suspect**. [object of a preposition]

P.S. As you write, you don't have to identify how noun clauses function in sentences. Think of them as just another tool to express ideas and vary sentence structure.

Sometimes, the introductory word of a noun clause is omitted because it is understood. The sentences below make sense if you read them with or without the bracketed word.

The prosecutor hopes [**that**] **the jury will convict the suspect**.

The defense lawyer knows [**that**] **he has a strong case**.

Editing Tip

Only omit the introductory word in a noun clause if it doesn't cause misunderstanding.

UNCLEAR
Tom didn't believe **Jerry would leave town**.

CLEAR
Tom didn't believe **that Jerry would leave town**.

UNCLEAR
Mom didn't say **you called**.

CLEAR
Mom didn't say **that you called**.

Exercise 9 Identifying Noun Clauses

Read these paragraphs from a report about free verse in American poetry. Underline all the noun clauses. **Hint:** There are more than ten noun clauses.

¹Twentieth-century American poetry is distinguished by <u>what is called free verse</u>. ²<u>Whoever wrote the first unrhymed poem</u> broke new literary ground. ³Free-verse sound patterns reflect <u>what the ideas of a poem are</u>. ⁴In other words, rhyme and meter are not <u>what determine how a poem sounds</u>. ⁵Robert Frost was a famous American poet who was opposed to

free verse. [6]He felt <u>that writing in free verse was like playing tennis without a net.</u>

[7]Robert Lowell in his *Life Studies*, writes <u>what he feels</u> without using formal patterns of rhyme. [8]His statement on free verse is clear: "The law says <u>that I am completely free.</u>" [9]In his free verse, Lowell examines <u>how experience affects him</u> by using a conversational tone. [10]This doesn't mean <u>that he rejects rhyme and meter outright.</u> [11]<u>What he questions</u> is <u>why a poet would give up either kind of writing.</u> [12]Both serve a purpose, depending on <u>who the poet is</u> and <u>what he or she wants to express.</u>

Exercise 10 Writing Sentences with Noun Clauses

Review the list of words that introduce noun clauses on page 153. Then fill in the blanks below with noun clauses. Exchange papers with a partner to check that you have written a noun clause, not an adjective clause or an adverb clause.
Students' sentences will vary.

1. I know _____ which is the right train _____.

2. Sam worries _____ that he won't get into college _____.

3. Jared will be happy with _____ whatever he gets for his birthday _____.

4. Has anyone checked _____ whose boots those are _____?

5. Do you really care _____ how the job gets done _____?

6. The most important problem is _____ where the dog has gone _____.

7. _____ How to find a job _____ is something to think about.

8. Natalie wondered _____ why the birds stopped singing _____.

9. Waldo learned _____ which chess players were unbeatable _____.

10. Kramer swung at _____ whatever ball was pitched _____.

Exercise 11 Create Your Own Exercise

With a partner, make up ten sentences that include noun clauses. Your sentences may be about any topic. Exchange sentences with another student pair and see if you can identify all of their noun clauses.
Students' exercises will vary.

On the blank before each numbered item, write *I* if the group of words is an
independent clause or *S* if it is a subordinate clause. On a separate piece of
paper, revise every subordinate clause to make it a complete sentence.
Students' revisions to subordinate clauses will vary. Samples are given below.

__S__ 1. Since there are $20 million worth of products with Duke's name
on them, university officials take a keen interest in where the products are manufactured.

__S__ 2. ~~Because~~ Duke University does not believe in unfair labor practices.

__I__ 3. To make clothes that say, "Duke University," manufacturers must
comply with fair industry practices.

__I__ 4. Duke officials claimed that this was the right thing to do.

__S__ 5. Whichever manufacturers do not pay legal wages or allow
factory inspections, are sanctioned and required to bring their wage scales up to standard.

__S__ 6. No matter whether underage workers work in factories, at home,
or abroad, , Duke University takes steps to correct the situation.

__I__ 7. Unless there are fair wages and safe working conditions, Duke
University won't license its name.

__S__ 8. ~~Who~~ Union representatives are the voices calling for better conditions for garment
workers.

__I__ 9. Whoever supports Duke officials supports healthy working
conditions in our global economy.

__S__ 10. ~~That~~ Ohio State applauds Duke as a model for its
licensing agreements.

Exercise B Identifying Adjective and Adverb Clauses

Underline the adjective clauses and the adverb clauses in the sentences
below. Write *ADJ* in the blank next to an adjective clause and *ADV* in the
blank by an adverb clause.

__ADJ__ 1. Ms. Cruz, who is a popular teacher, started an internship program.

__ADV__ 2. Because students want to learn about business, this program is
a success.

__ADV__ 3. Although students don't get paid, they get valuable
work experience.

__ADJ__ 4. The students, who work five hours a week, run a snack bar and
supply store.

___ADV___ 5. If the store makes a profit, a percentage goes to a local food pantry.

___ADV___ 6. Whenever the snack bar turns a profit, the money goes into a fund.

___ADJ___ 7. This fund, which Ms. Cruz oversees, supports after-school programs.

___ADV___ 8. A meeting will be called next week so that a second charity may be chosen.

___ADV___ 9. Unless the interns object, Ms. Cruz wants to donate money to a children's theater.

___ADV___ 10. Even though students may have other ideas, I like this idea.

Exercise C **Writing Sentences with Noun Clauses**

Create a full sentence for each numbered item by writing a noun clause to fill in the blank. **Remember:** Include introductory words, such as the ones listed on page 153, so that the meaning of each sentence is clear.
Students' sentences will vary. Sample answers are given.

1. My uncle said how he felt about my boyfriend .

2. My only relative is who saved me from the fire .

3. That the boys walked to school is completely true.

4. After adopting the cat, Maura knew where to shop for pet supplies .

5. Tara decided what to do after graduation.

6. She knows how to showcase her experience.

7. Renata explained why the mustard fell from the fridge .

8. Please listen to whatever the teacher says about the assignment.

9. They were absolutely sure about where to go for dinner .

10. How to fix a television is more important than when.

Exercise D **Writing a Paragraph**

Students' paragraphs will vary. Students should support their opinions with reasons and examples and should use clauses correctly.

In Exercise B, you read about a program in which students participated in a business internship under a teacher's guidance. On a separate piece of paper, write a few paragraphs in response to the following statement. Support your opinion with facts and examples.

All students should be required to gain work experience in the real world in order to graduate from high school.

Combining Sentences: Using Subordinate Clauses

When you combine sentences, you join ideas. By using a subordinate clause, you can combine related ideas from more than one sentence into a single sentence.

🔹 You can combine two sentences by turning one sentence into an adjective clause.

Use the introductory words from the list on page 149, such as *who*, *which*, and *when*. **Remember:** An adjective clause usually follows the noun or pronoun it modifies, and commas set off a nonessential adjective clause from the rest of the sentence.

ORIGINAL   Rita Dove became the youngest poet laureate of the United States. She was born in 1955.

COMBINED   Rita Dove, **who was born in 1955,** became the youngest poet laureate of the United States.

ORIGINAL   Grandparents are important in Rita Dove's poetry. Her grandparents appear in *Thomas and Beulah*.

COMBINED   Rita Dove's grandparents, **who appear in *Thomas and Beulah*,** are important in her poetry.

COMBINED   Grandparents, **who are essential to Rita Dove's poetry,** appear in *Thomas and Beulah*.

🔹 You can combine two sentences by turning one sentence into an adverb clause.

One way to combine sentences is by using a **subordinating conjunction** to create an adverb clause. Choose a subordinating conjunction that clearly expresses the relationship between the ideas. Note that adverb clauses may come at the beginning, middle, or end of a sentence.

ORIGINAL   Please don't throw that magazine away. It lists rules for a poetry contest.

COMBINED   Please don't throw that magazine away **because it lists rules for a poetry contest**.

ORIGINAL   I came in late. I still think I passed the test.

COMBINED   **Although I came in late,** I still think I passed the test.

P.S. When you write clauses, you don't need to identify which function they serve in a sentence, as long as each clause enhances the meaning and reads smoothly.

Some Subordinating Conjunctions

Cause-Effect Relationship
because   whereas
since

Time Relationship
after   when
as soon as   whenever
before   while
until

Resulting Relationship
in order that
so that

Conditional Relationship
although   if
even though   unless
provided that

Enriching Your Vocabulary

The root of *stagnate* is a Latin noun, *stagnum*, meaning "a swamp, or a pool of standing water." Metaphorically, the word can be used for any lack of motion. Without a high school diploma, one might get stuck in a *stagnant* career.

Exercise 12 **Combining Sentences with Adjective Clauses**

Work with a partner to combine each pair of sentences into a single sentence by changing the second sentence into an adjective clause. An introductory word is suggested in parentheses. Write your responses on a separate piece of paper, and underline the adjective clause in your combined sentence. See Answer Key.

EXAMPLE The stock market fascinates people. It fluctuates up or down. (when)
The stock market, <u>when it fluctuates up or down</u>, fascinates people.

Hint

Set off nonessential adjective and adverb clauses with commas.

1. The American workforce of the 1980s stagnated the economy. The workforce was considered too big and inefficient. (which)

2. In the next decade, the workforce became smaller and more efficient. The economy grew stronger. (when)

3. Many economists advise people not to spend too much or too little when the economy changes. Economists study spending habits. (who)

4. Sudden changes in the economy often change a person's spending patterns. Sudden changes in the economy occur from time to time. (that)

5. People should know that economists warn against going into debt in both good and bad economies. People fuel the economy. (who)

6. Optimism may shrink margins of safety and allow credit card debts to grow out of control. People try to maintain margins of safety. (which)

Exercise 13 **Combining Sentences with Adverb Clauses**

Combine each pair of sentences into a single sentence with an adverb clause. Use the subordinating conjunction suggested in parentheses—or one of your choice. Write your responses on a separate piece of paper, and underline the adverb clause in each of your combined sentences. See Answer Key.

EXAMPLE Virgil wrote often about Cupid. Cupid was a minor god. (although)
<u>Although Cupid was a minor god</u>, Virgil wrote about him often.

1. In Greek mythology, the leaves never fell from trees in autumn. Persephone made this happen. (until)

2. Odysseus finally finds his way home from the Trojan War. Many forces tried to stop him. (even though)

3. Greek gods and goddesses often helped humans. People respected and revered the gods and goddesses on Mt. Olympus. (as long as)

4. At times, the gods would punish people. People insulted a god. (if)

5. A person approached the gates of Hades. The three-headed guard dog, Cerberus, had to be confronted. (when)

6. The god Zeus threw thunderbolts. He wanted to display his strength or anger. (whenever)

Four Types of Sentence Structures

To express yourself well, you need to write with a variety of sentence structures. By understanding different sentence structures, you can vary the way you communicate information.

🔹 A **simple sentence** has one independent clause and no subordinate clauses. However, it may have a compound subject (s) or verb (v).

   S   V
She breathed.

    S   S   V
Shoshona and Raymond took in a deep breath of cold, fresh air.

🔹 A **compound sentence** has two (or more) independent clauses and no subordinate clauses.

   S V   S   V
She took in one long breath, yet she still didn't feel completely at ease.

🔹 A **complex sentence** has one independent clause and at least one subordinate clause.

      S   V   S   V
If your chest expands too much, you may not be breathing correctly.
[introductory subordinate clause]

    S   S   V   V
A teacher, who knows breathing exercises, can help a person relax.
[a subordinate clause within an independent clause]

🔹 A **compound-complex sentence** has two or more independent clauses and at least one subordinate clause.

      S   V   S   V
Three sisters took yoga so that they could learn relaxation techniques,

      S   V
but their brother was not interested. [a subordinate clause between two independent clauses.]

Writing Hint

Besides varying sentence structure, good writers vary the number of sentences in each paragraph. Most paragraphs should not include more than five sentences; some have only one. A one-sentence paragraph tends to stand out and add emphasis.

Exercise 14 Identifying Sentence Structure

Identify the sentence structure of each sentence in the paragraph below. In the blank before each numbered sentence, write *S* for simple, *Cd* for compound, *Cx* for complex, or *Cd-Cx* for compound-complex.

_____Cx_____ [1]Yoga, which was developed by Hindus in India, is a system of

exercises for mental and physical control. _____S_____ [2]For the millions of people who participate in yoga classes, breathing properly is essential.

_____Cd-Cx_____ ³Yoga masters believe that oxygen provides the body with energy, so they have developed exercises to increase oxygen intake. _____Cd_____ ⁴Anyone can benefit from simple yoga breathing techniques, but only healthy people should try the more intense exercises.

_____Cx_____ ⁵By learning proper breathing techniques, people improve their health, increase their life span, and even lose weight, yoga experts believe.

_____S_____ ⁶To breathe correctly, a person must take in air through the nostrils, not the mouth. _____Cx_____ ⁷Because the hair, or cilia, within the nostrils acts as a filter, yoga experts feel sure that this is a healthier way to breathe.

_____Cd-Cx_____ ⁸If you inhale correctly, your stomach will expand, and your chest will fill with air. _____Cd-Cx_____ ⁹When you breathe out, your chest should withdraw slightly, and your stomach should draw back toward your spine.

Exercise 15 Writing with a Variety of Sentence Structures

On a separate piece of paper, expand each item into a sentence with the structure indicated in parentheses—*Cd* for compound, *Cx* for complex, *Cd-Cx* for compound-complex. Students' sentences will vary.

EXAMPLE   (Cd) Arthur touches his toes.
            Arthur can touch his toes, and he can stand on his head.

1. (Cx) Betina does fifteen pushups in a row.
2. (Cd) Troy cycles daily.
3. (Cd-Cx) We skate for forty minutes.
4. (Cx) She gave us a lesson on the history of surfing.
5. (Cd) Dancing is good exercise.
6. (Cx) How many laps did he do?
7. (Cx) Walking increases your heart rate.
8. (Cd-Cx) Exercise is important for mental health.
9. (Cd) Juanita practices karate five times a week.
10. (Cd-Cx) I want to learn to dance.

Effective Sentences: Parallel Structure

🔹 When you express two or more closely related ideas in a sentence, each should follow a similar structure.

Parallel grammatical structure in a sentence signals that items are similar or closely related.

| NONPARALLEL | Food at the ballpark is greasy, doesn't taste very good, and I spend a lot of money on it. |
| PARALLEL | Food at the ballpark is greasy, tasteless, and expensive. |

Parallel structure applies to clauses and phrases as well as words. When you write a series of clauses in one sentence, the structure of the clauses should be parallel.

NONPARALLEL	Kansas City suffered in the Depression, when the drought came, and after the beginning of the war.
PARALLEL	Kansas City suffered when the Depression hit, when the drought came, and when the war began. [Each item in this series is an adverb clause.]
PARALLEL	Over the river, through the woods, and under the fence, the fox ran from the hounds. [Each item in this series is a prepositional phrase.]

Exercise 16 Identifying Parallel Structure in Sentences

On a separate piece of paper, rewrite the sentences below so that they contain correct parallel structure. See Answer Key.

1. Cross-country travel in 1870 was exhausting, not very comfortable, and cost a lot of money.

2. Stagecoaches were the fastest, you could rely on them, and they were the safest way to travel.

3. No one expected a woman to drive a stagecoach because taking a physical job was not what most women did, because men always drove stagecoaches, and no woman had ever applied for the job.

4. You may have heard of an unusual woman who lived in the 1870s, using the name "Charley," and a stagecoach was driven by her.

5. Charley kept her identity hidden by cutting her hair short, by scruffy men's clothes, and acting like the other drivers.

6. Charley was known among stagecoach drivers to be honest with money, working reliably, and she was always polite to passengers.

7. After her death, the stagecoach company, her co-workers, and whoever was one of her passengers were amazed to find out she was a woman.

8. Like the stagecoach drivers, Pony Express riders worked long hours, didn't eat very many meals, and sleeping was hard to do, too.

9. The Pony Express was a mail service lasting for only eighteen months and that the transcontinental railroad put out of business.

10. For a Pony Express rider, getting a letter from the East to the West required many horses changed, knowing how to avoid danger, and being able to sleep in the saddle.

Exercise 17 Writing Sentences with Parallel Structure

On a separate piece of paper, write five sentences with parallel structure that express two closely related ideas. For subject matter, write on the subject of travel, using the following questions to help you with ideas. Students' sentences should contain parallel structures.

1. What form of travel do you like best?

2. What are some of the most memorable trips you have taken, either to places close by or far away?

3. Where would you like to travel to if you could? Why?

4. How do you think traveling gives us insights into our own lives?

5. How do other people's customs and ways of life make us examine our own?

Exercise 18 Write What You Think

Write several paragraphs in response to the following position. Support your opinion with facts and examples. Reread your paragraphs to check for parallel structure.

■ **Refer to Composition, Lesson 3.2, to find strategies for persuasive writing.**

In the mid-1800s, the transcontinental railroad put the Pony Express and the stagecoaches out of business. Likewise, cars and trucks have almost put the railroads out of business. However, cars and trucks have had a negative impact on air pollution and energy conservation. Americans should revitalize the railroad system and do away with car and truck transportation.

Students' paragraphs will vary. Give students full credit if they have stated an opinion and attempted to support their opinions. They should also have written grammatically correct sentences that begin with a capital letter and end with an appropriate end punctuation mark.

Varying Sentence Beginnings, Structures, and Lengths

Now that you have experience with subordinate clauses, sentence structures, and other writing tools, you can express ideas in a variety of ways when you write paragraphs or longer papers.

● When you write a paragraph or a longer paper, vary the sentence structures.

ORIGINAL	Jack London entertained gold prospectors in Canada's frozen wilderness by telling adventure stories.
PREPOSITIONAL PHRASE	**In Canada's frozen wilderness,** Jack London entertained gold prospectors by telling adventure stories.
PARTICIPIAL PHRASE	**Telling adventure stories,** Jack London entertained gold prospectors in Canada's frozen wilderness.
ADVERB CLAUSE	**While telling adventure stories,** Jack London entertained gold prospectors in Canada's frozen wilderness.
ADJECTIVE CLAUSE	Jack London, **who entertained gold prospectors in Canada's frozen wilderness,** told adventure stories.

Like professional writers, you can also experiment with a variety of sentence lengths to create smooth, flowing paragraphs. The following paragraph begins with two medium-length sentences and then follows with one short sentence and one long sentence.

[1]Renata had written dozens of adventure stories, but she dreamed of traveling to the Yukon like the famous novelist Jack London. [2]After researching the frigid wilderness of Canada, she made plans for her own real-life adventure. [3]Her first stop would be at an old gold miners' camp. [4]She would end her journey at the finish line of the famous annual dogsled race, the Iditarod, before returning home to Minnesota.

Exercise 19 Varying Sentence Beginnings

On a separate piece of paper, rewrite each of the following sentences to change its structure. You may reword the sentence if necessary or use other forms of words in the sentence. Just be sure to express the same idea. See Answer Key.

1. Jack London was born in San Francisco in January 1876 to parents known by the San Francisco public as eccentrics.

2. He went to work at age thirteen due to a family financial crisis.

3. A voyage to the Bering Sea on a ship trying to catch seals became his first of many world adventures.

4. Earning a living as a "vendor of brain" rather than as a laborer was the motto of Jack London.

5. One night in 1895, he wrote a 4,000-word essay for a newspaper contest, which brought him his first earnings as a writer.

6. He was self-taught and successfully passed exams that allowed him to graduate from high school when he was nineteen.

7. On the *Klondike*, Jack London sailed off for his first Yukon adventure after a brief college experience.

8. The perilous conditions in the Yukon weakened Jack London's health but provided a wealth of material for his most famous work, *The Call of the Wild*.

9. *The Call of the Wild* is a novel he finished in five weeks, and it became famous.

10. He got married, then he had two daughters, but he continued to travel.

Exercise 20 **Writing a Paragraph with Varied Sentences**

On a separate piece of paper, write a paragraph about Jack London's life. Use information from the research notes below. You don't have to use all the information. Try to vary sentence beginnings, lengths, and structures in the paragraph. **Remember:** Subordinate clauses allow you to connect related ideas in sentences. Students' paragraphs will vary. See teacher pages for assessment rubrics.

> Traveled 2,000 miles on a raft down the Yukon River; then worked his way back to Oakland, California
>
> "The White Silence"—first story about the Yukon: rejected
>
> Short stories first published in 1899; begins to earn money
>
> Marries, has two daughters, but continues to travel
>
> In five weeks completes famous novel <u>The Call of the Wild</u> (1902)
>
> <u>Sea-Wolf</u> (novel) makes him more famous and richer.
>
> 1904: Writes about Russo-Japanese War for Hearst newspaper from the war front
>
> 1905: Poor health, divorce, then remarriage to Charmain Kitteridge
>
> More adventures—Hawaii
>
> Moves to Glen Ellen, California; plans dream house called "Wolf House"
>
> Fire destroys "Wolf House"; London dies in 1916—at age of 40

Revising and Editing Worksheet 1

On a separate piece of paper, revise the paragraphs below. Correct sentence fragments, combine sentences, add details, add or drop words, correct spelling and punctuation errors, and try to vary sentence structures and beginnings. Check for correct sentence structures and for the placement of subordinate clauses.

[1]The people of New Orleans are affected by their proximity to the Gulf of Mexico and the many channels and inlets called bayous. [2]Their French and Spanish cultural heritages also influence them. [3]The Creole and Cajun cultures of this region have been well preserved over the years. [4]The many bayous and waterways tend to isolate people. [5]People around New Orleans to this day still speak a form of French called Creole. [6]As well as English.

[7]Creoles are descendants of early French and Spanish settlers. [8]Creole dominates the famous cuisine people love to eat in New Orleans. [9]You won't know the pleasure of Creole culture until you try gumbo. [10]Gumbo is a rich and flavorful fish soup that is a signature Creole dish. [11]Hot sausage and peppers in gumbo from the Spanish influence. [12]Green peppers and okra show an African influence. [13]The word *gumbo* actually comes from *gombo*. [14]*Gombo* is the word for "okra" in the African language of Bantu.

[15]People who visit New Orleans also enjoy the wonderful music of the city. [16]New Orleans, which is sometimes called the Big Easy. [17]It is the home of jazz. [18]New Orleans celebrates it's native son. [19]That native son is Louis Armstrong. [20]He was a great trumpet player. [21]New Orleans is also the home of Cajun music. [22]The Cajun music is Zydeco. [23]Zydeco has a rich, complex sound. [24]Zydeco incorporates French, North American, and Caribbean sounds. [25]People love that sound. [26]Visitors to New Orleans praise it. [27]The culture in New Orleans earns more praise than its location or its business.

Revisions will vary but should contain only complete sentences and correct spelling. Check that students have varied sentence structures, beginnings and lengths.

Revising and Editing Worksheet 2

Work with a partner or small group to revise these paragraphs. Write your revised story on a separate piece of paper, and compare your revision to those made by other groups of classmates. Eliminate sentence fragments, combine sentences, add details, add or drop words, correct spelling and punctuation errors, and try to vary sentence structures and beginnings. Be sure to correct awkward sentence structures, including misplaced subordinate clauses.

¹No one, because this was the night before their departure from the weeklong train ride, slept. ²When Roselle looked out her window, she saw nothing moved or made a sound. ³Whatever project Sam attempted lost his concentration. ⁴So he looked out the window along with Roselle. ⁵Suddenly, a jolt disturbed the otherwise smooth ride of the sleek train. ⁶Flashing before their eyes Sam and Roselle, who were cousins. ⁷They envisioned their family get-togethers in Michigan. ⁸Hoping they would again see their parents, brothers, and sisters.

⁹Originally, the idea of the first student field trip. ¹⁰To Mars thrilled Roselle and Sam. ¹¹Whoever had signed up for the trip had high hopes. ¹²They had high hopes of one day earning a living as an astronaut or space scientist. ¹³It wasn't that Roselle had now changed her mind, but the length of the trip and the unexpected occurrences had worn her out. ¹⁴Without much sleep, as if it were filled with cotton, her brain barely worked. ¹⁵Nothing making sense.

¹⁶Sam had taken a good catnap earlier in the day. ¹⁷Sam took a catnap as the train traveled through the Martian fire desert. ¹⁸So Sam was rested! ¹⁹Never mind that his cousin kept shaking him to look at the fascinated landscape. ²⁰She entitled "a flamescape." ²¹He took Roselle by the arm. ²²They walked to the back of the train car. ²³The locked compartment that held the emergency escape map and for the protection of special breathing tanks had popped open in the thunderous jolt. ²⁴Sam and Roselle were born leaders. ²⁵They decided to lead their tour group on foot. ²⁶The brand new Martian Motel on Red Mars Lake. ²⁷Where they were to be the first occupants from Earth.

Revisions will vary but should contain only complete sentences and correct spelling. Check that students have varied sentence structures, beginnings, and lengths.

Chapter Review

Exercise A Identifying Types of Clauses

On the blank before each numbered item, identify the underlined clause in each sentence by writing *ADJ* for an adjective clause, *ADV* for an adverb clause, or *N* for a noun clause.

ADV 1. People don't notice whether it's winter or summer <u>when they're happy</u>. —Anton Chekhov

ADV 2. I only regret <u>that I have but one life to lose for my country</u>. —Nathan Hale

ADJ 3. I have a dream that my four little children will one day live in a nation <u>where they will not be judged by the color of their skin but by the content of their character</u>. —Martin Luther King, Jr.

ADJ 4. The man <u>who usually makes no mistakes</u> does not usually make anything. —Edward John Phelps

_N_ 5. I know not <u>what course others may take</u>; but as for me, give me liberty, or give me death! —Patrick Henry

ADJ 6. No matter where its seed falls, it makes a tree <u>which struggles to reach the sky</u>. —Betty Smith

ADV 7. Nothing is ever done in this world <u>until men are prepared to kill one another</u> if it is not done. —George Bernard Shaw

_N_ 8. Ask not <u>what your country can do for you</u>; ask what you can do for your country. —John F. Kennedy

ADJ 9. I had a dream <u>which was not a dream at all</u>. —Lord Byron

ADV 10. <u>When a man assumes a public trust</u>, he should consider himself a public property. —Thomas Jefferson

Exercise B Identifying Sentence Structure

Underline every subordinate clause in the sentences below. Then, in the blank before each numbered item, identify the sentence structure by writing *S* for simple, *Cd* for compound, *Cx* for complex, and *Cd-Cx* for compound-complex.

_Cx_ 1. <u>While reading American poetry</u>, you absorb American history and culture.

_S_ 2. Edward Taylor's poetry was in the "wilderness baroque" style and was full of word play and puns.

_____Cx_____ 3. The seventeenth-century poet Anne Bradstreet, <u>who was married to the governor of Massachusetts</u>, was one of the few women to publish poetry in colonial America.

_____Cd-Cx_____ 4. Phillis Wheatley, <u>who arrived on American shores in 1761</u>, was sold into slavery, and still she became a world-famous poet.

_____Cx_____ 5. <u>As a supporter of the antislavery movement</u>, African American poet Frances Harper lectured against slavery.

_____Cd_____ 6. The powerful songs of slaves were not sung for entertainment; instead, they played a crucial role in work and in social and religious gatherings.

_____Cd_____ 7. People enjoy the haunting tales of Edgar Allan Poe, but few know his poetry.

_____Cx_____ 8. *Song of Myself* was published numerous times <u>before the poet Walt Whitman felt that it was complete</u>.

_____Cx_____ 9. Over one thousand handwritten copies of poems were found in Emily Dickinson's home <u>after she died in 1886</u>.

_____Cx_____ 10. Speeches by Native American leaders, such as Chief Joseph, have <u>as much power and intensity as the greatest poetry</u>.

Exercise C **Combining Sentences with Clauses**

On a separate piece of paper, combine each pair of sentences into a single sentence by changing one sentence into a subordinate clause. An introductory word is suggested in parentheses. **Remember:** Use commas where they are needed (1) after an introductory adverb clause and (2) around a nonessential adjective clause. See Answer Key.

EXAMPLE   Students are trying out for the play. Those students should report to the auditorium after school. (whoever)
Whoever is trying out for the play should report to the auditorium after school.

1. There are few major parts in this play. The cast of characters is surprisingly long. (even though)

2. You receive a cue from the director. Please begin reading your lines. (when)

3. Martin Anderson received the lead male role. He had never performed on stage before. (who)

4. Critics from the school newspaper attended the opening performance. They could write reviews. (so that)

5. Students wrote and performed a play. The townspeople were willing to come. (whenever)

Cumulative Review

Exercise A Identifying Parts of Speech

Read the sayings and fortunes below. In the blank before each numbered item, identify the part of speech of the underlined word in each sentence. Use these abbreviations.

N = noun   ADJ = adjective   CONJ = conjunction
PRON = pronoun   ADV = adverb   INTER = interjection
V = verb   PREP = preposition

___PRON___ 1. Today will be <u>yours</u> for the asking.

___INTER___ 2. <u>Alas</u>, you are the apple of my eye.

___N___   3. Do you know that <u>beauty</u> is in the eye of the beholder?

___ADV___   4. It is <u>equally</u> good to give as it is to receive.

___PREP___ 5. You must choose one thing or another, one <u>at</u> a time.

___ADJ___   6. Success is like a <u>beautiful</u> sunrise, for it comes and goes.

___ADV___   7. The days and nights pass all <u>too</u> quickly when you are content.

___N___   8. <u>Success</u> occurs for those who believe in it.

___V___   9. In the still of the night <u>rises</u> the storm.

___CONJ___ 10. To choose <u>or</u> not to choose is always a question to ponder.

Exercise B Writing Complete Sentences

Revise the following paragraphs to correct sentence fragments and run-on sentences and to eliminate wordiness. Make any other changes that you think will improve these paragraphs. Write your revised paragraph on a separate piece of paper. **Hint:** Not every sentence needs revision. Students' revisions will vary.

[1]Whenever British soldiers sang the song "Yankee Doodle." [2]They insulted American patriots. [3]Ironically, the song became an anthem for George Washington's revolutionary army. [4]In one line of the song, a feather in a soldier's cap is calling "macaroni," an Italian pasta, considering "macaroni" was a derogatory term used in the eighteenth century to ridicule people who attempted to look and act as sophisticated as people from Europe. [5]The British thought of the Americans as uncultured people. [6]The British never thought of the Americans as capable. [7]The Americans would never triumph. [8]Over Britain. [9]Under the command of George Washington, the colonial army proving the British wrong. [10]When the British surrendered, the American military band struck up the tune of "Yankee Doodle." [11]The American military band enjoyed a last laugh about this song.

Exercise C **Identifying Phrases**

On the blank before each numbered item, identify each underlined phrase by writing one of these abbreviations in the space provided.

PREP = prepositional phrase   INF = infinitive phrase
PART = participial phrase   APP = appositive phrase
GER = gerund phrase

GER 1. You may not enjoy <u>focusing on mental fitness</u>.

APP 2. Coach Star, <u>the author of *Get Strong, Get Smart*</u>, believes in mental preparation for sports.

INF 3. <u>To believe that you can win</u>, you must think positively.

PREP 4. If you go <u>into a game</u> without mental preparation, the game is harder to win.

PART 5. Many athletes, <u>upset by a loss</u>, have to work on attitude.

GER 6. <u>Envisioning good results</u> is one way to prepare mentally for a sport.

Exercise D **Identifying Clauses**

Underline every subordinate clause in the sentences below. Then identify each clause by writing *ADJ* for an adjective clause, *ADV* for an adverb clause, or *N* for a noun clause in the space before each sentence.

ADJ [1]The United States Treasury released a new silver dollar <u>that commemorates African American soldiers from the American Revolution</u>.

ADJ [2]Crispus Attucks, <u>who was the first patriot to die at British hands</u>, is on one side of the coin. _ADV_ [3]<u>Because African American families suffered losses</u>, a family appears on the flip side. _ADJ_ [4]A man <u>who spied for George Washington</u>, James Armistead, was African American. _ADV_ [5]<u>Wherever the 1st Rhode Island regiment went</u>, African Americans joined in. _ADJ_ [6]Virginians <u>who died at Valley Forge</u> fought alongside African American patriots. _N_ [7]<u>That African Americans fought in the Revolution</u> is a little known fact. _ADV_ [8]Historians note <u>that more than 5,000 African Americans fought against the British</u>.

Grammar Test

Identifying Errors

Directions: Each of the numbered items either is totally correct or contains an error in one of the underlined word(s) or punctuation marks. In the answers section to the right of each item, circle the letter of the underlined word(s) or punctuation mark that contains the error. If the sentence is correct, circle *D* for NO ERROR.

EXAMPLE Among the states in the United States, only Texas <u>have</u> been named an <div align="center">A</div> independent republic with <u>its</u> own flag and government. <u>NO ERROR</u> <div align="center">B C D</div>	Ⓐ B C D

1. The Comanches, a Native American group in Texas. <u>Obtained</u> horses from
   A
   Spanish explorers. <u>This</u> occurred <u>during</u> the eighteenth century. <u>NO ERROR</u>
   B   C   D

   1. Ⓐ B C D

2. As <u>masterful</u> riders and <u>aggressively</u> fighters, the Comanches <u>successfully</u>
   A   B   C
   pushed the Apache from their Texas lands. <u>NO ERROR</u>
                                              D

   2. A Ⓑ C D

3. Spanish settlement slowed. <u>Just</u> as the population of Texas began to rise,
                              A
   Native American groups. <u>Including</u> the Comanche and Apache, <u>fought</u>
                           B   C
   over the land. <u>NO ERROR</u>
                   D

   3. A Ⓑ C D

4. Up until the late eighteenth century<u>, Texas</u> was part of Mexico<u>, which</u> was
                                        A   B
   ruled <u>from afar</u> by Spain. <u>NO ERROR</u>
         C   D

   4. A B C Ⓓ

5. The Louisiana Purchase of <u>1803, made</u> the United States a neighbor of
                             A
   Spanish Texas<u>; but</u> not <u>until</u> 1819 did a border exist that both sides could
                B   C
   recognize. <u>NO ERROR</u>
               D

   5. A Ⓑ C D

6. The Spanish <u>because they weren't welcomed</u> left Mexico <u>in 1821,</u>
               A   B
   when Mexico won its independence. <u>NO ERROR</u>
   C   D

   6. Ⓐ B C D

7. At this time<u>, Moses Austin</u> started a settlement of Americans. <u>Near</u>
               A   B
   San Antonio, Texas<u>, with</u> the permission of the Mexican government.
                      C
   <u>NO ERROR</u>
   D

   7. A Ⓑ C D

Exercise 2 Correcting Errors

Directions: Each numbered item contains one or more errors. Circle the letter of the correctly written revision. **Hint:** A numbered item may have more than one error.

EXAMPLE Hannah feels sickly. Her fever is going up real rapid

A   B   Ⓒ

    A. Hannah feels sickly. Her fever is going up rapid.
    B. Hannah feels sickly. Her fever is going up rapidly.
    C. Hannah feels sick. Her fever is going up rapidly.

1. When an illness is infectious, really students should stay home

1. A   B   Ⓒ

    A. When an illness is infectious, students should stay really home.
    B. When an illness is infectious. Students should stay really home.
    C. When an illness is infectious, students really should stay home.

2. If you want to recover quick from a cold rest is the best medicine

2. A   B   Ⓒ

    A. If you want to recover quick from a cold, rest is the best medicine.
    B. If you want to recover quickly from a cold. Rest is the best medicine.
    C. If you want to recover quickly from a cold, rest is the best medicine.

3. You often catching a cold through contact, it only takes shaking the hand of a cold victim.

3. A   Ⓑ   C

    A. You often catch a cold through contact, it only takes shaking the hand of a cold victim.
    B. You often catch a cold through contact. It only takes shaking the hand of a cold victim.
    C. You often catch a cold through contact; it only takes shake the hand of a cold victim.

4. Vaccines prevent disease easy. Including polio and other life-threatening illnesses.

4. Ⓐ   B   C

    A. Vaccines prevent disease easily, including polio and other life-threatening illnesses.
    B. Vaccines prevent disease easily; including polio and other life-threatening illnesses.
    C. Vaccines prevent disease easy. Include polio and other life-threatening illnesses.

5. Catching a cold, a person can often prevent by eating properly.

5. A   Ⓑ   C

    A. Catching a cold. A person can often prevent by eating properly.
    B. By eating properly, a person can often prevent catching a cold.
    C. By eating properly, a person can often preventing catching a cold.

6. Exercise has opened the door to health. And people rushed to their local gyms.

    6. A   Ⓑ   C

  A. Exercise has opened the door to health. And people have rushed to their local gyms.

  B. Exercise has opened the door to health, and people have rushed to their local gyms.

  C. Exercise have opened the door to health; and people have rushed to their local gyms.

Exercise 3 Combining Sentences

Directions: On a separate piece of paper, combine the sentences in each numbered item into a single sentence. There is more than one way to combine most sentences.   See Answer Key.

EXAMPLE   Eudora Welty is an American writer. She is a favorite American. She lives in the South.

    Eudora Welty is a favorite American writer who lives in the South.

1. Eudora Welty was born in 1909. She was born in Jackson, Mississippi. Her parents came from the North.
2. Have you read *The Optimist's Daughter*? Her novel is famous. *The Optimist's Daughter* won the Pulitzer Prize.
3. She began to write short stories in 1931. She moved home to Mississippi permanently in 1931.
4. Before 1931, Eudora Welty had graduated from the University of Wisconsin. She had taken a course in advertising at Columbia University. Columbia University is in New York City.
5. Readers gain an understanding of life in the South. This happens through Eudora Welty's characterizations. This happens through the vivid twists of humor in her writing.

Exercise 4 Identifying Parts of a Sentence

Directions: Answer each numbered question by circling, in the answer section, the letter of the sentence that contains the named sentence structure.

1. Which sentence contains a **direct object?**

    1. A   Ⓑ   C

  A. Is that the half-time buzzer for the basketball game?

  B. The referee usually blows a whistle at half-time.

  C. The players will rest during the half-time break.

2. Which sentence contains a **compound verb**?
   A. The wind pushes the boat forward and tips it into the cold surf.
   B. The boat looked strangely mysterious and somewhat frightening in the fog.
   C. A boat accident or an unfortunate mishap can occur in wind or rain.

   2. (A)　B　C

3. Which sentence contains a **gerund phrase**?
   A. She was riding her bike while he was flying a kite.
   B. Flying a kite or riding a bike are perfect park activities.
   C. They were enjoying their day at the park.

   3. A　(B)　C

4. Which sentence contains an **adjective clause**?
   A. The person that you hired is here.
   B. Please describe where I should go?
   C. For that job, you'll need advanced computer skills.

   4. (A)　B　C

5. Which sentence contains an **infinitive phrase**?
   A. Did you give the letter to the postal carrier yesterday?
   B. I brought the letter to the post office and mailed it in person.
   C. The post office clerk asked me to place an extra stamp on the heavy envelope.

   5. A　B　(C)

6. Which sentence contains a **participial phrase**?
   A. The audience, breaking into laughter, began to applaud.
   B. The actors had been rehearsing the humorous scene.
   C. Providing an intermission is usually a good idea.

   6. (A)　B　C

7. Which sentence contains an **adverb clause**?
   A. The governor who lives in our town is up for election.
   B. Was last's year election turnout as heavy?
   C. Because of polling, candidates know how voters feel about issues.

   7. A　B　(C)

8. Which sentence contains a **predicate nominative**?
   A. Ashley will remain a volunteer at the hospital.
   B. The patients seemed happy and satisfied.
   C. The doctors help train the volunteers in the hospital.

   8. (A)　B　C

9. Which sentence contains a **predicate adjective**?
   A. A scary mystery rates at the top of my reading list.
   B. The mystery story that I wrote yesterday was imaginative.
   C. Did you hear that terrific mystery play read on the radio?

   9. A　(B)　C

10. Which sentence contains an **indirect object**?
    A. Is this my decision to make?
    B. The Secretary of State spoke freely about her opinion
    C. The Vice-President brought the President the information.

    10. A　B　(C)

Using Verbs

Visit us at
www.sadlier-oxford.com

Direct students to chapter-specific portfolio projects on Sadlier-Oxford's website.

STUDENT WRITING
Narrative Essay

'Grounds' Brews a Delicious, Earful Experience
by Sara McCann
high school student, Gig Harbor, Washington

Plenty of pastries, exceptional espresso, and wailing harmonicas—all of these things comprise live jazz nights at Grounds for Coffee, a hip joint in Tacoma.

As I parked my car next to the Pantages Theatre, I was a little apprehensive about going through with this experience. I didn't know what to expect from live jazz . . .

As I approached the brick building, the aroma of coffee beans hung in the air. Through the large windows, I could see more than forty people lounging in couches, waiting in line, or sitting around tables talking intensely. It didn't look too scary yet.

Upon opening the door, my senses were overcome with joy. My nose was filled with the smell of pies and other desserts as well as the alluring scent of espresso. My ears were filled with dancing notes from the harmonicas and guitars coming from the room in the far end of the building.

I saw colorful posters clinging to the muted flamingo pink painted wall. I saw people of all ages, from eight to eighty-five, talking to one another, as well as all types of people sitting together. The barriers of diversity were overcome. It was nothing less than amazing.

I made my way to the coffee bar to order drinks. Espresso syrup flavors lined the walls, and the workers behind the counter looked eager to take my order. I took a seat at a table located in the middle of the building. At one end were couches and pillows, and at the other end of the building was the sitting room that has been turned into "jazz room" every Friday and Saturday night.

I sat for awhile, sipping my vanilla latte and listening to the conversations around me. This was perhaps as entertaining as anything else I saw or heard. The talk ranged from the weather to the subconscious state of mind. The thing that I found most interesting was that anybody could just sit down at any random table and be welcomed without introductions. That doesn't happen every day.

When I finished the foam at the bottom of my latte, I decided to join the crowd of people enjoying the music in the adjoining room. I was surprised to see that the people playing music were two men in their twenties who were very talented.

The wailing and moaning I expected to be exposed to turned out to be melodious notes floating and jumping up and down the scale. One man was playing a mean harmonica, while the other was strumming blues chords that made my heart ache. Their style was great, and their music was excellent—lively jazz with a twist of the blues.

I've never really listened to jazz, but after that night, I decided I just might broaden my horizons a bit.

Allow time for students to discuss the student writing. Suggest that they identify its strengths and propose possible improvements. Use the model to introduce the concepts in the chapter.

Sara McCann's narrative essay tells about an experience at a unique coffee shop. Sara includes many sensory details that help the atmosphere come alive.

As you reread the essay, notice how Sara uses mostly past tense verbs. Using verb tenses accurately helps your reader understand the progression of your thoughts. The exercises in this chapter will give you practice using verb tenses correctly.

Regular Verbs

🔹 All verbs have four basic forms, or **principal parts**. They are the present, the present participle, the past, and the past participle.

🔹 Regular verbs add *-d* or *-ed* to the present tense to form the past and past participle.

Principal Parts of Verbs			
PRESENT	PRESENT PARTICIPLE (Use with *am, is, are, was, were.*)	PAST	PAST PARTICIPLE (Use with *has, had, have.*)
discover study guess	(is) discovering (is) studying (is) guessing	discovered studied guessed	(had) discovered (had) studied (had) guessed

The **present participle** of regular verbs ends in *-ing.* It works with the verb *to be* (*am, is, are, was,* or *were*) to make a verb phrase.

   She **is looking** for proof.   He **was searching** for bones.

The **past participle** of regular verbs ends in *-d* or *-ed.* It works with the helping verb *have* (*has, have,* or *had*) to make a verb phrase.

   They **have asked** permission.   You **have** also **received** help.

When you add *-ing* and *-ed* to the present form of a verb, you must apply the spelling rules about dropping the final *-e,* changing the *-y* to *i,* and doubling consonants: *cope, coping, coped; marry, marrying, married; mop, mopping, mopped.* (For more about spelling rules, see Lesson 16.2.)

The past and past participle forms of some verbs may be spelled with two alternative endings: *-ed* or *-t.*

   I **have dreamed** that before.   You **burned** the toast.
   She **dreamt** about a train ride.   The fire **had burnt** through the night.

Editing Tip

When the verbs *use* and *suppose* appear before an infinitive, add the ending *-d,* even though it may be silent in conversation.

   used
I ~~use~~ to play the piano.
   supposed
Are you ~~suppose~~ to go to the concert?

 Don't get too worried about the labels for all the verb forms. It's their correct use that is important in writing.

Exercise 1 Using the Principal Parts of Regular Verbs

To complete each sentence, write in the blank the correct past form or past participle form of the verb in parentheses.

EXAMPLE   Parts of the fossil (resemble) **resembled** both a bird and a dinosaur.

1. Many paleontologists (study) _____studied_____ and (collect) _____collected_____ fossils as children.

2. Recently, paleontologists (unearth) _____unearthed_____ interesting evidence.

3. The evidence (indicate) _____indicated_____ an evolutionary link between birds and dinosaurs.

4. An ancient bird claw (look) _____looked_____ like the claw of a dinosaur.

5. One fossil (remind) _____reminded_____ paleontologists of a turkey.

6. A debate has (continue) _____continued_____ about the link between birds and dinosaurs.

7. Birds may have (descend) _____descended_____ from dinosaurs, or dinosaurs may have (develop) _____developed_____ from birds.

8. This question has (puzzle) _____puzzled_____ paleontologists for decades.

9. They (use) _____used_____ to look for evolutionary evidence of dinosaurs in birds.

10. Recently, however, paleontologists have (concentrate) _____concentrated_____ on evidence of birds in dinosaurs.

Exercise 2 Revising a Journal Entry

Revise this paragraph so that it describes an event that happened in the past. Use the past form and past participle form of the italicized verbs.

enjoyed
[1]I *enjoy* visiting Madagascar, a small island off the coast of east Africa. [2]With
worked   hoped
other paleontologists, I *work* at a dig where we *hope* to find fossils of ancient
uncovered
birds and dinosaurs. [3]One paleontologist *uncovers* a rare specimen in a previous
located   dated
dig. [4]She *locates* a fossil of a feathered meat-eater. [5]Strangely, the fossil *dates* to a
shipped
time after the mass extinction of dinosaurs. [6]The paleontologist *ships* the rock
created
containing the fossil back to the United States. [7]Our dig *creates* great interest in
discovered
these ancient feathered creatures. [8]We *discover* a tail similar to one on a dinosaur
spotted
called a theropod and also a forearm like one on a bird. [9]Paleontologists *spot*

similar discoveries in the United States.

Irregular Verbs 1

Not every past verb form or past participle ends in *-d* or *-ed*. Verbs that vary from the standard pattern are called **irregular verbs**.

🖌 Use the principal parts of these common irregular verbs correctly when you write and speak. The first verb on this chart is also the most irregular English verb—*be*. *Be* has singular and plural forms in both the present and past tenses. Notice that the word *be* by itself is not one of its principal parts. Students will encounter many irregular verbs in their own writing that are not listed on this chart.

Principal Parts of Common Irregular Verbs			
PRESENT	PRESENT PARTICIPLE (Use with *am, is, are, was, were.*)	PAST	PAST PARTICIPLE (Use with *has, had, have.*)
[be] is, are	(is) being	was, were	(had) been
become	(is) becoming	became	(had) become
begin	(is) beginning	began	(had) begun
bite	(is) biting	bit	(had) bitten
blow	(is) blowing	blew	(had) blown
break	(is) breaking	broke	(had) broken
bring	(is) bringing	brought	(had) brought
build	(is) building	built	(had) built
burst	(is) bursting	burst	(had) burst
buy	(is) buying	bought	(had) bought
catch	(is) catching	caught	(had) caught
choose	(is) choosing	chose	(had) chosen
come	(is) coming	came	(had) come
cost	(is) costing	cost	(had) cost
do	(is) doing	did	(had) done
draw	(is) drawing	drew	(had) drawn
drink	(is) drinking	drank	(had) drunk
drive	(is) driving	drove	(had) driven
eat	(is) eating	ate	(had) eaten
fall	(is) falling	fell	(had) fallen
feel	(is) feeling	felt	(had) felt
find	(is) finding	found	(had) found
fly	(is) flying	flew	(had) flown
forget	(is) forgetting	forgot	(had) forgotten; (had) forgot
freeze	(is) freezing	froze	(had) frozen
get	(is) getting	got	(had) gotten; (had) got
give	(is) giving	gave	(had) given
go	(is) going	went	(had) gone
grow	(is) growing	grew	(had) grown

 You can always use a dictionary to check a verb form. A dictionary entry word appears in the present form, but if a verb is irregular, its past, past participle, and present participle forms are listed after the pronunciation.

fly \ flī \ **flew, flown, flying**

Enriching Your Vocabulary

The adjective *indulgent*, as used in Exercise 3, comes from the Latin word *indulgens* which means "lenient." You would be considered *indulgent* if you listened to unceasing complaints from a friend.

Exercise 3 Using Irregular Verbs

To complete each sentence, fill in the blank with the correct past form or past participle form of the verb that appears in parentheses.

EXAMPLE   (forget) She had __*forgotten*__ to lock the door. *or* forgot

1. (give) This author ____gave____ away signed copies of her new novel.

2. (break) The speed skater had ____broken____ the record by a split second.

3. (buy) Had he ____bought____ the skis before the sale?

4. (feel) Yesterday ____felt____ like spring.

5. (build) The indulgent parents have ____built____ a tree house in the woods.

6. (bring) The tourist ____brought____ oranges home from Florida.

7. (grow) The farmer ____grew____ organic vegetables.

8. (catch) The shortstop ____caught____ the ball for the double play.

9. (be) What ____were____ the words to the school song?

10. (go) We ____went____ to Great Adventure last summer.

Exercise 4 Editing a Paragraph

Cross out each incorrect verb, and write the correct verb above it. Make any other changes you think will improve the article.

¹One state high school ~~gotted~~ got a special state award last week. ²The governor had ~~chose~~ chosen a school that developed a community involvement program. ³This program ~~brung~~ brought happiness to senior citizens. ⁴Because of this program, recipients have ~~ate~~ eaten hot, nutritious meals. ⁵Although volunteer chefs had cooked the meals, students with licenses had ~~drove~~ driven them to people's homes. ⁶One student participant in the program said, "I ~~feeled~~ felt my work was important. ⁷I always ~~catched~~ caught a glimpse of a broad smile on Ms. Tan's face when I ~~brung~~ brought her each meal." ⁸Another student noted, "I had ~~forgotted~~ forgotten *or* forgot how great volunteer work is. ⁹With this experience, I ~~felted~~ felt like a positive part of my community." ¹⁰Since the governor has ~~gived~~ given the award to Silver Creek High School, other schools have ~~became~~ become interested in developing community-based programs of their own.

Irregular Verbs 2

In addition to the twenty-nine irregular verbs from the previous lesson, here are another thirty-seven more commonly used irregular verbs.

● Use the principal parts of these common irregular verbs correctly when you write and speak. Students will encounter many irregular verbs in their own writing that are not listed on this chart.

Principal Parts of Common Irregular Verbs			
PRESENT	PRESENT PARTICIPLE (Use with *am, is, are, was, were*.)	PAST	PAST PARTICIPLE (Use with *has, had, have*.)
hold	(is) holding	held	(had) held
hurt	(is) hurting	hurt	(had) hurt
keep	(is) keeping	kept	(had) kept
know	(is) knowing	knew	(had) known
lay [to put or place]	(is) laying	laid	(had) laid
lead	(is) leading	led	(had) led
lend	(is) lending	lent	(had) lent
lie [to rest or recline]	(is) lying	lay	(had) lain
lose	(is) losing	lost	(had) lost
make	(is) making	made	(had) made
meet	(is) meeting	met	(had) met
put	(is) putting	put	(had) put
ride	(is) riding	rode	(had) ridden
ring [to make a sound]	(is) ringing	rang	(had) rung
rise [to stand up]	(is) rising	rose	(had) risen
run	(is) running	ran	(had) run
say	(is) saying	said	(had) said
see	(is) seeing	saw	(had) seen
sell	(is) selling	sold	(had) sold
send	(is) sending	sent	(had) sent
set [to put]	(is) setting	set	(had) set
show	(is) showing	showed	(had) shown
shrink	(is) shrinking	shrank; shrunk	(had) shrunk; shrunken
sing	(is) singing	sang	(had) sung
sink	(is) sinking	sank; sunk	(had) sunk
sit [to rest oneself on a chair]	(is) sitting	sat	(had) sat
speak	(is) speaking	spoke	(had) spoken
stand	(is) standing	stood	(had) stood
steal	(is) stealing	stole	(had) stolen
swim	(is) swimming	swam	(had) swum
swing	(is) swinging	swung	(had) swung
take	(is) taking	took	(had) taken
tell	(is) telling	told	(had) told
throw	(is) throwing	threw	(had) thrown
wear	(is) wearing	wore	(had) worn
win	(is) winning	won	(had) won
write	(is) writing	wrote	(had) written

Writing Hint

Here's a memory trick to help you distinguish *lay*, *raise*, and *set* from *lie*, *rise*, and *sit*. Remember that the first three take direct objects.

YOU CAN:

lay an egg if you are a chicken.

set an egg down on a counter.

raise an egg over your head before you throw it.

BUT YOU CANNOT:

lie an egg,

sit an egg, or

rise an egg.

Exercise 5 Using Irregular Verbs

Complete each sentence by writing the correct past form or past participle form of the verb in parentheses.

1. (rise) The first scene opened just after the moon had ____risen____.

2. (meet) Didi ____met____ Sam, the detective.

3. (take, speak) In the first scene, Sam ____took____ notes and Didi ____spoke____.

4. (win) Didi thought she had ____won____ Sam over.

5. (lay) When Sam left, Didi ____laid____ a canvas on a closet shelf.

6. (write) But first, Didi read a note she had ____written____ to her husband Al.

7. (lie) Al had ____lain____ down for a nap before Sam arrived.

8. (sing, run) When Al heard a loud voice that ____sang____ off key, he ____ran____ downstairs.

9. (throw, say, lose) Didi ____threw____ some towels over the canvas and ____said____ she had ____lost____ a painting.

10. (tell, lead) We wondered if Didi had ever ____told____ Al about Sam, who ____led____ the investigation.

11. (put) In Act 2, Sam ____put____ Al under suspicion.

12. (sit, steal) Then Al ____sat____ down to talk with Didi and discovered she had ____stolen____ the painting.

13. (sink, shrink) Al's heart ____sank____ and his world ____shrank or shrunk____ instantly.

14. (make) Sam had ____made____ remarks Didi didn't appreciate.

15. (show) Sam had ____shown____ his ignorance about art.

16. (see) Didi ____saw____ a chance to test Sam's abilities.

17. (steal, speak) That's why she had ____stolen____ her own artwork and ____spoken____ to Sam.

18. (rise) Sam ____rose____ to the occasion and solved the case.

Exercise 6 Writing Sentences with Irregular Verbs

For each of the following verbs, write a sentence that uses the past form or past participle form of each one: Sentences will vary.

lie (to rest or recline), *lose, make, ring* (to make a sound), *say, set, shrink, swim*

Mid-Chapter Review

Exercise A **Using Regular Verbs**

On a separate piece of paper, write the past or the past participle form of the verb in parentheses for each sentence.

1. Americans (elect) Thomas Jefferson President in 1800. elected

2. In 1762, after graduating from college, he (study) law. studied

3. As a writer and patriot, he (draft) resolutions for the colonies. drafted

4. From 1775 to 1776, he was on the committee that (produce) the Declaration of Independence. produced

5. During the Revolution, Virginia (elect) Jefferson as governor. elected

6. He later (join) the Continental Congress and (try) to establish laws such as freedom of religion. joined; tried

7. Then as minister to France, he (witness) the French Revolution, which he (support). witnessed; supported

8. Jefferson (believe) in a strong central government. believed

9. Jefferson and Hamilton (disagree) about many issues. disagreed

10. Jefferson (form) what later (turn) into the Democratic party. formed; turned

Exercise B **Using Irregular Verbs**

Complete the chart below by filling in the missing principal parts. When you've finished the chart, write two sentences for each verb on a separate piece of paper. Use the past form in one sentence and the past participle form in the other. Students' sentences will vary.

Principal Parts of Verbs			
PRESENT	PRESENT PARTICIPLE	PAST	PAST PARTICIPLE
1. is, are	(is) being	2. was, were	3. (had) been
become	4. (is) becoming	5. became	6. (had) become
7. buy	(is) buying	8. bought	9. (had) bought
catch	(is) catching	10. caught	11. (had) caught
12. eat	13. (is) eating	ate	14. (had) eaten
15. find	16. (is) finding	17. found	(had) found
forget	18. (is) forgetting	19. forgot	20. (had) forgotten *or* forgot
21. hold	22. (is) holding	held	23. (had) held
keep	24. (is) keeping	25. kept	26. (had) kept

Principal Parts of Verbs			
PRESENT	**PRESENT PARTICIPLE**	**PAST**	**PAST PARTICIPLE**
27. lay	28. (is) laying	laid	29. (had) laid
lend	30. (is) lending	31. lent	32. (had) lent
33. lie	(is) lying	34. lay	35. (had) lain
36. ring	37. (is) ringing	38. rang	(had) rung
sell	39. (is) selling	40. sold	41. (had) sold
42. show	(is) showing	43. showed	44. (had) shown
speak	45. (is) speaking	46. spoke	47. (had) spoken
48. tell	49. (is) telling	told	50. (had) told

Exercise C **Proofreading a Paragraph**

In each sentence, correct any mistakes you find in the use of the verb forms. **Hint:** Not every sentence has a verb error, and one sentence has more than one. *The irregular verb* hit *was not included on the charts in Lessons 8.2 and 8.3.*

¹Have you ~~heared~~ (heard) about ENSO? ²Scientists have ~~came~~ (come) up with that term for what most people call El Niño. ³This weather phenomenon ~~hitted~~ (hit) the Pacific Ocean in 1998 with a vengeance. ⁴It ~~begun~~ (began) with a warm southerly flow of ocean current off the west coast of Peru and Ecuador around Christmastime in 1996. ⁵People in southern California have not ~~forgot~~ (or forgotten) the last scrape with ENSO. ⁶During the 1982–1983 period, it ~~rided~~ (rode) through that area and caused over $100 million in damage. ⁷By August 1997, climate experts had ~~sended~~ (sent) a warning to the people of southern California, in particular, where El Niño ~~brung~~ (brought) torrential rains. ⁸Around that time, fishermen had ~~finded~~ (found) fish in deeper waters than usual because of the warm current. ⁹During the winter months, both southern and northern California experienced torrential rains and mud slides. ¹⁰At the same time, people living in Gulf Coast states and the South ~~loosed~~ (lost) homes and other property at record rates due to tornadoes.

Verb Tense

🖋 A **verb tense** expresses the time an action is performed.

Every English verb has three **simple tenses** (present, past, and future) and three **perfect tenses** (present perfect, past perfect, and future perfect).

The Six Verb Tenses		
TENSE	WHAT IT SHOWS	EXAMPLE
Present	action happening in the present; action that happens repeatedly	We **dance** in pairs. We **dance** all night.
Past	action completed in the past	We **danced**.
Future	action that will happen in the future	We **shall dance**. We **will dance**.
Present perfect	action completed recently or in indefinite past	I **have danced**.
Past perfect	action that happened before another action	I **had** already **danced** the foxtrot.
Future perfect	action that will happen before a future action or time	By nine o'clock, I **will have danced**.

Each tense also has a **progressive form**, which is made up of a helping verb and the present participle (the *-ing* form). The progressive forms show ongoing action.

The Progressive Forms for the Six Tenses	
PROGRESSIVE FORM	EXAMPLE
Present progressive	**(am, is, are) dancing**
Past progressive	**(was, were) dancing**
Future progressive	**will (shall) be dancing**
Present perfect progressive	**(has, have) been dancing**
Past perfect progressive	**had been dancing**
Future perfect progressive	**will have been dancing; shall have been dancing**

🖋 Don't switch verb tenses needlessly. Keep tenses consistent whenever possible.

INCONSISTENT   The referee **blows** a whistle, and we **stopped** the game.
CONSISTENT   The referee **blew** a whistle, and we **stopped** the game.

Sometimes, the meaning of a sentence requires a shift in verb tense. Use the verb tense that makes sense, based on what you're trying to communicate.

I **ordered** a sweater that **will arrive** tomorrow.

Editing Tip

Use present-tense verbs (the **literary present tense**) when you write about an author's writing.

In *Walden*, Henry David Thoreau **writes** about his two-year residence at Walden Pond. He **lives** by himself, and for these two years, he **views** the life of society as an outsider. He **comes** to the famous conclusion that people "lead lives of quiet desperation."

Writing Hint

There is yet another verb form that is used for showing emphasis in writing—the **emphatic form**.

I **do know** geography.

He **does know** the location of Guam.

We **did study** maps diligently.

Using Verb Tenses

Replace the italicized verbs either to show actions completed in the past or to show ongoing action, depending on the context.

[1]Last summer, we *take* (took) a vacation in New England. [2]The first stop *is* (was) Boston, Massachusetts. [3]On the way into the city, we *stop* (stopped) at Walden Pond. [4]The famous writer Ralph Waldo Emerson *owns* (owned) the land. [5]His friend Henry David Thoreau *builds* (built) a cabin on the land and *moves* (moved) in on July 4, 1845. [6]He *wants* (wanted) to live a simple life with as few possessions as possible. [7]He *hopes* (hoped) to turn back the clock to simpler times. [8]Industrialization and its effects on New England life *worry* (worried) him greatly. [9]Because of this, he *keeps* (kept) a journal of his experiment in living. [10]The ideas of Henry David Thoreau *affect* (affected) many people since the 1854 publication of his journal *Walden*.

Making Verb Tenses Consistent

On a separate piece of paper, revise any of the following sentences in which you find unnecessary shifts in verb tenses. **Hint:** Most of the sentences that do need revising can be fixed in more than one way.

1. If the temperature drops too low, we ~~wore~~ (will wear) heavy coats and hats.

2. They judged the speed-skating contest only when the finishing times ~~will have been~~ (were) confirmed.

3. I will be competing in the race only after I ~~sharpened~~ (sharpen) my skates.

4. When Mary ~~had already gone~~ (goes) to the starting line, the race will begin.

5. Mary has been training in the hopes that she ~~had made~~ (will make) the Olympic team.

6. The cloud has passed, and the sun ~~will be~~ (is) shining.

7. I lace up and tighten my skates as I ~~have prepared~~ (prepare) for the race.

8. I would have placed second, but I ~~will have been falling~~ (fell).

9. Mary is crossing the finish line that she ~~will have~~ planned to cross tomorrow.

10. If we ~~had been starting~~ (start) today, we will finish the book on time.

Using the Active Voice

📘 When a verb is in the **active voice**, the subject of the sentence performs an action. When a verb is in the **passive voice**, the subject receives an action. The passive voice always uses some form of the helping verb *be*.

ACTIVE	The outfielder **made** a spectacular play.
PASSIVE	A spectacular play **was made** by the outfielder.
ACTIVE	The runner **spiked** the second baseman.
PASSIVE	The second baseman **was spiked** by the runner.
ACTIVE	The relief pitcher **dazzled** the opposing team.
PASSIVE	The opposing team **was dazzled** by the relief pitcher.

📘 Use the active voice when you write because it is stronger and more direct. The passive voice is acceptable when you don't know the performer of an action or when you want to emphasize the action, not the performer.

The best players **were fielded** in the All-Star Game.
[The performer of the action is unknown.]
A glittering trophy **was presented** to the most valuable player.
[The object of the action is stressed instead of the performer.]

Writing Hint

Technical and scientific writers often use the passive voice because the emphasis is placed on the object of the study rather than on the performer.

The experiment **was designed** to test the ability of a cancer vaccine to attack only cancer cells— not healthy cells. The vaccine **was given** to people with advanced lung cancer in hopes that it would reverse the progress of the disease. [Emphasis throughout is on the experiment itself, not on those who performed it.]

Exercise 9 **Using the Active Voice**

On a separate piece of paper, rewrite the sentences below using the active voice. If the passive voice is acceptable, explain why.

EXAMPLE   An Oscar was presented to Gregory Peck for his performance as Atticus Finch.
Gregory Peck received an Oscar for his performance as Atticus Finch.

See sample answers in Answer Key.

1. The poem at President John F. Kennedy's 1961 inauguration was read by Robert Frost.

2. A poem for the 1997 inauguration of President Bill Clinton was recited by Miller Williams.

3. Poems have been read by their authors at various presidential inaugurations.

4. A new surgical procedure was tested by a team of doctors.

5. A cure for brain cancer was developed by researchers at UCLA.

6. Coverage of the experimental procedure was denied by the HMO.

7. Herbal treatments are recommended by some health professionals.

8. Some infectious diseases are cured by antibiotics.

9. Major diseases as well as simple aches or pains can be treated by practitioners of holistic medicine.

10. Herbal tea is drunk by many people as a remedy for anxiety.

11. A survey was done by Landmark Healthcare, Inc., to find out how many people used alternative medicine in the year 1998.

12. It was shown by the survey that health care is growing in popularity.

13. Some type of alternative medicine was used by forty-two percent of the adults surveyed in the study.

14. Herbal therapy, chiropractic care, and massage therapy were turned to most often by the people surveyed.

15. In general, alternative medicine is not usually employed by the people surveyed as a replacement for traditional care.

Exercise 10 Writing with the Passive and Active Voice

On a separate piece of paper, write a paragraph about a hobby or interest you enjoy, such as music, movies, or sports. Most of the sentences in your paragraph should be written in the active voice, but one or two may be in the passive voice. Identify the voice of each of your verbs by marking *ACT* for active voice or *PAS* for passive voice above each one.

Answers will vary. See teacher pages for assessment rubrics.

Exercise 11 Write What You Think

■ **Refer to Composition, Lesson 3.2, to find strategies for writing persuasively.**

On a separate piece of paper, write a paragraph in response to the following statement. State your opinion clearly, and support it with reasons and examples. After you finish, check your writing for the correct use of the passive and active voices.

Most doctors trained in traditional medicine are quick to prescribe drugs—some with serious side effects—for any medical complaint, but they discount the beneficial effects of holistic health care. Medical students should all be trained in such alternative health care methods as acupuncture, therapeutic massage, nutrition, and herbal remedies as well as traditional medicine.

Answers will vary. Give students full credit if they have stated an opinion and attempted to support their opinions. Look for grammatically complete sentences that begin with a capital letter and end with an appropriate end punctuation mark.

Mood

Mood expresses attitude in a sentence and affects the verb forms you use. The three moods you use all the time without even thinking about it are the indicative, the imperative, and the subjunctive.

◗ A verb is in the **indicative mood** when the sentence makes a statement or asks a question.

> The cowboy herds the cattle.
> Did she forget that calf in the field?

◗ A verb is in the **imperative mood** when the sentence makes a direct command or makes a direct request.

> Herd the cattle by noon.
> Please bring that calf to the corral.

The subject of an imperative sentence is omitted but is understood to be *you*.

Mood is something you don't need to worry about because you use mood instinctively and correctly. The only mood that causes writers trouble is the subjunctive mood. If you follow the rules listed below, you'll use the right mood all the time.

◗ A verb is in the **subjunctive mood** when the sentence expresses an indirect command, an indirect suggestion, an indirect statement of necessity, or a condition or a wish that is contrary to fact.

In a *that* clause expressing a requirement, necessity, or wish, the subjunctive calls for the use of the infinitive form of a verb without the word *to*. Use this form whether the subject is singular or plural.

INDIRECT COMMAND	My brother insisted **that** she **follow** him.
INDIRECT SUGGESTION	The rancher urged **that** he **learn** about young calves.
INDIRECT STATEMENT OF NECESSITY	It was necessary **that** she **wear** protective gear.

In a wish or a contrary-to-fact clause beginning with the word *if*, the subjunctive calls for using *were* instead of *was* whether the subject is singular or plural.

> One cowboy wished he **were** the owner of his own ranch.
> If the ranch **were** in Texas, they wouldn't worry about snow.

Writing Hint

Sometimes, the subjunctive mood sounds awkward in a sentence, even though it's grammatically correct. In such cases, rewrite the sentence using an infinitive.

AWKWARD
It was necessary that Kathy attend the workshop.

SMOOTH
It was necessary for Kathy to attend the workshop.

Editing Tip

When you're writing about a wish or something contrary to fact, make sure you use the verb form *were* rather than *was*.

were
If I ~~was~~ rich, I'd buy a huge ranch in Montana.

The verb forms for the subjunctive mood are the same as those for the indicative mood with three exceptions:

1. In the third person singular, the -s is omitted:
   I recommend that Blair **seek** additional tutoring. [not *seeks*]

2. In the present subjunctive mood, the verb form for *be* is always *be*:
   We suggest that the news anchor **be** present on camera during the report. [not *is*]

3. In the past subjunctive mood, the verb form for *be* is always *were*:
   If I **were** able to play an instrument, I'd be in a band. [not *was*]

Exercise 12 Using the Subjunctive Mood

In each sentence, fill in the blank with the correct subjunctive form of the verb in parentheses. Rewrite any awkward sentences on a separate piece of paper.

1. (be) If I _____were_____ a doctor, I would specialize in skin problems.

2. (study) The teacher suggested that Mara _____study_____ harder.

3. (be) Alex wished he _____were_____ in the band.

   The coach urged everyone to practice hard.
4. (practice) The coach urged that everyone _____practice_____ hard.

5. (be) If we _____were_____ professional athletes, we would be role models.

   It was necessary for Elena to work after school.
6. (work) It was necessary that Elena _____work_____ after school.

7. (be) My mother wished that she _____were_____ a professional dancer.

8. (memorize) The teacher insisted that Melanie _____memorize_____ the poem.

9. (be) "If I _____were_____ you, I would tell the truth," Sam said.

10. (take) Alicia demanded that her boyfriend _____take_____ her to the prom.

Exercise 13 Writing Sentences in the Subjunctive Moods

On a separate piece of paper, write sentences about places you would like to travel to, about how you would get there, about how long it would take, and about what you would like to do or see in those places. Write sentences in the subjunctive mood as much as possible. Then exchange papers with classmates or other student pairs to identify the verb's mood in each sentence and the correct verb form.   Students should use the subjunctive mood correctly in their sentences.

Revising and Editing Worksheet 1

Revise these paragraphs on a separate piece of paper. Focus especially on verb tenses, mood, and voice. Make any other changes that you think will improve the report.   Answers will vary. Sample answers given.

[1] Do you think that time ~~went~~ (goes) by more quickly for you now than it ~~does~~ (did) when you ~~was~~ (were) five years old? [2] The feeling that "time flies" is often ~~been~~ considered to be a psychological or emotional response. [3] The human response to time ~~lays~~ (lies) in the brain. [4] Recent studies (have) shown that changes in a person's sense of time relate to changes in a person's central nervous system. [5] People in different age groups were ~~suppose~~ (supposed) to estimate a time period of three minutes. [6] People who most often estimated the time ~~correct~~ (correctly) were in ~~there~~ (their) twenties. [7] People in ~~there~~ (their) sixties had estimated (that) three minutes ~~were~~ (was) closer to three minutes and forty seconds. [8] The perception of the passage of time ~~lie~~ (lay) somewhere between these amounts for people in their thirties and forties.

[9] Researchers think the brain contains a special clock. [10] ~~Researchers think the clock kept~~ (that keeps) track of time. [11] Imagine that every day you ~~had been rided~~ (ride) a bus to school. [12] ~~The bus stopped~~ (which stops) at a red light. [13] ~~The light always had remained red~~ for one full minute. [14] If the light ~~was~~ (were) to ~~remains~~ (remain) red for two minutes one day, the driver would probably ~~moves~~ (move) a foot off the brake after one minute ~~is passing~~ (had passed).

[15] Dopamine is a chemical produced in the brain. [16] ~~The human brain clock has been regulated by dopamine.~~ (that regulates the human clock.) [17] Studies ~~would~~ have ~~been~~ shown that by adding dopamine, the brain clock ~~runned~~ (runs) faster. [18] ~~By~~ (and that) removing dopamine, the brain clock ~~is ran~~ (runs) more slowly. [19] Where ~~does~~ (do) musicians and athletes get their sense of timing, and why do some people struggle with thinking or moving too fast? [20] The brain clock may hold answers to these and other questions.

Revising and Editing Worksheet 2

Work with a partner or small group to revise these paragraphs. Write your revised report on a separate piece of paper, and compare your response with those made by other pairs or groups of classmates. Focus especially on verb tenses, mood, and voice, but make other changes you think will improve the report as well. Answers will vary. Sample answers given.

¹In Bozeman, Montana, John Baden, a retired college professor and writer, was concerned about social issues. ²He suggested that he ~~meets~~ meet with other Montana writers. ³Bozeman ~~are~~ is located in Gallatin County. ⁴Gallatin County needs help, and John Baden ~~feeled~~ felt that writers might be part of a solution. ⁵The county ~~would~~ had been ~~struggled~~ struggling with a poor economy. ⁶In addition, people with ~~different~~ differing interests ~~was use to locking~~ locked horns like the cattle on the Montana range.

⁷It was necessary that writers ~~were~~ be involved with important issues affecting the county, such as land development. ⁸But how could writers influence land use? ⁹More than once in the past, public opinion has been influenced by a writer's words, and Baden hopes his writers ~~might could~~ will do the same. ¹⁰~~So~~ he and other writers in the state ~~meeted~~ met in a workshop that has ~~became~~ become a privately funded, popular project in Montana.

¹¹Writing by the Gallatin members ~~appear~~ appears in various newspapers throughout the West. ¹²Their words ~~has~~ have helped residents of Montana confront issues they have ~~been~~ disagreed on, including the environment.

¹³Lately, a new issue has ~~been~~ given the Gallatin writers an unexpectedly worthy subject: the modern cowboy. ¹⁴The modern cowboy is a person who ~~live~~ lives in Montana but who ~~is working~~ works on a computer. ¹⁵The modern cowboy is someone who doesn't ~~worked~~ work the land in a state noted for its ranchers, foresters, and miners.

Chapter Review

Visit us at
www.sadlier-oxford.com

Exercise A Using Verb Tenses

Change the italicized verb to the verb tense specified in parentheses. You may look back at the charts on page 185. Write your answers on a separate piece of paper.

1. I *set* the table for Thanksgiving dinner. (past perfect)   had set

2. Brad *stirred* the pumpkin soup. (past perfect progressive)   had been stirring

3. Suzy *throws* some flour onto the breadboard. (past)   threw

4. The bread dough *rises* for about an hour. (future perfect progressive)
   will have been rising

5. The guests *arrive* on time. (present perfect)   have arrived

6. The host *serve*s dinner exactly at 6 P.M. (future)   will serve

7. We *hang* our coats in the closet. (present perfect progressive)
   have been hanging

8. The meal *ends* by dark. (future perfect)   will have ended

9. One guest *told* hilarious jokes after dinner. (past progressive)   was telling

10. No one *forgot* this delicious meal. (future)   will forget

Exercise B Using the Active Voice

On a separate piece of paper, rewrite the sentences below to use the active voice whenever possible. If the passive voice is acceptable, explain why.
See Answer Key.

1. Experiments were conducted by a team of researchers.

2. The poem was recited by Margo after the break.

3. The sailboat was propelled by the strong wind.

4. The dam was built by beavers.

5. The Nobel Prize for Literature was won by Polish poets twice in the last twenty years.

6. The gold medal was earned by the world's fastest runner.

7. The shutter in my camera was repaired by the photo technician.

8. The play's set was created by an award-winning scenic designer.

9. A lifesaving drug was developed by the pharmaceutical company.

10. A calendar featuring illustrations of cats was produced by the animal shelter.

Exercise C **Revising a Paragraph**

On a separate piece of paper, revise the paragraph below. Use the active voice whenever possible. Decide whether the paragraph should be past or present tense, and make verb tenses consistent. Answers will vary. Sample answers given.

¹Tornadoes are also ~~knowed~~ known as twisters. ²Tornadoes often ~~had caused~~ cause damage when they touch down, ~~especially~~ if people ~~were~~ are in the path of one. ³~~They~~ it would be wise to dive into a ditch or hide under something heavy. ⁴~~It is suggested that~~ a person ~~hides~~ should hide from falling debris inside a house. ⁵After a tornado warning, people are ~~suppose~~ supposed to go into enclosed rooms without windows for protection. ⁶But where will a tornado ~~striked~~ strike? ⁷Tornadoes ~~would have struck~~ can strike anywhere and everywhere. ⁸Weather conditions, though, ~~had made~~ make areas of the Midwest and the South the most likely candidates for tornadoes. ⁹A tornado ~~formed~~ forms when a warm front hits a cold front during a thunderstorm. ¹⁰This crazy mix of cold and warm fronts ~~shall tilt~~ tilts the layers of air, creating the trademark funnel of a tornado. ¹¹Fortunately, scientists have learned how to predict many tornadoes so they can warn people to seek protection.

Exercise D **Using the Subjunctive Mood**

Write a verb in the subjunctive mood for each sentence below.

1. If I _____were_____ you, I'd return the money.

2. She suggested that the group _____remain_____ quiet during rehearsal.

3. It is necessary that Bill _____finish_____ his dinner.

4. I wish the movie _____were_____ more interesting.

5. If it _____were_____ sunny, we could eat outdoors.

6. The police officer demanded that the thief _____stop_____ running.

7. I require that Roger _____go_____ with us to the beach.

8. The engineer suggested that the astronaut _____put on_____ his space suit.

9. If Beth _____weren't_____ so busy, she would phone her Aunt Kate.

10. If I _____were_____ a carpenter, I would make you a shelf.

Subject-Verb Agreement

STUDENT WRITING
Expository Essay

Twin Towers
by Sara Wechter
high school student, Norwalk, Connecticut

To someone sitting at the top of the bleachers at a Norwalk High School girls' basketball game, it is easy to see why senior Heather Hanson and junior Ayanna Brown have been nicknamed the "twin towers." Standing at 6'3" each, they have been a major backbone in the undefeated 1999 season of girls' basketball. Heather and Ayanna grace the court with a confident air; but off the court, they are anything but cocky.

Both girls say that teamwork is a major component of the game, and one of the major reasons the team has done so well this year (compared to last season's 19–6 record) is that the talent is so spread out. There are many great players on the team who score consistently. Ayanna has an impressive game point average of 15.6, while Heather manages to contribute an average of 10 points per game.

With talent like this, one has to wonder where basketball can take them. Realistically, basketball should be used as a stepping stone to other opportunities, such as college. Heather and Ayanna have big plans for their futures, including a college education and steady careers. Heather has been accepted to Dartmouth, but she has not yet settled on a major. Will she join the WNBA? We will have to wait and see because college is her first priority.

With the talent, hard work, and encouragement of Coach English, these girls have the potential to achieve anything.

Sara Wechter's expository essay about two remarkable athletes is effective because it begins with an attention grabber, offers statistics about the two athletes' success, and tells about their future plans.

Several of Sara Wechter's sentences have two subjects, since she writes about two players. In such cases, subject-verb agreement can be especially tricky. You will learn more about subject-verb agreement as you do the lessons and exercises in this chapter.

Allow time for students to discuss the student writing. Suggest that they identify its strengths and propose possible improvements. Use the model to introduce the concepts in the chapter.

Person, Number, and Intervening Phrases

The subject of a sentence may be in the **first**, **second**, or **third person**, and it may be **singular** or **plural** in number. *I* and *we* are first person; *you* is second person; *he, she, it,* and *they* are third person.

🖋 A third-person **singular subject** takes a **singular verb**. A third-person **plural subject** takes a **plural verb**.

The following chart shows how present tense verbs change when the subject is third-person singular.

Subject-Verb Agreement in the Present Tense		
PERSON	**SINGULAR SUBJECT**	**PLURAL SUBJECT**
1ˢᵗ	I dream and wish.	We dream and wish.
2ⁿᵈ	You dream and wish.	You dream and wish.
3ʳᵈ	He dreams and wishes. Ann dreams and wishes.	They dream and wish. The boys dream and wish.

The verb *be* has three forms to match person and number in the present tense. (See the side column.)

🖋 In a **verb phrase**, the helping verb (HV) must agree with the subject.

  HV S   V   S HV   V
Have they sung that song?   She **has** read the novel.

When a negative construction follows the subject, use the number that agrees with the subject.

  S   V
Math, not social studies or English, **remains** her best subject.

                    S   S   V
Not Saul or Keith, but **Raif** and **Jason complete** the crossword puzzle in the newspaper.

🖋 Sometimes, a prepositional phrase or a clause comes between the subject and verb; this is referred to as an **intervening phrase** or **clause**.

Make sure the verb agrees with the subject of the sentence, not with the object of a preposition or the subject of a clause.

    S   V
The **room** to your right and down the hall **contains** a new computer.

  S   V
The **jobs** that the newspaper advertises **require** sales experience.

Editing Tip

Use *don't* (*do not*) with third-person plural subjects and *doesn't* (*does not*) with third-person singular subjects.

The girls **don't** swim this afternoon.

They **don't** require a signed pass.

Ralph **doesn't** have the assignment.

She **doesn't** support that opinion.

Step by Step

Subject-Verb Agreement in the Present Tense

1. Find the subject of the sentence. **Remember:** The subject of a sentence never appears in a prepositional phrase or clause.

2. Decide whether the subject is singular or plural.

3. Choose the verb form that agrees in number with the subject.

Exercise 1 Choosing the Correct Verb

Underline the subject of each sentence and the verb in parentheses that agrees with the subject. **Hint:** Watch out for intervening clauses or phrases.

1. <u>Students</u> (<u>volunteer</u>, volunteers) to teach minicourses after school.

2. One <u>student</u> (prepare, <u>prepares</u>) a course called Geometry in Art.

3. Eleventh-grade <u>teachers</u> from the same school (<u>supervise</u>, supervises) each instructor.

4. One <u>course</u> (teach, <u>teaches</u>) the history of political speeches.

5. A poetry <u>course</u> (present, <u>presents</u>) English sonnets and Japanese haiku.

6. One student <u>instructor</u> (challenge, <u>challenges</u>) all the math teachers.

7. A <u>course</u> that focuses on wellness (meet, <u>meets</u>) on Mondays.

8. <u>Ms. Shyre</u>, the principal, (hope, <u>hopes</u>) to visit each miniclass.

9. One <u>problem</u> for these classes (<u>is</u>, are) lack of room.

10. (<u>Have</u>, Has) new <u>programs</u> ever begun without a few problems?

Exercise 2 Proofreading a Paragraph

For each mistake in subject-verb agreement in the following paragraphs, cross out the incorrect verb and write the correct verb above it.

[1]How ~~does~~ do publishers decide which books to publish? [2]They hire experts in marketing who research the interests of readers and then report their findings to the editors of publishing companies.

[3]~~Doesn't~~ Don't authors influence what gets published? [4]For example, Aneela French, not John Alep or Elena Cayge, ~~hire~~ hires a literary agent to contact publishers about a book she wrote on sailing. [5]John Alep ~~don't~~ doesn't have an agent, so he participates in publishing contests advertised in magazines. [6]Elena Cayge, who has written five unpublished books, ~~send~~ sends a manuscript for a children's book directly to a publisher for consideration. [7]An editorial board of readers and marketing experts ~~decide~~ decides whether or not a manuscript, with merits as well as shortcomings, ~~become~~ becomes a published book.

Agreement with Indefinite Pronouns

An **indefinite pronoun** expresses an amount or refers to an unspecified person or thing. Some indefinite pronouns are always singular; others are always plural.

Always Singular

anybody	neither
anyone	nobody
each	no one
either	one
everybody	somebody
everyone	someone

Always Plural

both	many
few	several

◖ In the present tense, use a singular verb when the subject is a singular indefinite pronoun. Use a plural verb when the subject is a plural indefinite pronoun.

SINGULAR　　**Each** of the scientists **performs** experiments.

PLURAL　　**Several** of the experiment results **help** doctors treat illnesses.

SINGULAR　　**Either** of the laboratories **contains** lasers.

◖ Depending on how they're used in a sentence, the following indefinite pronouns may take a singular or a plural verb: *all*, *any*, *some*, *most*, *none*.

SINGULAR　　**Most** of the hospital **remains** open on weekends.

Some of this cake **belongs** to the nurses.

Is any of the medicine ready to be picked up?

All of the blood **is** donated by students.

PLURAL　　**Most** of the patients **complete** an information form.

Some of our doctors **work** the midnight shift.

Any of the diseases on this floor **are** contagious.

All of the rooms **are** clean.

The pronoun *none* is especially tricky. Use a singular verb only when you can think of the subject as "none of it." Use a plural verb when you can substitute "none of them."

None of the test **is** easy. [None of *it* is easy.]

None of your answers **are** right. [None of *them* are right.]

Exercise 3　Choosing the Correct Verb

Underline the subject of each sentence and the verb in parentheses that agrees in number with the subject.

1. <u>Many</u> (<u>participate</u>, participates) in volunteer programs throughout high school.

2. <u>Several</u> of my classmates (<u>belong</u>, belongs) to Youth Engaged in Service, or YES.

3. <u>All</u> of the communities (<u>benefit</u>, benefits) from YES's programs.

4. <u>One</u> of the schools (ask, <u>asks</u>) the entire freshman class to participate.

5. In YES, <u>everybody</u> who volunteers (choose, <u>chooses</u>) a charity to help.

6. YES provides grants, and <u>everyone</u> on YES teams (work, <u>works</u>) to match them.

7. <u>One</u> of the group's favorite charities (<u>is</u>, are) literacy.

Enriching Your Vocabulary

The verb *gratify* on page 200 means "to give pleasure or satisfaction to." Derived from the Latin word *gratificare*, meaning "to oblige or please," it has the same root as the word *grace*. The curator was *gratified* to see the excellent restoration of the ancient icons.

8. Everybody (is, are) encouraged to join the YES network.

9. All in the YES network (start, starts) with a phone call to Washington.

10. Most of the volunteers (reap, reaps) the rewards of helping others.

Exercise 4 Writing Complete Sentences

Working in pairs or small groups, write a complete sentence on a separate piece of paper for each numbered item. Use the group of words as the subject of the sentence. Use present tense verbs, and check your sentences for correct subject-verb agreement. Read your sentences aloud for extra practice in hearing the sound of correct agreement. Students' sentences will vary.

1. Everyone I know

2. Few of the students

3. None in this group

4. Most of my time

5. Several of us wandering through

6. All of the tutors

7. Nobody over there

8. Neither of these papers

9. Any of the group members

10. Both of the textbooks

Exercise 5 Proofreading a Paragraph

Proofread the paragraph below. Correct any errors you find in subject-verb agreement. **Hint:** One of the sentences contains no errors; two sentences have more than one error.

¹One of the many feelings student volunteers gain ~~are~~ is a sense of self-worth. ²How ~~do~~ does this feeling come about in teenagers who volunteer for community service? ³Well, many of them ~~says~~ say that raising money to help others ~~make~~ makes them feel that they are giving to rather than taking from their community. ⁴Based on student comments, everybody in such a volunteer group ~~feel~~ feels gratified by his or her efforts. ⁵There ~~is~~ are local organizations as well as national ones to help teenagers organize volunteer groups. ⁶Volunteers decide how to raise money for a charity or group. ⁷In time, everybody on the team ~~raise~~ raises money or ~~assist~~ assists the charity directly. ⁸These methods ~~serves~~ serve a community and the individual volunteers well. ⁹Volunteers often ~~says~~ say that they feel a new sense of connection to their communities.

Agreement with Compound Subjects

When two or more subjects share the same verb, a sentence has a **compound subject**. There are particular rules that apply to compound subjects and verb forms in the present tense.

Editing Tip

A singular subject followed by *as well as* or *together with* takes a singular verb form; the subject is not compound.

Hawaii as well as Alaska ~~are~~ *is* not part of the mainland United States.

Salt together with garlic ~~season~~ *seasons* the meat.

◗ When two or more singular subjects are joined by *and*, they take a plural verb.

> Arizona, New Mexico, Utah, **and** Colorado **meet** at an area known as the Four Corners.

◗ When two or more singular subjects are joined by *or* or *nor*, they take a singular verb.

> Neither Iowa **nor** Nebraska **borders** an ocean.
> Either Interstate 70 **or** 80 **spans** the United States.

◗ When a singular subject and a plural subject are joined by *or* or *nor*, the verb agrees with the subject closer to it.

> Corn **or** soybeans **grow** on most Iowa farms.
> **Is** barley **or** oats grown in Iowa, too?
> Neither the White Mountains **nor** Lake Winnipesaukee **disappoints** a visitor to New Hampshire.
> **Are** water skis **or** a surfboard easier to use in the ocean?

Step by Step

Agreement with Compound Subjects

1. Identify the compound subjects. **Remember:** The subject of a sentence never appears in a prepositional phrase.

2. Find the conjunction that connects the subjects: *and*, *or*, or *nor*.

3. When *or* or *nor* connects the subjects, use a singular verb only if the subject nearer the verb is third-person singular.

Exercise 6 **Choosing the Correct Verb**

Underline the subject of each sentence and the verb in parentheses that agrees with the subject. **Hint:** Not every sentence has a compound subject.

1. Vermont and New Hampshire (lie, lies) on the Massachusetts border.

2. Both the Atlantic and the Pacific (border, borders) the United States.

3. Neither the bus nor the trains (stop, stops) at every small town.

4. (Is, Are) buttes or a mesa visible from the banks of the Rio Grande?

5. The children or their guide (has, have) wandered off the trail.

6. Pike's Peak together with the Continental Divide (stun, stuns) me on every visit to Colorado.

7. San Francisco or the northern counties (is, are) where we'll visit.

8. The <u>Delaware River</u> as well as the Hudson River (form, <u>forms</u>) a state border.

9. Neither <u>Kansas</u> nor the two <u>Dakotas</u> (<u>produce</u>, produces) as much cattle as Texas.

10. Either my <u>brother</u> or my <u>parents</u> (<u>want</u>, wants) to tour NASA.

Exercise 7 **Writing a Description**

In one paragraph on a separate piece of paper, describe a place that means something special to you. It could be a waterfall, a wood, a library, a shop, a park, a stadium, even a city street—any place that you cherish. Describe how the place makes you feel. What makes it special to you? How does the place look, smell, and sound? Try to include compound subjects and at least one indefinite pronoun in your paragraph. When you're done, ask a classmate to look over your work to check it for subject-verb agreement.   Students' paragraphs will vary. Refer to the teacher pages for assessment rubrics.

Exercise 8 **Writing a Paragraph**

Based on the following notes, write a paragraph for a report about the structure of the U.S. government. Use present tense verbs. Then, get together in a small group to read your paragraphs aloud and to check one another's sentences for subject-verb agreement.   Students' paragraphs will vary.

Executive, Legislative, Judicial: 3 branches of U.S. government

Congress = legislative branch of federal government

Elected positions in Congress: 2 senators for each state in Senate, differing numbers of representatives for each state in House of Representatives

All federal courts and the Supreme Court = Judicial branch

President and Vice President of United States = Elected officials in executive branch

Make laws: legislative branch

Carry out laws: executive branch

Check fairness, decide punishment for breaking laws: judicial branch

Checks and balances—the three branches of government work together

Constitution and the Bill of Rights: documents allow for development of new laws by legislative branch; these documents check actions and behavior of people and groups by judicial branch

---

Agreement with Subjects Following Verbs and with Collective Nouns

◖ A verb (V) must agree with the subject (S) even when the subject follows the verb.

      V   S
Where **are** those **articles** about jogging from *Runners* magazine?
           V   S
Across the sky **scoot** the billowing **clouds**.

◖ A verb agrees with the subject, *not* with the predicate nominative.

        S   V   PN
Tonight's **topic is vacations**.
   S   V   PN
Vacations in Italy **seem** an **answer** to my prayers.

◖ **Collective nouns**, like those listed in the side column, name a group of people or things.

Use a singular verb when you think of a collective noun as one unit. Use a plural noun when you think of a collective noun as lots of separate individuals.

    The **committee votes** tomorrow. [*Committee* refers to a single unit and takes a singular verb.]
    The **press** usually **ask** a variety of questions. [*Press* refers to multiple members in the group and takes a plural verb.]

◖ Some nouns ending in *-s* function as singular subjects and take a singular verb. Some function as plural subjects and take a plural verb. A few may be either singular or plural, depending on the context and meaning.

Some nouns that end in *-s* are listed in the side column. The nouns that are always plural usually constitute a pair of something or an object made up of parts working together.

SINGULAR   **Physics explains** how you win a tug of war.
PLURAL   **Are** your **eyeglasses** too weak or too strong?

SINGULAR   **Statistics is** a tough course in college.
PLURAL   **Statistics are** the basis of this report.

SINGULAR   **Is politics** an interest of yours?
PLURAL   How **do** the **politics** affect the seating chart in the class?

Some Collective Nouns

audience	flock
class	group
club	herd
committee	pair
crowd	(the) press
family	(the) public
	team

Singular

mathematics	news
measles	physics
mumps	

Plural

binoculars	scissors
eyeglasses	shorts
pants	stairs

Singular or Plural

acoustics	statistics
politics	series

Exercise 9 | Choosing the Correct Verb

Underline the verb in parentheses that agrees with the subject.

1. Statistics (<u>support</u>, supports) the conclusions in her study.

2. If the audience (applaud, <u>applauds</u>), take a deep bow.

3. The press (tend, <u>tends</u>) to frustrate celebrities. *accept* tend

4. A pair of new speakers (cost, <u>costs</u>) more than I can spend.

5. The Rangers together with their coach (<u>agree</u>, agrees) on a strategy.

6. (Has, <u>Have</u>) mumps become a problem in the child-care center?

7. Those pants (<u>look</u>, looks) antique but fashionable.

8. These binoculars (<u>work</u>, works) well for bird-watchers.

9. Where (do, <u>does</u>) the club sell books at this sale?

10. (<u>Is</u>, Are) the crowd cheering for the Oscar-winning actress?

Exercise 10 | Writing Complete Sentences

Write a sentence using each word listed below as the subject. Makes sure that the verb in each sentence agrees in number with the subject. Write your sentences in the present tense. Students' sentences will vary.

EXAMPLE   politics

The politics in the race for mayor are nasty and embarrassing.

1. news

2. acoustics

3. stairs

4. class

5. flock

6. mathematics

7. scissors

8. crowd

9. measles

10. club

Exercise 11 | Write a Description

■ Refer to **Composition, Lesson 2.4, for tips on writing a descriptive paragraph.**

On a separate piece of paper, write a brief paragraph in response to the question below. Support your response with facts, reasons, and examples. Check to make sure you're using proper subject-verb agreement.

You are performing at a school fund-raiser with a heavy-metal rock group. The auditorium is packed with students, the school and local press, teachers, and parents. How would the audience and various members of it react to your performance?

In your writing, use collective, plural, and singular nouns to describe the action and reactions on stage and in the audience.

Other Problems in Agreement

Here are other situations in which subject-verb agreement may become problematic.

■ For more on adjective clauses, see **Grammar**, Lesson 7.2.

● For subject-verb agreement in an adjective clause, look for the antecedent of the relative pronoun. The antecedent is what determines whether the verb is singular or plural.

> She is one of those **athletes** who **compete** hard and **win** often. [The verbs agree with *athletes*.]
> This is the **game** that **tests** her strength. [The verb agrees with *game*.]

● The title of a work of art (painting, movie, literature, or music) is always a singular subject and takes a singular verb.
> *The Thirty-Nine Steps* **is** my favorite Hitchcock movie.
> *The Birds* **is** coming.

● Use a singular verb with a third-person subject that names a single amount or time. Use a plural verb with a third-person subject that refers to multiple items.
> **Two-thirds is** the answer to the division problem.
> [a single amount]
> **Three dollars is** not enough to buy an entire pizza.
> [a single amount]
> These three **dollars are** damaged. [multiple items]
> **Two weeks** of vacation always **passes** too quickly. [a single time period]
> **Six months equals** half of a year. [a single time period]
> These dark winter **days are** passing slowly. [multiple items]

● Use a singular verb with names of organizations that are plural in form.
> **The Campfire Girls is** an organization for young females.

Use a singular verb when *many a(n)* and *every* comes before a compound subject.

Many a student **and** tutor **meets** at the coffee shop.

Every Monday **and** Wednesday **is** soccer practice.

Exercise 12 Choosing the Correct Verb

Write the correct form of the verb in parentheses on the blank to complete each sentence.

1. (say) I agree with the speakers who ___say___ people should read.

2. (boast) *Luck Strikes* ___boasts___ a cast of happy actors and actresses.

3. (tell) *Green Hills and Winding Roads* ___tells___ a story about

   eighteenth-century Virginia.

4. (shine) The cars that ___shine___ in the showroom window are the most expensive models that the dealership sells.

5. (pitch) The campers who ___pitch___ their tents under a tree are sheltered from rain.

6. (begin) "Talk Counts," a radio show, ___begins___ at 3 P.M.

7. (represent) Three months ___represents___ the length of a season.

8. (seem) Three-eighths ___seems___ to be the right answer.

9. (listen) Many a boy and girl ___listens___ to tales told aloud.

10. (be) ___Is___ every first and third Monday a regular business day for our health club?

11. (help) Weight Watchers ___helps___ millions of people control their eating.

12. (sponsor) On the Fourth of July, the Teamsters ___sponsors___ the town parade.

13. (quarrel) Nearly every brother and sister ___quarrels___ over borrowing the car.

14. (make) Two weeks ___makes___ up a fortnight.

15. (grow) Many a flower and shrub ___grows___ best in the sun.

16. (make) Four score years ___makes___ up eighty years.

17. (be) *Wuthering Heights* ___is___ my favorite novel.

18. (work) My sister, who ___works___ as a nurse, is coming to visit.

19. (become) Every nook and cranny ___becomes___ filled with mud after a flood.

20. (scorn) Howard is one of the many who ___scorn___ bottled water.

Exercise 13 **Create Your Own Exercise**

On a separate piece of paper, write two sentences as examples of each of the four rules about subject-verb agreement in this lesson. Then, rewrite the sentences using the same format as in Exercise 12 above. Exchange papers with a classmate, and complete the sentences with the correct verb forms. Exchange papers again to check the sentences, and discuss questions you or your partner might have about subject-verb agreement.   Answers will vary.

Revising and Editing Worksheet 1

Revise these paragraphs on a separate piece of paper. Focus especially on subject-verb agreement, but make any other changes that you think will improve the report. Answers will vary. Subject-verb agreement errors are corrected.

[1] ~~Are~~ Is Yoknapatawpha County a real place? [2] Many a fan and critic ~~wonder~~ wonders about this while reading the novels of William Faulkner (1897–1962). [3] A series of novels by this author ~~take~~ takes place in this fictitious county, modeled after Jefferson County, Mississippi, Faulkner's real home.

[4] The politics of Yoknapatawpha County ~~reflect~~ reflects the politics of the real Mississippi in the century after the Civil War. [5] The aristocracy of the South ~~cling~~ clings to its pride with difficulty. [6] The poorer members of society ~~holds~~ hold on to the value of life with great difficulty.

[7] Faulkner himself ~~come~~ comes from a well-to-do Mississippi family. [8] The political and commercial exploits of his great-grandfather, Colonel William C. Falkner, ~~was~~ were legendary. [9] The twentieth-century author's ancestor, who lived life with great flair and style, ~~were~~ was killed by one of his political rivals. [10] Today, many still ~~loves~~ love the characters from Yoknapatawpha County. [11] ~~Many still admires~~ and admire Faulkner's unique writing style. [12] Almost all of Faulkner's novels—after his third novel—~~is~~ are set in this place. [13] One of them ~~include~~ includes a map. [14] All his novels ~~focuses~~ focus on the psychology of people. [15] The early novels ~~presents~~ present views that are different from those of the later ones.

[16] An earlier novel like *Sartoris*, which was written when Faulkner was a young man, ~~reveal~~ reveals his more negative views about people. [17] But by the time he won the Nobel Prize for Literature (1949), the mature Faulkner said, "Man will not merely endure; he will prevail."

[18] Which of the books written by William Faulkner ~~are~~ is your favorite?

Revising and Editing Worksheet 2

Work with a partner or small group to revise these paragraphs. Write your revised passage on a separate piece of paper, and compare your response with those made by other pairs or groups of classmates. Focus especially on subject-verb agreement, but make any other changes that you think will improve the passage. Answers will vary. Subject-verb agreement errors are corrected.

¹Casey, a book critic for the local newspaper, together with other journalists
eats
~~eat~~ lunch at the same café each day. ²A friend and Casey ~~begins~~ to talk about
begin
Have
books. ³"~~Has~~ there been many books written about the experience of Native

Americans in the recent past?" the friend, Amanda, asks. ⁴As a reviewer of
knows
current books, Casey ~~know~~ the answer immediately.
write
⁵"One of those authors who ~~writes~~ memoirs is William Least Heat Moon,"
write
Casey answers. ⁶Then, he continues, "Some, like this author, ~~writes~~ about
tells
unique experiences. ⁷*Blue Highways* ~~tell~~ about William Least Heat Moon's travels

around the United States in the 1970s."

⁸Casey explains how the author leaves a college in Columbia, Missouri. ⁹The
has
author ~~have~~ taught English and literature courses at the college. ¹⁰William Least
known
Heat Moon is also ~~know~~ as William Trogdon. ¹¹William Least Heat Moon heads

out to small towns throughout the United States. ¹²Either *Leaves of Grass* or
becomes
Black Elk Speaks ~~become~~ the author's reading companion as he travels. ¹³One
is
book ~~are~~ a series of poems; the other book is a Native American memoir.
represents
¹⁴Three months ~~represent~~ a small part of his coast-to-coast trip to places such as

Dime Box, Texas and Ninety-Six, South Carolina. ¹⁵Neither Igo nor Ono,
fades
California, ~~fade~~ from the author's memory because of their odd names.
attracts
¹⁶Casey tells Amanda that a community ~~attract~~ the author because William

Least Heat Moon thinks he might find something out about his own ancestry.
, which
¹⁷~~His ancestry~~ is part Native American. ¹⁸Several of the book's chapters ~~shows~~
show

how willingly people share their personal histories with a stranger such as

William Least Heat Moon.

Chapter Review

Exercise A Choosing the Correct Verb

Choose the verb in parentheses that agrees with the subject.

1. (Is, <u>Are</u>) the employer and her employees in a meeting?

2. Mathematics (cause, <u>causes</u>) many students to seek out tutors.

3. This bulletin board, not that pencil sharpener, (stay, <u>stays</u>) here.

4. Somebody on these school teams (<u>has</u>, have) many trophies.

5. Any of these books (<u>belong</u>, belongs) on the library reserve shelves.

6. How (<u>is</u>, are) the public responding to the new mayor?

7. Neither the dogs nor the cat (<u>has</u>, have) vaccination tags.

8. (Is, <u>Are</u>) the book, magazine, and pamphlet free?

9. Joe, as well as Mike and Tami, (create, <u>creates</u>) recipes.

10. Sal and Beth (is, <u>are</u>) among those students who (<u>get</u>, gets) high grades.

Exercise B Proofreading a Paragraph

For each mistake in subject-verb agreement in the following paragraph, cross out the incorrect verb, and write the correct verb above it. **Hint:** Not every sentence contains an error; one sentence has more than one error.

¹Because our school has students from many foreign countries, a special welcome committee ~~greet~~ (greets) newcomers. ²Some of the foreign students are children of diplomats who ~~works~~ (work) in embassies. ³Alida and Sarkis speak languages other than English. ⁴Russian and Armenian as well as English ~~is~~ (are) spoken in their homes. ⁵The parents of Akeem ~~works~~ (work) for a Nigerian newspaper. ⁶Each of his parents ~~write~~ (writes) a column about the United States. ⁷The international press ~~have~~ (has) many representatives in our city; therefore, the children ~~attends~~ (attend) our schools. ⁸International Kids ~~are~~ (is) the name of a club in our school that everyone is welcome to join. ⁹The group ~~consist~~ (consists) of students from four continents, including the United States. ¹⁰Every boy and girl ~~take~~ (takes) turns presenting something special about his or her language and culture.

Exercise C Writing Complete Sentences

On a separate piece of paper, write a complete sentence for each numbered item, beginning your sentence with the given word or group of words. Use present-tense verbs, and check your sentences for correct subject-verb agreement. Students' sentences will vary.

1. Both you and I . . .

2. Three ingredients in the soup . . .

3. The only reason that counts . . .

4. A flock of birds . . .

5. No one . . .

6. Few . . .

7. Neither English nor other languages . . .

8. The Forest Rangers of America . . .

9. She is one of those dancers who . . .

10. The public . . .

11. Each of us . . .

12. Either the judge or the jury members . . .

13. None of the contestants . . .

14. Anybody in the crowd . . .

15. *The Honeymooners* from the 1950s . . .

16. National politics . . .

17. Every car, truck, and van . . .

18. Which . . .?

19. Thirty-eight dollars . . .

20. *The Adventures of Huckleberry Finn* by Mark Twain . . .

Exercise D Write What You Think

On a separate piece of paper, write a paragraph in response to the statement below. Support your opinion with reasons and examples.

Today's young people spend so much time playing computer games and surfing the Internet that they ignore the beauty and grandeur of nature. Schools should make sure their teenagers spend a minimum of four hours a week outdoors doing physical activities such as hiking, playing sports, and even gardening while they learn about the environment. Such activities are just as important as English or math.

Answers will vary. Give students full credit if they have stated an opinion and attempted to support their opinions. Look for grammatically complete sentences that begin with a capital letter and end with an appropriate end punctuation mark.

Using Modifiers

STUDENT WRITING
Narrative Essay

Team Captain
by Adele Grundies
high school student, La Mesa, California

My first thought was "Cool: something for my college application." When I was appointed captain of my high school tennis team, I had no idea how much responsibility the new title would hold. After practice that first day, my coach asked me if I had any ideas about uniforms that year. Uh-oh. I had no clue what this job would consist of.

After practice every day, I was already worn out and did not need the additional burden of having to drive from one sports store to the next for tennis skirts. By the time I got home at 5:30 and tried to order shirts, I realized that all silk-screening stores had already closed. I also didn't realize that a white T-shirt cost $3 while a white tank top cost $25, a fact that was difficult to explain to the rest of the team.

Finally, we needed some kind of fund-raiser. In the hot days of September, with thirty energetic girls, I decided to have a car wash. I made up dozens of flyers, piles of tickets, and lists for people to bring buckets, signs, soap, sponges, and towels. The first weekend was so successful that we had a second car wash. Seeing everything come together was amazing because everyone was working together and having fun.

All of this work wore me down, but it also gave me the excitement of responsibility, which I loved. During our daily runs, instead of joking around with complaints of exhaustion, I would push myself to be a good example to the rest of the team, and I yelled my encouragement whenever possible. As the other seniors took their cue from me and began acting in the same manner, I saw the team come together in a way that had never happened in the past three years that I'd been on it. I felt like a captain.

Adele Grundies's essay is effective because she concisely explains a challenge she faced, how she confronted the challenge, and the effect it has had on her. As you write essays for college applications or other purposes, think about how these qualities can strengthen your own essay.

Reread the essay, and pay particular attention to Adele's pronouns. How many different kinds of pronouns does she use? How do they help create her casual style? In this chapter, you'll practice using pronouns correctly in various writing exercises.

Allow time for students to discuss the student writing. Suggest that they identify its strengths and propose possible improvements. Use the model to introduce the concepts in the chapter.

Using Subject Pronouns

This chart shows you subject pronouns. Notice that the second-person pronoun *you* is the same in both the singular and plural forms.

Subject Pronouns	
SINGULAR	**PLURAL**
I, you, he, she, it	we, you, they

◄ Use a **subject pronoun** when the pronoun functions as the subject (S) of a sentence or clause. Most mistakes are made when the pronoun is part of a compound sentence element.

      S   S
The artist and **I** took part in a panel discussion. [The pronoun is part of a compound subject.]

          S   S
The sculptor **whom you** and **I** met in the museum is famous. [The pronouns are subjects of the adjective clause.]

◄ Use a subject pronoun when the pronoun functions as the predicate nominative (PN) of a sentence or clause.

Remember: A **predicate nominative** is a noun or pronoun that follows a form of the verb *be* and renames or identifies the subject.

             PN   PN   PN
The volunteers were Sean, Yokiko, and **he**.

                    PN   PN
The co-chairs of the committee are Terri and **I**.

Exercise 1 · Choosing the Correct Pronoun

On a separate piece of paper, write a subject pronoun that correctly completes each sentence.

EXAMPLE   The teenagers in the tennis tournament are you and ___*she*___.

1. Venus Williams said that ___she___ and her sister are the top two female tennis players.

2. The sisters have proven that ___they___ can rise through the ranks quickly.

3. If ___you___ were a talented player, would ___you___ compete professionally?

Writing Hint

When someone on the phone asks, "Who is this?" you probably say, "It's me." But be sure to use a subject pronoun in writing or on grammar tests when the pronoun comes after a form of *be*: "It's **I**" or "It is **we**."

Step by Step

Use these steps to choose the correct pronoun in compound subjects:

Allie and (me, I) plan to run the marathon.

1. Say the sentence with just the pronoun:

   Me plan to run the marathon. [sounds wrong]

   I plan to run the marathon. [sounds right]

2. Use the pronoun that sounds right:

   Allie and **I** plan to run the marathon.

4. The girls' mother explains that ___she___ acts as coach and manager, too.

5. Their father calls them during tournaments because ___he___ can't attend their matches.

6. The exciting rivalry between Martina Hingis and Venus keeps ___them___ both in form.

7. Martina was ranked number one until ___she___ lost to Venus.

8. As a strong tennis player, Venus believes that ___she___ can beat any man.

Exercise 2 **Editing a Paragraph**

Edit the following paragraph to correct all errors in pronoun usage. **Hint:** Two of the sentences contain no errors.

¹Someone asked if Jeff and ~~me~~ [I] want to become professional athletes. ²Jeff and ~~me~~ [I] said, "No, thank you." ³Articles about teenage athletes explain how ~~them~~ [they] have to practice for hours after school. ⁴Take professional tennis players or ice skaters. ⁵~~Them~~ [They] must travel all the time while practicing and continuing an education. ⁶Would Jeff and ~~me~~ [I] like to live in hotels, away from friends and family all the time? ⁷A tennis player such as Martina Hingis, ranked number one in the world at sixteen, may not like the lonely hotel life, but she must enjoy the success. ⁸Venus Williams and ~~her~~ [she] need strong support from their families. ⁹Both players say that ~~them~~ [they] depend on their parents for coaching and personal guidance. ¹⁰Would Jeff or ~~me~~ [I] like to be at the top of the athletic world?

Exercise 3 **Write What You Think**

■ Refer to **Composition**, Lesson 3.2, to find strategies for writing persuasively.

On a separate piece of paper, write a one-paragraph response to the following statement. Support your opinion with facts, reasons, and examples.

Young athletes who compete professionally run the risks both of sustaining serious injuries to joints and bones that are not fully developed and of missing out on educational and social opportunities that are part of growing up. With this in mind, a rules committee has proposed the following rule: No one under the age of eighteen may compete professionally in tennis, figure skating, gymnastics, baseball, basketball, football, or hockey.

Answers will vary. Give students full credit if they have stated an opinion and attempted to support their opinions. Look for grammatically complete sentences that begin with a capital letter and end with an appropriate end punctuation mark.

Using Object Pronouns

This chart shows you object pronouns. Notice that the second-person pronoun *you* is the same in both the singular and plural forms, and it is the same for both subject and object pronouns.

Object Pronouns	
SINGULAR	**PLURAL**
me, you, him, her, it	us, you, them

◖ Use an **object pronoun** when the pronoun functions as the direct object (DO) or indirect object (IO) of a sentence or a clause. Most mistakes occur with compound-sentence structure.

                                  DO   **DO**
As part of the play, Derek pushes **you** and **me**.

                        IO   **IO**   **DO**
Nadine showed the **boys** and **us** her **souvenirs**.

       IO   **IO**   **DO**
Ian asked **you** and **him** a difficult **question**.

◖ Use an object pronoun when the pronoun functions as the object of a preposition (OP) in a sentence.

                       OP   **OP**
Please stand behind **Roger** and **him**.

       OP
Besides **me**, nobody has the combination to the safe.

◖ Use an object pronoun when the pronoun functions as an object complement (OC). (See Lesson 5.9 for more on object complements.)

                     DO   **OC**
The street mime made his **audience us**.

             DO   **OC**   **OC**
I consider the **winners you** and **me**.

When an object is a compound object, use the step-by-step approach you learned on page 213. Test each pronoun alone, and say the sentence aloud to yourself. Let your ear help you decide the correct pronoun to use.

Editing Tip

Be sure to use an object pronoun when the pronoun functions as an object of a preposition. Avoid these common errors:

                         me
This is just between you and ~~I~~.

I gave the tickets to Carly
    him
and ~~he~~.

Be especially alert with pronouns in a compound object.

Step by Step

To decide whether to use a subject pronoun or an object pronoun:

1. Decide what function the pronoun performs in the sentence.

2. If the pronoun is a subject or a predicate nominative, choose the subject pronoun.

3. If the pronoun is a direct object, an indirect object, an object complement, or the object of a preposition, choose the object pronoun.

Exercise 4 Choosing the Correct Pronoun

Underline the pronoun in parentheses that correctly completes each sentence.

1. Both Tran and (I, me) read a book about treasures on the *Titanic*.

2. The movie about the *Titanic* scared Raymond and (he, him).

3. Money and jewels on board the *Titanic* went down with (she, her) when (she, her) sank.

4. Between you and (I, me), I prefer the book to the movie.

5. The *Monitor*, the Civil War shipwreck, interested my father and (I, me).

6. J. L. Worden, the captain of the *Monitor*, was a hero to (us, we).

7. According to (he, him), Worden was wounded during a battle between the *Monitor* and the *Merrimack*.

8. My father and (me, I) talked about the battle between the *Monitor* and the *Merrimack*.

9. (She, Her) and her friend gave an oral book report about the sinking of the *Monitor* in 1862.

10. Recently, a naval officer showed (we, us) pictures (he, him) had taken of the wreck of the *Monitor* on the sea floor.

Exercise 5 Writing Sentences with Object Pronouns

Correct the following sentences. Each one includes a subject pronoun or an object pronoun. Cross out each incorrect pronoun, and write the correct one above it. If the sentence is correct, write *C* after it.

EXAMPLE   *She*
~~Her~~ and her friend went to the butterfly exhibits.

1. Jeff and ~~him~~ *he* got up early for the Christmas bird count.

2. When they got to the park, they saw Tom and ~~I~~ *me*.

3. ~~Him~~ *He* and ~~me~~ *I* had coffee at the boathouse.

4. Between you and ~~I~~ *me*, we counted fifty different birds.

5. For Norma and him, it was a high count.   C

Who or Whom?

Here are some tips to help you use the subject pronoun *who* and the object pronoun *whom*.

Subject Form	Object Form
who	whom

🖐 Use the subject pronoun *who* when the pronoun functions as a subject or as a predicate nominative in a sentence or in a clause.

Who painted the mailbox turquoise? [*Who* is the subject.]
Robbie is **who** gave the party. [*Who* is the predicate nominative.]
The carpenter **who** repaired the mailbox also painted it. [*Who* is the subject of the adjective clause *who repaired the mailbox*.]

🖐 Use the object pronoun *whom* when the pronoun functions as a direct object, an indirect object, or the object of a preposition in a sentence or a clause.

Whom do you trust? [*Whom* is the direct object.]
You handed **whom** the keys? [*Whom* is the indirect object of a sentence.]
For **Whom** *the Bell Tolls* is one of Ernest Hemingway's greatest novels.
[*Whom* is the object of the preposition *for*.]

P.S. Almost nobody uses *whom* today in everyday speech because it sounds so formal. However, in formal writing—and on grammar tests—follow the rules listed here and use *whom* as indicated.

In deciding whether to use *who* or *whom* in a sentence, try substituting *he/she* or *him/her* for *who/whom*. If *he* or *she* sounds right in the sentence, use the subject pronoun *who*. If *him* or *her* sounds right, choose the object pronoun *whom*. To do this for a question, flip the question around to make it a statement.

(**Who**, **Whom**) did you speak with? [Change the question into a statement.]
You spoke with (**who/whom** *or* **she/her**).
[The object pronoun **her** is correct, so use the object pronoun **whom**.]
Whom did you speak with?

🖐 Use *who/whom* to refer to people and *which* or *that* to refer to objects.

Sam was the one **who** played first base.
That was the ball **that** went over the wall.

Step by Step

When you need to choose between *who* and *whom*:

1. Decide what function the pronoun performs in the sentence.

2. Use *who* if the pronoun functions as a subject or a predicate nominative.

3. Use *whom* if the pronoun functions as a direct object, an indirect object, or the object of a preposition.

Complete each sentence by writing the correct pronoun form of *who* or *whom* in the blank.

1. Alexander Graham Bell, ___who___ invented the telephone, didn't work alone.

2. The person with ___whom___ he worked, Tom Watson, discovered how speech travels through wires.

3. Bell worked with people ___who___ were hearing impaired.

4. Bell also worked with his father, ___who___ had created a system of speech through signals.

5. Bell was the first scientist ___who___ believed speech could travel by electricity.

6. The first person to ___whom___ Bell spoke by telephone was Watson.

7. In 1876, people discovered ___who___ Bell was when he unveiled his new invention.

8. It was Bell ___who___ fought the hardest for his new invention.

Exercise 7 Editing a Paragraph

Work with a partner to edit the following paragraph to correct all errors in pronoun usage.

¹~~Whom~~ Who do you think would make a great inventor? ²Is it only a student ~~whom~~ who gets good grades in science? ³Do all students ~~which~~ who do well in science think of themselves as future engineers or inventors? ⁴A recent program, "Invention and Design," encourages students ~~whom~~ who might become inventors. ⁵A person ~~that~~ who taught high school physics guided the students through the program. ⁶Program developers decided who would work with ~~who~~ whom on each team, based on students' verbal, math, and artistic abilities. ⁷Students ~~whom~~ who participated said that teamwork was the most difficult and the most rewarding aspect of the program. ⁸Teams ~~whom~~ that failed in their first invention often succeeded with their second try. ⁹The second attempt often showed ~~whom~~ who persisted. ¹⁰This hands-on program inspired students ~~whom~~ who participated to comment: "It was inspiring; I plan to do more in this field" and "It was challenging, and that made it more exciting."

Mid-Chapter Review

Exercise A Choosing the Correct Pronoun

Underline the correct pronoun in parentheses to complete each sentence.

1. The tour guide and (<u>they</u>, them) decided what to see in Italy.

2. The students' travel committee members were Felix, Ashley, and (<u>he</u>, him).

3. For Lana and (she, <u>her</u>), the committee created a report on Italy.

4. The committee chair asked (they, <u>them</u>) and (we, <u>us</u>) to prepare a brochure.

5. For Rome, (<u>we</u>, us) and another group created dioramas of the Coliseum.

6. The brochure about Florence was written by Tim, Max, and (I, <u>me</u>).

7. Students asked (he and I, <u>him and me</u>) about a famous museum, the Uffizzi.

8. If not for Sam and (she, <u>her</u>), we wouldn't know about the Grand Canal of Venice.

9. The guide showed Andie and (I, <u>me</u>) books on Tuscany.

10. (<u>We</u>, Us) also wanted to go to Sicily.

Exercise B Editing a Dialogue

In the following dialogue from a formal telephone conversation, correct all errors in the use of the pronouns *who* or *whom*. **Hint:** Not every sentence has incorrect pronoun usage.

RECEPTIONIST: [1]With ~~who~~ ^{whom} would you like to speak?

CALLER: [2]Could you please tell me who is in charge of product development?

RECEPTIONIST: [3]The person for ~~who~~ ^{whom} you are looking is Ms. Martin. [4]Please hold.

MS. MARTIN: [5]Hello?

CALLER: [6]Is this Ms. Martin?

MS. MARTIN: [7]This is ~~her~~ ^{she}. [8]~~Whom~~ ^{Who} may I ask is calling?

CALLER: ⁹My name is Paul Osaya. ¹⁰I am the person ~~whom~~ ^{who} sent your company my idea for a computer game.

MS. MARTIN: ¹¹Oh, yes. ¹²Alica Peña, ~~whom~~ ^{who} is our vice president, and I discussed your idea.

CALLER: ¹³Is it Ms. Peña with ~~who~~ ^{whom} I should speak?

MS. MARTIN: ¹⁴Yes, may I ask ~~who~~ ^{whom} you work for, Mr. Osaya?

CALLER: ¹⁵I am an eleventh grade student ~~whom~~ ^{who} attends Morris High School.

MS. MARTIN: ¹⁶You are the youth ~~who~~ ^{whom} we're looking forward to hiring.

Exercise C Editing a Paragraph

Edit the following paragraph to correct all errors in pronoun usage.
Hint: One of the sentences contains no errors, and one sentence has more than one error.

¹To ~~who~~ ^{whom} would you hand a book of poetry for free? ²Take Madeline, Tony, and ~~she~~ ^{her}, who are standing at the entrance to the Alamo in San Antonio. ³Are ~~them~~ ^{they} the kind of readers for ~~who~~ ^{whom} poets write? ⁴For poets, ~~whom~~ ^{who} come from all walks of life, the answer is yes. ⁵To prove this point, Andrew Carroll, ~~which~~ ^{who} heads the Literacy Project, visited the Alamo on his cross-country poetry giveaway tour. ⁶Supported by the Academy of American Poets, ~~him~~ ^{he} and his literacy volunteers gave away over 4,000 free poetry books in a month. ⁷The project proves that people who like poetry are in supermarket checkout lines, jury rooms, and hotels, as well as in schools and libraries. ⁸~~Whom~~ ^{Who} would benefit from this program? ⁹Anyone ~~whom~~ ^{who} is touched by poetry would enjoy a free book of poems. ¹⁰If you ask me, poetry belongs to ~~we~~ ^{us} all.

Appositives and Incomplete Constructions

An appositive is a word or phrase that identifies or explains the noun or pronoun that comes right before it. (See Lesson 6.2.)

● For a pronoun appositive, use a subject pronoun if the word that the appositive refers to is a subject or a predicate nominative. Use an object pronoun if the word that the appositive refers to is a direct or indirect object or the object of a preposition.

The Wright brothers, Wilbur and **he**, made aviation history.

[*He*, a subject pronoun, refers to *brothers*, the sentence subject.]

The aviation pioneers are the Wright brothers, Wilbur and **he**.

[*He* refers to the predicate nominative *brothers*.]

Aviation history was made by the Wright brothers, Wilbur and **him**.

[*Him* refers to *brothers*, the object of the preposition *by*.]

The historian praised the Wright brothers, Wilbur and **him**.

[*Him* refers to *brothers*, the direct object.]

● When the pronouns *we* or *us* are followed by a noun appositive, choose the pronoun form you would use if the pronoun were alone in the sentence.

The era in which an event takes place matters to **us** historians.

[You would say, "The era . . . matters to *us*."]

Next, **we** athletes will participate in a state competition. [You would say, "Next, *we* will participate . . . . "]

The dog brought **us** teenagers the bone. [You would say, "The dog brought *us* the bone."]

● In an incomplete construction, choose the pronoun form you would use if the sentence were complete. An incomplete construction omits some words, which are understood. Usually, an incomplete construction appears at the end of a sentence and starts with the word *than* or *as*. In the following sentences, the omitted words appear in brackets.

Marly is a faster sprinter than **she** [is].

Jerome solves algebra equations as quickly as **he** [solves them].

● Be consistent in your choice of pronouns; don't shift pronouns unnecessarily.

INCORRECT **One** should research **your** family tree.

CORRECT **One** should research **one's** family tree.

CORRECT **You** should research **your** family tree.

Editing Tip

Pronouns ending in *-self* or *-selves* cannot be used as subjects. Use personal pronouns as subjects.

Victoria and ~~myself~~ *I* read

that book.

Has anyone sung better than ~~youself~~ *you*?

Exercise 8 Choosing the Correct Pronoun

Underline the pronoun in parentheses that correctly completes each sentence.

EXAMPLE   The composers of the song, Dana and (she, her), won the prize.

1. Why aren't the winners, Gena and (he, him), accepting the awards?

2. The M.C. handed Dana and (I, me) the microphone.

3. (We, Us) student council members won't vote for a longer school day.

4. Shannon and (she, her) are the hardest workers.

5. Yoko understands chess better than (I, me).

6. Nelson believes that when one reads, (one's, your) world opens up.

7. Jimmy played the sonata as well as (we, us).

8. It's not for (us, we) to decide.

9. Did anybody do better on that test than (you, yourself)?

10. It is (he, him) we trust.

Exercise 9 Create Your Own Exercise

Write five sentences on any subject, using an appositive with a pronoun in each sentence. Try to use appositives as different parts of a sentence, such as the subject, predicate nominative, direct object, indirect object, object complement, or object of a preposition. Then rewrite the sentences using the format in Exercise 8 above. Exchange papers with a classmate, and underline the pronoun that completes each sentence correctly. Check your answers with your partner.
Students' sentences will vary.

Exercise 10 Editing Sentences

Read each sentence for errors with pronouns. Cross out a pronoun that is incorrect, and write the correct pronoun above it. If a sentence is correct, write *C* after it.

EXAMPLE   Jefferson is as smart as ~~me~~.ⁱ   Students may also change
                                                      one doesn't to *you don't*.

1. If one doesn't forget the facts, ~~your~~ (one's) papers will need fewer corrections.

2. Was it Anne who sang in as high a key as I?   C

3. Let me remind you that ~~us~~ (we) citizens vote every November.

4. The mayor gave the teachers, Mr. Wiecker and ~~she~~ (her), an award.

5. It was the twins, Alaine and she, who greeted you.   C

6. Asher and ~~me~~ (I) would like to do this for our mother.

7. Why don't ~~us~~ (we) students have a seat on the school board?

8. If only our candidate could speak as well as ~~her~~ (she), we'd win.

Agreement with Antecedent

The word a pronoun refers to is its **antecedent**. Pronouns must agree with their antecedents in **gender** (male or female) and **number** (singular or plural). You may wish to review Lessons 9.2 and 9.3 on subject-verb agreement with indefinite pronouns and compound subjects.

Possesive Pronouns

my	our
your	your
his	their
her	
its	

◗ Use a plural possessive pronoun to refer to two or more antecedents joined by *and*.

> Therese, Carolina, and Michael enjoyed **their** mountain hike.

◗ Use a singular possessive pronoun to refer to two or more singular antecedents joined by *or* or *nor*.

> Neither Max nor Tony sent **his** stories to the magazine.

◗ Use a singular pronoun when the antecedent is a singular indefinite pronoun: *anybody, anyone, each, either, everybody, everyone, neither, nobody, no one, one, somebody, someone.*

> Someone in the girls choir sang **her** solo off key.
> Neither of the boys remembered **his** homework.

Use the expression "his or her" when a singular indefinite pronoun refers to both males and females.

> Each of the writers will read **his or her** story tomorrow.
> Nobody in the group wanted to voice **his or her** opinion.

◗ When a compound antecedent joined by *or* or *nor* contains a singular word and a plural word, use a pronoun that agrees with the nearer antecedent.

> Suzy or the **boys** volunteered **their** help.
> The dogs or **cat** played in **its** yard.

◗ Use *it* to refer to animals when the animal's gender is unclear. Otherwise, use *he/him* or *she/her*.

> Keep that tiger away from me! **It**'s dangerous! [gender unclear]
> My cat Marisa always licks **her** paws. [gender clear through name]

Writing Hint

To avoid having to repeat the phrase "his or her" too often, try either to use an article instead of a pronoun or to rephrase the sentence.

Nobody gives "~~his or her~~ *a*" locker combination away.

Most people don't tell their locker combination.

Exercise 11 **Choosing the Correct Pronoun**

Underline the pronoun in parentheses that agrees with its antecedent. **Hint:** First, find the antecedent(s).

1. One of the students refuses (<u>his</u>, their) assignment.

2. Matt, Karan, and Ed edit (her, <u>their</u>) school magazine.

3. Was either Tony or Nestor sitting in (<u>his</u>, their) assigned seat?

4. Princess enjoys burying (its, <u>her</u>) bones.

5. Anyone who reads (<u>a</u>, their) story receives extra credit.

6. None of the women gave (<u>her</u>, their) secret password away.

7. Each one of my friends has (<u>his or her</u>, their) own point of view.

8. Will the boys or that girl give me (<u>her</u>, a, their) pass to the library?

9. Jay and Jane wrote (his or her, <u>their</u>) play about life on Mars.

10. Janet and Dena ran to the park after (her, <u>their</u>) class was over.

Exercise 12 Editing Sentences

Edit the following sentences for errors with pronouns. Cross out a pronoun that is incorrect, and write the correct pronoun above it. If a sentence is correct, write *C* after it.

1. Kim and Sara left ~~her~~ ^{their} notebooks in the library.

2. Neither fathers nor mothers want their children to fail.   C

3. Can Marcia or John give ~~her~~ ^{his} report before lunch?

4. Somebody in the earth science class eats ~~their~~ ^{his or her} lunch outside.

5. Each of the boys uses his calculator to add large numbers.   C

6. Someone has left ~~their~~ ^{his or her} homework on the bus.

7. Each of my aunts and uncles volunteered ~~his~~ ^{his or her} time.

8. Felix, Bob, and Rayna buy ~~her~~ ^{their} lunch in the cafeteria.

9. Peter, Paul, and Mary harmonized ~~his or her~~ ^{their} parts.

10. Several members of the chess club will discuss ~~his or her~~ ^{their} strategies.

Exercise 13 Writing Sentences

Work with a partner to write a sentence using the words given below as the subject. Use a correct possessive pronoun in each sentence you write.

Students' sentences will vary.

1. Each of the singers

2. Everybody on the team

3. Antony and Cleopatra

4. Mrs. Murray or Mr. Fleury

5. Neither Cheryl nor Annette

6. The circus elephant

7. Our dog King

8. Neither of the runners

Clear Pronoun Reference

Personal pronouns must always agree with their antecedents in gender, number, and person.

● Avoid confusing or unclear pronoun references.

UNCLEAR	Alba and Zoe worked on the project until **she** had to go home. [*Who* had to go home? The pronoun reference is unclear.]
CLEAR	Alba and Zoe worked on the project until **Zoe** had to go home.
UNCLEAR	The collector admired the Elvis lamp on the table and bought **it**. [*It* could refer to either the *table* or the *Elvis lamp*.]
CLEAR	Because the collector admired the Elvis lamp sitting on the table, she bought it. [*It* clearly refers to the *Elvis lamp*.]
UNCLEAR	The cat chased the mouse and the hamster and caught **it**. [*It* could mean either the *mouse* or the *hamster*.]
CLEAR	The cat chased the mouse and caught it; the hamster got away. [*It* clearly indicates the *mouse*.]

● Avoid inexact or weak references, especially when a pronoun doesn't have a definite or clear antecedent.

A sentence that contains a weak pronoun reference is difficult for readers to decipher.

UNCLEAR	Rashid wrote tons of stories on a science fiction theme, but none of **it** was ever published. [What does the pronoun *it* refer to?]
CLEAR	Rashid wrote tons of science fiction stories, but none of **his writing** was ever published.
UNCLEAR	You missed both the party and the dinner, **which** was good. [What does the pronoun *which* refer to?]
CLEAR	You missed both the party and the dinner. It was a delicious meal.

● Avoid using *it, they*, and *you* in a vague, general way when a sentence has no clear antecedent.

UNCLEAR	**They** say that exercise helps the mind as well as the body. [What or who does *they* refer to exactly?]
CLEAR	**Fitness researchers** say that exercise helps the mind as well as the body.
UNCLEAR	The music was so loud, **you** couldn't hear yourself think.
CLEAR	The music was so loud, **we** couldn't hear ourselves think.
CLEAR	The music was so loud, **concert-goers** couldn't hear themselves think.

Writing Hint

Certain phrases are correct, even though pronouns appear without clear references—for example, *it's raining, it's late, it seems*.

Exercise 14 # Writing Sentences with Clear Pronoun References

Revise the following numbered items so that pronouns have clear references. Cross out words you want to replace, and write the replaced words above them. You may also need to change the order and wording in sentences for clarity. If a sentence has no errors, write a *C* after it. **Hint:** Some sentences have more than one error.

The candidates

EXAMPLE   ~~They~~ do whatever it takes to win an election.

                   citizens
1. In some countries, ~~you~~ can only praise but never criticize the government.

2. He really believes in art, but he doesn't believe that genius can be taught. C

                                             actor
3. We waited outside the actors' dressing rooms but didn't meet a single ~~one~~.

                marketing executives
4. In the boardroom, ~~they~~ make all kinds of decisions about how products

   will be advertised.

                                        the carrots
5. Pull the weeds and the carrots from the garden and wash ~~them~~.

                                 Ralph   them
6. Ralph and Denton shared the course materials before ~~he~~ had to return ~~it~~ to

   the college professor.

                  that Luther
7. Marc told Luther ~~he~~ was in line for an award.

8. Elaine made rabbits disappear, coins appear, and her own hat twirl in the
   These tricks
   air. ~~This~~ delighted the audience.

                                   they never performed any of them
9. Don and Juanita always composed songs, but ~~none of it was ever performed~~.

        the doctors
10. Did ~~they~~ tell you to take this medication three times a day?

Exercise 15 # Editing a Paragraph

Rewrite the paragraph below on a separate piece of paper. Use accurate and clear pronoun references in your edited paragraph.   See Answer Key.

   [1]They say the best cars are the old ones. [2]My friend Mike restored a 1969 Mustang. [3]That car had a shiny black paint job. [4]It was the kind with sparkles, so it shone and glittered when you saw him drive by. [5]The interior was immaculate. [6]Its upholstery was leather, and it crinkled with age. [7]It was a polished and gleaming dashboard. [8]When Mike turned the key, it made a low insistent rumble. [9]It was hard not to look at that beautiful car when it drove past.

Revising and Editing Worksheet 1

Revise the following paragraphs on a separate piece of paper. Focus especially on the correct use of pronouns, check for spelling mistakes, and make any other changes that you think will improve the passage.

Revisions will vary. A sample revision is given.

¹Many people think only of Ellis Island in New York harbor when ~~it comes~~ [they think about]
~~to~~ immigration [but] some also think of Angel Island in San Francisco Bay. ²The island processing centers for ~~immigrants~~ [immigration] were both in operation until 1940.

³The Chinese, Japanese, and other Asian immigrants ~~whom~~ [who] passed through this Western center between 1910 and 1940 told ~~his~~ [their] stories to immigration officials on Angel Island.

⁴More than 100,000 Chinese and other Asian immigrants ~~that~~ [who] passed through Angel Island suffered discrimination and internment. ⁵One Chinese immigrant ~~write~~ [wrote of the American officials] on the walls of the detention center. ~~⁶The immigrant wrote of the American officials,~~ " . . . They mistreat ~~we~~ [us] Chinese." ⁷~~Him~~ [He] and others had ~~his~~ [their] poems and pictures discovered by a California park ranger in 1970.

⁸A book of these poems, titled *Island*, has been published. ⁹The English versions of the poems may be just as powerful as ~~them~~ [they are] in their original ~~language~~ [languages]. ¹⁰~~A person~~ [One] ~~whom~~ [who] reads this book will find that ~~their~~ [one's] understanding of the Asian immigrant experience is deepening.

¹¹From 1863 to 1962, the American government and military services decided ~~whom~~ [who] would use ~~a~~ngel Island. ¹²The government and ~~them~~ [they] chose to use the island ~~as an army post, known as Fort McDowell.~~ [for a number of purposes.] ¹³[It was home to Fort McDowell, an army post.] During World War II, a number of American guards ~~and~~ [or] a foreign prisoner spent his war years on Angel Island. ¹⁴Before the island became a state park in 1962, ¹⁵~~Angel Island~~ [it] served as a missile base.

¹⁶If the ground on Angel Island could speak, ~~the land~~ [it] would spin endless tales of tragedy, suffering, and heartache.

Students should write complete sentences, fix fragments and run-ons, plus correct errors in pronoun usage.

Revising and Editing Worksheet 2

Work with a partner or small group to revise these paragraphs. Write your revised passage on a separate piece of paper, and compare your response with those made by other pairs or groups of classmates. Focus especially on the correct use of pronouns, but make any other changes you think will improve the passage. Revisions will vary. A sample revision is given.

¹Many of the Kennedy clan have contributed to american government. ²The second son of Joseph and Rose Kennedy was John Fitzgerald ~~Kennedy~~, who ~~whom~~ was president from 1961 until 1963. ³On November 22, 1963, he was assassinated. ⁴The parents of JFK and all his siblings gave ~~his~~ their support to John's political ambitions. ⁵As president, John chose who ~~whom~~ would be his attorney general without hesitation. ⁶He chose his younger brother Robert. ⁷The tragic fate of assassination was shared both by John and ~~he~~ him.

⁸When one thinks about John F. Kennedy, ~~your~~ one's focus also turns to his wife, Jacqueline. ⁹John F. Kennedy or ~~her~~ she always delighted the public with ~~their~~ his or her dynamic personality. ¹⁰~~Her~~ She and ~~their~~ her children Caroline and John, Jr., remained in the public eye long after JFK's death. ¹¹Later in Jacqueline's life, ~~she took on~~ the job of editing books for a publisher, ~~showing~~ showed her to be a talented individual, not just a famous one.

¹²The father of John, Robert, and Edward ~~were~~ was as prominent as ~~them~~ they. ¹³Joseph Kennedy rose from rags to riches in business and government. ¹⁴As ambassador to England, he served President Franklin D. Roosevelt. ¹⁵Before World War II. ¹⁶~~Joseph Kennedy believed~~ A belief that the United States should not intervene in the war and ~~approved~~ his approval of talks between England and Nazi Germany; carried their weight negatively back home subsequently, he was urged to resign ~~their~~ his post. ¹⁷Rose Kennedy ~~was~~ the wife of Joseph Kennedy. ¹⁸~~Rose~~ and ~~him~~ he encouraged their children to participate in government. ¹⁹Both of ~~they~~ them felt enormous pride when ~~her~~ their son became the first Irish American and the first Catholic President of the United States.

Chapter Review

Visit us at
www.sadlier-oxford.com

Exercise A Using Subject and Object Pronouns

Fill in each blank with the correct form of a pronoun that makes sense in
the sentence. Make sure that the word you add is a pronoun, not a noun.
The first answer is supplied.

¹Members of the Famous Arkansans Committee are Felicia, Wayne, and __I__ .

² __We__ are preparing an oral report for a class presentation. ³Felicia

developed a research and organization plan for __us__ . ⁴The plan is to

come up with a list of famous people from Arkansas. ⁵When __we__

accumulate fifteen names, __they__ will be divided between the three

committee members for further research. ⁶For Felicia, Wayne, and __me__ ,

this plans sounds good. ⁷To begin, Felicia tells __us__ several names of

important, contemporary people from Arkansas. ⁸ __She__ lists President

Clinton, the forty-second U.S. President; Maya Angelou, an author and poet;

and Johnny Cash, a country-western singer. ⁹Wayne admires prominent

people from the past, so __he__ places Sequoyah, a Cherokee who helped

develop an alphabet for his language, on the list. ¹⁰Between Felicia, Wayne,

and __me__ , there are fourteen names on the list; that means that

__we__ must come up with just one more.

Exercise B Choosing the Correct Pronoun

Underline the pronoun in parentheses that correctly completes
each sentence.

1. (<u>Who</u>, whom) painted *Portrait of the Artist's Mother*, known as *Whistler's Mother*?

2. The man (<u>who</u>, whom) painted (she, <u>her</u>) is James Whistler.

3. It was Whistler (<u>who</u>, whom) coined the phrase "Art for art's sake."

4. Would you consider (he, <u>him</u>) a modern painter?

5. London, the city in which he settled in 1859, never fully accepted (<u>him</u>, he).

6. Whistler's writing mentions painters (who, <u>whom</u>) he admired.

7. Whistler also noted the critics with (who, <u>whom</u>) he quarreled.

8. Whistler raged against John Ruskin, the English critic (<u>who</u>, whom) ruined (he, <u>him</u>).

9. French, Spanish, and Japanese painters were among those (<u>who</u>, whom) influenced (he, <u>him</u>).

10. It was (<u>they</u>, them) he turned to for inspiration.

Exercise C Correcting Pronoun Errors

Correct all pronoun errors in the following sentences.

1. The casting director gave the main roles to Nathan and ~~I~~. (me)

2. Raquel and ~~her~~ used their own zoom lenses. (she)

3. The prop person worked with Tracy and ~~she~~. (her)

4. Marta told the director that the editors have more work than ~~them~~. (the set designers)

5. The film producers were ~~us~~ three sisters. (we)

6. The title, "Three Sisters," amused ~~we~~ actors. (us)

7. The costume designer is as creative as ~~her~~. (she)

8. Is Morley a more experienced actor than ~~him~~? (he)

Exercise D Using Correct Pronouns

Fill in each blank with a pronoun that agrees with its antecedent(s).

1. Each of the women brought ___her___ child to the park.

2. Anyone in this group can present __his or her__ report.

3. The neighbors had ___their___ block-association picnic.

4. Fourth-grade boys and a second-grade boy recited ___their___ poems.

5. Either the students or Mr. Morano will present ___his___ views.

6. It was either Matt or Ben who forgot the words to ___his___ poem.

7. Everyone who reads __his or her__ report aloud will get extra points.

8. Three cheerleaders and Marlene share ___a___ locker in the gym.

9. Either Mel or Arthur makes ___his___ multimedia presentation today.

10. Neither the king nor the queen wore __his or her__ crown outside.

Using Modifiers

Visit us at
www.sadlier-oxford.com

STUDENT WRITING
Expository Essay

Driving: Teen Rite of Passage
The Benefits and Pitfalls of Teenage Driving Revealed
by Suzanne O'Kelley
high school student, Eugene, Oregon

Looking at the packed parking areas around South, one sees that driving is a major factor of student life. Though some students manage to remain oblivious to the call of the driver's seat, many fall prey and are captured by the ups and downs of driving.

The allure of the automobile hits as freshmen turn fifteen and attempt to pass their driver's permit test. Not knowing what to expect, nervous teens wait in the Department of Motor Vehicles building. Finally, the first nerve-racking driving test is over, and new drivers flood onto the open road . . . usually, still in the passenger's seat.

Parents seem to have a hormone that releases when their child can drive, forcing them to ruin the experience in every way possible. Their fingers lock in a white-knuckled position and their feet pound on an imaginary brake pedal as their son or daughter putters around a parking lot at the breakneck speed of ten miles per hour.

Driver's education is another infamous aspect of driving that parents say is "for the child's own good." The in-class sessions are filled with '80s videos worse than *Footloose*, but hey, there's no better remedy for insomnia. The behind-the-wheel courses are expensive and embarrassing, unless it suddenly becomes cool to drive two miles under the speed limit in a car covered with "Student Driver" signs. The only benefit from these classes is an insurance discount.

For most people, the actual driver's license test is a blur. But when the time comes to drive alone for the first time, all the hassles and worries of the past year of student driving vanish. Now there are new things to worry about. . . .

For those without a car, there's nothing more appealing than a new set of wheels. Less appealing, however, is the hundreds of hours put into buying and caring for a car, but as long as the car is still on the distant horizon, the problems that accompany a car are both out of sight and out of mind.

When a car is finally available, problems arise. Gas money, insurance money, parking money, and repair money flow out of wallets. Friends want rides, parents want errands, but drivers just want freedom.

The audience for Suzanne O'Kelley's essay about driving is her high school peers. Her humorous tone and witty descriptions hold a reader's attention and encourage him or her to read on. In addition, Suzanne discusses several aspects of her topic, including parents' reactions, driver's education classes, and car ownership.

As you reread the essay, pay attention to the modifiers—the adjectives and adverbs. Modifiers add color and freshness to your writing. As you do the writing exercises in this chapter, you'll practice adding modifiers to your own work.

Allow time for students to discuss the student writing. Suggest that they identify its strengths and propose possible improvements. Use the model to introduce the concepts in the chapter.

Forming the Degrees of Comparison

When you make comparisons, you use three **degrees of comparison**: the **positive**, the **comparative**, and the **superlative**. Imagine three days in a row without rain or snow, starting on Friday.

POSITIVE   On Friday, the sky was blue and the sun was **bright**.

COMPARATIVE   On Saturday, the sun was **brighter** than on Friday.

SUPERLATIVE   On Sunday, the sun was the **brightest** of all three days.

Here are some rules for forming comparative and superlative degrees.

🖉 **One-syllable modifiers** Add *-er* and *-est* to one-syllable modifiers.

short, short**er**, short**est**   great, great**er**, great**est**

🖉 **Two-syllable modifiers** Add *-er* and *-est* to most two-syllable modifiers.

simple, simpl**er**, simpl**est**   shiny, shini**er**, shini**est**

When an *-er* or *-est* ending for a modifier sounds clumsy, use *more* and *most* before the positive degree.

eager, **more** eager, **most** eager

🖉 **-ly adverbs** Use *more* and *most* for all adverbs that end in *-ly*.

rapidly, **more** rapidly, **most** rapidly

However, be careful since not all *-ly* words are adverbs.

ugly, ugli**er**, ugli**est**

🖉 **More than two syllables** For modifiers of three syllables or more, use *more* and *most* to form the comparative and superlative degrees.

capable, **more** capable, **most** capable
unappealing, **more** unappealing, **most** unappealing

🖉 **Decreasing degrees** For all modifiers, use *less* and *least* for decreasing degrees of comparison (regardless of the number of syllables).

humble, **less** humble, **least** humble
bravely, **less** bravely, **least** bravely

🖉 **Irregular modifiers** The modifiers listed in the side column form their degrees of comparison irregularly.

Irregular Degrees of Comparison

good	better	best
well	better	best
bad	worse	worst
badly	worse	worst
ill	worse	worst
many	more	most
much	more	most
little	less *or* lesser	least
far	farther	farthest
	further	furthest

Step by Step

To form the comparative and superlative degree of modifiers:

1. Count the number of syllables.

2. Apply the appropriate rule:
   one syllable = *-er* and *-est*
   two syllables = personal taste
   three syllables = *more* and *most*
   -ly adverbs = *more* and *most*

3. Memorize the modifiers with irregular degrees of comparison.

Enriching Your Vocabulary

The graphic verb *exude*, used in Exercise 1, is from the Latin word *exsudare*, meaning "to sweat out." It is defined as "to pass out in drops through pores," "to ooze," or "to discharge." It also means "to diffuse or seem to radiate," as in *exuding* great joy.

Exercise 1 Proofreading a Paragraph

Cross out any incorrect modifiers and write the correct form in the space above it.

¹If you want to find a ~~gooder~~ *(good)* ranch, where would you look? ²You'd probably expect to find the ~~authenticest~~ *(most authentic)* ranches in a place like Texas. ³But can you imagine a less ~~predictabler~~ *(predictable)* place for a ranch than England? ⁴In truth, it might take a ~~longest~~ *(longer)* time to get to Laredo, England, than to Laredo, Texas. ⁵In Laredo, England, though, just 5,139 miles from its namesake, you'll find a ranch ~~trulyer~~ *(more truly)* Western than ranches from frontier days in Texas! ⁶In Westphalia, Germany, one of the ~~more strange~~ *(strangest)* places you could visit would be Lubbock Town, named after another Texas cowboy location. ⁷Cowboy clubs have become popular throughout Germany, where people more ~~thoroughlyer~~ *(thoroughly)* enjoy experiencing the American West in re-created towns. ⁸The Munich Cowboy Club sponsors a Western museum, which exhibits one of the ~~most rare~~ *(rarest)* autographed photographs of Buffalo Bill Cody. ⁹From among the clubs and re-created towns that exude cowboy charm, Germans show ~~more keen~~ *(keener)* interest in cowboys and the frontier days than people from other foreign countries.

Exercise 2 Forming the Comparative and Superlative

Write the comparative and superlative degrees for each modifier.

1. beautiful	more beautiful	most beautiful	5. plain	plainer	plainest
2. highly	more highly	most highly	6. cautious	more cautious	most cautious
3. good	better	best	7. courageously	more courageously	most courageously
4. bad	worse	worst	8. industrious	more industrious	most industrious

Exercise 3 Writing a Travel Advertisement

You are a travel writer who has just taken an assignment to write a one-paragraph description of a great place to visit. On a separate piece of paper, write this paragraph, which will be included in a letter mailed to people interested in taking a trip. You may write about a real place or a made-up place. Use at least five comparative and superlative modifiers in your paragraph to make readers of this letter want to visit the place you're writing about.

Using the Degrees of Comparison

Use the following rules to help you use the comparative and superlative forms of modifiers correctly.

🖋 Use the **comparative degree** to compare two things. Use the **superlative degree** to compare three or more things.

COMPARATIVE   The San Francisco cable cars were a **better** means of transportation than the buses.

SUPERLATIVE   Our visit to Muir Woods was the **best** day of our trip.

In dialogue, you'll often hear the superlative used in a comparison between two things. In writing, though, use the comparative.

INCORRECT   Of the two places we visited, I liked the Golden Gate Bridge **best**.

CORRECT   Of the two places we visited, I liked the Golden Gate Bridge **better**.

🖋 **Avoid double comparisons.** Use either *more* (or *most*) or *-er* (or *-est*) but never the word and the suffix together.

INCORRECT   I tried to run **more faster** to gain on my opponent **more sooner**.

CORRECT   I tried to run **faster** to gain on my opponent **sooner**.

> ## Editing Tip
>
> Avoid misusing *less* and *fewer*. *Less* indicates "how much" and is used to modify a singular noun. *Fewer*, which specifies "how many," is used to modify a plural noun.
>
> *fewer*
> Boyd read ten ~~less~~ books than Rita did. [*Books* is plural.]
>
> Boyd eats **less** food when he isn't exercising. [*Food* is singular.]

Exercise 4 Editing Sentences

Edit these sentences for the correct use of modifiers. If the sentence has no errors, write *C* after it. If you find an error, cross out the incorrect word(s), and write the correct form of the modifier above the line.

EXAMPLE   The Sound Surround pays students ~~higher wages than~~ *the highest wages of* any place else in town.

most
1. Stephanie has the ~~more~~ interesting job of anyone I know.

2. Nestor and Michelle work in a store that sells the ~~most~~ latest music.

better
3. Between rock and jazz, Michelle likes jazz ~~best~~.

most
4. Nestor is the ~~more~~ knowledgeable about music among all his friends.

fewer
5. The *Clothes Horse* hires ~~less~~ high school students in winter than

in summer.

most

6. The *Sports Shack* is the ~~more~~ difficult place in town for students to get work.

7. Of the two debates, the one about jobs was more relevant. C

less

8. Lemar has ~~fewer~~ time in his schedule for studying now that he's working.

most

9. Deciding to work after school is one of the ~~more~~ difficult decisions

students must make.

10. The law should be more indifferent to the hours students work. C

Exercise 5 · Editing a Paragraph

Improve the following paragraph by correcting all the incorrect modifiers.

¹People think that scooping ice cream during the summers would be the most

fun

~~funnest~~ job. ²However, these people don't think about the hazards of the job.

³First, pushy tourists have to consider every flavor before they choose the

best   most

~~more better~~. ⁴They can get nasty if you are not the ~~more~~ patient of all the

hottest

servers. ⁵Second, on the ~~hotter~~ day of the summer, an ice cream shop is packed

with customers looking for quick service. ⁶Finally, even if you thought that the

~~most~~ tastiest food was ice cream, you'll never enjoy it after scooping it all day.

Exercise 6 · Writing Sentences with Comparisons

On a separate piece of paper, write a paragraph in which you compare two or more objects, people, places, or activities. Here are some possible topics:

three books	two states	three parks
two famous people	three sports	three advertisements

Include at least four comparative or superlative forms in your paragraph, and underline each one. Students' paragraphs will vary.

Exercise 7 · Write What You Think

On a separate piece of paper, write your response to the statement below in a paragraph. Include reasons and examples to support your opinion.

Students should not be allowed to work after school or during the summer until they are at least eighteen years of age.

Answers will vary. Give students full credit if they have stated an opinion and attempted to support their opinions. Look for grammatically complete sentences that begin with a capital letter and end with an appropriate end punctuation mark.

Illogical Comparisons and Double Negatives

◗ Avoid illogical comparisons. Use the words *other* or *else* to compare something with others in its group.

ILLOGICAL	Chicago is larger than any city in the Midwest. [Chicago is a city in the Midwest. Chicago can't be larger than itself.]
LOGICAL	Chicago is larger than any **other** city in the Midwest.
ILLOGICAL	Molly can run farther than anyone on the track team.
LOGICAL	Molly can run farther than anyone **else** on the track team.

◗ Avoid unclear comparisons. Add whatever words are necessary to make a clear comparison.

UNCLEAR	Eduardo is more interested in writing stories than Judy.
CLEAR	Eduardo is more interested in writing stories than Judy is.
CLEAR	Eduardo is more interested in writing stories than he is in Judy.

◗ Avoid using two negative words together. Only one negative word is necessary to express a negative idea. Count the contraction *-n't* (for *not*) as a negative word.

Note that there is more than one way to correct a double negative. Use the correct form that sounds best to you and fits the tone and style of your writing.

INCORRECT	I haven't never read a science fiction story that I didn't like.
CORRECT	I've never read a science fiction story that I didn't like.
CORRECT	I haven't yet read a science fiction story that I didn't like.
INCORRECT	Ryan didn't have no room for nothing except a small suitcase.
CORRECT	Ryan didn't have room for anything except a small suitcase.
CORRECT	Ryan had no room for anything except a small suitcase.

Did you notice that you sometimes need to change words when correcting a double negative? For example, you change *nobody* to *anybody*, *nothing* to *anything*, *never* to *ever*, *no one* to *anyone*, *nothing* to *anything*, and *none* to *any*.

Below you'll find examples of ways in which two negatives may be used correctly in one sentence. These kinds of situations occur infrequently.

I wouldn't not read a book by Sigrid Nuñez just because I've never heard of her.

Jamie couldn't not go to his sister's recital after she practiced so hard.

Writing Hint

Some modifiers must stand alone because they are at the highest degree of comparison already. For example, how can something be more perfect than perfect?

That is a ~~very most~~ unique hairstyle.

Tacos are my ~~most~~ favorite food.

Editing Tip

In colloquial speech, some people say *ain't* as a contraction for *am not*, *is not*, and *are not*. In formal writing, however, *ain't* is widely considered to be inappropriate.

Enriching Your Vocabulary

The noun *prodigy*, used in Exercise 9, is derived from the Latin word *prodigiosus*, which means "marvelous." The related word *prodigious* can mean "amazing" or "enormous, huge." A *prodigious* weight was lifted from his shoulders when the recital was postponed to next month.

Exercise 8 Editing Sentences for Double Negatives

In the following famous quotations, fix all the double negatives. Eliminate or change words as necessary.

1. Nothing ~~can't~~ ^{can} be created from nothing. —Lucretius, 99–55 B.C.

2. He ~~hasn't never~~ ^{has not} aquired a fortune; the fortune has acquired him.
   —Bión, 325–255 B.C.

3. I ~~couldn't not~~ ^{could not} know whether I was then a man dreaming I was a butterfly, or whether I am now a butterfly dreaming I am a man. —Chang-tzu, 369–286 B.C.

4. His only fault is that he ~~hasn't~~ ^{has} got no fault. —Pliny the Younger, c. A.D. 100

5. An argument doesn't need ~~no~~ ^a reason, nor a friendship. —Ibycus, c. 580 B.C.

6. What ~~ain't~~ ^{is no} good for the swarm ~~ain't~~ ^{is} no good for the bee.
   —Marcus Aurelius Antonius, A.D. 131–180

Exercise 9 Proofreading a Paragraph

Correct all errors with illogical or unclear comparisons and double negatives in the paragraph below.

¹As classical composers, Beethoven (1770–1827) and Mozart (1756–1791) stand out from everyone ^{else} in the eighteenth century. ²No one ~~couldn't never~~ ^{else could ever} come close to their musical brilliance or popularity. ³Their home of Vienna, Austria, boasted more musical talent than any ^{other} European city of its day. ⁴Nobody ~~never~~ ^{ever} had a father as supportive of his talent as Mozart's. ⁵Leopold Mozart didn't let ~~nobody~~ ^{anybody} important in Europe accept his son as less than a child prodigy, or genius. ⁶On the other hand, Beethoven's childhood was more ~~difficulter~~ ^{difficult} than Mozart's. ⁷Beethoven's father ~~hadn't none of the~~ ^{had no} desire to help his son; instead, he used the boy's talent for his own gain. ⁸There wasn't ~~nothing~~ ^{anything} as lucky for the young Beethoven as his support by Count Waldenstein of Bonn, Germany. ⁹This aristocrat was more interested in Beethoven than his father ^{was}. ¹⁰When they grew old, both composers ended in the ~~most~~ saddest of circumstances. ¹¹Mozart ~~didn't have~~ ^{had} no money, which made his life harder than ^{other} people's lives. ¹²Beethoven became deaf and ~~couldn't~~ ^{could} hear no music, forcing him to compose from memory.

Misplaced Modifiers

If a sentence is not written correctly, a modifier may accidentally modify the wrong word. A **misplaced modifier** is a word, phrase, or clause that's in the wrong place. It modifies a word that is different from the one it's meant to modify.

🞑 Correct a misplaced modifier by moving it as close as possible to the word it is meant to modify.

MISPLACED	Smiling with delight, the trophy was handed to Jenine.
CORRECTED	The trophy was handed to Jenine, who was smiling with delight.
MISPLACED	They imagined an extraordinary space trip in their classroom.
CORRECTED	In their classroom, they imagined an extraordinary space trip.
MISPLACED	From the ocean floor, Andy gave me a seashell.
CORRECTED	Andy gave me a seashell from the ocean floor.
MISPLACED	Fidgeting and fussing, the nurse calmed the sick child.
CORRECTED	The nurse calmed the sick child, who was fidgeting and fussing.

> ## Writing Hint
>
> Always check that the word *only* modifies the word you really intend it to modify in a sentence. Place *only* before the word or phrase it modifies.
>
> **MISPLACED**
> I **only** play tennis on Tuesdays. [This implies that you do nothing else but play tennis on Tuesday.]
>
> **CORRECTED**
> I play tennis **only** on Tuesdays. [Now it's clear that when you play tennis, it's on Tuesday.]

Exercise 10 Editing Sentences

Correct the misplaced modifiers in each sentence below.

1. ^On her way to work, My sister saw the girl climbing the mountain ~~on her way to work.~~

2. ~~As a baby,~~ my mother sang lullabies to me as a baby.

3. ~~Gliding on air currents,~~ she observed two hawks gliding on air currents.

4. ~~From the top bookshelf,~~ he read *Green Mansions*, a long-forgotten book from the top bookshelf.

5. ^In the canoe, We enjoyed watching the lake ~~in the canoe.~~

6. ~~Lumpy and sour,~~ my father baked the lumpy and sour loaf of bread incorrectly.

7. Rufus ~~only~~ hides under the bed only during a thunderstorm.

8. ^In her studio one day, Sara drew a cartoon of a rhinoceros ~~in her studio one day~~.

9. ~~Loud and shrill,~~ Max turned off the loud and shrill car alarm.

10. ~~At the age of twelve,~~ Zoe's parents took her to the Everglades at the age of twelve.

Exercise 11 **Editing a Scene from a Play**

Work with a partner to correct misplaced modifiers in this passage from a play. Write your revision on a separate piece of paper. Compare your changes with those made by other pairs of classmates.

In the moonlight,
SCENE 1: ¹Elisa, the main character, thinks about her future ~~in the moonlight.~~

who is howling.
²In the background, ~~howling,~~ her father tries to quiet Bailey, the family dog.

flying in the dark
³~~Flying in the dark,~~ Elisa and her father see a bat. ⁴Elisa's ideas about her

Once inside the house,
future are at once forgotten ~~inside the house.~~

ELISA

at the age of four
⁵~~At the age of four,~~ you gave me Bailey, remember?

FATHER

In your bedroom,
⁶You always drew pictures of dogs ~~in your bedroom~~; so I

had to give you a real one.

(⁷Scared, Elisa closes the door to keep the bat outside.)

ELISA

with the fresh night air surrounding me,
⁸Dad, I was thinking about my future career; but I forgot all

about the career I'd like to pursue ~~with the fresh night air~~

~~surrounding me.~~

FATHER

clever
⁹~~As a clever girl,~~ my journal is full of your ideas about what

Inside a desk drawer,
you will do one day. ¹⁰You will find some old entries in my

journal about your aspirations to become a veterinarian.

~~inside a desk drawer.~~

Dangling Modifiers

Sometimes, a modifier appears that isn't logically attached to any word in a sentence. A **dangling modifier** is a word, phrase, or clause that doesn't connect to or logically modify any word in the sentence.

DANGLING	Refreshed but hungry, the fried egg tasted great.
CORRECTED	I got out of bed refreshed but hungry, and the fried egg tasted great.

● Correct a dangling modifier by rewording the sentence. Add a word or words that the phrase or clause can modify.

DANGLING	Walking home from school, the wind blew over a pine tree.
CORRECTED	Walking home from school, we saw the wind blow over a pine tree.

In the corrected sentence, the phrase *walking home from school* modifies the noun *we*.

DANGLING	Struggling to complete the marathon, an ankle was sprained.
CORRECTED	Struggling to complete the marathon, Greta sprained her ankle.

In the corrected sentence, the phrase *struggling to complete the marathon* clearly modifies *Greta*.

DANGLING	Using DNA evidence, the ex-con was implicated in the burglary.
CORRECTED	DNA evidence implicated the ex-con in the burglary.

The corrected sentence make it clear that it was not the ex-con who was using the DNA evidence.

Writing Hint

Some dangling modifiers used in everyday speech are acceptable as introductory phrases. Examples include *generally speaking, strictly speaking, considering the alternative, to tell the truth,* and *to be perfectly frank.*

Generally speaking, cats make good pets.

Cats can't speak, so the phrase *generally speaking* is technically a dangling modifier.

Exercise 12 **Editing Sentences**

Rewrite each sentence to correct the dangling modifiers. If a sentence is correct, write *C* after it. **Hint:** You may want to use the second-person pronoun *you* to rewrite sentences that contain dangling modifiers.

EXAMPLE	To become an architect, ~~the study is hard~~. *you must study hard.*

1. After ~~circling~~ the stadium for an hour, a parking spot opened up

   near the west entrance.

   we circled

2. ~~Stuck between the sofa cushions,~~ he lost the remote control. *between the sofa cushions*

           you
3. To tell ^the truth, my stereo is secondhand.   Students may also mark this *C*

    As we were
4. ^~~S~~trolling along the beach this afternoon, the sun set.

    As I was   *my*
5. ^~~B~~icycling up Tug Hill, ~~the~~ tire went flat.

                           you should find it
6. By paying close attention to your surroundings, ^~~it's~~ easy to write a good story.

                            flying overhead last night.
7. ~~Flying overhead last night,~~ I saw two long-eared owls ^.

          my keys   *I never lose them.*
8. By always putting ~~them~~ in the same place, ~~my keys are never lost.~~

                            to the west
9. ~~Looking to the west,~~ the moon rose over Cleopatra's Needle ^.

       I was
10. While ^talking on the phone, my mother knocked on my door.

Exercise 13 Revising a Paragraph

Revise the following paragraph from a biography by correcting dangling modifiers. Write your revised biography on a separate piece of paper. **Hint:** Some sentences may include introductory phrases that are acceptable English even though they are also dangling modifiers. Consider using second person pronouns when you rewrite sentences with dangling modifiers. You may need to add words as well as change arrangements of words in some sentences.

                        you study
[1]To understand great architects, ^Frank Lloyd Wright (1867–1959) ~~is one of the~~

                                                 you discover
~~most famous modern architects.~~ [2]Visiting Chicago and its suburbs, ^many of his

designs ~~are evident in various structures.~~ [3]By following the lines of nature, ~~the~~

                                      the prairie style of architecture
~~prairie style of~~ Frank Lloyd Wright's ~~architecture was~~ invented ^. [4]Attempting to

                            Wright removed
create an open feeling in homes, ^unnecessary walls ~~were removed in Wright's~~

                  homeowners welcomed   *as a*
~~homes~~ . [5]Considering the alternative, ^open spaces ~~were a welcome~~ change ^

~~for homeowners.~~ [6]Using his ideas for construction, ~~Taliesin,~~ Frank Lloyd Wright's

built Taliesin, his   *experiencing fire twice*,
^own house, ~~was built~~ in Spring Green, Wisconsin. [7]Although ~~destroyed twice~~

                                        Wright constructed
~~by fire~~, Wright rebuilt Taliesin both times. [8]Concerning Taliesin, ^a second

structure, Taliesin West, ~~was constructed~~ in Scottsdale, Arizona. [9]For learning

       architecture students use
about design, ^this building ~~is used~~ as a school ~~for architecture students~~ today.

                           the Guggenheim family erected
[10]Upon selecting Wright's architectural plans, ^a unique, circular museum in New

York City ~~was erected and is called the Guggenheim Museum.~~

Revising and Editing Worksheet 1

Read the following report carefully. Correct errors in the use of modifiers. Make any other changes you think will improve the report. Write your revised report on a separate piece of paper. Revision will vary. Sample revision is given.

[1]~~This report is on waves of energy.~~ [2]Light waves may travel ~~fastest~~ (faster) than sound waves, but the principle by which all waves of energy travel is the same. [3]To understand this idea, you don't have to do ~~nothing~~ (anything) more complicated than experiment with a rope. [4]To create a rope wave, ~~a hand is moved~~ (move your hand) while holding onto one end of the rope. [5]The high and low spots on the rope waves are no different from the crests and troughs of water. [6]The ~~more~~ harder you move the rope, the ~~more~~ greater the amount of energy created that travels through the wave. [7]The ~~gentler~~ (more gently) you move the rope, the ~~lesser~~ (fewer) number of waves you create.

[8]Can you name more kinds of waves than anyone (else you know)? [9]After reading this selection, you ~~wouldn't not~~ (would) include light waves, sound waves, rope waves, and water waves on a list of waves of energy, (but) think ~~more~~ harder to make your list ~~more~~ bigger. [10]Did you consider musical instruments?

[11]~~Vibrating wildly,~~ a musician's plucked guitar strings are examples of (vibrating wildly) sound waves. [12]Those strings don't ~~never~~ (ever) stay still when you hear music. [13]Think about your ~~favoritest~~ (favorite) singers in the world. [14]To make their music, ~~vocal chords are vibrated~~ (they vibrate their vocal chords). [15]Waves of energy from the vocal chords (, which we hear as the human voice,) are what we enjoy listening to ~~as the human voice~~ from a stage.

[16]There ~~aren't~~ (are) scarcely ~~no~~ (any) instruments that don't send out ~~no~~ waves of energy, from air blown through wind instruments to strings ~~vibrated~~ (vibrating) on string instruments. [17]Some people enjoy the waves of energy produced by surfaces being tapped on percussion instruments ~~most~~ (more) than any (other) instruments ever invented.

Students should use modifiers correctly in complete sentences.

Revising and Editing Worksheet 2

Read the following biographical sketch carefully. Correct errors in the use of modifiers. Make any other changes you think will improve the biographical sketch. Work with a partner or small group to revise the biography. Write your revised biographical sketch on a separate piece of paper, and compare your response with those made by other pairs or groups of classmates.

¹This biographical sketch is ~~on~~ about the Shawnee leader Tecumseh (1768?–1813); he led one of the most surprising and ~~baddest~~ worst raids against American forces in the War of 1812. ²Why couldn't he ~~not~~ side with the Americans? ³Being forced to live like white people in North America, Shawnee beliefs ~~were threatened~~ threatened.

⁴No less than five times during Tecumseh's childhood did his people confront white soldiers. ⁵While fighting for Shawnee land around the Ohio River, Tecumseh's father and two brothers were killed. ⁶Through a dream he had, Tecumseh hoped to unite all Native Americans in a multitribal alliance ~~through a dream he had~~. ⁷The ~~dreamed-of~~ alliance wouldn't let ~~no~~ any tribes be moved from their land or be denied their way of life. ⁸Letting his brother, known as the Prophet, or Tenskwatawa, address fellow Native Americans, strengthened the alliance ~~The alliance was strengthened~~. ¹⁰Tenskwatawa's style of speaking was more ~~fiercer~~ fierce than Tecumseh's style of speaking. ¹¹Some listeners thought of him as wiser but stranger than any other speakers to come before him. ¹²In addition, Tenskwatawa didn't preach ~~no~~ nonviolence. ¹³In the fight for independence from the United States.

¹⁴Young Native Americans ~~knowed~~ knew of Tecumseh's ~~capturing~~ capture of Detroit during the War of 1812 before he was fifty. ¹⁵At Tippecanoe, in 1811, ~~a battle was lost by Tenskwatawa~~ Tenskwatawa lost a battle. ¹⁶The British hadn't ~~never~~ ever intended to support Tecumseh or his brother. ¹⁷The British eventually trapped Tecumseh in a ~~more~~ brutal battle at Moraviantown, Canada. ¹⁸There, Tecumseh ~~only~~ died with only his dream of Native American unity and independence.

Students should use modifiers correctly in complete sentences, fix fragments and run-ons, plus combine subjects, verbs, and simple sentences into compounds whenever appropriate for sense and the flow of ideas.

USAGE
Chapter 11

Visit us at
www.sadlier-oxford.com
Internet

Chapter Review

Exercise A Using Degrees of Comparison

Proofread the following sentences for the correct use of modifiers. If you find an error, cross out the word or phrase, and rewrite it correctly in the space above. If a sentence is correct, write *C* after it.

1. One of the ~~fascinatingest~~ *most fascinating* ways in which animals communicate is

   through pheromones.

2. A pheromone is one of the ~~most~~ best ways to signal location.

3. Pheromones are one of nature's more intriguing class of chemicals. C

4. In animals, the sense of smell is often the ~~more higher~~ *most highly* developed sense.

5. Animals can sense windborne pheromones from a ~~farthest~~ *far* distance away.

6. A bee sting that releases a pheromone causes more ~~aggressiver~~ *aggressive* behavior

   in nearby bees.

7. A bee sting's odor most ~~oftenest~~ *often* incites other bees to sting in the

   same place.

8. A bombardier beetle's pheromone is ~~least~~ *less* likely to cause harm than to

   attract a potential mate.

9. A skunk's pheromone-produced spray is the ~~less~~ *least* pleasant smell to me.

10. Chemists believe that pheromones are ~~the more~~ *a* better way to protect

    crops than artificial pesticides.

Exercise B Correcting Double Negatives and Illogical Modifiers

Correct problems with double negatives and illogical comparisons in the sentences below. Cross out words that aren't necessary, and add words that might be needed to correct each sentence.

1. Tony ~~hadn't~~ *had* hardly done anything unusual when his hard drive crashed.

2. Couldn't ~~nobody nowhere~~ *anybody anywhere* figure out how to fix his computer?

3. Marcia, who is better than anyone ∧ *else* with computers, fixed it.

4. Marcia hasn't ~~never~~ *ever* been stumped by a computer problem.

5. Her computer was ~~more old~~ *older* than mine.

6. Tony couldn't find ~~no~~ ^{any} Internet site to diagnose his problems.

7. Marcia suggested a library site, saying "Well, maybe I'm ~~most~~ ^{more} interested in libraries than you_∧." ^{are}

8. He tried ~~more~~ harder to find ~~more~~ better information through the site.

9. The library's electronic catalog didn't have ~~none~~ ^{any} of the information.

10. Then, Marcia chose a different database and found an article ~~more~~ better than anything Tony could find.

Exercise C Writing Sentences with Comparisons and Clear Modifiers

On a separate piece of paper, write five sentences about your experiences using a computer and the Internet. The sentences do not have to follow one another as they would in a paragraph. Use one comparison or clear modifier in each sentence.   Students' sentences will vary.

Exercise D Revising a Paragraph

On a separate piece of paper, rewrite the paragraph to correct misplaced and dangling modifiers. **Hint:** You may need to change the wording or to add words to correct some modifiers.   See Answer Key.

¹Roaring and leaping, Professor Michael Bleyman was not afraid of tigers or lions. ²To provide a home for abandoned or abused big cats, Bleyman founded a special farm in North Carolina. ³Named as the successor to Bleyman after his death, Nancy Schonwalter's old job as a video producer was abandoned. ⁴The Carnivore Preservation Trust is maintained by Schonwalter and only volunteers, without government funds. ⁵Wandering freely around the preservation, neighboring farmers aren't afraid of the big cats. ⁶Having escaped its cage, Bleyman once had to catch a tiger roaming around his neighbor's land when he began saving big cats. ⁷Now over twenty years old, a chain-link fence surrounds the animal preserve. ⁸Emaciated and tied to a tree, people from the Carnivore Preservation Trust once rescued a tiger found in downtown Houston, Texas. ⁹Newly rescued, Nancy Schonwalter might approach a tiger without fear in order to gain its acceptance. ¹⁰One of the major problems for the Trust is only finding enough big-cat food for the animals, which costs around $350,000 a year.

CHAPTER REVIEW

Choosing the Right Word

STUDENT WRITING
Expository Essay

Swing Is Back
by Michael Arcaro
high school student, Scarsdale, New York

Gentlemen, put on your zoot suits and wide-brimmed hats. Ladies, put on those knee-length skirts and beaded cardigans—because swing is back. The old smooth West Coast swing and bouncy East Coast swing have merged with newer beats to form neoswing. This version of swing has stormed America. Mosh pits are changing into swing floors. The fun beats seem to attract all ages. Swing classes are packed with young swingers eager to learn hip moves. An amazing quarter of those who swing dance today are under the age of twenty. Ten years ago, it was nearly impossible to find a swinging teen.

So what turned swing from an almost dead music to the mainstream style of today? This neoswing era emerged in small Los Angeles clubs and spread to the East Coast. Advertisements such as the jeans commercial featuring the Brian Setzer Orchestra covering Louis Prima's "Jump, Jive 'n' Wail" have created a national swing craze. As a result, swing lessons are packed; clubs have swing nights weekly; and vintage, hepcat clothes are back in style.

Many bands have emerged, giving their versions of classic hits and adding a whole new style of songs to the swing scene. Big Bad Voodoo Daddy has made its mark on the neoswing era with its big-band-style music. Royal Crown Revue adds its punk/swing style to the swing craze. The Brian Setzer Orchestra is known for having a whole orchestra behind a lead guitarist. Squirrel Nut Zippers has added a Dixieland spin to swing. Other groups have grown in popularity with similar styles. Many of them pay tribute to the old swingers—including Benny Goodman, Louis Prima, Duke Ellington, and the Glenn Miller Orchestra—by covering hit songs such as "Sing, Sing, Sing."

Another reason for this booming swing era is movies: *Swing Kids* and *Swingers* have created a hip, fun image of swingers. They've inspired teens to imitate the stylish look of the characters. Modern swing is filled with fun beats that make people just want to get up and dance. With hundreds of swing moves and personal touches, pretty much anything goes, as long as it follows the beat. This horn-tooting music is here to stay.

Michael Arcaro's essay explains the swing-dance craze. He gives background information, statistics about the dancers, and plenty of examples of the craze in television ads, in clothing trends, in new band sounds, and in recent movies.

Michael's lively word choice imitates the lively rhythm of the music he's writing about. Choosing words carefully is part of the art and creativity of writing. In this lesson, you'll find many suggestions for choosing the right word in your own writing.

Allow time for students to discuss the student writing. Suggest that they identify its strengths and propose possible improvements. Use the model to introduce the concepts in the chapter.

From *accept* to *beside*

● **accept, except** *Accept* is a verb that means "to receive" or "to agree to." *Except* is a preposition that means "but."

The committee decided to **accept** the senator's proposal. All the committee members **except** the senator from Iowa voted in favor of it.

● **adapt, adept, adopt** *Adapt* is a verb that means "to make fit or modify for use." *Adept* is an adjective meaning "very skilled or proficient." The word *adopt* is a verb that means "to take as one's own; to take by choice."

If you **adopt** a dog, you'll have to **adapt** your schedule to walk it. Soon, you'll become **adept** at teaching the dog tricks.

● **advice, advise** *Advice* is a noun that means "an opinion, or a recommendation regarding a decision." *Advise* is a verb that means "to give advice or counsel."

Brian usually listens to the counselor's **advice**.
I **advise** you to drive slowly around the curve.

● **affect, effect** *Affect* is a verb that means "to influence." The noun *effect* means "the result of an action." The verb *effect* means "to cause" or "to bring about."

Drinking coffee **affects** my sleep.
An **effect** of the oil shortage is the rising gas prices.
The new school dress code has **effected** major changes in the classroom.

● **all ready, already** *All ready*, an adjective phrase, means "completely ready." *Already* is an adverb meaning "previously" or "by now."

I have **already** seen *Romeo and Juliet*.
The room is **all ready** to be painted.

● **all the farther, all the faster** Use "as far as" instead of "all the farther." Use "as fast as" instead of "all the faster."

That's **as far as** I'll go to win the match.
His mind works **as fast as** a computer.

● **amount of, number of** Use *amount of* when you write about a general quantity of something. Use *number of* to refer to something that can be counted.

The **amount of** food Gary consumed surprised me.
The **number of** laps Helena swims every day is impressive.

Enriching Your Vocabulary

The adjective *adept*, which means "highly skilled or expert," comes from the Middle Latin *adeptus*, meaning "one who has attained." It's usually followed by the word "at" and then by a gerund. The carpenter was *adept* at working with her hands.

Writing Hint

Use *being that* rather than *being as* for a clause that acts as an adjective. However, *being that* is somewhat awkward and clumsy. In your writing, try to substitute *since* or *because* for *being that*.

Since
~~Being that~~ it's been overcast, my flowers haven't bloomed.

because
He took the job ~~being that~~ he felt qualified.

Editing Tip

Even though English includes both *altogether* and *all together*, don't assume that it also includes both *alright* and *all right*. There is only one *all right*; *alright* is not a word.

● **anywheres, everywheres, nowheres, somewheres** These words are all spelled incorrectly. None of them should be spelled with an *-s* at the end.

> **Everywhere** we went on vacation, it rained.
>
> **Nowhere** did it pour as it did that day in Portland.

● **bad, badly** Use *bad*, which is always an adjective, after a linking verb such as *be*, *seem*, and *feel*. Use *badly*, an adverb, to modify an action verb.

> Even though it was a **bad** connection, I told Ming Yen how **badly** I missed her.
>
> Hector felt **bad** about missing Kathy's call.
>
> Fortunately, Peg's trailer wasn't **badly** damaged in the hurricane.

● **beside, besides** *Beside* means "by the side of." *Besides* as a preposition means "in addition to." *Besides* as an adverb means "moreover."

> **Beside** the reservoir is a small grove of locust trees.
>
> **Besides** joining the soccer team, I joined the drama club.
>
> It's too cold to swim; **besides**, the pool is closed.

Exercise 1 Editing a Paragraph

Proofread the following newspaper article from a high school newspaper to correct all errors in word choice. **Hint:** Not every sentence contains an error; some sentences contain more than one error.

[1]~~Somewheres~~ Somewhere in the halls of Clarkson High School, Julie Browne is giving ~~advise~~ advice. [2]Her goal—to become a family therapist—encouraged her to get involved in the Talk Shop. [3]In this program, nobody ~~accept~~ except peers gives ~~advise~~ advice. [4]~~Nowheres~~ Nowhere else have students set up a peer counseling program like the one at Clarkson. [5]~~All ready~~ Already, students are lining up before homeroom when the Talk Shop opens. [6]The faculty and administration have ~~adapted~~ adopted this method of peer counseling. [7]~~Accept~~ Except for certain problems that demand adult or professional intervention, peer counseling has been very ~~affective~~ effective. [8]Peers trust one another, ~~being as~~ because they have many of the same concerns. [9]Any student who feels ~~badly~~ bad about a problem at home or in school may seek the ~~advise~~ advice of a Talk Shop counselor. [10]Sometimes, students are advised to see the guidance counselor. [11]Other times, a problem is ~~all ready~~ already resolved by the end of a ten-minute Talk Shop session. [12]Will the other local schools ~~adapt~~ adopt a peer counseling program?

From *between* to *fewer*

◗ **between, among** Use *between* to compare two people or things. You may also use *between* when comparing three or more items if the sentence implies that only two of them will be compared at a time. Use *among* to refer to a group or to three or more people or things.

> **Between** shrimp and lobster, I'll take shrimp any day.
> Do you know the difference **between** a crustacean, a bivalve, and a fish?
> **Among** fishermen, crabbing is considered an art.

◗ **borrow, lend, loan** *Borrow* means "to take something temporarily that must be returned." *Lend*, the opposite of *borrow*, means "to give something temporarily with the expectation that it will be returned." Don't confuse *loan* and *lend*. *Loan* is always a noun; it's the thing that is *lent*.

> Ali will **lend** you his copy of *The Martian Chronicles* to read.
> He already **borrowed** another science fiction novel from Hank.
> Was that Isaac Asimov book you gave me a **loan** or a gift?

◗ **can, may** Use *can* to show that something is possible. Use *may* when the subject is asking permission to do something or there's a possibility of doing something.

> You **can** have a window seat, but you **may** not be able to see the peak of Mt. Hood.

◗ **could have, could of** Always use *could have*; *could of* is incorrect.

> Natasha **could have** been a rock star.

◗ **different from, different than** In most cases, *different from* works better than *different than*. However, in certain instances, *different than* eliminates an awkward construction and streamlines a sentence.

> How are crocodiles **different from** alligators?
> The zoo looks **different than** it did ten years ago.

◗ **disinterested, uninterested** *Disinterested* means "impartial or lacking interest in something or someone." *Uninterested* means "bored, indifferent, showing no interest in someone or something."

> The lawyers selected only **disinterested** individuals for the jury.
> The defendant appeared strangely **uninterested** in the verdict.

◗ **eager, anxious** Use *eager* to show hopeful excitement. Use *anxious* to show worry about the future.

> Sara was **anxious** about her test results.
> She was **eager** to hear that she passed.

Enriching Your Vocabulary

The noun *detritus*, used in Exercise 2, comes from the Latin *deterere* meaning "to rub off." The word refers to fragments of rock produced by disintegration or wearing away, as well as any accumulation of debris. Rock climbers must be particularly cautious as they approach the *detritus* on rock cliffs.

● **emigrate, immigrate** *Emigrate* means "to leave one country and go to another." *Immigrate* means "to enter a country and live there."

> Gambrowitz, the writer, **emigrated** from Poland during World War II. She **immigrated** to Argentina and worked as a bank clerk.

● **farther, further** *Farther* refers to physical distance. *Further* refers to additional degree or time.

> Nevil walked **farther** on the Appalachian Trail than Joan.
> His understanding of Freanch goes **further** than I will ever know.

● **fewer, less** *Fewer* modifies plural nouns that can be counted. *Less* modifies singular nouns that can't be counted.

> Use **fewer** peppers in the sauce. **Less** tabasco sauce would also improve the flavor.

Exercise 2 Editing a Paragraph

Make corrections in the choice of words in the following paragraph. Cross out words that are incorrect, and write the correct words above them. **Hint:** Not every sentence has an error. Answers will vary. Sample corrections are given.

¹In 1985, underwater diver Robert Ballard found the ruins of the ship *Titanic* ~~between~~ (among) the detritus on the ocean floor. ²The success of the 1997 movie *Titanic* does not suggest that Ballard ~~can~~ (may) never again find another treasure or shipwreck. ³Pushing himself even further, he's planning to investigate the ocean floor for evidence of the biblical floods. ⁴His study of two tectonic plates is different ~~than~~ (from) any previous project. ⁵The next project he wants to direct ~~bad~~ (badly) is to find shipwrecks from World War II ~~somewheres~~ (somewhere) in the South Pacific. ⁶Who could ~~of loaned~~ (have lent) him the sophisticated, expensive equipment for these explorations? ⁷In truth, Ballard has no need to ~~lend~~ (borrow) anything; he ~~all ready~~ (already) has everything he needs. ⁸~~Being as~~ (Because) he's director of Marine Exploration at Woods Hole, Massachusetts, Ballard ~~may~~ (can) have access to the latest equipment. ⁹Actually, Ballard wishes ~~less~~ (fewer) people linked him to the *Titanic*. ¹⁰It's not that he can't ~~except~~ (accept) fame or that he's ~~disinterested~~ (uninterested) in that ship. ¹¹He simply wishes the public's interest would go ~~farther~~ (further) than the *Titanic*.

From *hopefully* to *percent*

● **hopefully** Use *hopefully* as an adverb to mean "in a hopeful manner." Do not use it in place of "I hope."

> The volunteers waited **hopefully** for the election results.
> I **hope** I will arrive before it rains.

● **imply, infer** *Imply* means "to hint or suggest." *Infer* means "to understand a hint or suggestion."

> I **infer** from your report that you enjoy cooking.
> Did she **imply** that she planned to become a chef someday?

● **inside of, outside of, off of** Don't use *of* after the prepositions *inside*, *outside*, and *off*. Also, use *from*, not *off* or *off of*, when you're referring to the source of something.

> You'll find a ring **inside** ~~of~~ the box.
> He leapt **off** ~~of~~ the diving board.
> Here's the calculator I borrowed **from** Tina.

● **in, into** *In* is a preposition that refers to a sense of belonging, location, or position within specified boundaries. *Into* is a preposition that refers to entry, introduction, or movement from one place to another.

> Sea turtles leave the ocean to lay their eggs **in** the sand.
> There are bass **in** this lake. The bass jumped **into** the net.
> After hatching, the baby turtles rush **into** the surf.

● **kind of a, sort of a, type of a** Drop the *a*. Use *kind of*, *sort of*, or *type of*. But keep in mind that *kind* (*sort, type*) *of* can usually be omitted without changing the meaning of a sentence and, in fact, should be avoided unless truly necessary.

> The **kind of** ~~a~~ guitar I like most is acoustic.
> The guitar I like most is acoustic.

● **lay, lie** *Lay* means "to set something down," and it takes a direct object. *Lie* means "to place oneself or remain in a horizontal position," and it does not take a direct object.

> Don't **lay** the blanket on the bed.
> Make sure you **lie** down and rest before the swim meet.

● **learn, teach** *Learn* means "to gain knowledge." *Teach* means "to instruct."

> Tim can **teach** Betty how to drive on weekends.
> She will **learn** to drive this summer.

Step by Step

To decide whether to use *good* or *well*:

1. Decide how the word is used in the sentence.

2. If the word is an adverb (telling how something is done), use *well*. *Good* is never used as an adverb.

3. If the word is an adjective, look at its meaning in the sentence. If it means "in good health," use *well*. For all other meanings, use *good*.

Kim is doing **well** at her new job.

She is in very **good** health.

---

leave, let *Leave* means "to depart" or "to allow to remain." *Let* means "to allow."

> They won't **let** you **leave** the country without a passport.
> I never **leave** the dishes in the sink.

like, as, as if, as though Don't use *like* to introduce a subordinate clause. Use *as*, *as if*, or *as though*. Use *like* to express similarity, sameness, or near sameness.

> The dog runs **as if** it's being chased.
> He performed well, **as** I knew he would.
> Pat and Anna look **like** sisters.

most, almost *Most* is an adverb that means "greatest in quantity." *Almost* is an adverb that means "not quite; nearly but not completely."

> **Most** of my clothes fit into this suitcase.
> The airplane is **almost** full.

percent, percentage *Percent* is an adverb that means "per hundred." *Percentage*, a noun, means "a part of a whole expressed in hundredths."

> What Caribbean country has a 90 **percent** literacy rate?
> The **percentage** of dual income families is increasing.

Exercise 3 Choosing the Right Word

Underline the word in parentheses that correctly completes each sentence.

1. What (percent, <u>percentage</u>) of the school's budget goes to the arts?

2. Approach a new book (like, <u>as</u>, as if) you would a new friendship.

3. (Leave, <u>Let</u>) bankers help you apply for college loans, but don't (<u>leave</u>, let) decisions until the last minute.

4. The children in that class act (like, <u>as if</u>) they're better than we are.

5. Don't (<u>let</u>, leave) your application (<u>lay</u>, lie) around too long.

6. Annabelle had to get (<u>off</u>, off of) the student council because of her grades.

7. (<u>I hope that</u>, Hopefully,) the movie won't start before we arrive.

8. The nasty tone of that letter (infers, <u>implies</u>) that the student council is to blame for the mistake.

9. I scraped (most, <u>almost</u>) all the cake batter out of the bowl.

10. As we turned (in, <u>into</u>) the wind, some dirt flew (in, <u>into</u>) my eye.

From *raise* to *who*

raise, rise *Raise* is a verb that means "to lift up," and it takes a direct object. *Rise*, a verb that means "to go up; to get up," does not take a direct object.

I **raise** the shade when I **rise** in the morning.

real, really *Real* is an adjective that means "actual." *Really* is an adverb that means "actually" or "genuinely."

I **really** like movies based on **real** events or people.

seldom, seldom ever Strictly speaking, *ever* is redundant after *seldom*.

We **seldom** review the math concepts the same day that we learn them.

set, sit *Set* means "to place or put down," and it takes a direct object except when referring to the sun. *Sit* means "to occupy a seat," and it does not take a direct object.

I will **set** the table before dark.
We can **sit** down for dinner and watch the sun **set** in the west.

slow, slowly *Slow* is an adjective. Other than in the expressions *Drive slow* and *Go slow*, which have become acceptable because of their wide use on road signs, don't use *slow* as an adverb. *Slowly* is always an adverb.

The conductor said to beat the drum **slowly**.
Painting with oils is a long, **slow** process.

sure, surely Use *sure* as an adjective. Use *surely* as an adverb to mean "certainly" or "without a doubt." Do not use *sure* as an intensifier.

Longer days are a **sure** sign of spring. **Surely**, you must be relieved that winter is over. These tulips ~~sure~~ look beautiful on Cedar Hill.

than, then *Than* is a conjunction that introduces a subordinate clause. *Then* is an adverb meaning "therefore" or "next in order or time."

The cougar leapt higher **than** the antelope.
Then the cougar showed her **prowess** at tree-climbing.

who, whom, which, that Each of these relative pronouns has its own job. Use *who* (a subject pronoun) or *whom* (an object pronoun) to refer to people. Use *which* or *that* to refer to animals and objects, not to people.

The twins, **who** left their sandals in the hotel room, were the same teenagers **whom** we met in the lobby. Walking barefoot toward the pool, they dropped their goggles, **which** they needed for swimming.

Enriching Your Vocabulary

Prowess has two meanings—bravery, or superior ability and skill. Derived from the Old French word *prou*, meaning "brave," *prowess* conveys a sense of special skill or overarching, commanding ability.

Writing Hint

Use *that* to introduce a clause that is essential to the meaning of the sentence. Use *which* to introduce a nonessential clause.

Editing a Paragraph

Cross out the words that are used incorrectly, and write the correct words above them. **Hint:** Some sentences have more than one error, and one sentence has no errors.

[1]A book ~~which~~ _that_ you like often says something about who you are in terms of your interests. [2]For example, a person ~~that~~ _who_ is fascinated with history, especially World War I, may ~~sure~~ _surely_ be a fan of Ernest Hemingway. [3]A ~~real~~ _really_ good novel is _The Sun Also Rises_. [4]You begin to think the characters in the story are ~~really~~ _real_, not imagined. [5]Another novel ~~who~~ _that_ is recommended by teachers and students is _A Separate Peace_ by John Knowles. [6]Readers ~~that~~ _who_ enjoy this book read it ~~real slow~~ _really slowly_ on purpose. [7]An English boy recounts his experience in an American boarding school. [8]In addition, the book is set during World War II, in the 1940s. [9]On a rainy day, ~~set~~ _sit_ yourself down with a novel ~~which~~ _that_ you are ~~real~~ _really_ interested in. [10]There ~~sure~~ is no telling what you may discover about yourself when you ~~raise~~ _rise_ from your chair. [11]You may find that book better ~~then~~ _than_ any you've ever read before. [12]A good reader can seldom ~~ever~~ resist the characters created by a skillful author, characters ~~which~~ _who_ are as real as people ~~that~~ _whom_ we know. [13]Reading a novel set during a historical event is also a ~~real~~ _really_ good way to visit the past.

Write What You Think

On a separate piece of paper, write your response to the following statement. Remember to include examples and anecdotes to support your opinions and ideas.

■ **Refer to Composition, Lesson 3.2, to find tips for writing persuasively.**

Your local school board has proposed the following policy: No student will be allowed to read a novel, short story, or book of nonfiction unless that book has been approved by the school board, a committee of parents, and all the teachers in the school.

Answers will vary. Give students full credit if they have stated an opinion and attempted to support their opinions. Look for grammatically complete sentences that begin with a capital letter and end with an appropriate end punctuation mark.

Revising and Editing Worksheet 1

In the following draft of a personal narrative, correct errors in the choice of words, and make any other changes you think will improve the paragraphs. Write your revised narrative on a separate piece of paper.

Revisions will vary. Sample revisions are given.

¹There ~~sure~~ are surprises in ~~most~~ ^{almost} everyone's life, and mine ~~ain't~~ ^{is} no ~~acception~~ ^{exception}. ²Surprises can happen ~~anywheres~~ ^{anywhere}, at ~~anytime~~ ^{any time}. ³~~Between~~ ^{Among} all the extraordinary events ~~which~~ ^{that} have happened ~~of~~ ⁱⁿ my lifetime, ⁴Øne in particular is different ~~than~~ ^{from} all the others.

⁵The event I will describe ~~effects~~ ^{affects} me to this day. ⁶With time, I have ~~excepted~~ ^{accepted} what happened one day, way back in 1986. ⁷I was home from school and not feeling ~~too good~~ ^{well}. ⁸I was ~~kind of laying~~ ^{lying} on a couch in the living room. ⁹The television was on, but ~~being that~~ ^{since} my memory is ~~real~~ ^{really} bad, I don't know what program was on. ¹⁰~~Anyways~~ ^{Anyway}, I was falling asleep when I ~~rised~~ ^{raised} myself up to watch the space shuttle *Challenger* take off.

¹¹I ~~all ready~~ ^{already} knew something about the crew ~~which~~ ^{that} would fly the

Challenger. ¹²The day before, my class had discussed a special crew member, Christa McAuliffe‿^{who} ~~that~~ was a teacher from New Hampshire. ¹³Christa was ~~adapted~~ ^{adopted} by school children ~~everywheres~~ ^{everywhere} as a model astronaut. ¹⁴~~Anyways~~ ^{Anyway}, I could ~~of~~ ^{have} slept through this live broadcast ~~accept~~ ^{except} for my mother's insistence that I watch it. ¹⁵On her ~~advise~~ ^{advice}, I watched the television ~~real close~~ ^{really closely}.

¹⁶No one could ~~of~~ ^{have} been ~~disinterested~~ ^{uninterested} in what was happening on the live broadcast. ¹⁷The rocket fuel flamed ~~as~~ ^{like} a special ~~affect~~ ^{effect} in a Hollywood movie. ¹⁸But this scene was ~~real~~ ^{really} different ~~than~~ ^{from} a movie. ¹⁹As the *Challenger* moved ~~further~~ ^{farther} away from Earth, ~~less~~ ^{fewer} people could take their eyes off ~~of~~ its ascent. ²⁰Suddenly, seventy-three seconds later.‿²¹Ã huge explosion spelled a ~~real~~ ^{really} bad disaster. ²²I have never felt so ~~badly~~ ^{bad} about a news event before.

²³Christa McAuliffe is the one astronaut ~~that~~ ^{who} will never be forgotten by schoolchildren ~~anywheres~~ ^{anywhere}.

In the following draft of a play review, correct errors in the choice of words, and make any other changes you think will improve the paragraphs. Work with a partner or small group to revise the paragraphs. Write your revised review on a separate piece of paper, and compare your revisions with those made by your classmates.   Revisions will vary. Sample revisions are given.

[1]*Our Town* by Thorton Wilder is a ~~real~~ *really* popular play about life in an American town. [2]Many schools and theater companies continue to ~~adopt~~ *adapt* this play to their stages and actors. [3]*Our Town* tells the story of two young people ~~that lives~~ *who live* in a small New Hampshire town about one hundred years ago. [4]The play is set in Grover's Corners, which wasn't much different ~~than anywheres~~ *from anywhere* else in the United States. [5]The action takes place in the local high school, and the dramatic tension is ~~among~~ *between* George Gibbs and Emily Webb. [6]Emily is the person ~~which~~ *whom* George has loved for much of his life. [7]Audiences are ~~sure effected~~ *surely affected* when Emily and George ~~ends~~ *end* up marrying. [8]Things go ~~bad~~ *badly* for Emily, ~~which~~ *who* dies in childbirth. [9]Her family ~~excepts~~ *accepts* her death and ~~lies~~ *lays* her to rest in the local cemetery.

[10]The play ~~sure~~ gets interesting when Emily meets others in the cemetery ~~which~~ *who* lived in Grover's Corners in the past. [11]Everyone has affecting stories to tell. [12]The experiences of those ~~that~~ *who* lived before is ~~sure~~ chilling for audiences and readers. [13]~~Them~~ *Those* in Grover's Corners speak to who we are and about the good and the bad ~~of~~ *in* our people and towns; both past and present. [14]When audiences ~~raises~~ *rise* from their seats, they understand ~~how~~ *that* people today are no different ~~than~~ *from* people one hundred year ago. [15]They are often deeply ~~effected~~ *affected* at the end of the play, ~~being as~~ *since* the characters experience life ~~like~~ *as* the audiences themselves do. [16]Audiences ~~imply~~ *infer* that people, wherever and whenever they live, share the same basic concerns and needs. [17]We ~~can~~ *may* fly to the moon, but we have no ~~less~~ *fewer* problems ~~then~~ *than* we ever did before.

Chapter Review

Exercise A **Choosing the Right Word**

Underline the word in parentheses that correctly completes each sentence.

1. Everyone (accept, <u>except</u>) Yoko volunteered to tutor on Wednesdays.

2. (<u>Seldom</u>, Seldom ever) did we go to museums last year.

3. Isn't there a saying that goes, "Let sleeping dogs (lay, <u>lie</u>)"?

4. Ms. Willis wants to (learn, <u>teach</u>) us rules for algebraic equations.

5. Simi became (<u>adept</u>, adapt) at playing the tuba.

6. We got (in, <u>into</u>) a dispute over which color to paint the scenery.

7. Where do you want to (set, <u>sit</u>) at the dining room table?

8. Customers (that, <u>who</u>) leave satisfied, usually return.

9. The window (which, <u>that</u>) you broke was the principal's.

10. Do you know what (percent, <u>percentage</u>) of students took drivers education?

11. When should we (leave, <u>let</u>) the animals out of their cages?

12. The director will (<u>adapt</u>, adopt) my story for an after-school television special.

13. Winners were chosen from (between, <u>among</u>) many entries, but first place was (<u>between</u>, among) two juniors.

14. You (<u>can</u>, may) drive downtown, but you (can, <u>may</u>) not find parking.

15. Readers (imply, <u>infer</u>) the meaning that authors (infer, <u>imply</u>) through the details the authors include.

16. If you do (bad, <u>badly</u>), you'll be grounded.

17. The team needed (<u>fewer</u>, less) hitters (being as, being that, <u>since</u>) the ones they (<u>already</u>, all ready) had were excellent.

18. To resolve the dispute between these two families, a (<u>disinterested</u>, uninterested) party was brought in to hear both sides of the story.

19. On the (<u>advice</u>, advise) of his aunt, Yuri (<u>emigrated</u>, immigrated) to Canada.

20. (<u>Nowhere</u>, Nowheres) else will travelers find a hotel that (<u>accepts</u>, excepts) pets.

Exercise B **Editing a Paragraph**

Cross out the words that are used incorrectly on the next page, and write the correct words above them. **Hint:** Some sentences have more than one error.

Answers will vary. Sample corrections are given.

¹The Great Depression had ~~all ready~~ ^{already} begun when the stock market

crashed in 1929. ²The crash ~~effected~~ ^{affected} the United States economy for years

to come. ³There were ~~less~~ ^{fewer} dollars available to the average person, and ~~less~~ ^{few}

people had money to ~~loan~~ ^{lend}. ⁴President Franklin Roosevelt, with the ~~advise~~ ^{advice}

and consent of Congress, ~~adapted~~ ^{adopted} a program called the New Deal to spark

the economy. ⁵~~Between~~ ^{Among} the many New Deal programs, one stands out:

Social Security. ⁶To this day, people ~~everywheres~~ ^{everywhere} feel that they will be hurt

~~real bad~~ ^{really badly} if Social Security is not protected. ⁷In addition to Social Security,

the New Deal ~~rose~~ ^{raised} the incomes of Americans through work-related

projects. ⁸Members of Congress ~~which~~ ^{who} supported the New Deal believed

in a strong federal government. ⁹Other members of Congress believed that

a strong federal government would only ~~infer~~ ^{imply} higher taxes. ¹⁰~~Hopefully,~~

the New Deal ~~learned~~ ^{taught} Americans how government programs can help in

hard times. ¹¹~~Somewheres~~ ^{Somewhere} in your neighborhood, you might see the

~~affects~~ ^{effects} of the New Deal—for example, your public swimming pool or a

public mural in your school may have been created by a ~~new~~ ^{New} Deal program.

Exercise C   ## Writing Correct Sentences

For each of the words below, write an interesting and complete sentence.
You may change the verb form to fit the sentence. Underline the word in
each sentence, and then exchange sentences with a partner. Check to see
if the underlined words have been used correctly. Students' sentences will vary.

EXAMPLE   immigrate

Nevil Behari <u>immigrated</u> to Jamaica and settled in Kingston.

1. advise	6. into	11. bad	16. teach
2. fewer	7. percentage	12. infer	17. slow
3. all ready	8. which	13. except	18. who
4. well	9. really	14. farther	19. rise
5. uninterested	10. lay	15. between	20. surely

Cumulative Review

Exercise A Using Verbs Correctly

On a separate piece of paper, correct all the errors in verb usage in the following sentences. Look for incorrect verbs and verb forms, unnecessary shifts in verb tense, and unnecessary use of the passive voice. **Hint:** A sentence may have more than one mistake.

1. If I ~~was~~ were you, I would have screamed with joy when I ~~winned~~ won the award.
2. As the master of ceremonies ~~speaked~~ spoke, I ~~holded~~ held my breath.
3. I might ~~has~~ have stayed ~~freezed~~ frozen in my seat at the idea of giving a speech.
4. You ~~do~~ did well to have ~~choosed~~ chosen a quotation from Shakespeare.
5. No one will ever ~~forgot~~ forget the way you ~~had~~ thanked your drama coach.
6. To hear every word you ~~was~~ were saying, we ~~keeped~~ kept quiet.
7. Your poise ~~teached~~ taught me an important lesson.
8. You ~~rised~~ rose to the occasion and ~~gaved~~ gave credit to your fellow actors.
9. If I had ~~sit~~ sat in the front row, you could ~~had seed~~ have seen me smile.
10. When you ~~have~~ went back to your seat, you ~~was~~ were on cloud nine.

Exercise B Subject-Verb Agreement

Underline the verb in parentheses that agrees with the subject.

1. Astronomers (was, <u>were</u>) shocked to find evidence of water in space.
2. Conditions on Titan, a moon of Saturn, (resembles, <u>resemble</u>) those that led to the creation of life on Earth.
3. One of the scientists (<u>guesses</u>, guess) that life could emerge on Titan.
4. Researchers at a European Space Observatory (has, <u>have</u>) been using new techniques to study our solar system.
5. Water, a sign of life, (<u>has</u>, have) been spotted all over the cosmos.
6. Water apparently (<u>exists</u>, exist) where temperatures are extremely cold.
7. What (<u>is</u>, are) the source of this water among planets and stars?
8. Comets, some think, (has, <u>have</u>) brought water to the solar system.
9. (<u>Is</u>, Are) the United States or other countries conducting research about water?
10. The press often (writes, <u>write</u>) articles on the search for water.

Exercise C Using Pronouns Correctly

Underline the pronoun in parentheses that correctly completes each sentence.

1. Carson and (<u>I</u>, me) will be lifeguards this summer.

2. The beverage vendors at the lake will be Koko, Ali, and (<u>he</u>, him).

3. The store owner hired Otis and (I, <u>me</u>) as summer cashiers.

4. It's all right to call the dog (he, <u>him</u>) instead of *it*.

5. Was Ms. Chen the executive to (who, <u>whom</u>) you wrote?

6. Between you and (I, <u>me</u>), I liked the root beer better.

7. The best summer employees, Luz and (<u>she</u>, her), got a raise.

8. The employees gave the factory managers, Lily and (he, <u>him</u>), a gift.

9. Few realize how much (<u>we</u>, us) volunteer ushers enjoy the films we see.

10. The janitors and (her, <u>she</u>) cleared the displays from her classroom walls.

Exercise D Using Modifiers Correctly

On a separate piece of paper, edit the following sentences to correct all errors in the use of modifiers, including dangling modifiers. **Hint:** Some sentences have more than one error.

1. Which cuisine do you like ~~more~~ better, Chinese or Korean?

2. The ~~most fresh~~ freshest ingredients make the ~~bestest~~ best soup.

3. Of these four restaurants, the Pasta Palace is the ~~less expensivest~~ least expensive.

4. She cooked the ~~most~~ greatest meal of all time in her mind.

5. The Afghan Kebab House is smaller than any other restaurant in this city.

6. The chef worked ~~more~~ harder to create the ~~most~~ perfect dessert.

7. Didn't ~~nobody never~~ anybody ever tell you that the dish contained hot peppers?

8. While stir-frying the vegetables, ~~the recipe belonging to Dave was lost.~~ Dave lost his recipe.

9. ~~Floating in the soup, the customer spotted a clove of garlic.~~ The customer spotted a clove of garlic floating in the soup.

10. The ~~deliciouser~~ more delicious the dish, the ~~popularer~~ more popular an item becomes on the menu.

Usage Test

Identifying Errors

Directions: Each of the numbered items either is correct or contains an error in one or more of the underlined parts of the sentence. In the answer section to the right of each item, circle the letter of the underlined sentence part that contains the error. If the sentence is correct, circle *E* for NO ERROR.

EXAMPLE   It's <u>me</u> who <u>has taken</u> out the library book about Anne Bradstreet. She
            A   B

           is <u>known</u> for her poetry, which <u>was written</u> in seventeenth-century
              C   D

           Massachusetts.   <u>NO ERROR</u>
                           E

          (A) B C D E

1. Do you know of <u>whom</u> I speak when I <u>mention</u> Anne Bradstreet? Of her
              A   B

   many poems, I <u>believes</u> that "Prologue" is her <u>best</u> verse.   <u>NO ERROR</u>
              C   D   E

          1. A B (C) D E

2. Anne Bradstreet <u>married</u> in England, then <u>came</u> to America. <u>Her,</u> four sons
               A   B   C

   and four daughters <u>lived</u> a settler's life.   <u>NO ERROR</u>
                D   E

          2. A B (C) D E

3. Her father <u>hisself</u> <u>encouraged</u> Bradstreet <u>to write</u> poems. That <u>was</u> unusual,
            A   B   C   D

   considering Puritan beliefs of the time.   <u>NO ERROR</u>
                           E

          3.(A) B C D E

4. <u>One</u> finds when reading the poems of Anne Bradstreet that <u>your</u> mind
   A   B

   <u>enjoys</u> the ideas while your ear <u>welcomes</u> the rhymes.   <u>NO ERROR</u>
      C   D   E

          4.(A) B C D E

5. The poems "Contemplations" <u>and</u> "Prologue" <u>acts</u> as strong statements for
                          A   B

   women's rights. <u>They address</u> Bradstreet's place in life as a woman and a
                    C

   Puritan.   <u>NO ERROR</u>
             D

          5. A (B) C D E

6. <u>She</u> and other neighbors <u>who</u> also <u>were writers</u> <u>had builded</u> a strong
   A   B   C   D

   intellectual community in Ipswich, Massachusetts, in the 1630s.   <u>NO ERROR</u>
                                                     E

          6. A B C (D) E

7. Anne Bradstreet would often <u>lay</u> down with illness. <u>Her</u> last poem, <u>written</u>
                      A   B   C

   in 1669, <u>is even entitled</u> "As Weary Pilgrim."   <u>NO ERROR</u>
          D   E

          7.(A) B C D E

8. One of Anne Bradstreet's <u>brother-in-laws</u>, <u>brought</u> a manuscript
                                     A   B

   of <u>her poems</u> to England that <u>was published</u> in 1650.   <u>NO ERROR</u>
          C   D   E

                                  8. Ⓐ B C D E

9. *The Tenth Muse Lately Sprung Up in America* <u>was</u> the first printed book
                                            A

   of <u>English poems</u> from America. <u>It</u>, along with her other unpublished
           B   C

   poems, <u>presents</u> a picture of Puritan life.   <u>NO ERROR</u>
             D   E

                                    9. A B C D Ⓔ

10. If a jury <u>vote</u> for best writer from early colonial days, Anne Bradstreet
                A

   <u>would be</u> a candidate. <u>Her</u> work <u>stands</u> the test of time.   <u>NO ERROR</u>
        B   C   D   E

                                  10. Ⓐ B C D E

Exercise 2   Correcting Errors

Directions: In the following sentences, the underlined part may contain one or more errors. In the answer section to the right of each item, circle the letter of the choice that correctly expresses the idea in the underlined part of the sentence. If you think that the original wording is correct, circle *D* for NO ERROR. **Hint:** A sentence may have more than one error.

EXAMPLE   The Tigers and the Mustangs <u>are the best local teams.</u>   A B C Ⓓ
                       A. is the most bestest local teams
                       B. are the most best local teams
                       C. are the more best local teams
                       D. NO ERROR

1. <u>Either you or Alex have won</u> the student body election.   1. Ⓐ B C D
   A. Either you or Alex has won   B. Either your or Alex has won
   C. Either your or Alex have won   D. NO ERROR

2. Elvia performs that dance <u>really good, much better then me.</u>   2. Ⓐ B C D
   A. really well, much better than I.
   B. really well, much better than me.
   C. really well, much better then I.
   D. NO ERROR

3. Simon <u>dove into the pool and swim</u> for first place in the competition.   3. A B Ⓒ D
   A. dove into the pool and swummed
   B. dived into the pool and swum
   C. dived into the pool and swam
   D. NO ERROR

4. <u>Everyone know who's</u> in charge of this gym.   4. A B Ⓒ D
   A. Everyone knowed whom is   B. Everyone knows whose
   C. Everyone knows who's   D. NO ERROR

5. Until Eli Whiel wrote that book, no one <u>had never written</u> about   5. A B Ⓒ D
   teenage businesses.
   A. had never wrote   B. had ever writed
   C. had ever written   D. NO ERROR

6. The students <u>couldn't hardly wait for their</u> test results to be announced.   6. A Ⓑ C D
   A. couldn't hardly wait for their   B. could hardly wait for their
   C. could hardly wait for his or her   D. NO ERROR

7. <u>Ramon or her usually, but not always, lead</u> a class review before the   7. A Ⓑ C D
   chemistry test.
   A. Ramon or her usually, but not always, leads
   B. Ramon or she usually, but not always, leads
   C. Ramon or she usually, but not always, lead
   D. NO ERROR

8. They <u>has never rang no bells</u> in the orchestra before.   8. Ⓐ B C D
   A. have never rung any bells   B. has never rang any bells
   C. have never rung no bells   D. NO ERROR

Exercise 3 Identifying Errors

Directions: In each numbered group of sentences, *one or more* of the
sentences may contain usage errors. In the answer section to the right of each
item, circle the letter of *every* sentence that contains an error.

EXAMPLE   A. The second stew I cooked was far better than my first attempt.   A Ⓑ Ⓒ D
          B. Neither James nor she write poetry with rhymes.
          C. Few in these classes answers as many questions as Felix.
          D. Much of the mural is based on the theme of harmony.

1. A. Because of help from David and her, everyone has solved the   1. A B Ⓒ Ⓓ
      algebra problem.
   B. The flock of birds imitate each other's calls and movements.
   C. Along with you and I̶, the Nguyen twins are the best musicians I know. me
   D. Todd and h̶e̶r̶ sent an e-mail from San Francisco to you and I̶. Todd and she...
                    was   adopt   to you and me.
2. A. Neither Martha nor I w̶e̶r̶e̶ able to a̶d̶a̶p̶t̶ the puppy.   2. Ⓐ Ⓑ C D
   B. Both the basketball and baseball teams had to l̶o̶a̶n̶ uniforms from   borrow
      other schools.
   C. Everyone in the company is trained to perform his or her job efficiently.
   D. Kim or his brothers run the hundred-yard dash in record time.

3. A. We were ~~all ready~~ late when the bus pulled away from the station.   _already_

   B. The fleet waits in the harbor for the fog to lift.

   C. Therese had ~~sang~~ a solo first, then she sang with the entire choir. _sung_

   D. You're invited to enjoy a day at the beach with us.

3. Ⓐ B Ⓒ D

4. A. We haven't ~~never~~ been camping or hiking in the mountains. _ever_

   B. Juan's family sponsored a family that wanted to immigrate to the United States.

   C. Jody draws worse than ~~me~~ or anyone else I know. _I_

   D. Sonya and Michael have caught enough fish for us to eat at dinner.

4. Ⓐ B Ⓒ D

5. A. It's wonderful to watch the sun rise over water.

   B. If you and I plan this correctly, we'll get to the movies on time.

   C. Could you tell me to ~~who~~ I should deliver this message? _whom_

   D. The ~~most~~ greatest actor of all time is in the movie.

5. A B ⒸⒹ

6. A. During most storms, the snow would barely cover the porch steps.

   B. In this display, we show the brightest, most interesting paintings.

   C. If I ~~was~~ to plan an amazing journey, I'd include a trip down the Amazon. _were_

   D. Did you want ~~least~~ to eat than he? _less_

6. A B ⒸⒹ

7. A. We have forgotten the canteens filled with water.

   B. He dreamt an incredible dream about the high school of the future.

   C. Once you have taken the test, you can't take it again.

   D. She will ~~loan~~ him the book if he returns it tomorrow. _lend_

7. A B C Ⓓ

8. A. When my sister does well on a test, she gets to choose a video for the weekend.

   B. If nothing else, he plays the guitar ~~good~~. _well_

   C. I feel worse today than I did yesterday, but far better than I did last week.

   D. He has never done ~~nothing~~ but good deeds. _anything_

8. A Ⓑ C Ⓓ

Exercise 4 Correcting Errors

Directions: Look back at each item in Exercise 3, and double-check your answers. Make sure you have identified all of the sentences with errors. On a separate piece of paper, rewrite correctly all of the incorrect sentences in each numbered item. Write the entire sentence. **Hint**: A sentence may have more than one error.

Punctuation: End Marks and Commas

STUDENT WRITING
Expository Essay

Student Copes with Disability
by Alex Zane

high school student, Pottsville, Pennsylvania

To some students, walking to school, learning to drive, and running laps in gym class are all challenges; but to sophomore Robert Heffner, these "challenges" would be welcome.

Heffner, who attended the Intermediate Unit 29 in Mar Lin before attending Pottsville, has cerebral palsy, which leaves him unable to walk without the assistance of crutches.

This challenge may affect his walking ability, but it doesn't change his attitude, which always seems to be positive.

"With all that he is dealing with, he never complains, and he never tries to go home sick. Meanwhile, other students are always in my office trying to go home. I just think he is such a positive example of what people can overcome," PAHS school nurse Janine Tobash said.

Heffner's upbeat attitude can be seen in how he feels about this school. "PAHS is a very good school. The students and faculty help me sometimes by carrying my books in between classes and by helping me get my lunch," Heffner said.

Also, when the school elevator is running slowly and causing him to be late, his teachers "always understand."

An example of a student who helps Heffner can be found in senior Robert Yarnell, who helps out by getting and carrying Heffner's lunch every day—although Yarnell himself doesn't feel that the act deserves attention.

"Rob is a nice guy. I help him because he is my friend, not because I want to look like some Good Samaritan," Yarnell said.

Faculty member Ms. Lucy Portland noticed the atmosphere Heffner created when she had him in study hall during his freshman year. She noticed that wherever he was, fellow students were always there to give a helping hand, whether it was in class, at school dances, or at sporting events. "Rob has become an active member of the school community. People enjoy helping him because he is so personable. In study hall, students would clear the aisle for him and help him with his books," Portland said.

With an optimistic attitude, Heffner is able to create a cheerful atmosphere wherever he goes by showing students that it's possible to overcome anything.

Alex Zane's expository essay explains the qualities of a remarkable person. He has organized his essay logically starting out with background information and including quotations from faculty members and friends.

Reread Alex's essay, and notice how he uses punctuation accurately in quotations, clauses, and phrases. In this chapter, you'll practice using commas and end marks accurately in your own writing.

Allow time for students to discuss the student writing. Suggest that they identify its strengths and propose possible improvements. Use the model to introduce the concepts in the chapter.

End Marks and Abbreviations

◖ Use a **period** at the end of a statement (declarative sentence). Use either a period or an exclamation mark at the end of a command (imperative sentence).

DECLARATIVE   The Metroliner takes you to the state capital**.**

IMPERATIVE   Take the Metroliner**.** It's coming**!**

◖ Use a **question mark** at the end of a direct question (interrogative sentence). An indirect question ends with a period.

DIRECT   Could you tell us which bus stops near the White House**?**

DIRECT   Wanda asked, "Which bus stops near the White House**?**"

INDIRECT   I wonder which bus stops near the White House**.**

◖ Use an **exclamation point** at the end of an exclamation (exclamatory sentence).

That's the President**!** He's walking toward us**!**

◖ Use a period after many abbreviations.

In general, avoid using abbreviations when you write a paper or report for school or work. Instead, spell out the word(s). The following chart shows the exceptions to this rule.

Periods in Abbreviations		
Initials and Titles	Dr. P. Tano, Jr. Tia F. Lyn, Ph.D. Ms. E. Jones	
Times	A.M. P.M. B.C. A.D.	
Addresses	83 Shadow Ave. P.O. Box 99 32-10 Elm Blvd.	
Others	Inc. Co. Assn. etc. vs.	

◖ Some abbreviations should not have a period. One familiar form of abbreviation is the **acronym**, a word formed from the first letter(s) of several words. Acronyms do not use periods.

RADAR   **Ra**dio **D**etecting **A**nd **R**anging

SCUBA   **S**elf-**C**ontained **U**nderwater **B**reathing **A**pparatus

A modern tendency is to omit the period following common abbreviations, such as *ft* (*foot* or *feet*) and *lb* (*pound*). State abbreviations used as postal addresses don't take periods (*NY*, *TX*, *CA*). Some other common abbreviations that don't take periods include *mph* (miles per hour), *AM* or *FM* radio, *TV*, *FBI*, and *IRS*.

 Dictionaries differ in punctuating some abbreviations, including the abbreviations for United States (*US* or *U.S.*). Whichever style you choose, use it consistently throughout your writing.

When an abbreviation with a period, such as *etc.*, falls at the end of a sentence, don't use another period.

INCORRECT
We liked Washington, D**.**C**..**

CORRECT
We liked Washington, D**.**C**.**

However, don't omit a comma, question mark, or an exclamation point following an abbreviation.

Did the play begin at 8:00 P.M**.?**

Writing Hint

Follow the style in a style manual for using periods, commas, and abbreviations in a bibliography.

Martin**,** John**,** and Samantha Schwartz**.** *Writing With the Reader in Mind***.** Englewood Cliffs**,** NJ**:** Prentice Hall**,** 1989**.**

Proofreading a Paragraph

Proofread the following paragraphs for problems with end marks and punctuation in abbreviations.

¹By 5 P.M. on October 29, 1929, the stock market had plunged the U.S. into the *or US*

biggest banking crisis of its history! ²In 1932, Mr. Franklin D. Roosevelt was

elected President! ³Roosevelt, or F.D.R, had a plan called the New Deal to help *FDR*

the nation recover from the Depression. ⁴His plan was to get people working

again through govt. programs. ⁵Some of his most successful programs still exist *government*

today? ⁶You've heard of the F.D.I.C, haven't you? ⁷That was a plan to protect

bank deposits up to $5,000! ⁸Another program that still exists is Social Security.

⁹The SS Act was set up to provide retirement funds and unemployment *Social Security*

insurance. ¹⁰If you live in TN., you have heard of the TVA, or the Tennessee *Tennessee*

Valley Authority. ¹¹This agency, which was begun under the New Deal, was

designed to increase the productivity in, and prosperity of, the T.N. Valley. *Tennessee*

¹²One of the reasons FD.R was able to begin so many programs was that he

hired a dynamic group of advisors? ¹³Among those on his panel were Dr.

Raymond Moley, Rexford G. Tugwell Ph.D, and Dr. Adolph A. Berle Jr. ¹⁴In

addition, Ms. Frances Perkins was appointed as Secretary of Labor. ¹⁵All

contributed to solving the natl. crisis of the Great Depression. *national*

Writing an Expository Paragraph

■ **Refer to Composition, Lesson 2.4, for tips on writing an expository paragraph.**

On a separate piece of paper, write a paragraph that explains the functions of a club or organization in your school. You may choose to talk about a group that you might join, such as the student council or the marching band, or one that operates as part of the school administration, such as the teachers' union or the guidance center. In your explanation, be sure to identify the leaders and administrators of the group. Use abbreviations correctly, and end all sentences with an appropriate end punctuation mark.

Answers will vary. See teacher pages for assessment rubrics.

Commas in a Series

You know what a period means when you're reading: You've come to a complete stop, one that signals the end of a complete idea. A **comma** is trickier because it represents a slight pause within a complete sentence. The next few lessons will help you review the most important rules for commas.

🔹 Use commas to separate items in a series. A series contains three or more similar items in a row.

> We fished, hiked, and biked in Idaho.
> I want mushrooms, peppers, and sausage on the pizza.

See also Lesson 14.2, which explains when to use semicolons rather than commas in a series.

🔹 When a coordinating conjunction (such as *and* or *but*) connects a series of items, phrases, or clauses, *don't* add commas. Commas are needed between independent clauses.

> Tony dove for the ball **and** caught it **but** dropped it when he tried to throw it to first base.
> Tony dove for the ball**,** **and** he caught it.

🔹 Use a comma to separate two or more adjectives that precede and modify the same noun.

> The **tall, majestic** mountain appeared in the distance.

> ## Step by Step
>
> To decide whether to put a comma between two adjectives preceding a noun:
>
> 1. Put *and* between them. If *and* makes sense, use a comma.
>   [and]
>   They walked to the old**,** spooky building
>
> 2. If *and* doesn't make sense, don't use a comma.
>   ~~and~~
>   The fat mother hen clucked wildly.

However, don't use a comma when the last adjective in a series is really part of a compound noun. You can tell if one of the adjectives belongs to the noun if you can't reverse the position of the adjectives.

> My **favorite second** cousin lives in Tulsa, Oklahoma. [*Second cousin* is a compound noun.]

Exercise 3 Proofreading Sentences

This student writer forgot to use commas in sentences. Insert all necessary commas. If a sentence is already correct, write C after it.

1. It can be called the Midwest the bread basket the Middle West or the heartland.

2. People think of the Midwest as endless amber fields of grain.

3. Others focus on the wild, destructive storms that rip through the Midwest.

4. East of the Mississippi are endless corn fields. C

5. Enormous, black clouds gather over the Midwest and bring frequent torrential downpours.

6. Crop destruction can result from a tornado, a hailstorm, or a blizzard.

7. Willa Cather, Carl Sandburg, and James Fenimore Cooper set their poems and stories in the Midwest.

8. The soil, the climate, and adequate rainfall create good farming conditions.

9. South Dakota's vast, endless, open space is featured in the movie *Badlands*.

10. Does *The Wizard of Oz* take place in Kansas, Ohio, or Idaho?

 Working Together

Exercise 4 **Proofreading a Paragraph**

Proofread the following paragraph. Insert commas where they are needed, and correct end punctuation marks. When you are finished, exchange your work with a classmate, and check each other's work for correct punctuation.

Hint

Same sentences need more than one correction. One sentence doesn't need any.

¹The last word that is spelled correctly at the Scripps Howard National Spelling Bee determines the winner each year. ²The winning words from 1966, 1983, and 1984 were no more than six letters. ³Those words were *ratoon, Purim,* and *luge.* ⁴Have you ever heard of these words? ⁵Some winning words are words for illnesses or bacteria, such as *narcolepsy, staphylococci,* and *eczema.* ⁶Others are familiar words that have tricky spellings, such as *kamikaze, sarcophagus,* and *croissant.* ⁷How about *chihuahua* and *incisor?* ⁸Even my kid brother can spell those words!

Compound Sentences and Introductory Elements

🍂 Use a comma before a coordinating conjunction that joins two independent clauses.

The coordinating conjunctions (*and*, *but*, *or*, *nor*, *for*, *so*, and *yet*) join independent clauses to form a **compound sentence**.

> The children wanted to stay at the beach**,** **but** the sun had set.

🍂 Use a comma in compound interrogative or imperative sentences in which the subject either does not appear first or is an implied *you*.

> Finish writing your report now**,** or the teacher won't accept it.
> What did your parrot say**,** and how did you train it?

🍂 Use a comma after an introductory participle or participial phrase.

> **Alerted,** the firefighters raced to the cineplex.
> **Alerted by 911,** the firefighters raced to the cineplex.

🍂 Use a comma after an introductory infinitive or infinitive phrase.

> **To relax,** Clarke does needlepoint.
> **To swim the English Channel,** you'll need to train for over a year.

🍂 Use a comma after an introductory adverb clause.

> **When you give a speech,** look at your audience.

See also Lesson 13.5 for how to use commas following introductory words such as *yes*, *no*, and *well*.

🍂 Use a comma after an introductory prepositional phrase or a series of introductory prepositional phrases.

> **With regrets,** I turned down Justin's invitation.
> **By four o'clock on Thursday,** I'll be at the beach.

P.S. A comma is not always necessary after a short, introductory prepositional phrase. However, your meaning will be clear if you use a comma after most introductory prepositional phrases, and the comma will be correct in most cases.

Exception: Don't use a comma after an introductory prepositional phrase if it is immediately followed by the verb of the sentence.

> Inside the bag on the bedroom door **is** the **tape recorder**.
> $\overset{v}{}$ $\overset{s}{}$

Between two short main clauses, a comma may sometimes be omitted, according to some books; but, in this book grammar rules are kept as simple and as consistent as possible.

Don't confuse a compound sentence with a sentence that has a compound subject or a compound verb. You don't need a comma between parts of a compound subject or a compound verb.

COMPOUND VERB
The party started at 7 P.M. and ended by midnight. [no comma]

COMPOUND SENTENCE
Tina will marinate the chicken, and Tony will grill it. [comma]

On a separate piece of paper, revise each sentence so that it begins with an introductory element. Add commas where necessary. You may need to add, drop, or change some words. See Answer Key.

1. Study the dining habits from the past to understand today's table manners.

2. Ancient Romans ate their meals using only their fingers.

3. Aristocrats also ate with their hands using every finger but the pinkie and ring finger.

4. The fork shocked aristocrats when it was introduced in the eleventh century.

5. Aristocrats still resisted the fork in the 1500s.

6. Everybody carried knives before tableware was mass-produced.

7. An ivory spoon was unearthed in Egypt and estimated to be six thousand years old.

8. The Welsh give a fiancée a carved, wooden spoon to celebrate an engagement.

9. I always ask for chopsticks at Chinese and Japanese restaurants.

10. Innkeepers did not provide cutlery before the eighteenth century.

 Exercise 6 **Writing Sentences with Commas**

Work with a partner or small group to write a paragraph based on the following notes. Proofread your paragraph to make sure you've used commas correctly.
Answers will vary. See teacher pages for assessment rubrics.

> Christopher Columbus sought a commercial route to Asia for Spain, 1492.
>
> Columbus was inspired by Marco Polo's journals from 13th century
>
> Journals describe Polo's travels to court of Kublai Khan in China
>
> Columbus made four voyages to New World between 1492–1502
>
> Columbus thinks New World is really Asia
>
> He lacked knowledge of Earth's geography
>
> Columbus's book—Book of Prophecies—describes imagined passage to India
>
> Amerigo Vespucci sails from Portugal to Brazil (1501)
>
> Vespucci was the first European to recognize the New World
>
> Vespucci's book is Mundus Novus (The New World)

Sentence Interrupters and Nonessential Elements

When you add ideas or information to the main idea of your sentence, those **sentence interrupters** are set off by commas. If a sentence interrupter is at the beginning or the end of a sentence, set it off with a comma. If a sentence interrupter is located in the middle of a sentence, set it off with two commas.

🖊 Use commas to set off a **noun of direct address**, the name of the person being spoken to.

Abraham, please recite the Gettysburg Address.

🖊 Use commas to set off nonessential appositives and appositive phrases.

Did you see *The Civil War*, **the public television documentary**?
Glory, **a Civil War movie,** features an African American regiment.

🖊 Use commas to set off nonessential adjective clauses. Do not use commas with an essential adjective clause.

Essential adjective clauses are necessary to the meaning of sentences and usually answer the question *Which one(s)*. **Nonessential adjective clauses** add information but do not help the sentences make sense.

ESSENTIAL   The man **who led the Union** was Abraham Lincoln.
NONESSENTIAL   Walt Whitman, **who wrote "O Captain! My Captain!,"** honored Lincoln.

ESSENTIAL   The battle **that officially began the war** was at Ft. Sumter.
NONESSENTIAL   The Battle of Antietam, **which took place in 1862,** was one of the bloodiest of the war.

🖊 Use commas to set off parenthetical expressions and transitional expressions that interrupt a sentence.

Walt Whitman's brother, **in fact,** was wounded in the war.

🖊 Use commas to set off contrasting expressions that begin with the words *not* or *yet*.

Preserving the union, **not bringing an end to slavery,** was Lincoln's initial aim for the war.

Step by Step

To decide if an adjective clause should be set off with commas:

1. Try saying the sentence aloud without the adjective clause.
2. If the sentence makes sense without the adjective clause, that clause is **nonessential**. Use commas.
3. If the sentence doesn't make sense without the clause, that clause is **essential**. Do not use commas.

Some Common Parenthetical and Transitional Expressions

as a result · incidentally
by the way · in fact
for example · moreover
for instance · nevertheless
furthermore · of course
however
on the other hand
unfortunately

Exercise 7 Proofreading Sentences

Proofread the following sentences, adding commas where they are needed. Write *C* if the sentence is correct.

1. The first inaugural address that Abraham Lincoln gave preceded the Civil War. C

2. Lincoln who confronted secession was our sixteenth President.

3. Lincoln deployed the militia which numbered 75,000 men to uphold the Union.

4. Incidentally the words "All men are created equal" come from the Gettysburg Address.

5. The Gettysburg Address Lincoln's famous speech was written to dedicate a cemetery.

6. Lincoln said that in fact the dead did not die in vain.

7. Mrs. Lydia Bixby a woman from Boston lost two sons in the war.

8. Lincoln wrote a letter to tell her that her sons died on the "altar of freedom." C

9. The thirteenth amendment which prohibited slavery was passed in 1865.

10. Lincoln's second inauguration was the first that African Americans attended. C

Exercise 8 Revising Sentences

On a separate piece of paper, revise each sentence by inserting at the caret mark (∧) the words in parentheses. Also insert commas where they are needed.

EXAMPLE   Lincoln's second inaugural address∧was attended by African Americans. (which was in 1865)
Lincoln's second inaugural address, which was in 1865, was attended by African Americans.   See Answer Key.

1. Abraham Lincoln's assassin∧was an actor. (John Wilkes Booth)

2. Booth∧shot the President at Ford's Theater. (unfortunately)

3. On the day∧friends and foes mourned him. (that Lincoln died)

4. Lincoln was a great President∧. (as well as a gifted lawyer and writer)

5. In Whitman's eulogy∧Lincoln is called our great martyr chief. ("When Lilacs Last in the Dooryard Bloom'd")

6. The Lincoln Memorial∧includes thirty-six columns representing the states in the Union at the time the memorial was built. (which is in the U.S. capital)

7. Only one of his four sons∧lived beyond childhood. (Robert Todd Lincoln)

8. Robert Todd Lincoln∧later became Secretary of War. (who never ran for office)

Other Comma Uses

▌ Use commas to set off *well, yes, no, first, second, next, finally, last,* and single-word or compound adjectives or adverbs that begin a sentence.

JACKSON:	First, ring the doorbell.
PEDRO:	Well, I did.
JACKSON:	Next, knock on the door.
PEDRO:	Yes, I did that, too.
JACKSON:	Finally, remember to leave a note.
PEDRO:	No, I forgot to do that.

Frustrated, Pedro walked back to the house and left a note for Carol.
Satisfied and happy, he again joined Jackson.

▌ Use commas to separate the date and year. No comma is needed between the month and date or between the month and year. You do need a comma after a year. No comma is needed when a span from one year to another year is specified.

I first visited Berlin on July 24, 1988. I visited the Berlin Wall on July 25. The Berlin Wall came down a year later, in October 1989, at the end of the Cold War. The Cold War lasted from 1945 until 1989.

Editing Tip

Do not use commas between subjects and verbs or between verbs and objects.

Berlin, is a great capital city.

W.G. Sebald translates, his own books.

▌ Use commas to separate smaller parts from larger parts of plays or other literary works.

In Act 3, scene ii, the President meets the Queen.

▌ Use commas following the greeting and closing of a friendly letter and after the closing of a business letter.

Dear Latisha,   Dear Uncle Henry,   Best,   Sincerely,

▌ Use a comma to set off a name followed by an abbreviation.

I admire both Martin Luther King, Jr., and Malcolm X.

▌ Use commas to set off direct quotations but not indirect quotations.

DIRECT	Josie repeated, "Our assignment is to research the Cold War."
	"Escape over the Berlin Wall could be fatal," William explained.
INDIRECT	Rolfe says that he has a small piece of the Berlin Wall.

▌ Use commas to set off tag questions.

Rolfe was born in East Berlin, **wasn't he**?
I like sauerkraut with my sausage, **don't you**?

Exercise 9 **Using Commas Correctly**

Circle the letter of *all* the correct answers for each question.

1. Which of the following sentences is not punctuated correctly?
   (a) Ms. Rosa Carr Ph.D reviewed our text. (b) He's gone to lunch hasn't he?
   (c) Arthur Blick, D.D.S, is my dentist. (d) First run to the store.

2. Which of the following sentences is punctuated correctly?
   (a) Many consider the Middle Ages to span the years 600 to 1250. (b) No, I
   don't care if you're lost. (c) I don't know how to get in do you? (d) Edward
   Jones, Jr., is the pitcher.

3. Which of the following sentences is punctuated correctly?
   (a) Thanksgiving is on November 23 this year. (b) On October 31, 1999,
   I went to a masquerade party. (c) Summer goes from June, to September.
   (d) On July, 4, 1776 the United States declared independence.

4. Which dateline for a friendly letter is correctly punctuated?
   (a) October 19 1979 (b) August 1, 1983. (c) December 27, 1964 (d) May. 13, 1959

Exercise 10 **Proofreading a Friendly Letter**

Proofread the friendly letter below. Add commas and end punctuation marks
where necessary.

¹March 12, 1999

²Dear Rachel,

³Did Mom or Dad tell you about the state JCT, Juniors
Championship Tour? ⁴Last week I was accepted on the tour from our high
school along with Tran, Carl, and Floyd. ⁵Victor asked, "They'll let girls play
golf, won't they?" ⁶I told him, that I'm the first girl on the tour, but not
the last. ⁷The event begins on June 7 and goes through June 12, but I
won't be on the course until June, 8.

⁸Oh, by the way, I did read Act III, scene 2, of Shakespeare's <u>King
Lear</u> as you recommended. ⁹I can't believe that the poor guy can't figure
out what's up with his daughters, can you? ¹⁰To read that kind of terrific
play makes me excited about college. ¹¹Do you have any tips to help me do
well on the ever-popular verbal SAT?

¹²We all miss you. ¹³Hope you can make it to the JCT.

¹⁴Your loving sister,
¹⁵Erin

Correcting Run-on Sentences and Sentence Fragments

Chapter 5 provides practice in fixing sentence fragments and run-on sentences. This lesson briefly covers the strategies for correcting these common sentence errors.

◗ To correct a **run-on sentence**, use the following strategies.

1. Add end punctuation and a capital letter to break up the run-on sentence.

RUN-ON	The dinosaurs and woolly mammoths once roamed the earth, they are now extinct.
CORRECTED	Dinosaurs and woolly mammoths once roamed the earth. **T**hey are now extinct.

2. Change the run-on sentence into a compound sentence. Note the different corrections that are possible.

RUN-ON	Dinosaurs became extinct millions of years ago, the bald eagle nearly died out during our own lifetime.
CORRECTED	Dinosaurs became extinct millions of years ago**, but** the bald eagle nearly died out during our own lifetime.
CORRECTED	Dinosaurs became extinct millions of years ago**;** the bald eagle nearly died out during our own lifetime.
CORRECTED	Dinosaurs became extinct millions of years ago**; however,** the bald eagle nearly died out during our own lifetime.

3. Turn one of the sentences into a subordinate clause.

CORRECTED	**Although dinosaurs became extinct millions of years ago,** the bald eagle nearly died out during our own lifetime.

◗ To correct a **sentence fragment**, use these three strategies.

1. Add the missing subject, verb, or both.

FRAGMENT	The bald eagle "a free spirit, high-soaring, and courageous."
CORRECTED	**To Jefferson**, the bald eagle **was** "a free spirit, high-soaring, and courageous."

2. Attach the fragment to a complete sentence before or after it.

FRAGMENT	The bald eagle is recovering. From near extinction.
CORRECTED	The bald eagle is recovering from near extinction.

3. Drop a subordinating conjunction.

FRAGMENT	Because the bald eagle may come off the endangered species list.
CORRECTED	The bald eagle may come off the endangered species list.

Writing Hint

If you always correct a sentence fragment or run-on sentence in the same way, your paragraphs will sound monotonous and singsongy. In a paragraph or essay, read the sentences silently in your head or quietly aloud. See how they sound together in sequence. Aim for variety.

Enriching Your Vocabulary

The word *auspicious*, which appears in Exercise 12, comes from the Latin root *auspicium*, which means "omen." It is used to describe a good omen or to mean "favorable." Our athletes were confident and strong, so the race got off to an *auspicious* start.

Proofreading a Paragraph

Proofread the following paragraph to correct run-on sentences and sentence fragments. Also, check the use of commas and end punctuation marks.
Answers will vary. A sample revision is given.

¹The Endangered Species Act began to list and protect animals and plants in 1973, it originally documented 170 species whose existence was threatened. ²More and more animals and plant species are about to be erased from the list, but what does this say about the way we protect our environment? ³The 1972 banning of the insecticide DDT was helpful. ⁴In 1962, in her classic book *Silent Spring*, Rachel Carson described the devastation DDT caused she told us that DDT was killing off the bald eagle our nation's symbol. ⁵Look at the chart in Exercise 12, it shows those species that are to be removed from the Endangered Species Act list. ⁶Can you determine ⁷Which states have benefited most from the efforts?

 Exercise 12 **Writing Sentences**

The chart below includes species whose recovery looks favorable. Working with a partner, write at least five sentences in response to the list.
Answers will vary. See teacher pages for assessment rubrics.

Auspicious Species	
Some species proposed to be removed or downgraded from the Endangered Species Act list between 1998 and 2000:	
American Peregrine falcon	North America
Bald eagle	48 coterminous states
Aleutian Canadian goose	Alaska, Washington, Oregon, California, Canada
Columbia white-tailed deer	Washington, Oregon
Hawaiian hawk	Hawaii
Brown pelican	Texas, Louisiana, Mississippi, Alabama, Florida
Gray timber wolf	Minnesota, Michigan, Wisconsin
Dismal Swamp Southeastern shrew	Virginia, North Carolina
Ash Meadows Amargosa pupfish	Nevada
Tidewater goby	California
Virginia Northern flying squirrel	Virginia, West Virginia
Island night lizard	California

Source: *Houston Chronicle,* Wednesday, May 6, 1998

Editing and Proofreading Worksheet 1

Correct sentence fragments and run-on sentences, and make any other changes you think will improve the paragraphs. Check for the correct use of commas and other punctuation marks. Proofread carefully.

Answers will vary. A sample revision is given.

[1]Can you imagine how maps might connect to poems? [2]An American poet, Elizabeth bishop, made this connection often; she wrote and lived in both North and South America. [3]A map that helps you locate a place is like a poem. [4]That helps you to pinpoint emotions and thoughts. [5]In Elizabeth Bishop's first book of poems, *North and South,* the first poem of the collection is, in fact, entitled "The Map." [6]Subsequent books, *Questions of Travel* and *Geography III,* reflect her geographic life patterns. [7]For her work, she won a National Book Award as well as the Pulitzer Prize for poetry.

[8]Elizabeth Bishop grew up in Massachusetts with an aunt but spent each summer in Nova Scotia, Canada, with her grandparents. [10]After graduating from Vassar College, she lived in Florida, France, and then Mexico. [12]From around 1951 until 1970 she lived in Brazil, worked as a translator turning Portuguese language texts into English, and wrote her own poetry. [13]One translation, *The Diary of Helena Morley,* is an actual diary of a fascinating young Brazilian girl who made diary entries between 1893 and 1895.

[15]For Elizabeth Bishop, every word in a poem counts. [16]She often chose to write poems about simple concrete objects, as in "The Iceberg," "The Armadillo," and "Roosters." [17]For example, in "The Fish," a famous poem about a fish, she describes its eyes, "They shifted a little, but not to return my stare."

[18]Along with other admirers, I remember attending a reading Ms. Bishop gave in March, 1973, in Cambridge, Massachusetts. [19]At the time, she was teaching at harvard university; I believe, that the date was March 20, 1973. [20]Nevertheless, it was a memorable night, and I place it firmly on my own map of important life experiences.

Editing and Proofreading Worksheet 2

Correct sentence fragments and run-on sentences in the following paragraphs, and make any other changes you think will improve the paragraphs. Check for the correct use of commas, periods, and other punctuation marks. Proofread carefully. Work with a partner or small group. Write your paragraphs on a separate piece of paper, and compare your response with those made by other pairs or groups of classmates. Answers will vary. A sample revision is given.

¹For a long time, experts believed the first permanent farmers. ²In the
western United States or northern Mexico didn't arrive until around 1000 A.D.
³Surprisingly it now appears that their was a farming community in Texas three
thousand years ago. ⁴Evidence of maize (corn) and squash has been found on an
ancient site Cerro Juanaqueña an article published in March 13 1998 described
the discovery for the first time.

⁵Most experts believe ancient people survived by hunting and gathering
edible plant foods such as nuts fruits and berries. ⁶The discovery at Cerro
Juanaqueña challenges that theory. ⁷Because its terraced land indicates
cultivated or farmed crops.

⁸One of the experts said he couldn't believe his eyes at first and thought that
nature must have created the terraces not human labor. ⁹Not only terraced land
was found. ¹⁰But ancient remains of leftover food were also uncovered. ¹¹Ancient
garbage heaps or *middens*, contained the leftovers from meals eaten around
campfires over 3,070 years ago.

¹²How did ancient people create terraced land for farming and how long did
the process take! ¹³Each terrace is about sixty feet long. ¹⁴Each terrace is about
twenty feet wide. ¹⁵It would take a human approximately 26 years to move
20,000 metric tons of dirt rock and debris to create a terrace. ¹⁶Based on this
fact experts conclude that hundreds of residents lived at Cerro Juanaqueña for
a long period of time but for how long they cant say for sure.

Chapter Review

Exercise A Proofreading Dialogue

Proofread the following dialogue between two characters in a screenplay. Add commas and the appropriate punctuation marks as needed.

RAMON: [1]By the way, what time does rehearsal begin?

JACKIE: [2]Get there at three o'clock sharp.

RAMON: [3]Oh, no! [4]Didn't you tell me five o'clock, Jackie?

JACKIE: [5]No way! Believe it or not, I reminded you yesterday.

RAMON: [6]Of course, it just slipped my mind.

JACKIE: [7]Please, Ramon, can you make it on time? [8]Incidentally, the director is springing for pizza.

RAMON: [9]Great! [10]Is my costume ready?

JACKIE: [11]What do you think, Hamlet?

Exercise B Using Commas and End Marks Correctly

In the following sentences, insert all missing commas, periods, and other end punctuation marks, or delete incorrect punctuation, as needed.

1. Birthdays, religious celebrations, and historical events are often celebrated as federal holidays.

2. On federal holidays, the post office and other government offices are closed.

3. Ralph, did you march in the Fourth of July parade last year?

4. I enjoy celebrations, such as Thanksgiving, that involve special foods.

5. We celebrate the birthday not only of George Washington but also, Abraham Lincoln on President's Day.

6. My friends think Memorial Day, not Labor Day, is a better holiday because on Memorial Day the swimming pools and beaches open.

7. To truly appreciate Groundhog Day, it's best to find out whether or not a groundhog is asleep.

8. On the birthday of Martin Luther King, Jr., I remember his words, "I have a dream. . . ."

9. Dr. Henry spoke to me after the surgery.

10. Surprisingly, our entire village gathered on December 31, 1999, to celebrate the new year.

CHAPTER REVIEW

Exercise C **Revising Sentences**

Revise each sentence by inserting the words shown in parentheses at the caret mark. Add commas where necessary. Check to see that your sentences are punctuated correctly. See Answer Key.

1. The Chicago Symphony Orchestra‸was founded in 1891. (which is the third oldest symphony in the United States)

2. Samuel Barber wrote music for the poems of Pablo Neruda‸ (the Chilean poet)

3. The cymbals‸are considered percussion instruments. (not only the drums)

4. David Del Tredici‸wrote many pieces of music based on *The Adventures of Alice in Wonderland.* (who studied music in California and New York)

5. Pablo Casals‸founded a yearly festival in Puerto Rico. (not only became a master cellist but also)

6. Yo-Yo Ma‸gave his first recital at six years of age. (the famous cellist)

7. *Rhapsody in Blue*‸was written by George Gershwin in the 1920s. (the first musical composition to combine jazz with classical music)

8. The classical concert pianist‸was Vladimir Horowitz. (whom many consider to be the greatest of the twentieth century)

Exercise D **Proofreading a Paragraph**

The following mess of words is a puzzle for you to figure out. Make it into a paragraph by separating it into sentences on a separate piece of paper. Add commas, periods, and other end punctuation marks. Be sure to begin each sentence with a capital letter. See Answer Key for a sample revision.

How can you demonstrate that light travels faster than sound well do you experience thunder or lightning first most people will say lightning and they're correct you may not know it but thunder and lightning occur at the same time yet light travels faster than sound doesn't it consequently we see the lightning bolt which strikes first before we hear the crash of the thunder to discover how far away lightning is striking you can use a formula first you count the seconds between a lightning strike and the sound of thunder that follows next you divide by three your quotient tells you the approximate distance to the lightning in kilometers

Punctuation:
All the Other Marks

STUDENT WRITING
Narrative Essay

One Teen Can Make a Difference
by Emily Broxterman
high school student, Overland Park, Kansas

I had an amazing surge of energy that morning as I leapt from my bed. It was still dark, and I looked forward to the rising sun. I quickly showered and dressed and anxiously waited for my parents to drive me to City Hall in downtown Topeka.

As I arrived, I saw hordes of students ready to begin the day. When my partners on the executive planning committee saw me, they ran to me screaming, "Today's the day!" I smiled back. "Let's do it!" I said.

We had planned all year for the first annual Smoke-Free Teens Are Rising (STAR) Rally, and it was finally going to happen. It was an idea that grew from wanting to educate other students about the legislative process and the detrimental effects of tobacco use.

A few months before we conceived of the rally concept, I testified before the Kansas legislature on behalf of the Smoke-Free Class of 2000 (SFC2000) in support of a bill that would limit youth access to tobacco. My fellow SFC2000 members and I continued to rally in support of this bill (I even called one of the senators at home!) until the bill was finally signed into law in May 1996. I learned so much from that experience about policy making, legislation, and advocacy. Most important, I learned that with persistence and dedication, I could make a difference. I wanted to share these important lessons with other kids my age.

The STAR Rally program of events lasted all day, beginning with mock Senate hearings and ending with over seven hundred students marching to the capitol, where the governor of Kansas greeted us. He praised our efforts and wished us well.

In retrospect, the first rally was definitely fulfilling. Since that day three years ago, we have held two more rallies and are planning our fourth. I had originally hoped that STAR participants would feel empowered to fight tobacco in their own communities. As my peers come out in droves each year and as the size of the rally continues to grow, I know they are realizing the strength of the message: One teen *can* make a difference.

Emily Broxterman's narrative essay describes events that have made a big impact on her life. Her title and her ending message help explain the significance of the events.

As you reread the essay, notice how Emily has used punctuation around quotations and abbreviations. In this chapter, you'll practice using punctuation accurately in your own writing.

Allow time for students to discuss the student writing. Suggest that they identify its strengths and propose possible improvements. Use the model to introduce the concepts in the chapter.

Colons

A **colon** (:) indicates that a list, a long quotation, or a formal statement will follow.

● Use a colon before a list of items, especially after the words *the following* or *the following items*.

> Henry James wrote about Americans living in Europe in the following novels: *The Portrait of a Lady*, *The American*, and *The Ambassadors*.

● Use a colon before a formal statement or quotation and before a long quotation that is set off as a block (any quotation of more than three lines).

> A book reviewer pointed out how Henry James's view of the United States is embodied in his characters: "The innocence of a young America is reflected in the almost foolish innocence with which James's American characters make decisions in Europe."

A long quotation of more than three lines is indented and set off as a block. Don't use quotation marks for block quotations.

> In the following passage from *The Europeans*, Robert Acton tries to impress a baroness from Europe:
>
> > Acton wished her to think highly of American scenery, and he drove her great distances, picking out the prettiest roads and the largest points of view . . . . It seemed to the Baroness very wild, as I have said, and lovely; but the impression added something to the sense of the enlargement of opportunity, which had been born on her arrival to the New World.

● Use a colon to emphasize a word or a phrase.

> Some people describe Henry James in one word: snob.
> The James family produced three brilliant writers: Henry (literature), William (psychology and philosophy), and Alice (a journal writer).

● Use a colon in the following situations: (1) between the hour and minutes, (2) between the chapter and verse in a reference to the Bible, and (3) after the greeting of a business letter.

> 7:45 P.M.   Genesis 12:1–3   Dear Dr. Demar:

Editing Tip

Don't use a colon before a list when the list follows a verb, a preposition, or the phrases *such as*, *including*, or *especially*.

Henry James's novels take place in ⁊London, Venice, and Rome.

My favorite authors are ⁊ Mark Twain, F. Scott Fitzgerald, and Ernest Hemingway.

Depending on the style you choose for bibliographical references, you may need to use colons in your Works Cited list. Refer to a model in Composition Lesson 3.5.

Exercise 1 Adding Colons to Sentences

Insert colons where they are needed in the following sentences. If no colon is needed write *C* after the sentence.

1. Tyrone liked the following books by Edith Wharton: *The House of Mirth, The Age of Innocence,* and *Ethan Frome.*

2. The first paragraph of *Ethan Frome* begins as follows: "In a sky of iron the points of the Dipper hung like icicles. . . ."

3. Ruby reads *Ethan Frome* at exactly 8:30 every evening.

4. Edith Wharton picked the perfect name for the setting of *Ethan Frome:* Starkfield.

5. Ethan Frome, a farmer, finds himself crushed by many forces: the cold, the isolation, and the small-town prejudices.

6. Two women complicate life for Ethan Frome: Mattie and Zeena.

7. *Ethan Frome* was a departure for Edith Wharton; her usual subject was high society. C

8. Edith Wharton owned two stately homes: one in Lenox, Massachusetts, called "The Mount"; and another in Newport, Rhode Island.

9. Edith Wharton spent time in the following cities: New York, Paris, and London.

10. Chapter 3 opens with a description of farmwork: "There was some hauling to be done at the lower end of the wood-lot, and Ethan was out early the next day."

Exercise 2 Writing a Travel Diary Entry

Imagine that you could visit any region of the United States that interests you, such as New England, the Southwest, the Pacific Northwest, or the Gulf Coast. What would a day be like during this trip? Jot down what you would do during the day, beginning each entry with the time. This is called an itinerary. Write in complete sentences. Answers will vary. See teacher pages for assessment rubrics.

EXAMPLE   6:45 A.M. I wake up and have breakfast on the patio, enjoying the view of the sun over the Sandia Mountains.

8:00 I make a list of what I will visit: Tío Pepe's restaurant, Old Town in Albuquerque, Georgia O'Keeffe's adobe house.

Semicolons

Use a **semicolon** (;) for a pause that's longer than one signaled by a comma but shorter than one signaled by a period or colon.

◖ Use a semicolon to join independent clauses in a compound sentence that doesn't have a coordinating conjunction.

> Minneapolis is a city in Minnesota; its twin city is St. Paul.

◖ Use a semicolon between independent clauses joined by a coordinating conjunction if either clause contains commas.

> We'll visit Chicago; **but** first we'll stop in Gary, Indiana.

◖ Use a semicolon before a conjunctive adverb or a transitional expression that joins independent clauses. A comma follows the conjunctive adverb or transitional expression.

> Kansas City is located on the Kansas border; **however,** a portion of the city lies on the Missouri border.
> I need to get to Kansas City; **that is,** I need to get to Kansas City, Missouri.

◖ Use a semicolon to separate items in a series when one or more of the items contains a comma.

> Tina lives in Ovid, New York; Wanda lives in Rome, New York; and Tony lives in Ithaca, New York.

Some Common Conjunctive Adverbs

accordingly	meanwhile
also	moreover
besides	nevertheless
consequently	otherwise
furthermore	still
however	then
indeed	therefore

Some Common Transitional Expressions

as a result	in addition
for example	in fact
for instance	that is
from that point on	
in other words	
on the other hand	

Exercise 3 **Using Semicolons and Colons**

Some of the following sentences need a semicolon; others require a colon. Review the rules for colons in Lesson 14.1, and then add or correct punctuation marks in the sentences below. If a sentence is correct, write *C* after it.

Editing Tip

Do not use a semicolon between an independent clause and a dependent clause or phrase.

I saw the Statue of Liberty, which is in New York Harbor.

1. Ada's ancestors immigrated from Kiev, Ukraine; Bari, Italy; and Warsaw, Poland.

2. Ellis Island processed immigrants landing in New York; that is, it processed them until 1954, when it closed.

3. Ellis Island was part of New York; now most of it belongs to New Jersey.

4. Respond to this statement: Ellis Island should belong to New York, not to New Jersey.

5. The Supreme Court made the final decision about the island; this decision is one that many dislike.

6. At the Supreme Court, a bystander commented, "It's a national shrine; it doesn't belong to any state."

7. The people of New Jersey were elated by the news; Ellis Island was part of their heritage, too.

8. Tax revenues now go to New Jersey and not to the people in New York; New York has lost a big income.

9. The Statue of Liberty may cause the next dispute; however, no lawsuits have been filed yet.

10. The national monument containing the Statue of Liberty is made up of two islands; Ellis Island and Liberty Island.

11. The Statue of Liberty has been administered by several government entities since its construction; the Lighthouse Board, the War Department, and the National Park Service.

12. The Statue was originally administered by the Lighthouse Board; its torch was considered an aid for navigation.

13. An elevator takes tourists to an observation deck; however, only a skinny staircase goes to the statue's crown.

Exercise 4 Write What You Think

Historic sites such as Ellis Island in New York Harbor, the Liberty Bell in Philadelphia, and Little Big Horn in Montana resonate with meaning for local residents and tourists alike. Write to the National Park Service and nominate a local landmark, building, store, or other place in your area as a National Historic Site, citing reasons why this place deserves to be accorded this honor.

Answers will vary. Give students full credit if they have nominated a place and attempted to support their nomination with reasons. Look for grammatically complete sentences that begin with a capital letter and end with an appropriate end punctuation mark.

Underlining (Italics)

Italics is slanted type: *It looks like this.* You can use italic type on a computer. If you are writing a word or phrase in longhand or on a typewriter that should be in italics, underline these words or phrases instead. Make sure, however, that you do not use both italics and underlining at the same time.

● Use **underlining** (or **italics**) for the following kinds of titles and names:

BOOKS	*The Day of the Locust* *The Moviegoer*
	Do Androids Dream of Electric Sheep?
MAGAZINES	*Newsweek* *Sports Illustrated* *Rolling Stone*
NEWSPAPERS	*Des Moines Register* *USA Today*
	San Francisco Chronicle
PLAYS	*Death of a Salesman* *The Iceman Cometh*
	Angels in America
MOVIES	*To Kill a Mockingbird* *2001: A Space Odyssey*
	Five Easy Pieces
TV/RADIO SERIES	*I Love Lucy* *All Things Considered* *Dateline*
ALBUMS/	*Meet the Beatles*
LONG MUSICAL WORKS	Beethoven's *Fifth Symphony*
WORKS OF ART	Leonardo da Vinci's *Mona Lisa*
	Grant Wood's *American Gothic*
SHIPS, PLANES,	U.S.S. *Arizona* *Spirit of St. Louis*
SPACECRAFT	*Challenger*

The abbreviation for "**U**nited **S**tates **S**hip (U.S.S)" or "**H**er (or **H**is) **M**ajesty's **S**hip (H.M.S)" before a ship's name is not underlined (or italicized): U.S.S. *Arizona*.

● Use italics for foreign words and expressions as well as for words, letters, and numbers referred to as such.

FOREIGN WORDS	*Tabula rasa* means "clean slate."
WORDS AS WORDS	Does *rise* or *raise* mean "to lift up"?
LETTERS	The word *separate* contains two *e*'s and two *a*'s.
NUMBERS	Binary code uses only *0*'s and *1*'s.

Editing Tip

Use italics when you want to place special emphasis on a word or phrase. But be careful not to overdo it, or the italics loses its impact.

UNACCEPTABLE
Do not walk on the grass.

ACCEPTABLE
Do *not* walk on the grass.

Exercise 5 **Revising a Log**

Read the following log, which is a daily journal kept during a ship's voyage. Add underlining to indicate italics, and check for mistakes in punctuation.

¹Our three-masted schooner, the Zephyr, set sail promptly at 4:30 for a sunset cruise. ²Advertisements in a popular magazine, Shipping News, and the Bangor Daily, a Maine newspaper, lured many passengers, young and old.

³The passengers were delighted as always with the ship's accommodations. ⁴Art prints hang in the cabins, such as: Swimmer under the Stars by Brian Lynch, the Irish American painter; and Island Magic by Teresa Hurley, a Native American painter. ⁵Our library holds over two thousand titles, among them the entire collection of seafaring novels by Patrick O'Brian, Moby Dick by Herman Melville, and Heart of Darkness by Joseph Conrad. ⁶Over the loudspeaker, we played George Gershwin's Rhapsody in Blue during dinner. ⁷Dinner was great; we had lobster, corn on the cob, and blueberry pie.

⁸At first, our guests believed they would endure a primitive sailing experience on an old wooden ship; now they find themselves enjoying modern conveniences as well. ⁹Tonight on deck, we'll show a humorous film, McHale's Navy; later, we crew members will perform songs from the musical H.M.S. Pinafore.

¹⁰Two young passengers asked me what the abbreviation H.M.S. before a ship's name means. ¹¹I told them that the abbreviation H.M.S. stands for "Her or His Majesty's Ship." ¹²One French Canadian passenger remarked, "C'est belle (it's beautiful)," as he gazed at the full moon.

Exercise 6 **Writing a Journal Entry**

On a separate piece of paper, write a journal entry about your reaction to a movie you've just seen or to a television program. Or choose a book, magazine article, or news item to discuss. Your journal entry should include specific names and titles related to your reaction (made-up or factual). Try to use as many direct quotes as you can. You may quote friends, teachers, or family members; or you may quote directly from the work you have selected. When you're finished writing, check your work with a partner to make sure you used italics and other punctuation marks correctly.

Answers will vary. See teacher pages for assessment rubrics.

Quotation Marks

🔹 Use **quotation marks** for titles of short works.

POEMS	"Wall" "This Is Just to Say" "The Emperor of Ice Cream"
SHORT STORIES	"The Open Boat" "Paul's Case" "The Lottery"
ARTICLES	"An Interview with Rita Dove" "Firefighter Saves Child"
SONGS	"Candle in the Wind" "Battle Hymn of the Republic" "America the Beautiful"
SINGLE TV/RADIO PROGRAM	"NBA Western Conference Championship: Game Three"
PARTS OF BOOKS	Section II, "A Way Home"

P.S. Everyone gets confused. You don't have to memorize which titles to underline (or italicize) and which to place in quotation marks. Check a punctuation guide such as this one or books such as *The Chicago Manual of Style* or *Words Into Type* when you're not sure which to use.

🔹 Use quotation marks at the beginning and end of a direct quotation. When a direct quotation is a complete sentence, begin the quote with a capital letter.

Alice said, "I don't live here anymore."

If a direct quotation is a phrase or just a word or two, use a lowercase letter if the quoted words do not begin the sentence.

Alice called the writer "the best in the business."

Introduce a short quotation with a comma. A direct quotation of three or more lines does not need quotation marks. Set it in a separate paragraph, and indent it from the margin of your writing.

🔹 Use single quotation marks for a quotation within a quotation or for a quoted title of a work within a quotation.

Moesha said, "Martin told me, 'Don't feed the elephants.'"
One critic remarked, "Robert Frost's poem 'Birches' is underappreciated."

Step by Step

Quotation Marks with Other Punctuation Marks

- Commas and periods always go inside closing quotation marks.
- Semicolons and colons always go outside quotation marks.
- For a quoted question or exclamation, the question mark or exclamation point goes inside the quotation mark.

  "Go Cardinals!" Melissa shouted.

- When a full sentence communicates a question or exclamation—but the quotation itself doesn't—the question mark or exclamation point goes outside the quotation mark.

  Does Marta understand Frost's "The Road Not Taken"?

Exercise 7 **Punctuating Sentences**

Write the following sentences on a separate piece of paper, and add or change punctuation marks as needed. You may wish to review the rules for italics in Lesson 14.3.

1. Kofi read and enjoyed the short story "The Waltz" by Dorothy Parker.

2. The novel "Seize the Day" by Saul Bellow begins, "When it came to concealing his troubles, Tommy Wilhelm was no less capable than the next fellow."

3. Robert Lowell's poem "For the Union Dead" was inspired by a Civil War memorial commemorating African American soldiers.
   (no italics)

4. Hemingway's short story "The Snows of Kilimanjaro" astonished Latisha.

5. Although Hemingway is known as "a man's writer," women read him too.

6. In the article "How to Tell a Story," Mark Twain says he was influenced by "the most expert storytellers."

7. Tanya exclaimed, "how retro, Dad!" when her father played the song "Norwegian Wood" by the Beatles.

8. Leo watched every episode of the television series Star Trek.

9. The radio announcer asked, "Do you think this new song is what one critic calls 'jungle rock?'"

10. "Can you remember the plot of the novel The Way to Rainy Mountain?" asked Shauna.

Exercise 8 **Write Your Own Exercise**

On a separate piece of paper, write one or more complete sentences in response to each of the instructions below. Leave out all punctuation marks. Then exchange papers with a classmate, and see if you agree on how to punctuate each sentence.   Students' sentences will vary.

1. Name a song that's popular now, and tell why you like or dislike it (mention the title and the performer).

2. Write a direct quotation (an actual quotation or a made-up one) at the beginning of a sentence.

3. Explain the meaning of a chapter title from a book.

4. Name a poem you've read and how it relates to you (give the poem's title, author, and a quotation from a line of the poem).

5. Explain why you watch a particular television program regularly.

6. Identify a newspaper or magazine article (an actual article or a made-up title) about a subject that interests you, and tell why you feel the way you do.

Punctuating Dialogue

Spoken words, or **dialogue**, give your reader an immediate sense of the people and events in your writing. A **dialogue tag** is the words that identify the speaker.

◖ Begin a new paragraph every time the speaker changes.

Note: The following rules also apply to punctuating other kinds of direct quotations, not only dialogue.

◖ Place quotation marks at the beginning and end of a speaker's exact words.

> "There's a planet I've never seen before," Jason said.

◖ When a dialogue tag interrupts a quoted sentence, a comma follows the tag and the second part of the quotation begins with a lowercase letter.

> "It's probably a satellite," Anita said, "or, possibly, an asteroid. Let's look at an astronomy map."

If the second part of a divided quotation is a complete sentence, it should begin with a capital letter.

> "I just saw a shooting star!" Herman shouted. "No one will believe it."

◖ When a direct quotation comes at the beginning of a sentence, use a comma, question mark, or exclamation point—but *not* a period—to separate it from the dialogue tag that follows.

> "Did you find the moons of Jupiter on the map?" Jason asked.
> "I sure did, Jason," Anita said, laughing.
> "It's headed this way," Jason screamed. "Look!"

◖ When the word *that* precedes a direct quotation, do *not* use a colon or a comma.

> Shakespeare said that "[a] light heart lives long."

Writing Hint

When a long quotation extends over two or more paragraphs, punctuate it as follows: Place an opening quotation mark at the beginning of the quote; no quotation mark at the end of the first paragraph; another opening quotation mark at the beginning of the next quoted paragraph(s); and then a closing quotation mark at the end of the quoted passage.

Editing Tip

Write dialogue so that it imitates real-life speech. Use less formal language, sentence fragments, slang, and contractions to make it sound natural. However, don't overuse the word *said* in dialogue tags. Use verbs that express the speaker's tone of voice, such as *whispered, laughed, complained, sniped,* or *insisted.*

Exercise 9 **Writing a Dialogue**

Work with a partner or small group to create one or more of the following dialogues. Write the dialogue on a separate piece of paper, following the conventions for punctuating dialogue. Find a partner or partners to role-play your dialogue for a small group or for the whole class. Students' dialogues will vary.

1. Write a conversation between a teacher and a student on why students should study a foreign language.

2. Write a dialogue in which a family discusses and maybe argues about what color to paint the inside or outside of their home.

3. Write a conversation among three friends who are on their way to a brand new school that's either much larger or much smaller than their previous school.

Exercise 10 Punctuating Dialogue

Change or add appropriate punctuation marks to the dialogue below, and insert a paragraph symbol (¶) to show where a new paragraph should begin. Make any other changes you think will improve the passage. See Answer Key.

[1]As Dora and Alex walked along the lake shore, they heard a strange and haunting sound. [2]What's that? Dora asked. [3]Do you hear that, Alex? [4]It's probably just the wind on the water Alex answered nothing to worry about.

[5]Dora and Alex continued walking along the water's edge and talking about the band they hoped to form in September when they got back to the city. [6]Okay. [7]Alex muttered to himself. [8]A bass guitar, a rhythm guitar, a keyboard player, and a drummer will be enough. [9]Well, Dora sniped. [10]Don't forget the lead singer. [11]I mean, that's my part, isn't it?

[12]Alex walked quietly ahead, then he broke the silence. [13]The band needs a name and a really good song. [14]If we can get a good beat, we can come up with some lyrics, Dora added. [15]Isn't that a weird sound, she said, referring to the wind rustling in the background, a sound that seemed to follow them. [16]I think it's the wind whipping up the lake water. [17]Alex answered. [18]Hey! he exclaimed, What about that for our name. [19]You're right! [20]Dora immediately agreed. [21]We can call our band Cool Breeze, she said, and we should add a wind instrument to our band. [22]How about a flute, a piccolo, or a harmonica. [23]Alex asked her, How's this for a song title, Wind Over Water?

Apostrophes

The **apostrophe** (') is used in contractions, in possessive forms of nouns and indefinite pronouns, and in certain kinds of plurals.

🖋 Use an apostrophe to show where letters, words, or numbers have been omitted.

I'll	o'clock	o'er	sayin'	we're
he's	they've	class of '70 reunion		

🖋 Add an apostrophe and -s ('s) to a singular noun to show possession or ownership.

my best friend's wedding	the eagle's nest	Trisha's wallet
the boss's desk	the mouse's tail	

🖋 Add only an apostrophe to a plural noun that ends in -s.
Add an apostrophe and -s ('s) to a plural noun that does not end in -s.

babies' cries	five dollars' worth	teachers' lounge
men's	sheep's	mice's

🖋 Use an apostrophe and -s ('s) to show the possessive form of indefinite pronouns.

anyone's guess	everyone's problem	someone's backpack

🖋 Use an apostrophe to show possession with expressions ending in -s or the sound of s.

old times' sake   the Red Sox' coach

🖋 Use an apostrophe and -s ('s) for the last name listed when two or more persons or groups possess something jointly.

Marcy, Ann, and Carol's team

The Electricians, Carpenters, and Plumbers' Association

🖋 Use an apostrophe and -s ('s) after each noun in a series of possessives to indicate that each one possesses something separately.

Both Jan's and Eliza's science projects won prizes.

🖋 Use an apostrophe and -s ('s) to form the plurals of letters, numbers, and words referred to as words.

Mississippi has four *s*'s, four *i*'s, and two *p*'s.

You've included too many *but*'s in this paragraph.

Exception

To make pronunciation easier, add only an apostrophe after ancient Greek names of more than one syllable and after the names *Moses* and *Jesus*.

Euripides' plays
Jesus' disciples

Certain dates are acceptable with or without apostrophes:

1900s and 1900's
'80s and '80's

A common spelling mistake is to put apostrophes in possessive personal pronouns. Don't! The following pronouns are already possessive and don't need apostrophes:

hers	his	yours
its	ours	theirs

Exercise 11 Using Apostrophes

In the following sentences, write the contraction wherever possible.

1. ~~I am~~ (I'm) going to leave a message on your answering machine.
2. ~~You are~~ (You're) not what you seem to be.
3. ~~We would~~ (We'd) visit our grandmother more often if ~~she would~~ (she'd) invite us.
4. I ~~did not~~ (didn't) know that you were going to Spain.
5. She ~~would have~~ (would've) asked me to her party if I ~~were not~~ (weren't) working.
6. We all know ~~he will~~ (he'll) do well at the swim meet.
7. Sue ~~will not~~ (won't) discuss what ~~she is~~ (she's) writing.
8. ~~They are not~~ (They're not *or* They aren't) what ~~I had~~ (I'd) ordered.
9. ~~Who is~~ (Who's) afraid of Virginia Manning?
10. Guess ~~who is~~ (who's) coming for dinner tomorrow night?

Exercise 12 Correcting Apostrophes

Read the following paragraphs. Correct all errors in the use of apostrophes. Also correct spelling mistakes. **Hint:** Not every sentence contains an error; some sentences have more than one.

¹For old times' sake, we hiked up Mt. Washington, one of the east coast's highest mountains. ²The mountain named after the first president isn't easy to climb. ³Our efforts were rewarded when we reached the mountain's summit at exactly two o'clock in the afternoon. ⁴At that point Cass's, Jerry's, and Anna's group visited the meteorological station. ⁵My subgroup's decision was simple: To continue hiking as long as possible. ⁶Several families stopped to rest at the Visitors' Center.

⁷For those of us who kept hiking, Mount Washington's highest peak didn't deter us. ⁸We marched along at our leader Mr. Bass's pace. ⁹The path's narrow and twisting course continued for miles. ¹⁰My heart's beating increased until we reached the top. ¹¹Mt. Washington's popularity began back in the mid-1800s; I can understand why.

Hyphens, Dashes, Parentheses, and Brackets

◖ Use **hyphens** in compound adjectives, some compound nouns, and numbers from twenty-one to ninety-nine.

COMPOUND ADJECTIVE	The high-powered attorney questioned the witness.
COMPOUND NOUNS	The daughter-in-law testified against her father-in-law.
NUMBERS	He was the eighty-second person to board the plane at gate forty-one.

◖ Use a **dash** to signal either an abrupt break or an unfinished statement. If you're writing in longhand or on a computer, a dash—known as an *em dash* because it's the width of a capital *M*—appears as one long solid line. On a typewriter, a dash is two hyphens in a row--like this, with no space on either side.

The judge chastised the jurors—even those who weren't late.
"But, Mom—," Rosa stammered.
"No excuses—we're going home now," interrupted her mother.

◖ Use **parentheses** to enclose either an explanation of material of less importance or an aside. Use a period inside parentheses only when the words make a complete sentence. Otherwise, place a period outside the parentheses.

Think about adding adjectives (words that describe a noun or pronoun) in your poem.
Yesterday, I was talking about Marta (my cousin from Illinois).
I have followed the MLA bibliographical style. (See the Works Cited list on page 14.)

◖ Use **brackets** to enclose an inserted explanation in a quotation. Also use brackets for added material of less importance that's already in parentheses.

"Tom Sawyer, created by Mark Twain [Samuel Clemens], was a close friend of Huckleberry Finn."
The jackalope (a fictitious animal [part rabbit, part antelope] and a popular legend in the Southwest) appeared on the postcard.

Writing Hint

Some compound nouns take hyphens; others don't. Still others are formed by running two words together. In certain cases, more than one usage is correct. Check your dictionary if you are unsure.

one-half sister-in-law
coup d'état masterpiece
attorney general
boardinghouse
vice president *or* vice-president
policy maker *or* policymaker

Enriching Your Vocabulary

The verb *chastise* means "to scold or condemn sharply; to punish, especially by beating." It is derived from the Latin word *castigare*, meaning "to punish." That teacher never *chastises* a student for asking a question.

Exercise 13 Using Hyphens, Dashes, Parentheses, and Brackets

Complete each sentence by adding hyphens, dashes, parentheses, and brackets where they are needed. **Hint**: A sentence may require more than one punctuation mark.

1. In the first act, the audience is sure that the most obvious suspects—the nephew and niece—are guilty.

2. I have a long subscription—two years—to *Turntable Magazine*.

3. Did you see that osprey (also called a fish hawk) dive into the water?

4. "I'll never—," the athlete muttered.

5. For my research, I wrote the quotation and page number as follows: "I pledge you, I pledge myself, to a new deal for the American people [(page 398)]."

6. Class is suspended—in other words, school's out.

7. Her letter stated, "Last year's event [she means the Reunion] was the best I can remember."

8. Barb loves to ride on this merry-go-round—it was built in the 1890s.

9. She may have the skills—namely, speed and agility—but can she win?

10. The play *The Weir* takes place in County Leitrim, Ireland—that's where my grandfather was born.

Exercise 14 Create Your Own Exercise

On a separate piece of paper, write three sentences that use hyphens, dashes, parentheses, and brackets—twelve sentences in all. This paper will be the answer key. Then rewrite the sentences on another piece of paper, this time leaving out the hyphens, dashes, parentheses, or brackets. Exchange papers—minus the punctuation marks—with another classmate, and fill in the missing punctuation marks on his or her paper. Use the answer key to check your sentences.
Students' sentences will vary.

Editing and Proofreading Worksheet 1

Add punctuation marks to the following paragraphs. Correct all run-on sentences and sentence fragments, and make whatever other changes you think will improve the paragraphs. Look for errors in spelling. **Hint:** All proper nouns are spelled correctly. Answers will vary.

[1]Many Native American leaders are famous for there eloquent and powerful speeches, Powhatan an Algonquin, Cochise an Apache, Chief Joseph a Nez Percé, among others. [2]For Cochise—from a long line of Apache warriors, a speech was part political communication and part personnel expression.

[3]Today we can appreciate Cochises' speeches in the following book by A. N. Ellis; "Recollections of an Interview with Cochise" 1913. [4]One of Cochises famous speeches "I Am Alone," was recalled by Henry Stuart Turrill a brigadier general in the U.S. Army who was present at Cochises original speech. [5]At a gathering in New York, Turrill tried to recreate it, he admitted though that it was difficult "after a lapse of thirty five years.

[6]Interestingly, the I Am Alone speech was originally translated from Apache into Spanish, Cochise was a fluent Spanish speaker. [7]In his speech, he describes the Spanish, Mexican, and American invasions of Apache territory. [8]He then expresses his sadness over the destruction of his people in these tragic lines. [9]But where I have destroyed one white man, many have come in his place"; "where an Indian has been killed, there has been none to come in his place".

[10]Native American's attempts to make peace with the white man may be summed up by Cochise words in this speech "I here pledge my word, a word that has never been broken". [11]In fact the United States government and army made and often broke it's treaties and promises. [12]During the 1800s. [13]Today, we can still be moved by the plight of what won critic called "the brave Apache".

Editing and Proofreading Worksheet 2

Work with a partner to change or add punctuation marks to the following paragraphs. Correct all run-on sentences and sentence fragments, and make whatever other changes you think will improve the paragraphs. **Hint:** Look for errors in spelling.   Answers will vary.

[1]Legends of the Old West continue to inspire books songs and films. [2]Perhaps you've seen the movie The Life and Times of Judge Roy Bean? [3]You may have heard the song *The Ballad of Roy Bean* or read the novel "Streets of Laredo?" by the contemporary novelist Larry McMurtry. [4]All these works have one thing in common. [5]They center around a famous real-life Western character called Roy Bean of the Bean Brothers. [6]The Bean Brothers were sometimes referred to by the Spanish phrase "Los Frijoles" the Beans. [7]The Beans lived just over the border from Mexico in Langtry Texas.

[8]Essentially Roy Bean was a self-appointed judge in a wild West town. [9]As legend goes The judge he held court in a saloon The Jersey Lily (named after the famous English singer Lillie Langtry). [10]He ruled by the one law book he owned "The Revised Statues of Texas, 1879" for company he kept a pet a bear named Bruno. [11]A sign hung outside his saloon that read, "Justice of the Peace. Law West of the Pecos. Billiard Hall." [12]In truth, the law of the land was not decided by right or wrong but to line Roy Beans pockets, the judge was easily bribed.

[13]Roy Bean and his brothers originally from Kentucky had shady reputations so did most of Langtry's citizens. [14]A Texas ranger had this to say about Langtry. [15]There is the worst lot of roughs, gamblers, robbers and pickpockets collected here I ever saw.

[16]Judge Bean always concluded court with the words Thats my rulin. [17]A word used to describe the judge was reprobate, namely, a corrupt or depraved person.

[18]Judge Roy Bean reprobate though he may have been, possessed other qualities, a quick mind, a sharp wit and a way with words.

Chapter Review

Exercise A Using Colons and Semicolons

Insert colons and semicolons where they belong in the following sentences.
Hint: Some sentences may need more than one punctuation mark. If a
sentence is correct, write *C* after it.

1. I have just read Exodus 4:10 from the Old Testament.

2. My favorite paintings include *Starry Night*, *The Lacemaker*, and *Mona Lisa*. C

3. The bus is late; however, before I hail a cab, I will wait five more minutes.

4. In her preface, the author says she invented some words; accordingly, I
   studied the glossary at the end of the book.

5. These are cities I would like to include on my trip: Tacoma, Seattle,
   and Portland.

6. Will the double feature begin at 5:15 or 5:30?

7. Robert Frost, my favorite poet, said, "Poets are like baseball pitchers.
   Both have their moments." C

8. My report is about Manchester, England; Gene's is about Dijon, France;
   and Ray's is about Canton, China.

9. I recommend these Southern writers: Eudora Welty, Flannery O'Connor,
   and Walker Percy.

10. The auto-repair hotline was busy; nevertheless, I redialed many times.

Exercise B Using Italics and Quotation Marks

Insert the appropriate punctuation for each item. Underline words that
should be in italic type. Make sure you place quotation marks in the right
place in relation to other punctuation marks. Remember to include commas
where necessary. If a sentence is correct, write *C* after it. Before you start,
review the summary in the margin on page 293.

1. Cary and Ingrid took us fishing on their father's boat, the <u>Bessie Mae</u>.

2. Mr. Robb had us read Elizabeth Bishop's poem "The Fish" in class today.

3. Hal's article about training astronauts appeared in today's <u>Daily News</u>.

4. In 1941, my Uncle Oliver was on the U.S.S. <u>Arizona</u>, a Navy ship that
   sank at Pearl Harbor.

5. <u>Horowitz in Moscow</u> is the name of Lauren's favorite recording of the
   pianist Vladimir Horowitz.

6. The first line of T. S. Eliot's poem "The Wasteland," "April is the cruelest
   month," describes how some taxpayers feel.

Chapter 14 • Punctuation: All the Other Marks **303**

7. Ramón believes that the Spanish word <u>qué</u> means "what."

8. Freddie watched the TV show "Hike Pike's Peak" from the series called <u>Peak Experiences</u>.

9. The operator asked Tim, "Did you say your name began with a <u>D</u> or a <u>T</u>?"

10. Kate Riley, the author of the novel <u>Cold Water Flat</u>, admitted to the audience, "I write from my own experience."

Exercise C Adding Punctuation to Dialogue

Read the following dialogue. On a separate piece of paper, insert quotation marks, other punctuation marks, and new paragraphs where they are needed. You may want to review Lesson 14.5.   See Answer Key.

¹Watch out for the spiders webs, Vladimir warned, this place is full of them. ²Lucy slowly turned the doorknob of the old fishing cabin, opened the creaky door, and exclaimed Wow! ³No ones been here for ages. ⁴Vladimir asked, Have you ever seen such old stuff before? ⁵No, never Lucy answered. ⁶She walked over to the bookshelves and looked at the dusty books on the shelves and said Theyre ancient. ⁷Vladimir opened one cracked, leather-bound book to page thirty three, where he found a handwritten note. ⁸He turned to Lucy and blurted out. ⁹This note says: the Vlonsky family that's my mothers maiden name came to this fishing cabin with their neighbors, the Nicholas family in 1965. ¹⁰Vladimir wondered aloud, Could it be that no one has been here since then? ¹¹I can't believe it Lucy gasped. ¹²Then Vladimir said, my parents and grandparents often told me about this place. ¹³When Lucy picked up another book To The Memory of Childhood by Lydia Chukavskaya she found another handwritten note. ¹⁴She read aloud We, the Vlonsky family, have enjoyed our first American holiday in this cabin: Memorial Day May 30, 1965.

Capitalization

Internet

Visit us at
www.sadlier-oxford.com

Direct students to
chapter-specific
portfolio projects
on Sadlier-Oxford's
website.

STUDENT WRITING
Narrative Essay

In the Corps Now:
Why I Am Set to Become a Marine
by Matisa Childs
high school student, Coral Gables, Florida

"Attention, forward march!" the sergeant yelled.

As I marched with other future recruits toward the South Dade Marine Recruiting Station, my heart ached with fear and confusion. I knew one thing: My mind was set on becoming a Marine.

After being scatterbrained throughout the past years of high school, the time came to figure out what I was going to do after graduation. I thought about college, but I did not know what to study. Then I began to joke about the military and finally decided to approach the recruiters on campus with an open mind. I figured it would not hurt. After learning of the benefits and career choices the military had to offer, I wanted in.

Being enlisted in the Delayed Entry Program (DEP) of the U.S. Marine Corps is a challenge. If I were going into the military, I wanted to be one of the best, so I chose the Marine Corps to earn respect and to gain pride.

After the first "poolee" meeting (a poolee is what the Marines call "to be" recruits), I realized this was not going to be an easy task. Poolee meetings are held at least once a month at Tropical Park; all-female poolee meetings are held every quarter at South Florida's main Marine recruiting station in Fort Lauderdale.

"Meetings" require poolees to get up at 5:30 A.M. on a meeting day and run, do crunches, pull-ups (flex hang for ladies), push-ups, and side-straddle hops (jumping jacks). Having been sore after this somewhat painful ordeal, we all seem to enjoy the chanting as we jog back to the recruiting station: "Hey Army, pick up your jets and follow me, we are Marine Corps proud to be; hey Navy, pick up your ships and follow me, we are Marine Corps proud to be; hey Air Force, pick up your jets. . . ."

Often, I ask myself why I want to be one of the few. The Marine Corps puts my mental and physical ability to the test to create discipline and a sort of humbleness. Because of this, my mind is set on becoming a Marine.

Matisa Childs's personal narrative explains why she has chosen to join the Marine Corps after high school. She gives background information and then tells about her experience in the preliminary training meetings.

As you reread the essay, notice how capital letters are used in words such as Marine Corps and Air Force. You'll review the rules for capital letters in the lessons and exercises in this chapter.

Allow time for students to discuss the student writing. Suggest that they identify its strengths and propose possible improvements. Use the model to introduce the concepts in the chapter.

Proper Nouns and Proper Adjectives

You've already learned (Lesson 4.1) that a **proper noun** names a particular person, place, thing, or idea. A **proper adjective** (Lesson 4.4) is the adjective form of a proper noun. Both proper nouns and proper adjectives are capitalized.

🖊 Capitalize the names of people.

Oscar de la Hoya   Susan B. Anthony
Frederick Douglass   Albert Einstein

🖊 Capitalize geographic names.

PLANETS,	Earth Neptune Big Dipper
CONSTELLATIONS	Andromeda galaxy Milky Way
CONTINENTS	South America Europe Antarctica
ISLANDS	Windley Key Guam Manhattan .
COUNTRIES	Vietnam South Korea Albania
STATES	Alabama New Mexico Oregon Idaho
CITIES, TOWNS	Houston Santa Fe Orlando Kansas City
BODIES OF WATER	Pacific Ocean Gulf of Mexico Lake Champlain
LOCALITIES, REGIONS	Black Hills Southwest the Everglades New England
	Rio Grande Valley the Pacific Northwest
STREETS, HIGHWAYS	Canal Street Route 66 Pacific Highway
BUILDINGS	Sears Tower Empire State Building the Eiffel Tower
PARKS, MONUMENTS	Yellowstone National Park Eleanor Roosevelt Memorial

Note: In the examples above, articles (*the*) and short prepositions (*of*) that are part of the name are *not* capitalized.

🖊 In street names or any other place where numbers are spelled out, lowercase the second number of a hyphenated number.

Eighty-fifth Street   Forty-second Stop Café

🖊 Regions named after directions are capitalized, but compass directions are *not* capitalized.

the deserts of the Southwest   northeast of Chicago

🖊 Common nouns that refer to two or more proper nouns are *not* capitalized.

Mississippi and Missouri rivers   Main and Grand streets

🖊 Capitalize proper adjectives formed from proper nouns.

Persian rug   Italian restaurant   Shakespearean sonnet

Writing Hint

Foreign last names that consist of more than one word often follow the capitalization rules of the foreign language. Check a biographical dictionary or other reference book for accuracy.

Cecil B. DeMille

Robert De Niro

Ludwig van Beethoven

Leonardo da Vinci

Charles de Gaulle

Walter de la Mare

Writing Hint

Sometimes, the dictionary gives two possibilities regarding capitalization. For example, both the terms *venetian blinds* and *Venetian blinds* are correct. In cases like this, pick one and be consistent in your writing.

Proofreading Sentences

Insert capital letters where they belong in the following sentences. To indicate a capital letter, use the proofreading symbol of three underscores beneath the letter: (t).

EXAMPLE   You'll find the bakery on the southwest corner of thirty-ninth street.

1. Christopher columbus crossed the atlantic ocean from spain to the americas.

2. leif ericsson from norway and possibly voyagers from ireland successfully sailed to north america before columbus.

3. Ancient people may have crossed the bering strait from asia to america on a land bridge that once connected siberia and alaska.

4. The southwest and west have many settlements that once were missions, such as santa fe, san francisco, and san diego.

5. north america has geological features like no other place on earth.

6. settlers along the mississippi and columbia rivers lived with the threat of floods.

7. Immigrants traveling to the united states might have seen the statue of liberty on liberty island in new york harbor.

Exercise 2 **Writing Sentences**

Working with a partner, write ten sentences based on information given on the chart. Pick a statistic from the chart, and describe, explain, compare, or contrast it.
Students' sentences will vary.

Superlative U.S. Statistics		
Largest state	Alaska	591,004 sq. mi.
Smallest state	Rhode Island	1,212 sq. mi.
Largest county (excludes Alaska)	San Bernardino County, California	20,064 sq. mi.
Smallest county	Kalawo, Hawaii	14 sq. mi.
Highest settlement	Climax, Colorado	11,560 ft.
Lowest settlement	Calipatria, California	-185 ft.
Longest river	Mississippi-Missouri	3,710 mi.
Highest mountain	Mount McKinley, Alaska	20,320 ft.
Lowest point	Death Valley, California	-282 ft.
Deepest lake	Crater Lake, Oregon	1,932 ft.
Rainiest spot	Mt. Waialeale, Hawaii	Annual aver. rainfall 460 inches
Tallest building	Sears Tower, Chicago, Illinois	1,454 ft.
Largest building	Boeing 747 Manufacturing Plant, Everett, Washington	205,600,000 cu. ft.; covers 47 acres
Tallest structure	TV tower, Blanchard, North Dakota	2,063 ft.

Source: U.S. Geological Survey, U.S. Bureau of the Census

Titles

◖ Capitalize titles and abbreviations of titles when they are used before names. Also capitalize abbreviations of academic degrees after a name.

President Franklin D. Roosevelt, former president of the United States
Justice Ruth Ginsberg, one of the nine Supreme Court justices
Edward Euing, M.D., a family-practice doctor

Some titles are generally capitalized even without a person's name.

the President of the United States   the Prime Minister   the Pope
the Chief Justice of the Supreme Court

◖ Capitalize a word that shows a family relationship only when that word is used before a name but without a possessive pronoun.

Grandma Moses   Uncle Remus   my grandmother Alice   her grandfather

◖ Capitalize the first and last word and all important words in the titles of works.

Note: Unless they are the first word in a title, do not capitalize the following small words: articles (*a*, *an*, *the*), coordinating conjunctions, and prepositions with fewer than five letters.

BOOKS	*The Call of the Wild* *Of Mice and Men*
PERIODICALS	*The Brooklyn Eagle* *Atlantic Monthly*
STORIES, ESSAYS	"The Comforts of Home"
	"The Narrow Bridge of Art"
POEMS	"Mending Wall" "Song for the Rainy Season"
PLAYS	*The Importance of Being Earnest*
	The Glass Menagerie
TV SERIES	*All in the Family* *The Honeymooners*
WORKS OF ART	*Whistler's Mother* *American Gothic*
MUSICAL WORKS	"Bridge over Troubled Water" "Rock Around the Clock"
MOVIES	Full Metal Jacket The Last Picture Show
	Gone with the Wind

> ## Writing Hint
>
> When you're not sure which words to capitalize or italicize in a title, check a dictionary, style manual, or handbook.
>
> *around the world in*
> *eighty days*

Exercise 3 Proofreading a Paragraph

Insert capital letters where they belong in the following paragraph. To indicate a capital letter, use the proofreading symbol of three underscores beneath the letter: (s).

[1]Camille's assignment was to write an article about recycling for her school newspaper, *the midtown monitor*. [2]She browsed through the *reader's*

guide to periodical literature and found an article entitled "collecting cans: house to house, block by block" from an issue of _the good news about garbage_. [3]She also looked in the _new york times index_. [4]On her way to the reference desk, she saw a copy of _a tale of two cities_. [5]Her thoughts drifted to paris, france, where dickens's great novel takes place. [6]She had enjoyed watching the Public Broadcasting Service (PBS) film version of the novel. [7]Eventually, Camille snapped out of her daydream of faraway places when she heard a student reciting a poem called "wake up the day." [8]Camille remembered her recycling report and, like reporters on _60 minutes_, she got to work.

Exercise 4 Writing About Research

On a separate piece of paper, write a few paragraphs about how you researched a subject for a report. You can base your paragraph on a real-life experience, or you can make up a story about doing research. Include titles of various works that you came across or thought about during your research experience. When you've finished writing, proofread your paragraph carefully to make sure you've used capital letters correctly. Students' paragraphs will vary. Refer to the writing rubrics in the teacher pages for help with assessment.

Exercise 5 Create Your Own Exercise

Work with a partner or small group. On a separate piece of paper, write ten sentences. In each sentence, include a title of a work or person's name with a title. (This paper will be your answer key.) You may choose books, magazine articles, stories, poems, plays, television series, works of art, musical works, or movies. Don't forget to include the titles of people (senators, kings, queens, doctors, coaches, etc.). You may also include geographic locations (such as Times Square) in your sentences. Try to vary your sentences by using a different kind of title in each sentence.

Rewrite your sentences on another piece of paper, this time without capital letters. Exchange papers with other student pairs or groups, and insert capital letters, where needed, by using the proofreading symbol of three underscores beneath the lowercase letter: (x). Students' sentences will vary.

First Words, Organizations, Religions, School Subjects

◖ Capitalize the first word in every sentence. Capitalize the first word in a direct quotation when the quotation either was originally or, as quoted, makes a complete sentence.

Do *not* capitalize the first word in an indirect quotation.

DIRECT QUOTATION   Waldo said, "This Web site contains Wallace Stevens's poem 'The Emperor of Ice-Cream.'"

INDIRECT QUOTATION   Waldo added that the site also contains biographical facts about Wallace Stevens.

If a quoted sentence is interrupted, begin the second part with a lowercase letter unless that second part is a complete sentence.

"I'm surprised," said Waldo, "that the poet Wallace Stevens was an insurance salesman."

Note: When you're quoting lines from literature, follow the writer's style. Some modern writers of fiction and poetry, such as E. E. Cummings or Bell Hooks, an African American poet, don't follow the usual rules for using capital letters.

◖ Capitalize the names of languages, nationalities, peoples, races, and religions.

In India, many languages are spoken, including Hindi and English.
The Baha'i faith is of Iranian origin and emphasizes spiritual unity.

◖ Capitalize the names of groups, teams, businesses, institutions, and organizations.

Amnesty International   Los Angeles Lakers   The Colorado School of Mines
Cornell University   The Red Cross   The Audubon Society   General Motors

◖ Capitalize the names of government agencies, groups (including the military), and organizations.

Environmental Protection Agency   The National Trust for Historic Preservation
Social Security Administration   U.S. District Court for Western Texas

◖ Capitalize the names of school subjects that are followed by a number.

Noah is taking Trigonometry 2, creative writing, United States history, and woodworking.

Editing Tip

Capitalize the first word of a complete sentence in parentheses if the sentence stands alone. If a parenthetical sentence is part of another sentence, lowercase the first word.

Answer the questions. (Use a number two pencil only.)

Answer the questions in pencil (use a number two pencil only), and erase unwanted pencil marks thoroughly.

Some style books capitalize the terms *black* and *white* when referring to people's race; some do not. Whichever style students use, have them use it consistently.

Enriching Your Vocabulary

The verb *aspire*, as used in Exercise 6, means "to be ambitious; to yearn or seek." Derived from two Latin words— *ad*, meaning "to," and *spirare*, meaning "to breathe"—*aspire* has a connotation of reaching toward a lofty or grand goal.

Insert capital letters where they belong in the following sentences. To indicate a capital letter, use the proofreading symbol of three underscores beneath the letter: (m̲).

1. Rory bragged, "it's easy to remember the famous first line of moby dick: 'call me ishmael.'"

2. in israel, many jews and muslims speak hebrew, arabic and/or english.

3. in some american cities, there are asian, african american, and hispanic cultural centers.

4. The new york stock exchange is in the financial district of new york city.

5. the united nations and the united states congress occasionally disagree.

6. new prescription drugs are tested by the food and drug administration (FDA).

7. aspiring doctors take chemistry 1 and 2, biology, and latin courses.

8. willa cather, author of *o pioneers!*, was a graduate of the university of nebraska.

Exercise 7 **Create Your Own Exercise**

Working with a partner, write one or more complete sentences in response to each numbered item. Students' sentences will vary.

1. Write about a school subject you would like to study.

2. Identify a favorite movie, and explain why you like it.

3. Share an expression or word from another language. Identify the language, and explain what the word or expression means.

4. Name a performing group you like and a song, dance, or play that it has performed or recorded.

5. Reproduce a direct quotation that someone you know said recently.

6. Take the same quotation you wrote in item number 5, and turn it into an indirect quotation.

7. Choose a local organization, group, or agency in your town or neighborhood, and explain its purpose.

8. Write down a dialogue you had recently with a teacher, parent, or friend. Each character should speak at least three times.

I and *O*; Historical Events, Documents, and Periods; Calendar Items; Brand Names; Awards

🔹 Capitalize the words *I* and *O*.

The first-person pronoun *I* is always capitalized. The poetic interjection *O* is rarely used today. Instead, we use the modern interjection *oh*, which isn't capitalized unless it's the first word in a sentence.

"O cursed ambition, thou devouring bird."—Havard

Oh, isn't it a beautiful morning.

🔹 Capitalize the names of historical events, documents, and periods.

The Seneca Falls Declaration of Sentiments was first drafted at the 1848 Women's Rights Convention.

Furniture from the Victorian Era is characterized by flowery carving and patterned upholstery.

🔹 Capitalize calendar items but not seasons.

CALENDAR ITEMS   Passover Presidents' Day Monday, October 19

SEASONS   spring break summer solstice autumn leaves

When you refer to a century, however, do not use capital letters.

Coco Chanel changed the course of twentieth-century fashion.

🔹 Capitalize brand names for manufactured products.

Buick Skylark   Kleenex   Xerox   Word for Windows

But do not capitalize the common noun that follows a brand name.

Take a Kleenex tissue.   Use some Dial soap.

🔹 Capitalize names of awards.

Schindler's List by the **prolific** Steven Spielberg won an Academy Award.

Writing Hint

Some writers use capital letters for emphasis. Using all capital letters represents urgency.

The officer shouted, "STOP!"

WHY HAVEN'T YOU RETURNED MY MESSAGE?

Exercise 8 Proofreading a Paragraph

Insert capital letters where they belong in the following sentences. To indicate a capital letter, use the proofreading symbol of three underscores beneath the letter: (p).

[1]On december 10, people celebrate the anniversary of the death of alfred nobel, the twentieth-century swedish chemist and inventor. [2]The nobel prize is awarded to individuals for their outstanding contributions

Enriching Your Vocabulary

The adjective *prolific* means "fruitful or turning out many products of the mind." Artists such as writers, composers, painters, and choreographers, are called *prolific* if they produce many works of art.

in chemistry, physics, medicine, and literature. ³In 1968, a nobel prize for economics was added. ⁴Sometimes, an organization wins the prize; the nansen international office for refugees won the 1938 nobel peace prize for its efforts before the outbreak of world war II in europe. ⁵Writers in various languages have won the literature prize: octavio paz from mexico, who writes in spanish; wole soyinka from nigeria, who writes in english; and w. b. yeats from ireland, who also writes in english. ⁶The 1978 winner in literature was joseph brodsky. ⁷Brodsky was born in st. petersburg, russia, and emigrated to the united states in 1972. ⁸His poems were written in russian, then they were translated into english. ⁹The american academy and institute of arts and letters elected Brodsky as a member the year after he won the nobel prize.

Exercise 9 **Proofreading a Dialogue**

With a partner, make corrections in the use of capital letters in the dialogue below. Use the proofreading symbols of a slash to indicate a lowercase letter and three underscores to indicate a capital letter.

Spring = lowercase letter   friday = capital letter

1. marcy said, "i need one hundred copies of this poem by shakespeare."

2. "i can do that," martin kidded her, "As easy as Apple Pie."

3. "If you could," marcy smiled, "i would be as excited as a kid on the fourth of july."

4. Martin said, "i'll do it if the xerox machine is working."

5. Sipping her dr. pepper, Marcy replied, "i don't really need one hundred, but i could use at least ten for the potsdam poetry club meeting on tuesday."

6. Martin asked, "do you want me to copy the love poem with the line, 'How can it? o how can Love's eye be true?'"

7. "This is the line i like," marcy said, reading aloud. "'but, o my sweet, what labor is't to leave.'"

8. "what a beautiful line!" martin exclaimed. "everyone likes shakespeare."

Editing and Proofreading Worksheet 1

Improve the paragraphs below by correcting sentence fragments and making any other changes you think will improve them. Write your revised report on a separate piece of paper, and compare your response with those made by other pairs or groups of classmates. Revisions may vary. A sample revision is given.

¹the american poet wallace stevens (1879–1955) was born in reading, pennsylvania. ²he went to college at harvard university on the banks of the charles river in cambridge, massachusetts. ³after college, stevens studied law at new york law school. ⁴After law school, he lived in new york city and was a reporter with the *new york herald tribune*. ⁵beginning in 1916, he worked for the hartford accident and indemnity company and lived in hartford, connecticut. ⁶in 1934, he was promoted to vice president of the company. ⁷throughout his business career, he wrote poems. ⁸when his volume *collected poems* came out in 1954, ⁹he won the pulitzer prize for poetry. ¹⁰The rich and successful businessman was now an esteemed american poet.

¹¹in his poems, stevens attempts to create order out of chaos. ¹²Read, for example, his poem "the idea of order in key west." ¹³His search for solid ground is evident in his last volume of poetry, *the rock*. ¹⁴wallace stevens also enjoyed a playful use of french, as in the poem title "le monocle de mon oncle." ¹⁵Although stevens had a victorian upbringing, he was a modernist in his writing. ¹⁶he had limited relationships with the most influential poets of his day, such as t. s. eliot and ezra pound.

¹⁷many students have read his poem "the emperor of ice-cream," ¹⁸which appears in anthologies of american literature. ¹⁹(of course, stevens is not talking about breyers or sealtest ice cream.) ²⁰today, many working poets and readers of poetry look to stevens for his wit, clear thinking, and philosophical approach to the world through his lyrical and very american poems. ²¹In his own words, Stevens said, "poetry means not the language of poetry but the thing itself, wherever it may be found."

Editing and Proofreading Worksheet 2

Work with a partner or small group to proofread and revise these paragraphs from a book summary. Correct sentence fragments and run-on sentences, eliminate wordiness, change verb tenses, and make any other changes you think will improve the paragraphs. Write your revised report on a separate piece of paper, and compare your response with those made by other pairs or groups of classmates. **Hint:** Watch out for spelling mistakes.

Revisions may vary. A sample revision is given.

[1]our story begins in the first half of the twentieth century, around 1920.

[2]many immigrants are arriving daily in the united states. [3]they come from all over the world, europe, asia, and the caribbean. [4]the family we will focus on comes from the ukraine, which was then a part of russia. [5]the popov family
left
~~leaves~~ russia to escape the terror that followed the 1917 russian revolution.

[6]when the family arrives in the united states, they travel across the country and settle in san francisco, california. [7]the father ivan goes from door to door.
selling   but   opens
[8]~~He sells~~ pots and pans. [9]he struggles for many years, ~~he is~~ finally ~~able to open~~ his own store. [10]only then does he begin to feel at home in the united states.

[11]the coming of the great depression causes trouble. [12]Ivan holds onto his
                                                 selling
business. [13]by earning extra income. [14]~~He sells~~ brown cow milk products from door to door. [15]his sons, dimitri and alexi, sell newspapers on street corners. [16]to
                                                                              arrive
raise money for the family, too. [17]by the early 1940s, success and security ~~arrives~~ at the popov house. [18]when Ivan invents an oven he calls the magic bake. [19]the store can't sell enough of these amazing machines. [20]dimitri and alexi enlist in
                                    breaks
the u.s. army just as world war II ~~brakes~~ out at the end of 1941.
                              survive.
[21]as always, the popovs ~~survives,~~ Alexi comes home with a new wife, the
                                        her
former maria von klemp. [22]~~that~~ he met in austria where he was a reporter for the army newspaper *stars and stripes*. [23]upon his dismissal from active duty in
                                        speak
france, dimitri travels to the ukraine. [24]he can ~~spoke~~ russian, and he wants to see where his parents came from. [25]He realizes during his visit how different his life would have been if his parents had not come to live in america.

Chapter Review

Visit us at
www.sadlier-oxford.com

Exercise A Proofreading Sentences

Insert capital letters where they belong in the following sentences. To indicate a capital letter, use the proofreading symbol of three underscores beneath the letter: (w).

1. the oglala sioux lived in the black hills of south dakota.

2. the bronx and harlem rivers are now used for recreation.

3. the empire state building was once the tallest building on earth.

4. Will the senator from iowa become the president of the united states?

5. mrs. de la cruz owned an apartment on madison and west end avenues.

6. we saw senator inouye interviewed on the television show *meet the press*.

7. "carried away" is my favorite story by the canadian writer alice munro.

8. My dog, fido, looked up and saw the ad for alpo dog food.

9. I called the environmental protection agency (EPA) about a gas leak.

10. we celebrated winter solstice in december by lighting candles in the snow.

Exercise B Writing Sentences

On a separate piece of paper, write a complete sentence as a response for each item. Use capital letters correctly.   Students' sentences will vary.

1. Identify a town, city, state, region, or foreign country where a friend or relative lives.

2. What are the names of two streets near your home?

3. In what other state would you like your pen pal to live?

4. How would you describe two natural features of your environment in a letter to the pen pal?

5. Write a quotation based on something the pen pal from item number 3 might write in a letter to you.

6. Now write the quotation from item number 5 as an indirect quotation.

7. Write a sentence about a senator from your state, using the senator's exact name and title.

8. Write about an article in a newspaper that focuses on an organization or government agency, using the titles of both the article and the newspaper.

9. What club or organization would you like to volunteer for and why?

10. What company would you like to work for and why?

Exercise C · Proofreading a Paragraph

Insert capital letters where they belong in the following sentences. To indicate a capital letter, use the proofreading symbol of three underscores beneath the letter: (d).

[1]During the first year of world war I, one of the most adventurous twentieth-century anthropologists and explorers was born—thor heyerdahl. [2]He grew up in norway, the northernmost scandinavian country, which borders the atlantic and arctic oceans. [3]He became famous after his 1947 trip across the pacific ocean from peru to the tuamotu islands of polynesia. [4]Along with five companions, he sailed on a primitive raft to prove his theory that the first polynesians were actually from south america. [5]The name of the raft, *kon tiki*, became the name of his famous book about this journey. [6]In 1970, heyerdahl set out to prove another theory about the way people migrate. [7]He believed that ancient people from the mediterranean could have sailed to the americas in reed boats. [8]He created a boat made from papyrus and sailed from morocco, which is located on the northwest coast of africa, to barbados, an island in the caribbean sea. [9]This journey became the subject for another book. [10]That book, entitled *ra expeditions*, was translated from his native Norwegian into english, and it was published in 1971.

Exercise D · Writing a Paragraph

On a separate piece of paper, write a paragraph about an imaginary hot-air balloon trip you would make in the summer with two or three companions. In a paragraph or two, describe how you would travel and what route you would take. Include the sights you would hope to see on your trip, and, depending on where you live, name the geographical features and any landmarks or buildings you might see.

Students' paragraphs will vary. See teacher pages for assessment rubrics.

Spelling

STUDENT WRITING
Research Paper

Julia Morgan: Blueprint for Social Change
by Pia Lindstrom Luedtke
high school student, Pasadena, California

In the latter half of the nineteenth century, a fresh wave of pioneers and dreamers came to California on the newly built railroads. These people continued the state's tradition of exploration, discovery, and social innovation and brought with them distinctive ideas that rapidly redefined frontier California. This massive population influx was reflected in an increasingly urban state. . . .

In the midst of this transformation, two reform movements became prominent by the turn of the century. The first, the women's suffrage and rights movement, peaked between 1900 and 1920 and caused many women to question their traditional roles as wives and mothers. However, they often faced hostility when they strove for professional recognition and equality in a male-dominated world. The second, the Beaux-Arts movement, put the focus of architecture back on the individual. This was particularly significant because, during this time of expansion, architecture played an important role in the creation of the state's regional identity. Though seemingly different, both movements shared a belief in the freedom of personal expression.

Julia Morgan (1872–1957), an integral yet apolitical figure in both movements, had been the first of her gender to be accepted into the École des Beaux-Arts architecture school in Paris in 1898 and was California's first woman to receive a state architect's license. She was, in essence, a reflection of California's changing times. Though Morgan has been overlooked in the past, her determined and courageous response to the resistance to her entrance into a male-dominated profession made her one of the twentieth century's most significant California pioneers.

Reprinted by permission of *The Concord Review*.

The paragraphs above are the introduction to a research paper. Pia Lindstrom Luedtke builds her topic by supplying background information on the two movements that are relevant to her topic.

Can you find any misspelled words in Pia's essay? Look again. The essay is effective partly because it is error-free. In this chapter, you'll cover the rules and be given advice that will help you spell words correctly whenever you write.

Allow time for students to discuss the student writing. Suggest that they identify its strengths and propose possible improvements. Use the model to introduce the concepts in the chapter.

Using a Dictionary

If you have ever talked to a professional writer or journalist, you learned that such people use dictionaries on a daily basis. No matter how much you write or read, the dictionary will always be your most trusted guide to spelling. Remember that spelling counts—and not just in school. In the work world, correct spelling is essential. When you write cover letters to prospective employers, always check your spelling. On the job, make it a lifelong habit. You want your writing to be a positive, not a *pejorative*, reflection of who you are.

🔖 If you're in doubt about how to spell a word, use a dictionary.

Besides showing each entry word's definition and etymology (word history), a dictionary offers many kinds of spelling help.

Entry word with syllable breaks

Pronunciation

Past tense with alternate past; and past participle with alternate

in·doc·tri·nate \in-ˈdäk-trə -ˌnāt\ *vt* **-nat·ed;** **-nat·ing** [prob. fr. ME *endoctrinen,* fr. MF *endoctriner,* fr. OF, fr. *en- + doctrine* doctrine] (1626) **1** : to instruct esp. in fundamentals or rudiments : TEACH **2** : to imbue with a usu. partisan or sectarian opinion, point of view, or principle — **in·doc·tri·na·tion** \(ˌ)in-ˌdäk-trə -ˈnā-shən\ *n* — **in·doc·tri·na·tor** \in-ˈdak-trə -ˌnā-tər\ *n*

Related words

Part of speech

strive \ˈstrīv\ *vi* **strove** \ˈstrōv\ *also* **strived** \ˈstrīvd\; **striv·en** \ˈstri-vən\ *or* **strived; striv·ing** \ˈstri-viŋ\ [ME, fr. OF *estriver,* of Gmc origin; akin to MHG *streben* to endeavor] (13c) **1** : to devote serious effort or energy: ENDEAVOR **2** : to struggle in opposition : CONTEND **syn** see ATTEMPT—**striver** \ˈstri-vər\ *n*

—from *Merriam Webster's Collegiate Dictionary,* Tenth Edition

People often ask, "If I can't spell a word, how can I find it in the dictionary?" It's not as hard as you think. Try sounding out the word and looking it up according to the sounds of each syllable. If you don't find it at first, try imagining what other letter or combinations of letters form the sound(s) of the word, and scan up and down the dictionary page. As a last resort, ask someone else for help.

Enriching Your Vocabulary

The adjective *pejorative* means "having a disparaging effect or force." The word *pejorative* casts a negative feeling over whatever it's attached to. My brother used the *pejorative* phrase "What a clown!" in reference to his college professor.

Editing Tip

1. When you come across a new or unfamiliar word, check its meaning, spelling, and pronunciation.

2. If a word looks similar to another word, write down both words with their meanings.

3. When you're learning to spell a new word, learn it syllable by syllable or by word parts.

4. Add the words you misspell to your proofreading log, and use that log as a quick reference. Underline the letter or letters that cause you trouble.

Exercise 1 **Using a Dictionary to Check Spelling**

Work with a partner to write the letter of the correct spelling in the blank. If you're not sure of the correct spelling of a word, take turns looking up the word in a dictionary to check the correct spelling.

_b_   1. (a) portible   (b) portable   (c) portibel   (d) portabel

_b_   2. (a) resonably   (b) reasonably   (c) reasonabley   (d) reasonibly

_a_   3. (a) murmur   (b) mermur   (c) murmer   (d) mermer

_a_   4. (a) circumference   (b) curcumfrence
       (c) cercumference   (d) circumfrance

_c_   5. (a) piculiar   (b) paculiar   (c) peculiar   (d) peculier

_a_   6. (a) minimum   (b) minamum   (c) minemum   (d) minimem

_b or c_   7. (a) jugement   (b) judgment   (c) judgement   (d) judgemint

_b_   8. (a) recomendation   (b) recommendation
       (c) reccomendation   (d) reccommendation

_c_   9. (a) sycology   (b) pscheology   (c) psychology   (d) physcoligy

_d_   10. (a) temprament   (b) tempurment   (c) tempurament   (d) temperament

Exercise 2 **Using a Dictionary**

Answer the following questions. If you're not sure about how to spell your answer, look up the word in a college dictionary.

1. What is the plural of *thesis*? ___theses___

2. Assume that you have to break the word *permeable* with a hyphen at the end of a line. Show all the points where you could place a hyphen. ___per-me-a-ble___

3. How do you spell the plural of the noun *millennium*? ___millennia *or* millenniums___

4. How do you spell the middle day in a school week? ___Wednesday___

5. How do you spell the past tense and past participle of the verb *sink*? ___past: sank *or* sunk; past participle: sunk___

6. When a word has alternate spellings, the one listed first in a dictionary is preferred. Underline the preferred spellings.

     a. <u>humor</u> or humour   d. theatre or <u>theater</u>

     b. analyse or <u>analyze</u>   e. honour or <u>honor</u>

     c. <u>dialogue</u> or dialog   f. <u>appendixes</u> or appendices

Spelling Rules

As you know, irregular spellings are not uncommon in English. But by learning a few simple rules, you'll always have guidelines to follow. Although these rules may have exceptions, with practice the exceptions will become second nature.

🔖 Write *i* before *e* except after *c*.

Note that most of these words have a long *e* sound.

I BEFORE E	achieve	believe	chief	niece	piece
AFTER C	ceiling	conceit	deceive	receive	receipt
EXCEPTIONS	either	neither	leisure	seize	weird

🔖 Write *ei* when these letters are not pronounced with a long /e/, especially when the sound is a long /a/, as in *neighbor* and *weigh*.

	height	their	foreign	forfeit	surfeit
SOUNDS LIKE *AY*	eight	freight	neighbor	reign	
	sleigh	veil	weigh		

🔖 For words of more than one syllable that end with the sound /*seed*/, only one word is spelled with -*sede*. Three words end in -*ceed*. All other /*seed*/ words end in -*cede*.

-SEDE	supersede				
-CEED	exceed	proceed	succeed		
-CEDE	concede	intercede	precede	recede	secede

🔖 Spell out the words for numbers between one and one hundred when writing sentences. Numbers that are compound words between twenty-one and ninety-nine are hyphenated.

> She watched Hitchcock's ***Thirty-nine*** *Steps* on channel **fifty-seven**.
> Middle-aged people like to joke that **fifty** is the new **forty**.

Note: Always spell out a number that begins a sentence.
> **One hundred** schools volunteered in the clothing drive.

When a sentence begins with a large number, reword the sentence to avoid spelling out the number.

> *A total of 467*
> ~~Four hundred sixty-seven~~ students donated money to Doctors Without Borders.
> *It was in 1999*
> ~~Nineteen ninety-nine was the year~~ that I learned the meaning of giving.

Writing Hint

A good way to remember something is to make up a mnemonic, or memory, device. Here are some nonsense phrases to help you remember some of the exceptions to the *i*-before-*e* rule:

Neither weird dog can **seize either** bone at its **leisure**.

Newspapers and some magazines write out numbers from one to nine only; ten and up are written as numerals. Either style is correct as long as it's used consistently.

Exercise 3   Remembering Spelling Rules

Work with a partner or small group to complete each item below. Write your answers on a separate piece of paper. Then compare your answers with those of other student pairs or groups in your class.

1. What rule does this mnemonic device help you remember: "The weight of this freight train equals eight sleighs?" Write *e* before *i* when the letters are pronounced with a long /a/ sound.
2. Make up your own mnemonic device (a sentence like the one either in item number one or in the Writing Hint on page 323) to help you remember the three words that end in *-ceed*. Answers will vary. If you *succeed* as a writer, you can *proceed* to *exceed* your wildest dreams.
3. Write all the two-syllable words you can think of that end with *-cede*. Check your list with a partner or small group. Possible words include *concede*, *precede*, *recede*, *secede*.
4. Write a sentence that tells something about the number of students in your class. Use the number in the sentence. Twenty of the thirty-two students in this class have brown eyes.

Exercise 4   Proofreading a Newsletter

The person who wrote these brief articles for a community newsletter needs a proofreader. Find and correct all of the spelling mistakes below. Write the corrected articles on a separate piece of paper. See Answer Key.

[1]Wierd Sounds

[2]Niether the city police cheif nor the residential nieghbors of the Tip Top Bread Factory can locate exactly where a wierd, high-pitched sound is coming from. [3]A group of Tip Top employees has decided to interceed in the investigation. [4]These employees will report thier findings in the next issue or conceed defeat.

[5]Procede Without Caution

[6]Without a doubt, the hieght of our success as a community is demonstrated in the way we spend our liesure time together. [7]To acheive this goal, our citizens place no cieling on what they can do to succede in creating fun activities for everyone, young and old. [8]So, on Saturday, don't receed into the background and riegn as a couch potato king or queen, or make an excuse like "My neice is visiting." [9]There's no reason to wiegh your options carefully, eiether. [10]Sieze the moment and join one of eight community groups—from the foriegn film club to the woodworking club (which made the sliegh for last year's winter parade) to the bongo club.

Prefixes and Suffixes

A **prefix** is a group of letters added to the beginning of a word; a **suffix** is a group of letters added to the end of a word. Adding a prefix or a suffix changes a word's meaning.

🌢 Adding a prefix does not change the spelling of a word.

uncertain	**dis**trust	**mis**guided	**ill**egitimate

🌢 If a word ends in *-y* preceded by a consonant, change the *y* to *i* before adding a suffix.

	glorious	saltiness	loneliest	shininess
EXCEPTIONS	dryness	shyly		

Keep the *y* when adding the suffix *-ing*, as in *trying* or *staying*. Keep the *y* when adding the suffix *-ly* or *-ness* to one-syllable adjectives, such as *shyness* and *wryly*.

🌢 If a word ends in *-y* preceded by a vowel, keep the *-y*.

	buoyant	destroyer	betraying	employable
EXCEPTIONS	daily	said		

🌢 Drop a word's final silent *-e* before adding a suffix that begins with a vowel.

	retrievable	enclosure	cringing	adorable
EXCEPTIONS	mileage	canoeing	hoeing	acreage

Note: American dictionaries give *likable, lovable, movable,* and *sizable* as the preferred spellings but also include *likeable, loveable, moveable,* and *sizeable.* The preferred spelling is always listed first in your dictionary.

🌢 Keep a word's final silent *-e* before adding a suffix that begins with the vowels *a-* or *o-* when the word ends in *-ge* or *-ce*.

advantageous	noticeable	changeable	courageous

🌢 Keep the final silent *-e* before adding a suffix that begins with a consonant.

	statehood	falsehood	boredom	management
EXCEPTIONS	argument	ninth	truly	wisdom

Note: American dictionaries list *judgment* and *acknowledgment* as the preferred spellings but also include *judgement* and *acknowledgement*.

Editing Tip

Some exceptions help you distinguish between two different words to which a suffix has been added.

sing + -ing = singing and *singe + -ing = singeing*

die + -ing = dying and *dye + -ing = dyeing.*

Writing Hint

Use hyphens with prefixes before a proper noun or adjective. Examples include *un-American, sub-Sahara, pro-Vietnam.*

Sometimes, a hyphen is used when a double consonant or vowel occurs, for example, *pre-election.* But watch out; others take no hyphen, such as *preempt.*

In other cases, hyphens are used after a prefix to distinguish it from a word that looks just like it.

The **recreation** group teaches tennis. I participated in a **re-creation** of the Battle of Gettysburg.

Here are the rules for doubling a final consonant before adding a suffix that begins with vowel.

When the suffix begins with a vowel, double the final consonant in one-syllable words that end in a consonant preceded by a single vowel.

pegged, strapping, planning, skimmed, baggage

Double the final consonants in words of more than one syllable when the word ends in a single consonant preceded by a single vowel and the new word is accented on the next-to-last syllable. Don't double the final consonant when the new word is not accented on the last syllable.

DOUBLE CONSONANT   *beginner, occurrence, referral*
SINGLE CONSONANT   *preference, reference*

Exercise 5   Adding Prefixes and Suffixes

Combine these words with their prefixes or suffixes (you may use a dictionary).

1. outrage + -ous ___outrageous___
2. un- + able ___unable___
3. re- + enter ___reenter___
4. dye + -ing ___dyeing___
5. live + -ly ___lively___
6. reply + -ed ___replied___
7. employ + -able ___employable___
8. state + -ly ___stately___
9. prefer + -ed ___preferred___
10. contrite + -ness ___contriteness___
11. flip + -ing ___flipping___
12. anti- + French ___anti-French___
13. sub- + continent ___subcontinent___
14. retrieve + -able ___retrievable___
15. amaze + -ment ___amazement___
16. post- + trial ___post-trial___
17. occur + -ence ___occurrence___
18. singe + -ing ___singeing___
19. control + -er ___controller___
20. anti- + establishment ___antiestablishment___

Exercise 6   Writing New Words

With a partner, write as many words as you can that contain one of the prefixes or suffixes (or both) listed below. Try to use at least four different prefixes and suffixes. Compare your list with those of other groups, and classify words together with the same prefix or suffix. Try to define your words. **Hint:** Look up the prefix or suffix in a college dictionary for help. See Answer Key.

PREFIXES   anti-, pre-, post-, un-, sub-, re-
SUFFIXES   -ment, -er, -able, -ence, -ness, -ous

Noun Plurals

There are several guidelines for forming noun plurals. Most are straightforward and easy to follow. As shown below, you start with the singular noun form and then follow the directions to form the plural.

Making Nouns Plural		
KINDS OF NOUNS	**WHAT TO DO**	**EXAMPLES**
Most nouns	Add -s to the singular.	cat**s**, car**s**, pencil**s**
Nouns that end in -s, -x, -z, -ch, -sh	Add -es to the singular.	mass**es**, tax**es**, waltz**es**, bench**es**, dish**es**
Family names	Follow the two preceding rules.	the Burton**s**, the Marx**es**, the Ruiz**es**, the Ross**es**
Family names that end in -y	Add -s to the name.	the Kennedy**s**, the Brady**s**
Nouns that end in -y preceded by a consonant	Change the -y to i, and add -es.	flurr**ies**, worr**ies**, observator**ies**
Nouns that end in -y preceded by a vowel	Add -s.	turkey**s**, valley**s**, guy**s**, replay**s**
Most nouns that end in -f or -fe	Add -s.	bluff**s**, sheriff**s**, belief**s**, proof**s**
A few nouns that end in -f or -fe	Change the f to v and add -s or -es.	shel**ves**, li**ves**, wol**ves**, thie**ves**, wi**ves**, lea**ves**
Nouns ending in -o preceded by a vowel	Add -s.	radio**s**, cameo**s**, scenario**s**
Most nouns ending in -o preceded by a consonant	Add -es.	hero**es**, tornado**es**, tomato**es**, innuendo**es** **Exceptions:** memos, silos
Most musical terms ending in -o	Add -s.	soprano**s**, alto**s**, solo**s**, piano**s**, piccolo**s**
Compound nouns	Make the most important word plural.	editor**s**-in-chief, passer**s**by, bill**s** of sale, father**s**-in-law, merry-go-round**s**
Letters, numbers, and words referred to as words	Use an apostrophe (') + -s.	P**'s**, 4**'s**, no if**'s**, and**'s**, or but**'s**
Irregular plurals, foreign plurals, and words that stay the same for both singular and plural	No rules apply! Memorize these forms.	men, children, mice, geese, feet, oxen, teeth, crises, series, parentheses, species, sheep, curricula, fungi

Editing Tip

Many word processing software applications can check your spelling. However, don't rely solely on these spell checkers. They cannot determine whether you should use *to, two,* or *too.* Only you can do that.

A few nouns have two acceptable forms: hoof**s** or hoo**ves**, scarf**s** or scar**ves**, dwarf**s** or dwar**ves**.

A few nouns have two acceptable forms: volcano**s** or volcano**es**, mosquito**s** or mosquito**es**, flamingo**s** or flamingo**es**, memento**s** or memento**es**.

Enriching Your Vocabulary

In geography, *promontory,* used in Exercise 7, means "a peak of high land that juts out into a body of water; headland." In anatomy, it refers to "a prominent body part." From the Marin Headland *promontory,* you can see the island of Alcatraz, the Golden Gate Bridge, and the city of San Francisco.

Exercise 7 **Forming Plurals Nouns**

Write the plural form of each noun. Check a dictionary if you're unsure. If the dictionary doesn't list irregular plurals or alternate plural forms, follow the rules in the chart on page 327.

1. Estavaz   Estavazes
2. mouse   mice
3. hanger-on   hangers-on
4. employee   employees
5. dynamo   dynamos
6. kazoo   kazoos
7. staff   staffs
8. convoy   convoys
9. promontory   promontories
10. alibi   alibis
11. Horowitz   Horowitzes
12. giraffe   giraffes
13. loaf   loaves

14. ratio   ratios
15. zero   zeros *or* zeroes
16. Murphy   Murphys
17. genius   geniuses
18. tooth   teeth
19. fungus   fungi *or* funguses
20. *ABC*   *ABC*'s
21. cupful   cupfuls *or* cupsful
22. stadium   stadia *or* stadiums
23. medium   mediums or media
24. brother-in-law   brothers-in-law
25. virtuoso   virtuosos
26. memo   memos

Exercise 8 **Writing with Plural Nouns**

Imagine a pair of identical twins who go to your school. Write a paragraph or two about the twins who have two of everything, and who go everywhere and do most things together. Students' paragraphs will vary. See teacher pages for assessment rubrics.

EXAMPLE   Timmy and Tommy received watch**es** for their birthday**s**.

Remember to use two of every item. When you've finished writing, check to see that all noun plurals are spelled correctly.

Editing and Proofreading Worksheet 1

Correct any spelling and capitalization errors that you find in the following classified advertisements of a newspaper.

WANTED [1] ~~Typeist~~ *Typist* for either Tuesday or ~~wenesday~~ *Wednesday* afternoons. [2] ~~Inter-national busness~~ *International business* company. [3] Student ~~applicationes~~ *applications* ~~acceptted~~ *accepted*. [4] ~~Foriegn~~ *Foreign* ~~languageses~~ *languages* a plus in all employees! [5] ~~Aplications~~ *Applications* should be ~~submited~~ *submitted* by March 20.

LOST [6] Diamond ring on ~~nineth~~ *ninth* of ~~febuary~~ *February*, near ~~sub-way~~ *subway* ~~entrence~~ *entrance* at Eighty-sixth street ~~dureing~~ *during* snow ~~fluries~~ *flurries*. [7] Information from ~~passerbys~~ *passersby* or people in ~~nieghboring~~ *neighboring* buildings appreciated. [8] Contact this newspaper's ~~managment~~ *management* with ~~writen~~ *written* description of ring for ~~referal~~ *referral* to ~~hopful~~ *hopeful* owner.

RENT [9] ~~Amazeing~~ *Amazing* value! [10] Award-~~wining~~ *winning* house builder to rent model home. [11] ~~Luxuryous~~ *Luxurious* ~~viewes~~ *views* of ~~mountaines~~ *mountains* and ~~vallies~~ *valleys* from second story ~~windowes~~ *windows*. [12] This model contains ~~noteable~~ *notable* ~~improvments~~ *improvements* over ~~earlyer~~ *earlier* models. [13] All real ~~estates~~ *estate* ~~agent~~ *agents* as well as possible renters welcome. [14] Sorry, ~~niether~~ *neither* cats nor dogs allowed.

INTERESTED? [15] Unusual ~~liesure~~ *leisure* vacations for both ~~childs~~ *children* and adults. [16] See ~~videoes~~ *videos* of ~~extremly~~ *extremely* ~~beautyful~~ *beautiful* vacation ~~Islandes~~ *islands* or ~~fascinateing~~ *fascinating* hikes up ~~snowey~~ *snowy* mountains. [17] All kinds of ~~tripps~~ *trips* ~~availible~~ *available*. [18] We are a long-time provider of fun for ~~familys~~ *families*. [19] Write to request an ~~outragous~~ *outrageous* ~~brosure~~ *brochure* of our many, ~~varyied~~ *varied* trips. [20] Each ~~brosure~~ *brochure* is ~~writen~~ *written* by our preeminent travel ~~writeing~~ *writing* staff.

Editing and Proofreading Worksheet 2

Work with a partner to correct any spelling, punctuation, and capitalization errors that you find in the following paragraphs. Make any other improvements that you think will improve the writing. Compare your revision to those of other pairs of students. Answers may vary. A sample revision is given.

[1]Langston Hughes (1902–1967) spent his teenage years~~yeares~~ between the cities~~citys~~ of Detroit and cleveland. [2]After high school and one year of college, Langston Hughes began his travels~~traveles~~, experiencing~~experienceing~~ Paris france, Washington D.C., and other locations~~locationes~~. [3]Wherever he lived, his writing abilities~~righting abilites~~ were unstoppable~~unstopable~~.

[4]Some of his early work appeared in African American anthologies~~anthologys~~. [5]One of Hughes's earliest~~earlyest~~ essays appeared~~appearred~~ in the magazine the *Nation*. [6]Through the support of a wealthy fan, Amy Spigarin, Hughes received~~recieved~~ funds to complete his college~~collage~~ education~~educatshun~~. [7]Around the same time, his poems~~poemes~~ were published in a volume entitled The Weary Blues (1926). [8]His novel *Not without laughter* (1930) established~~iestablished~~ his reputation, giving~~giveing~~ him the title "the bard of Harlem."

[9]As a popular writer, Langston Hughes seized~~siezed~~ the opportunity~~oportunity~~ to actively~~activily~~ speak out about~~for~~ the African American experience~~experiance~~ and to voice his beliefs~~beliefes~~ in racial~~raciel~~ justice and workers' rights~~writes~~. [10]Due~~Dew~~ to his political beliefs~~believes~~, he went to the soviet union. [11]In the 1930s, where he studied the Soviets' policies~~they're policees~~. [12]Hughes later wrote~~rote~~ wrote that he was pro American, denying~~denieng~~ that he was unpatriotic~~un patriotic~~.

[13]Langston Hughes's ~~Hughes~~ books line the shelves~~shelfs~~ of libraries~~librarys~~ and universities and range from poetry to stories~~storys~~ for children~~childrens~~. [14]He hoped his work would help the march toward civil rights proceed~~precede~~ for African Americans. [15]He included everyday speech and the evocative language of the blues in poems such as "Mother to Son," a work in which the mother speaks this unforgettable~~unforgetable~~ line:

"life for me ain't been no crystal stair."

Chapter Review

Exercise A Proofreading a Letter

The newspaper that published the following letter needs a better proofreader. Find and correct all of the spelling mistakes in it.

See Answer Key.

> [1] Dear Editer:
>
>   [2] As a citazen, let me sieze this oportunity to thank you for your peice on recycleing aluminum cans. [3] I have ofen attempted to interceed in my nieghborhood's recyleing plans—but without sucess. [4] For people to suceed with this kind of environmental effort, they must be truely dedicated to thier cause. [5] Our local eforts to recycle have been less than enthusiastic, if not down right distresing. [6] You're article in last Wenesday's paper opened people's eyes to the importence of provideing new stratagees for saving and re-using natural resources. [7] Let me comend you on some of your recomendations. [8] In particuler, I endorse the exciteing idea of enlisting ninty-five student volunteeres during summer vacations.
>
>   [9] I look forward to the next reciept of my newspaper, which I hope unviels more information on this important subject.
>
>   [10] Sincerly yours,
>
>   *E. L. Wichester*
>   E. L. Wichester

Exercise B Using a Dictionary

Answer the following questions. If you're not sure about how to spell your answer, look up the word in a college dictionary.

1. Which is the correct spelling: *pecular, peculir, peculiar, peculair?* _____peculiar_____

2. What do you call a person who owes a *debt*? _____debtor_____

3. How do you spell the past tense and past participle of the verb *ride*? __rode *and* ridden__

4. When you need to make a skirt or pants a couple of inches longer, what do you do to the skirt or pants? __lengthen them__

CHAPTER REVIEW

5. Underline the preferred American spelling for the following words:
   a. judgement or <u>judgment</u>   c. <u>mementos</u> or mementoes
   b. <u>canceled</u> or cancelled   d. <u>cooperate</u> or co-operate

6. How do you spell the present participle of the verb *singe*?
   <u>singeing</u>

7. "Three feet deep" tells the depth. "Four feet high" tells the
   <u>height</u>. "Eight feet wide" tells the <u>width</u>.

8. What is the plural of *thesis*? <u>theses</u>

9. At forty miles to the gallon, my car gets good gas <u>mileage</u>.

10. Hyphenate the word *fundamentally*. <u>fun-da-men-tal-ly</u>

Exercise C **Adding Prefixes and Suffixes**

Write the word that results when the following prefixes or suffixes
are added.

1. like + able <u>likable *or* likeable</u>   6. emancipate + -tion <u>emancipation</u>

2. please + ant <u>pleasant</u>   7. liquefy + -ing <u>liquefying</u>

3. ninety + th <u>ninetieth</u>   8. allot + -ed <u>allotted</u>

4. anti + social <u>antisocial</u>   9. ir- + reversible <u>irreversible</u>

5. pre + paid <u>prepaid</u>   10. lonely + -est <u>loneliest</u>

Exercise D **Writing Plurals**

Complete each sentence by writing the plural form of the word
in parentheses.

1. Claudia tried on three different (scarf) <u>scarves *or* scarfs</u>.

2. Two working (radio) <u>radios</u> will be more than enough.

3. Many (observatory) <u>observatories</u> are open only to scientists.

4. Until the calf injury heals, please use those (crutch) <u>crutches</u>.

5. The alpha male is the strongest member in a pack of (wolf) <u>wolves</u>.

6. Did you know that this house on Cape Cod belonged to the
   (Kennedy) <u>Kennedys</u>?

7. Environmental (crisis) <u>crises</u> happen all over the world.

8. The violin and piano (virtuoso) <u>virtuosos</u> performed a duet.

9. The (alumnus) <u>alumni</u> association met at noon.

10. You lengthened the (cuff) <u>cuffs</u> of my pants perfectly.

Cumulative Review

Exercise A Using Commas and End Marks Correctly

In the following sentences, insert all missing commas, periods, and other end punctuation marks.

1. Have you ever viewed a planet, star, or comet through a telescope, and have you ever been to a planetarium?

2. News of the sighting of a possible planet in TMR-1, an outer space system, was reported in a May 28, 1998, newspaper in Miami, Florida.

3. In fact, the dot, or what might be a planet, shows similarities to Jupiter.

4. Jupiter, also known as a gas giant, can't sustain life.

5. Incidentally, the dot, which was viewed through the Hubble telescope, was 450 light-years from Earth.

6. This possible planet turned out to be debris spun off from a developing star—a common process.

Exercise B Adding Punctuation to Dialogue

Add punctuation, capital letters, paragraph breaks and any other changes necessary to the following dialogue. Write your corrected version on a separate piece of paper.

[1]Steve asked Laura have you read The Red Badge of Courage the civil war novel by Stephen Crane. [2]Laura answered "No but I have read two of his short stories The Open Boat and The Blue Hotel. [3]"Do you know anything about Crane"? Laura asked "because I'd like to know". [4]Steve opened their textbook and read aloud Stephen Crane was born on November 1 1871 and died on June 5 1900. [5]His short life was full of questions and mysterys. [6]At times he lived the high life, other times he was penniless. [7]Scholars and readers are continually interested in his life, which few completely understand".

[8]Laura was interested in what Steve read. [9]You know Laura said I have a music CD called The Open Boat. [10]Steve asked "Is the name taken from the Stephen Crane story"? [11]Laura exclaimed "I bet it is"! [12]Steve stated "Writers titles should remain there's alone, I think unless they give the title to someone else.

See Answer Key.

Exercise C Proofreading a Paragraph

Proofread the paragraphs on the following page for the correct use of capital letters. Use the proofreading symbol of three underscores to indicate a capital: (m̲̲̲)

¹No one ever won a nobel prize for building a skyscraper, but the people who built the empire state building in 1930 deserve one. ²On September 17, 1930, governor alfred e. smith of the state of new york laid the cornerstone. ³It was on this site that the elegant waldorf-astoria hotel had stood. ⁴In its place, the architects—shreve, lamb & harmon associates—along with the builders—starrett brothers & eken, inc.—created a 102-story building that stood 1,472 feet tall up to the top of the antennae.

⁵This skyscraper is made out of indiana limestone and granite. ⁶Marble from france, italy, belgium, and germany lines the interior. ⁷The construction cost was originally estimated at $50 million; but because of the great depression, the cost actually went no higher than $25 million.

⁸Construction took one year and forty-five days. ⁹On may 1, 1931, in washington, d.c., president herbert hoover pressed a button to turn on the building's lights to celebrate its completion.

Exercise D   Using a Dictionary to Check Spelling

Work with a partner to write the letter of the correct spelling in the blank. If you're not sure of the correct spelling of a word, take turns looking up the item in a dictionary to check the correct spelling.

<u>a</u>   1. (a) achievement (b) acheivement (c) achievment (d) acheivment

<u>b</u>   2. (a) disapoint (b) disappoint (c) dissapoint (d) dissappoint

<u>c</u>   3. (a) preecede (b) preeceed (c) precede (d) preceed

<u>b</u>   4. (a) annonymous (b) anonymous (c) anonimous (d) anonymis

<u>c</u>   5. (a) hight (b) hieght (c) height (d) heite

<u>d</u>   6. (a) embarasment (b) embarrasment (c) embarassment (d) embarrassment

<u>a</u>   7. (a) mistakable (b) mistakeable (c) mistakible (d) mistakeible

<u>a</u>   8. (a) buoys (b) bouys (c) buoyes (d) bouyes

<u>d</u>   9. (a) ocurence (b) ocurance (c) ocurrence (d) occurrence

<u>b</u> 10. (a) comodites (b) commodities (c) commodites (d) comodities

Mechanics Test

Exercise 1 Identifying Errors

Directions: Each of the numbered items is either correct or contains an error in one of its underlined parts. In the answer section to the right of each item, circle the letter of the sentence part that contains the error. If the sentence is correct, circle E for NO ERROR.

EXAMPLE   Although she was not the first American poet; Phillis Wheatley was the
            A   B   C

first published African American poet of either sex. NO ERROR
                D   E

A B (C) D E

1. Phillis Wheatley arrived at Boston Harbor, Massachusetts, in 1761.
                        A   B

Supposedly, the seven-year-old African girl was wrapped only
  C   D

in a carpet. NO ERROR
          E

1. A B C D (E)

2. Do you know that Phillis Wheatley was sold as a slave. A tailor from
                                     A

Boston, Massachusetts, named John Wheatley, bought her. NO ERROR
  B   C   D   E

2. (A) B C D E

3. Before Phillis turned ten, the Wheatley's taught her to read and write
                    A   B

English using selections from English literature. NO ERROR
  C   D   E

3. A (B) C D E

4. In addition to English, Phillis studied latin; she also composed her own
                  A   B

English poems. Luckily, the Wheatleys appreciated her talent and
        C   D

encouraged her work. NO ERROR
            E

4. A (B) C D E

5. Phillis wrote poems through stretchs of nighttime. By day, she performed
         A   B   C

light domestic duties in the Wheatley household. NO ERROR
                D   E

5. A (B) C D E

6. Phillis was enslaved, however, she also was a highlight of Boston society,
         A   B   C

which recognized her as a prodigy of extraordinary literary talent.
                    D

NO ERROR
  E

6. (A) B C D E

7. At age seventeen, in 1770, one of her poems was published widly, both
      A   B   C

in England and throughout the colonies. NO ERROR
              D   E

7. A B (C) D E

8. The poem <u>"On the Death of Mr. George Whitefield,"</u> memorialized a

                A

   noted minister from Boston. Because of this <u>publication,</u> Phillis

                                   B

   received an invitation to go to <u>England;</u> it was here, in England,

                          C

   that she was given her treasured copy of John Milton's book

   <u>*Paradise Lost.*</u>   <u>NO ERROR</u>

    D   **E**

8. Ⓐ B   C   D   E

9. <u>"Poems on Various Subjects, Religious and Moral,"</u> <u>published</u> in <u>1773,</u>

                A   **B**   **C**

   was Phillis <u>Wheatley's</u> first and last published book. <u>NO ERROR</u>

            D   **E**

9. Ⓐ B   C   D   E

10. When the Wheatleys died, Phillis was freed, but the <u>American Revolution</u>

                                                          A

    halted <u>Phillis</u> career. She lived the rest of her life in <u>poverty;</u> her copy

          B   **C**

    of <u>*Paradise Lost*</u> was sold at auction to pay off her debts. <u>NO ERROR</u>

            D   **E**

10. A Ⓑ C   D   E

Exercise 2   Correcting Errors

Directions: In the following sentences, the underlined part may contain one or more errors. In the answer section to the right of each item, circle the letter of the choice that correctly expresses the idea in the underlined part of the sentence. If you think that the original version is correct, circle D for NO ERROR. **Hint:** A sentence may have more than one error.

  EXAMPLE   "What have you <u>there," she asked.</u>

            A. there?" she asked.   C. there"? she asked.

            B. there," she asked?   D. NO ERROR

Ⓐ B   C   D

1. Believe me, <u>Chris's computer skills</u> are extraordinary.
   A. Chris computer skill'   C. Chris's computers skills
   B. Chris' computer skills   D. NO ERROR

1. A   B   C   Ⓓ

2. The <u>milage on their van</u> indicates that they drove across the country.
   A. mileage on their van   C. milage on they're van
   B. milige on their van   D. NO ERROR

2. Ⓐ B   C   D

3. We ask that you please <u>bake a cake make a poster or bring old</u>
   <u>books</u> to sell.
   A. bake a cake, make a poster or bring, old books
   B. bake a cake make a poster or, bring old books
   C. bake a cake, make a poster, or bring old books
   D. NO ERROR

3. A   B   Ⓒ D

4. Your <u>actions, not your words</u> concern me.   4.(A) B C D
   A. actions, not your words,   C. actions not your words,.
   B. actions—not your words   D. NO ERROR

5. I was told she wouldn't come to the <u>prom; yet she arrived</u>   5. A B C (D)
   before dark.
   A. prom, yet; she arrived   C. prom, yet, she arrived
   B. prom yet she arrived   D. NO ERROR

6. The narrator <u>announced My saga begins</u> long before winter set in,   6. A B (C) D
   yet after the leaves had turned into an autumnal blaze of color."
   A. announced, "my saga begins: C. announced: "My saga begins
   B. announced: My saga begins   D. NO ERROR

Exercise 3 Identifying Errors

Directions: In each numbered group, one or more of the items may contain errors. Circle the letter of every item that contains an error. **Hint:** An item may have more than one error.

EXAMPLE   A. Those are real weapons!   A B (C)(D)
         B. She said softly, "I'm here."
         C. Did you hang your coat in the closet.
         D. We can join you for the game but we can't stay on for the picnic.

1. A. The fan asked, "May I have your autograph?"   1. A B (C) D
   B. "In a moment," the famous mystery writer replied.
   C. The table contained stacks of two books:*Haunted Hill* and "The
      Watson Question."* (italics)
   D. "I often experience writer's block," the fan overheard the writer say.

2. A. The Primavera pasta company opened <s>it's</s> its doors to the public.   2.(A)(B) C D
   B. The chef is a m<u>em</u>ber and officer of the <u>g</u>olden <u>s</u>poon
      Gourmet Society.
   C. The owner, who's originally from Rome, Italy, suggested we try
      the lasagne.
   D. An excellent review appears in the November issue of
      Food Lover's Journal.

3. A. The small fire caused the singeing of the curtains.   3. A (B) C D
   B. <s>Proceeding</s> the performance, please check your tickets before
      <s>preceding</s> to your seats.   Preceding, proceeding
   C. They appreciated the teacher's acknowledgement of their efforts.
   D. During the debate, there were signs with anti-Russian slogans.

4. A. Have you read the poem "Ode to a Grecian Urn" by the English poet John Keats?   "The Love Song of J. Alfred Prufrock" (no italics)

   B. ~~The Love Song of J. Alfred Prufrock~~ is the poem that made T. S. Eliot famous.

   C. The movie *Titanic* was based on the sinking of the "Titanic" a luxury ship. (italics)

   D. The Beatles, an English musical group from the 1960s, became famous with an album entitled *Meet the Beatles*.

4. A Ⓑ Ⓒ D

5. A. We volunteered after the flood for our conscience' sake. consciences'

   B. The ~~wolve's~~ den had been invaded by the photographers. wolves'

   C. Did you read ~~Carlos'~~ persuasive editorial? Carlos's

   D. I would've caught the bus if I had set the alarm.

5. Ⓐ Ⓑ Ⓒ D

6. A. We studied buddhism and shintoism, two religions found in Japan.

   B. I read the published letters from a seventeenth-century duke of York.

   C. The Congress is made up of the Senate and the House of Representatives.

   D. In the Twentieth Century, man first set foot on the moon.

6. Ⓐ Ⓑ C Ⓓ

7. A. Did you hear the ~~sheeps~~ crying in the distance? sheep

   B. The lamb was served with roasted tomatoes and potatoes.

   C. All the athletes hoped for gold medals in the upcoming Olympics.

   D. How many ~~strategys~~ do you have for catching ~~mices~~? strategies, mice

7. Ⓐ B C Ⓓ

8. A. "Will you be ~~rakeing~~ the leaves every autumn?" the child asked. raking

   B. The movie "Gone With the Wind" tells about the south during the Civil war. (italics)

   C. The Catskill and Adirondack mountains are in New York State.

   D. The curtains made from Belgian lace in Sonya's room are delicate.

8. Ⓐ Ⓑ C D

Exercise 4 Correcting Errors

Directions: Look back at each item in Exercise 3, and double-check your answers. Make sure you have identified *all* of the sentences with errors. On a separate piece of paper, rewrite correctly *all* of the incorrect sentences in each numbered item. Write the entire sentences. **Hint:** A sentence may have more than one error.

Errors in sentences in Exercise 3 are corrected above.

Glossary

absolute adjective   modifiers, such as *unique* or *flawless*, that do not take comparative or superlative forms.

absolute phrase   a phrase that consists of a noun and either a participle or a participial phrase. It stands alone; it is neither the subject nor the verb.

abstract noun   a noun that names ideas.

acronym   a word, such as *laser*, formed from the first letters of several words ("*l*ight *a*mplification by *s*timulated *e*mission of *r*adiation").

active voice   the form of a verb that shows the subject performing an action.

adjective   a word that modifies (tells more about) a noun or pronoun.

adjective clause   a subordinate clause that functions as an adjective and that modifies a noun or pronoun.

adjective phrase   a prepositional phrase that modifies a noun or pronoun.

adverb   a word that modifies (tells more about) a verb, an adjective, or another adverb.

adverb clause   a subordinate clause that modifies a verb, an adjective, or another adverb. In an **elliptical adverb clause**, some words are omitted (or understood).

adverb of manner   an adverb that ends with the suffix *-ly*.

adverb phrase   a prepositional phrase that modifies a verb, an adjective, or another adverb.

agreement   the correct relationship between subjects and verbs in number and person or between pronouns and antecedents in number and gender.

analyze   to carefully consider each part or element of a subject. This is a key word to look for in an essay test question; it tells you how to approach the topic.

anecdote   an incident that actually happened, often based on personal experience or observation. It is one type of evidence that may be used in persuasive writing (also called **incident**).

antecedent   the word or words that a pronoun refers to.

appositive   a noun or pronoun that identifies or explains the noun or pronoun that precedes it. Appositives are either **essential** or **nonessential**.

appositive phrase   a phrase made up of an appositive and all of its modifiers.

articles   three common adjectives. *A* and *an* are **indefinite articles**; *the* is the **definite article**.

audience   the person or persons who will read a written work.

autobiographical incident   a true story about something that happened to you.

body   the part of an essay that explains the information introduced at the beginning of the essay.

brainstorming   a step in the prewriting process; the method of generating ideas for writing by focusing on a single word and listing every related idea regardless of its quality.

call to action   a statement or statements in a persuasive essay that tell the reader what to do.

cause   a condition, situation, or event that makes something happen (the **effect**).

character   a person who appears in a story; an element of all fiction.

chronological order   the order in which events occurred; a method of organizing used by writers of fiction and nonfiction.

clause   a group of words that contains a subject and a verb but does not express a complete thought. There are several types of clauses: **independent**, **subordinate** or **dependent**, **essential**, **nonessential**, **adjective**, **adverb**, and **noun**.

clause fragment   a subordinate clause incorrectly punctuated as a sentence. It does not express a complete thought.

clincher sentence   a restatement or summary of the main idea of a paragraph that was expressed in the topic sentence. It ends the paragraph.

clustering   a step in the prewriting process; the method of generating ideas for writing by creating a diagram to explore a topic, to break a large topic into smaller parts, or to gather details (also called **mapping** or **webbing**).

coherence   the logical organization of ideas.

collective noun   a noun that names a group of people, animals, or things.

comma splice   a run-on sentence with only a comma separating the independent clauses.

common noun   a noun that names a general, rather than a particular, person, place, thing, idea, or event.

compare   to identify the way two or more topics are similar.

complement   a word that completes the meaning of a sentence.

complete predicate   in a sentence, the verb and all of its modifiers (such as adverbs and prepositional phrases), objects, and complements.

complete subject   the simple subject of a sentence and all of its modifiers (such as adjectives and prepositional phrases).

complex sentence   a sentence that has one independent clause and at least one subordinate clause.

compound-complex sentence   a sentence that has two or more independent clauses and at least one subordinate clause.

compound noun   a noun that consists of two or more words. It may be hyphenated, written as one word, or written as two words.

compound preposition   a preposition that contains several words.

compound sentence   a sentence that has two or more independent clauses joined by a conjunction and no subordinate clauses.

compound subject   two or more subjects sharing the same verb.

compound verb   two or more verbs sharing the same subject.

conclusion   the part at the end of an essay that summarizes the main ideas.

concrete noun   a noun that names an object you can see, hear, smell, taste, or touch.

conjunction   a word that joins other words or groups of words. There are three kinds of conjunctions: **coordinating**, **correlative**, and **subordinating**.

conjuctive adverb   an adverb (such as *however*, *moreover*, and *therefore*) used to combine two simple sentences into a compound sentence.

connotation   the emotional associations attached to a word.

contrast   to identify the way two or more topics are different.

coordinating conjunction   a conjunction (such as *and*, *but*, and *for*) that joins words or groups of words that are of equal importance.

correlative conjunctions   a pair of onjunctions (such as *either . . . or* and *neither . . . nor*) that are always used together.

dangling modifier   a modifier that does not describe or limit any word or group of words in a sentence.

declarative sentence   a sentence that makes a statement and ends with a period.

degrees of comparison   the forms of a modifier that indicate the extent of a quality. The three degrees are **positive** (used to describe one thing), **comparative** (used for two things), and **superlative** (used for three or more things).

demonstrative pronoun   a pronoun (such as *this*, *that*, and *those*) that points to a specific thing or person.

denotation   the meaning of a word given in a dictionary.

dependent clause   a clause that has a subject and a verb but that does not express a complete thought (also called **subordinate clause**).

descriptive paragraph   a paragraph that uses sensory details and spatial order to give the reader an image of a person, place, object, or animal.

dialect   a way of speaking in certain regions or among certain groups of people.

dialogue   the spoken words of a person.

dialogue tag   the words that identify the speaker.

direct object   a noun or pronoun that receives the action of an action verb. It answers the question *whom* or *what* following the verb.

discuss   to write about a topic in any way you choose. This is a key word to look for in an essay test question; it tells you how to approach the topic.

double negative   two negative words used together incorrectly to convey a negative meaning.

drafting   in the writing process, the step of putting thoughts into sentences and paragraphs.

editing   the process of correcting grammatical and usage errors in a piece of writing.

effect   the result of a **cause**.

elaboration   the process of adding details to support the main idea (also called development).

elements of fiction   the basic components of a work of fiction. These components include **character**, **plot**, **point of view**, **setting**, and **theme**.

emphatic form   a verb form that is made up of the verb *do* and another verb to provide emphasis.

essay   a piece of writing on a limited topic. All essays have an **introduction**, a **body**, and a **conclusion**.

essential adjective clause   an adjective clause that provides information necessary to an understanding of the sentence. Essential adjective clauses are not set off by commas.

essential appositive   an appositive that provides information necessary to an understanding of the sentence. Essential appositives are not set off by commas.

essential clause a clause that adds information necessary to an understanding of the sentence. It is not set off by commas.

evaluation essay an essay that evaluates a work of literature according to established criteria, such as believability of plot.

evidence information supplied to support an opinion. Types of evidence include **anecdotes**, **examples**, **facts**, **incidents**, **quotations**, and **statistics**.

example a type of evidence used as an illustration to support an opinion.

exclamatory sentence a sentence that expresses strong feeling and ends with an exclamation point.

explain to help a reader understand something by giving reasons or information. This is a key word to look for in an essay test question; it tells you how to approach the topic.

expository paragraph a paragraph that explains or informs.

eyewitness report a firsthand account of an incident that focuses more on the significance of the incident to the community or the society than on the writer.

fact a statement that can be proven. It is a type of evidence used to support an opinion.

5W-HOW? **questions** the questions *Who? What? When? Where? Why?* and *How?* Asking these questions about a topic will help you narrow (or limit) your essay.

fragment a group of words that is not grammatically complete and is incorrectly punctuated as a sentence.

freewriting a step in the prewriting process; the method of generating ideas for writing by recording ideas for a specified time without stopping, while ignoring grammatical and mechanical rules.

fused sentence a run-on sentence with no punctuation separating its independent clauses.

gender a quality of pronouns, which are either male (*he, his*), female (*she, her*), or neuter (*it, its*).

general-specific order a method of organizing an essay in which the writer presents ideas by making a general statement first and then specific statements to back up the generalization.

gerund a verb form that acts as a noun and always ends in *-ing*.

gerund phrase a phrase made up of a gerund and all of its modifiers and complements. The entire phrase functions as a noun.

grammar in any language, the rules that govern how words are arranged to form meaningful structures.

imperative mood the imperative mood is used to give a direct command or to make a request.

imperative sentence a sentence that issues commands or makes a request. It ends with either a period or (if the command shows strong feeling) an exclamation point.

incident a ministory that has a plot, characters, and a setting. It is a type of evidence that can be used to support an opinion.

indefinite pronoun a pronoun (such as *everyone, all,* and *none*) that refers to an unspecified person or thing, or that expresses an amount.

independent clause a clause that has a subject and a verb and expresses a complete thought (also called **main clause**).

indicative mood the indicative mood is used to state a fact or opinion, or ask a question.

indirect object a noun or pronoun that answers the questions *to whom, for whom, to what,* or *for what* following an action verb.

infinitive a verb form that is almost always preceded by the word *to* (the *sign,* or *marker,* of the infinitive). In a sentence, an infinitive can act as a noun, adjective, or adverb.

infinitive phrase a phrase made up of an infinitive and all of its modifiers and complements.

intensifier an adverb that answers the question *to what extent.*

intensive pronoun a pronoun that ends in *-self* or *-selves* and adds emphasis to a noun or pronoun.

interjection a word that expresses mild or strong emotion. It has no grammatical connection to the rest of the sentence.

interpret to support an idea about the meaning of a statement or event by using **examples**, **facts**, or **quotations**.

interrogative pronoun a pronoun (such as *who, whom,* and *whose*) that begins a question.

interrogative sentence a sentence that asks a question and ends with a question mark.

intervening clause a clause that comes between the subject and the verb.

intervening phrase a prepositional phrase that comes between the subject and the verb.

intransitive verb an action verb that stands without a direct object.

introduction the part of an essay that identifies the subject and lets the reader know what will be discussed. It is the first paragraph of the essay.

inverted sentence a sentence in which the verb comes before the subject.

irregular verb a verb that does not form its past and past participle by adding -d or -ed to the present tense.

I-search paper the story of how and why you wrote your research paper and what you experienced in the process.

linking verb a word that joins the subject of a sentence with a word that identifies or describes it.

literary analysis a discussion of one or more of the elements of a work of fiction (**character**, **plot**, **point of view**, **setting**, and **theme**).

loaded words words that carry positive or negative connotations that may sway emotions.

logical order a method of organizing an essay in which the writer presents ideas in a way that makes sense to the reader.

mechanics the correct use of capital letters, punctuation marks, and spelling rules.

misplaced modifier an adjective or adverb placed far from the word it modifies.

modifier a word that describes or limits another word or group of words. Adjectives and adverbs are modifiers.

mood the mood of a verb shows the speaker's intent. There are three moods: **indicative**, **imperative**, and **subjunctive**.

narrative paragraph a paragraph that tells a fictional or true story.

narrator a person who tells a story.

nonessential adjective clause an adjective clause that provides information not necessary to an understanding of the sentence. Nonessential adjective clauses are set off by commas.

nonessential appositive an appositive that provides information not necessary to an understanding of the sentence. Nonessential appositives are set off by commas.

nonessential clause a clause that adds information not necessary to an understanding of the sentence. It is set off by commas.

noun a word that names a person, place, thing, or idea. Nouns that name ideas are **abstract nouns**. **Concrete nouns** name things that can be seen, heard, smelled, tasted, or touched. There are four types of nouns: **proper**, **common**, **collective**, and **compound**.

noun clause a subordinate clause that functions as a noun.

noun of direct address a proper noun that names the person being spoken to. It has no grammatical relation to the rest of the sentence. It is set off by a comma or commas.

noun phrase a noun and all of its modifiers. A noun phrase acts as a noun in a sentence.

number pronouns are either singular or plural.

object complement a noun, pronoun, or adjective that follows the direct object and renames or describes it.

object pronoun a pronoun that functions as the direct object, the indirect object, or the object complement in a sentence, clause, or phrase.

opinion statement a clear expression of the writer's point of view (also called **thesis statement**).

order of importance a method of organizing an essay in which the writer presents ideas according to their increasing or decreasing order of importance.

outline the bare bones (or skeleton) of a piece of writing. It includes the most important points that will be discussed in the piece.

paragraph a block of text that includes a sentence stating the main idea and other sentences supporting that idea. There are four types of paragraphs: **descriptive**, **expository**, **narrative**, and **persuasive**.

paraphrase to restate in your own words every idea in the same order as in an original source.

participial phrase a phrase made up of a participle and all of its modifiers and complements. The whole phrase acts as an adjective.

participle a verb form that acts as an adjective (modifies a noun or a pronoun). **Present participles** always have an -ing ending. **Past participles** of regular verbs end in -d or -ed, but those of irregular verbs have different endings.

parts of speech the eight categories into which English words are classified according to their function in a sentence. The eight parts of speech are **adjectives**, **adverbs**, **conjunctions**, **interjections**, **nouns**, **prepositions**, **pronouns**, and **verbs**.

passive voice the form of a verb that shows a subject receiving an action.

person pronouns are either first person (*I*, *we*), second person (*you*), or third person (*he*, *she*, *it*, *they*).

personal pronoun a pronoun (such as *I*, *we*, *she*, *he*, and *you*) that refers to the speaker or to another person. The personal pronouns have **subject**, **object**, and **possessive** forms.

personal response essay   a discussion in which you share the thoughts and emotions that strike you as you read a particular passage in a work.

persuade   to try to make someone agree with your opinion or to take action.

persuasive paragraph   a paragraph that aims to convince the reader that the writer's opinion is correct or to take action.

phrase   a group of related words that has no subject or predicate. There are several types of phrases: **adjective**, **adverb**, **appositive**, **gerund**, **infinitive**, **noun**, **participial**, **prepositional**, and **verb**.

plagiarism   using someone else's words or ideas without acknowledgment.

plot   an element of fiction; the sequence of events in a fictional work.

point of view   an element of fiction; the perspective of the person who tells the story.

possessive form   a form of nouns or pronouns that indicates possession. Most nouns form the possessive case by adding an apostrophe and -s ('s).

predicate   the part of the sentence that tells what the subject does, what it is, or what happens to it. A predicate may be **complete** or **simple**.

predicate adjective   an adjective that follows a linking verb and modifies (or describes) the subject of a sentence.

predicate nominative   a noun or pronoun that follows a linking verb and renames or identifies the subject.

prefix   a meaningful group of letters added at the beginning of a word to form a new word.

preposition   a word that connects another word in a sentence to a noun or pronoun (and its modifiers, if any) to form a prepositional phrase.

prepostitional phrase   a phrase that begins with a preposition and ends with an object (a noun or pronoun). There are two types of prepositional phrases: **adjective** and **adverb**.

prewriting   the step of the writing process that includes all of the thinking, planning, and organizing that is done before writing begins.

primary source   an original text or document, such as a literary work, diary, letter, speech, interview, or historical document.

principal parts   the four basic forms of a verb. They are the present, the present participle, the past, and the past participle.

pronoun   a word that takes the place of a noun or another pronoun. There are eight kinds of pronouns: **personal**, **indefinite**, **demonstrative**, **interrogative**, **reflexive**, **intensive**, **relative**, and **reciprocal**.

proofreading   a step in the writing process; reading a piece of writing to look for and correct mistakes in spelling, punctuation, and capitalization.

proper adjective   an adjective formed from a proper noun. It begins with a capital letter.

proper noun   the name of a particular person, place, thing, or idea.

publishing   sharing or presenting what you've written.

purpose   the reason for writing, such as to describe, to inform, to tell a story, to persuade, or a combination of these reasons.

quotation   exact spoken or written words. It is a type of evidence used to support an opinion.

reciprocal pronoun   a pronoun that expresses mutual action or relation.

reflexive pronoun   a pronoun that ends in -self or -selves and refers to an earlier noun or pronoun in the sentence.

regular verb   a verb that forms its past and past participle by adding -d or -ed to the present.

relative adverb   an adverb (such as *when* or *where*) that introduces an adverb clause.

relative pronoun   a pronoun (such as *who, whom, whose, that,* and *which*) that introduces an adjective clause.

research paper   a written work based on a thorough investigation of a limited topic.

revising   the process of improving the content, organization, and style of a piece of writing.

run-on sentence   a sentence made up of two or more sentences that are incorrectly run together as a single sentence (also called stringy sentence).

secondary source   a writer's comments on a primary source. Some types of secondary sources are reference books, biographies, works of literary criticism, and textbooks.

sentence   a grammatically complete group of words that expresses a thought. A sentence may be **simple**, **compound**, **complex**, **compound-complex**, **declarative**, **exclamatory**, **imperative**, **interrogative**, **inverted**, or **run-on**.

sentence fragment   a group of words that is not grammatically complete and is incorrectly punctuated as a sentence.

setting an element of fiction; the place and time of the events in a story.

simple predicate a verb or verb phrase that tells something about the subject of a sentence.

simple sentence a sentence that has one independent clause and no subordinate clauses.

simple subject the key word or words in the subject of a sentence.

spatial order a method of organizing a piece of writing in which the writer describes the physical placement of someone or something (for example, from left to right or from inside to outside).

statistics facts expressed in numbers. Statistics are a type of evidence that may be used in persuasive writing.

stereotyping overlooking individual differences among members of a group.

story map a graphic device that can be used for gathering details when you write a story or report on an autobiographical incident.

style the manner in which you express your thoughts.

subject the part of the sentence that names the person, place, thing, or idea that the sentence is about. A subject may be **complete** or **simple**.

subject complement a noun or pronoun (**predicate nominative**) or an adjective (**predicate adjective**) that follows a linking verb and is necessary to express a complete thought.

subject pronoun a pronoun that functions as the subject of a sentence or clause.

subjunctive mood the subjunctive mood is used to state a wish, a requirement, or a condition contrary to fact.

subordinate clause a clause that has a subject and a verb but that does not express a complete thought (also called a **dependent clause**).

subordinating conjunction a conjunction (such as *so that*, *although*, *because*, and *unless*) that introduces an adjective or adverb clause.

suffix a meaningful group of letters added at the end of a word to form a new word.

summarize to give the most important ideas in your own words. This is a key strategy to use in writing a research paper.

synthesize to put together to form a new whole.

theme an element of fiction that conveys a message (for example, about people or life).

thesis statement a summary of an essay's main or controlling idea (also called **opinion statement** or position statement). It belongs in the introduction and may be one or two sentences.

tone refers to your word choice and attitude toward your topic.

topic sentence a sentence that states the main idea of a paragraph. In an essay, it also ties the paragraph in which it appears to the preceding paragraph.

transitive verb an action verb that is followed by a direct object.

unity a paragraph has unity when all of its sentences focus on a single main idea.

usage in any language, the customary rules governing the use of words and groups of words to communicate ideas.

Venn diagram a useful prewriting graphic organizer for identifying similarities and differences.

verb a word that expresses an action or a state of being. Some action verbs express an action that can be observed; others express an action that usually cannot be seen. **Linking verbs** join the subject of a sentence with a word that identifies or describes it. A **verb phrase** contains a main verb plus one or more helping (or auxiliary) verbs.

verbal a verb form that functions as a different part of speech. There are three kinds of verbals: **gerunds**, **infinitives**, and **participles**.

verb phrase a verb and all of its modifiers.

verb tense a form of a verb that expresses the time an action is, was, or will be performed. The three simple tenses are present, past, and future. The three perfect tenses are present perfect, past perfect, and future perfect. Each tense also has a progressive form made up of a helping verb and the present participle (the -*ing* form).

voice verbs have two forms of voice: the **active voice**, in which the subject of a sentence performs an action, and the **passive voice**, in which the subject receives an action.

Works Cited list a list that provides information about each source you have used in a research paper.

writing process the method of creating and finalizing any piece of writing. The steps in this process include **prewriting**, **drafting**, **revising**, **editing**, and **proofreading**.

you **understood** the understood subject of a command or request (an imperative sentence).

Index

capitalization (*continued*)

conjunctions (*continued*)
    and interjections, 95–96
    subordinating, 95, 151, 157
conjunctive adverbs, 111
    in combining sentences, 111
    commas after, 289
    listing of common, 289
    and semicolons, 279
content, in revising, 15
contractions, 105
    apostrophes in, 297
contrast. *See also* comparisons
    transitions to show, 28
controlling idea, 33
coordinating conjunctions, 95, 111, 115
    in combining sentences, 111, 289
    in correcting run-on sentences, 115, 279
    in forming compound subject or verb, 111
    and need for commas, 271, 273
correlative conjunctions, 95, 111, 115
    in combining sentences, 111
    in correcting run-on sentences, 115
    in forming compound subject or verb, 111
could have, could of, 251
critical reviews, 48–52
    writing strategies in, 50–51

D

dangling modifiers, 241
dashes, 299
dates
    commas to separate from year, 277
    use of apostrophes with, 297
declarative sentences, 103
    punctuation for, 103, 269
definite article, 87
degrees of comparison
    comparative, 233, 235
    decreasing, 233
    forming, 233–34
    irregular forms of, 233
    positive, 233
    superlative, 233, 235
demonstrative pronouns, 81
dependent clauses, 147. *See also* subordinate clauses
descriptive writing, 30, 32, 202, 204
dialogue
    adding, as writing strategy, 39

proofreading, 314
punctuating, 295–96
writing, 295–96
dialogue tags, 295
dictionary, 321
    abbreviations in, 269
    capitalization in, 307, 309
    hyphen use in, 299
    spelling in, 321
    verb forms in, 179
different from, different than, 251
direct address, noun of, 275
direct objects, 83, 117–18, 121, 215, 221
direct question, punctuation for, 269
direct quotations
    capitalization of first words of, 311
    commas to set off, 277
    quotation marks at beginning and end of, 293
discussion, 75
disinterested, uninterested, 251
doesn't as singular verb, 197
don't as plural verb, 197
double comparisons, avoiding, 235
double negatives, avoiding, 237–38
"Down with Curfews; Up with Children" by Nadine Strossen, 42–43
drafting, 13–14
    conclusions, 35
    defined, 13–14
    introductions, 34
dramatic analysis, 58–61
"Dust Storm," from *The Invisible Thread* by Yoshiko Uchida, 37–38

E

eager, anxious, 251
editing, 15–17. *See also* revising
    for fragments, 108
    paragraphs, 256
    peer, 16, 17
    strategies in, 16
effect, affect, 249
-ei, spelling rules for, 323
elliptical adverb clause, 151
emigrate, immigrate, 252
emotional appeals, in persuasive writing, 44, 45, 48
emphasis, transitions to show, 28
emphatic form of verb, 185
end marks, 269–270. *See also* exclamation points; periods; question marks

essays, 73–76
    body in, 33–34
    capitalization of titles of, 309
    conclusion in, 34
    introduction in, 33
    key words for, 74–75
    personal response, 58
    persuasive, 42
    problem-solution, 53–57
    selecting questions for, 75–76
    thesis statement in, 33
    topic sentence in, 33
    transitions in, 75
    writing strategies for, 74–75
essential adjective clause, punctuation with, 275
essential appositive clause, punctuation with, 275
essential appositives, 129
essential clause, 149
evaluation, 58
every, and subject-verb agreement before compound noun, 205
everywheres, nowheres, somewheres, anywheres, 250
except, accept, 249
exclamation points, 269
    to end exclamatory sentences, 103, 269
    to end imperative sentences, 103, 269
    in punctuating dialogue, 295
    with quotation marks, 293
    after strong interjections, 95
exclamatory sentences, 103, 269
expository writing, 31. *See also* problem-solution essay; research papers
    problem-solution essays as, 53–57
    research papers as, 62–72

F

farther, further, 252
fewer, less, 252
fewer in degrees of comparison, 235
first person, 39, 197
formal writing, 237
fragments. *See* sentence fragments
freewriting, 10, 12
friendly letters, commas following greeting and closing of, 277
further, farther, 252
fused sentences, 115
future perfect progressive tense, 185
future perfect tense, 185

future progressive tense, 185
future tense, 185

G
gender, agreement of pronouns with antecedents in, 223, 225
gerund phrases, 135–36
    in combining sentences, 139
gerunds, 135–36
good, well, 253

H
helping verbs, 83
hopefully, 253
hyphens, 299
    in compound adjectives, 87
    in compound nouns, 79
    proofreading for, 18
    when adding prefixes to proper nouns/adjectives, 325

I
-ie, spelling rules for, 323
illogical comparisons, 237–38
immigrate, emigrate, 252
imperative mood, 189
imperative sentences, 103, 109
    compound, 273
    punctuation after, 103, 269
    subject in, 109
imply, infer, 253
in, into, 253
incomplete constructions, 221–22
indefinite articles, 87
indefinite pronouns, 81, 199, 297
    apostrophes to show possessive form of, 297
    plural, 199
    singular, 199
    subject-verb agreement with, 199–200, 223
independent clauses, 147–48
    comma between, in forming compound sentence, 111
    semicolons between, in forming compound sentence, 289
indicative mood, 189
indirect objects, 117–18, 215, 221
indirect quotations, 311
    punctuation for, 269
infer, imply, 253
infinitive(s), 137–38
    commas after introductory, 273
infinitive phrases, 137–38
    commas after introductory, 273
inside of, off of, outside of, 253
intensifiers, 89
intensive pronouns, 81

interjections, 95–96
    capitalization of *O*, 313
    commas to set off mild, 95
    exclamation points to set off strong, 95
interrogative pronouns, 81
interrogative sentences, 103, 109. *See also* questions
    compound, 273
    punctuation after, 103, 269
    subject in, 109
intervening phrases, 197–98
into, in, 253
intransitive verb, 117
introductions, 75
inverted sentences, placement of subject in, 109
irregular verbs, 179–82
italics, 291–92
items in series
    commas to separate, 271–72
    semicolons to separate, 289

K
kind of a, sort of a, type of a, 253

L
lay, lie, 181, 253
learn, teach, 253
leave, let, 253
lend, loan, borrow, 251
less, in degrees of comparison, 235
less, fewer, 252
let, leave, 253
letters. *See* business letters; friendly letters
letters as letters
    apostrophes to form plurals of, 297
    italics for, 291
lie, lay, 181, 253
like, as, as if, as though, 254
linking verbs, 83, 119
list of items, colon before, 287
"Literacy: A Family Affair" by Anita Merina, 53–54
literary analysis, 58
    questions for, 60
literary present tense, 60, 185
literature, writing about, 58–61. *See also* evaluation; literary analysis; personal response essay
loaded words, supporting emotional appeals with, 45
loan, borrow, lend, 251
logical appeals, 44
logical order, 27
    in expository writing, 31

M
main clause. *See* independent clauses
main ideas
    in expository writing, 31
    in prewriting for research papers, 71
many a(n), and subject-verb agreement before compound subject, 205
may, can, 251
misplaced modifiers, 239
mnemonics, 323
modifiers. *See also* adjective(s); adverb(s)
    dangling, 241–42
    irregular, 233
    misplaced, 239
    one-syllable, 233
    two-syllable, 233
mood, 30, 189–90
most, almost, 254
movie reviews, 51. *See also* critical reviews

N
narrative writing, 30–31, 37–41. *See also* personal narratives
negatives, double, 237–38
no, comma to set off, 277
nominatives, predicate, 119–20, 213
none, as indefinite pronoun, 199
nonessential adjective clauses and commas to set off, 275
nonessential appositives, 129
nonessential clauses, 149
    and commas to set off, 275
noun(s), 79–80
    abstract, 79
    appositives as, 129
    capitalization rules for, 307, 309
    collective, 79, 203
    common, 79
    compound, 79
    concrete, 79
    defined, 79
    of direct address, 275
    forming plural, 327
    gerund/gerund phrases as, 135
    hyphens in compound, 299
    identifying, 80
    infinitive/infinitive phrases as, 137
    plural, 327, 328
    possessive, use of apostrophes in, 297

noun(s) (*continued*)
    as predicate nominative, 213
    proper, 79, 307–8
noun appositive, 221
noun clauses, 153–54
noun of direct address, commas to set off, 275
nowheres, somewheres, anywheres, everywheres, 250
number(s)
    agreement of pronouns with antecedents in, 223, 225
    apostrophes to form plurals of, 297
    hyphens in compound, 299
    italics for, 291
    spelling out names of, 323
    and subject-verb agreement, 197, 205
number of, amount of, 249

O

O, capitalization of, 313
object complements, 121, 215
object pronouns, 215–16, 217, 221
objects
    direct, 83, 117, 121, 215
    indirect, 117, 215
off of, outside of, inside of, 253
only, as misplaced modifier, 239
opinion statement, in persuasive writing, 32
organization of writing
    chronological, 26
    general to specific, 27
    of importance, 26, 28, 32
    logical, 27
    spatial, 26
    specific to general, 27
organizations
    capitalization of names of, 311
    and subject-verb agreement, 205
original research, 62
outline, 13
outside of, inside of, off of, 253

P

paragraphs
    adverb clauses in, 152
    clincher sentence in, 22, 23
    coherence in, 26–29
    descriptive, 32
    expository, 31
    narrative, 32
    persuasive, 32
    topic sentences in, 22, 23
    unity in, 22–23, 24

varying sentence beginnings and structure in, 164
parallel structure in effective sentences, 16, 161–62
paraphrasing, in research papers, 69
parentheses, 299
parenthetical citations, in research papers, 62, 70
parenthetical expressions
    commas to set off, 275
    listing of common, 275
participial phrases, 131–32, 273
    in combining sentences, 139
    commas after introductory, 273
participles, 131–32
    commas after introductory, 273
    past, 131, 177
    present, 131, 177
part of speech. *See* adjective(s); adverb(s); conjunctions; interjections; noun(s); preposition(s); pronoun(s); verb(s)
passive voice, 187
past participles, 131, 177
past perfect tense, 185
past progressive tense, 185
past tense, 177, 185
peer editing, 16, 17
percent, percentage, 254
perfect tenses, 185
periods
    after abbreviations, 269
    to end declarative sentences, 103, 269
    to end imperative sentences, 103, 269
    with parentheses, 299
    with quotation marks, 293
person(s)
    in pronoun-antecedent agreement, 225
    in subject-verb agreement, 197
personal narratives, 30–31, 37–41
personal pronouns, 81
personal response essay, 58
persuasive writing, 32, 42–47
    arguments in, 42
    attention grabber in, 32
    call to action in, 32, 45
    choosing topics in, 45
    clincher sentence in, 22, 23
    comparisons in, 48
    counterarguments in, 45
    critical review as form of, 48–52
    emotional appeals in, 44
    loaded words in, 45
    logical appeals in, 44

opinion statement in, 32
vocabulary in, 44
writing strategies in, 44–45
phrases
    adjective, 127–28
    adverb, 127–28
    appositive, 129–30
    colon to emphasize, 287
    in combining sentences, 139–40
    gerund, 135–36
    infinitive, 137–38
    intervening, 197–98
    participial, 131–32, 273
    prepositional, 93, 127, 273
    verb, 83, 197
plagiarism, 70
plot in narrative writing, 39
plot summary, 60
plural nouns, 327–28
    apostrophes in, 297
plural pronouns, 197
plural subjects, 197
plural verbs, 197
position statements, 44
positive degrees of comparison, 233
possessive nouns, apostrophes in, 297
possessive pronouns, 81, 223, 297
predicate adjectives, 87, 119–20
predicate nominatives, 119–20, 213, 221
predicates, 105–6
    complete, 105
    simple, 105
prefixes, 325–26
    and use of hyphens with, 325
preposition(s), 93–94
    and capitalization rules, 307
    compound, 93
    defined, 93
    distinguishing from adverbs, 93
    listing of common, 93
    pronouns as objects of, 215, 221
prepositional phrase, 93, 127, 273
    in combining sentences, 139
    commas after introductory, 273
    and subject-verb agreement, 197
present participles, 131, 177
present perfect progressive tense, 185
present perfect tense, 185
present progressive tense, 185
present tense, 177, 185
    literary, 60, 185
    subject-verb agreement in, 197

prewriting, 9–12
    brainstorming in, 9–10
    clustering in, 10–11
    defined, 9
    freewriting in, 10, 12
    outlines in, 71
    what if? questions in, 11
    writer's notebook in, 9, 12
primary sources, 68
principal parts of verbs, 177–78
problem-solution essay, 53–57
    writing strategies for, 55–56
pronoun(s), 81–82
    as appositives, 129, 221
    capitalization of *I*, 313
    defined, 81
    demonstrative, 81
    in editing, 16
    indefinite, 81, 199, 297
    intensive, 81
    interrogative, 81
    object, 215–16, 217, 221
    in objective case, 119
    personal, 81
    plural, 197
    possessive, 81, 223, 297
    as predicate nominative, 119,
        213
    reflexive, 81, 221
    relative, 81, 149, 205
    singular, 197
    subject, 213–14, 215, 217, 221
    as subject complement, 119
    in subjective case, 119
pronoun-antecedent agreement,
    223–24
    clearness of reference in,
        225–26
    with indefinite pronouns,
        199–200
proofreading, 18–20
    for consistency, 18
    defined, 18
    dialogue, 314
    essays, 76
    for hyphens, 18
    newsletters, 324
    for punctuation, 18
    questions in, 18
    sentences, 271–72, 276, 308,
        312
    symbols for, 19
proofreading log, 19, 76, 321
proper adjectives, 87, 307–8
    adding prefixes to, 325
    capitalization of, 307

proper nouns, 79, 307–8
    adding prefixes to, 325
publishing, 18–20
punctuation. *See also* specific marks
    in dialogue, 295–96
purpose, 13, 30–32
    for descriptive writing, 30
    for expository writing, 31
    identifying, 13
    for narrative writing, 30–31, 39
    for persuasive writing, 32
    for research paper, 71

Q

question(s). *See also* interrogative
sentences
    for analysis, 60
    beginning with interrogative
        pronouns, 81
    commas to set off tag, 277
    essay, 73, 74
    for peer editors, 16
    in proofreading, 18
    in revising, 15
    what if?, 11
question mark(s), 269
    to end interrogative sentences,
        103
    in punctuating dialogue, 295
    with quotation marks, 293
quotation(s)
    block, 287, 293
    capitalization of first words of
        direct, 311
    colons to introduce, 287
    commas to set off direct, 277
    enclosing inserted explanation
        in parentheses in, 299
    in expository writing, 31
    indirect, 311
    in introductions, 33
    punctuation with long, 295
    quotation marks at beginning
        and end of direct, 293, 295
    within quotations, and single
        quotation marks with, 293
    in research papers, 72
    setting off long, 287
    in supporting details, 24
quotation marks, 293–94
    at beginning and end of
        dialogue, 295
    at beginning and end of direct
        quotations, 293
    single, for quotations within
        quotations, 293
    for titles of short works, 293

R

raise, *rise*, 181, 255
readers. *See also* audience
    knowing, as writing strategy, 50
*Readers' Guide to Periodical
Literature, The*, 68
real, *really*, 255
reflexive pronouns, 81, 221
"Reform and the Triangle Shirtwaist
    Company Fire" by Hadley Davis,
    63–66
regular verbs, 177–78
relative adverbs, 149
relative pronouns, 81, 149, 205
relevance, in evaluating sources, 68
research, original, 62
research papers. *See also* expository
writing
    accuracy in, 68
    acknowledging sources in, 70
    audience for, 71
    bibliography source cards for,
        69
    choosing and limiting topics in,
        67, 70–71
    cross-reference notes in, 69
    direction statement in, 71
    explanation in, 62
    mapping ideas in, 70
    notes in, 69
    outline for, 70, 71
    paraphrasing in, 69
    parenthetical citations in, 62,
        70
    plagiarism as problem in, 70
    primary sources in, 68
    purpose of, 71
    relevance of, 68
    reviewing sources in, 68
    schedule for, 67
    source cards for, 69
    sources for, 68
    summary in, 62, 69
    survey of literature, 62
    synthesization of, 62
    thesis statements for, 70
    timeliness of, 68
    tracking sources in, 69
    Works Cited in, 62, 70
    writing strategies in, 67
revising, 15–17. *See also* editing
    for coherence, 28
    content in, 15
    defined, 15
    organization in, 15
    questions in, 15
    sentences, 276

T

tag questions, commas to set off, 277
teach, learn, 253
tense. *See* verb tenses
than, then, 255
that, which, who, whom, 255
the, 87
then, than, 255
thesis statement, 33, 44, 46
    in essays, 33
    in literary analysis, 60
    in research papers, 70
third person, 197
time
    colon between hour and minute in, 287
    and subject-verb agreement, 205
    subordinating conjunctions showing, 157
    transitions to show, 28
timeliness in evaluating sources, 68
time order. *See* chronological order
titles, 309–10
    capitalization rules for, 309
    identifying, in writing about literature, 60
    italics for long works, 291
    quotation marks for short works, 293
tone
    in problem-solution essay, 56
    in writing about literature, 60
topics
    freewriting in exploring, 12
    generating, 12
    narrowing, 12
    in persuasive writing, 45
    for problem-solution essay, 56
    in research papers, 67
topic sentence, 22, 23, 33
transitions, 28, 111
    commas to set off, 275
    in essays, 75
    listing of common, 275, 289
    semicolons before, when joining independent clauses, 279
transitive verbs, 117
type of a, kind of a, sort of a, 253

U

underlining. *See* italics
uninterested, disinterested, 251
unity, 22–23

V

verb(s), 83–84, 105–6. *See also* mood, subject-verb agreement, verb tenses, voice
    action, 83, 117
    compound, 111, 273
    emphatic form of, 185
    helping, 83
    intransitive, 117
    irregular, 179–82
    linking, 83, 119
    past participle as, 177
    plural, 197
    present participle as, 177
    principal parts of, 177, 178
    regular, 177–78
    singular, 197
    transitive, 117
    voice, 187–88
verb phrases, 83, 197
verb tenses, 185–86
    future, 185
    future perfect, 185
    future perfect progressive, 185
    future progressive, 185
    literary present, 60, 185
    past, 177, 185
    past participle, 131, 177
    past perfect, 185
    past perfect progressive, 185
    past progressive, 185
    perfect, 185
    present, 177, 185
    present participle, 131, 177
    present perfect, 185
    present perfect progressive, 185
    present progressive, 185
    progressive form of, 185
voice
    active, 187–88
    passive, 187–88

W

webbing, 10–11
well
    comma to set off, 277
well, good, 253
what if? questions in prewriting, 11
which, who, whom, that, 255
who, whom, 217–18, 255
words
    capitalization of first, 311–12
    choice of, in revising, 15
    choosing the right, 254
    colon to emphasize, 287
    determining part of speech of, 97
    inserting single, in combining sentences, 91
    loaded, 45
words as words
    apostrophes to form plurals of, 297
    italics for, 291
Works Cited in research papers, 62, 66, 70
works of art as subject
    agreement with verb, 205
    capitalization rule for, 309
writer's notebook, 9, 12
writing. *See* descriptive writing; expository writing; narrative writing; persuasive writing
writing process. *See* drafting; editing; prewriting; proofreading; publishing; revising
writing style, 13

Y

year, commas to separate dates from, 277
yes, comma to set off, 277
you, as understood subject, 109